International Secured Transactions Law

This book focuses on international harmonisation and the law of secured transactions by distilling and analysing the unifying principles of various significant international conventions and instruments such as the UN Convention on the Assignment of Receivables, the Unidroit Convention on International Factoring, the EBRD Model Law on Secured Transactions, the Unidroit Convention on the International Interests in Mobile Equipment and the UNCITRAL Legislative Guide on Secured Transactions.

International secured transactions conventions and instruments facilitate credit and promote economic activity through the creation of harmonised rules. Therefore, given the increasing globalisation of markets, international reform efforts for the harmonised modernisation of secured transactions law have gained pace over recent years. *International Secured Transactions Law* draws on experiences in both English and US laws in order to identify and illustrate the existing problems that need to be addressed, as well as to identify potential solutions.

International Secured Transactions Law will be of interest to scholars and students interested in international commercial law, corporate law or comparative secured transactions, and practitioners involved in international commercial transactions.

N. Orkun Akseli is a Lecturer in Law at Newcastle University Law School, UK. His primary research interests are Secured Transactions, Corporate Law, and Commercial Law. He has published research in these areas.

Routledge Research in Finance and Banking Law

Available titles in this series include:

European Prudential Banking Regulation and Supervision
The Legal Dimension
Larisa Dragomir

Forthcoming titles in this series include:

The Legal and Regulatory Aspects of Islamic Banking
A comparative look at the United Kingdom and Malaysia
Abdul Karim Aldohni

International Secured Transactions Law

Facilitation of credit and international conventions and instruments

N. Orkun Akseli

Routledge
Taylor & Francis Group
LONDON AND NEW YORK

First published 2011
by Routledge
2 Park Square, Milton Park, Abingdon, Oxon, OX14 4RN

Simultaneously published in the USA and Canada
by Routledge
270 Madison Avenue, New York, NY 10016

Routledge is an imprint of the Taylor & Francis Group, an informa business

Typeset in Baskerville by
RefineCatch Limited, Bungay, Suffolk
Printed and bound in Great Britain by
CPI Antony Rowe, Chippenham, Wiltshire

British Library Cataloguing in Publication Data
A catalogue record for this book is available
from the British Library

Library of Congress Cataloging in Publication Data
Akseli, Orkun.
International secured transactions law : facilitation of credit and international conventions and instruments / Orkun Akseli.
p. cm.
Includes biliographical references and index.
ISBN 978–0–415–48810–5
1. Security (Law) 2. Export sales contracts. I. Title.
K1100.A93 2011
\346.07'4–dc22 2010031926

ISBN 13: 978–0–415–48810–5 (hbk)
ISBN 13: 978–0–203–83161–8 (ebook)

For Erbil, Sevil, Ilgaz, Nicola and Ela Taylor

Contents

Preface

This book grew out of a doctoral thesis I wrote at the University of Manchester. Harmonisation of secured transactions law is critical both on a global basis and domestically. Small businesses are in need of liquidity to expand their businesses. International instruments that aim to harmonise secured transactions are the focus of this book. The book does not intend to employ an article-by-article analysis of international instruments nor does it for English and American laws. It simply provides an overview in which the international instruments, their *travaux preparatoires*, English Law and UCC Article 9 are used as a vehicle to illustrate and distil the unifying principles in creating a harmonisation process in secured transactions law and some of the problems that may be experienced, and some of the conclusions that might be drawn. One of the more feasible methods in achieving this is to use, generally, English and American laws to illustrate problems in secured transactions. The book also does not cover all secured transactions instruments, but deals only with the most influential ones. It is hoped that the resulting distillation of underlying principles may provide a conceptual, and maybe analytical, framework to further the debate on the utility and efficacy of international secured transactions instruments. It is hoped the monograph will be useful to academics, students, law reform agencies and, maybe, practitioners.

At various stages of both my doctoral research and the writing of this book, and in various other forms, I have engaged in many thoughtful discussions with a number of colleagues. My foremost debt is to Gerard McCormack and Andrew Bell, my PhD supervisors, who provided invaluable inspiration and guidance. Spiros Bazinas, Frederique Dahan, Franco Ferrari, Harry Sigman, Richard Hyland and Loukas Mistelis also have provided insightful criticism and encouragement. I have no doubt that their help and suggestions have added substantially to whatever value there is to the arguments made here. While the credit is given to people who have helped me, all that may be found to be unwise in this book remains my responsibility and mine alone. I also would like to thank my Editor, Ms. Katie Carpenter, and my Assistant Editor, Ms. Khanam Virjee, for their wholehearted dedication and for being extremely patient during the publication process regarding my requests of extension of deadlines, and for administering a very smooth publication process. I would like to extend my gratitude to my colleagues and the Newcastle University

Law School for granting me a semester of research leave that enabled me to finalise the monograph.

Finally, I would like to thank my parents Erbil and Sevil, and my brother Ilgaz, without whose support and encouragement during the whole process the project would not have been finalised. Especially, I would like to doubly thank my mother and former boss, Sevil, from whose experience as a lawyer spanning four decades and from whose guidance, I have learned a lot as a lawyer and as a colleague. Certainly my wife, Nicola, and my wonderful daughter, Ela Taylor, deserve my deepest gratitude for their immense patience and assistance in this long and winding road. I love all of them more than they think. I promised to play hop-scotch with my two-and-a-half-year-old daughter once the book is finished. I think I am now free to do that.

N. Orkun Akseli
Newcastle-upon-Tyne, 10 July 2010

Foreword

With his present book, Dr. Nazmi Orkun Akseli achieves a maturity rare for his age and makes another significant contribution to a better understanding of international instruments dealing with secured transactions law, which is a necessary condition for their implementation. His citation in the Introduction from the Institutes of Justinian shows clearly that he understands very well the key to secured transactions law, which many, lost in the tensions between debtor and creditor interests, often miss; that is, that security is good for both the debtor (to borrow more and at better terms) and the creditor (to obtain repayment in a more time- and cost-efficient way).

His choice of instruments is a very wise one. The Unidroit Convention on International Factoring (Ottawa, 1988) may not have been widely adopted, but it paved the way for another bold step in the field of receivables financing law, the United Nations Convention on the Assignment of Receivables in International Trade (New York, 2001).

The latter Convention may not have been widely adopted yet either, but I agree with Dr. Akseli that it will soon become a success (for those that measure success of a convention by the number of ratifications or accessions) and that it is already having an impact to the extent that it influenced national law in several countries and set the standards for national secured transactions law in line with the recommendations of the UNCITRAL Legislative Guide on Secured Transactions (2007).

Having already influenced secured transactions laws around the world, the Guide is becoming the general standard and a common point of reference for law reform in the field of secured transactions law. To mention just some examples, the new Personal Property Security Act of Australia, similar draft legislation in the Republic of Korea, the Draft Common Frame of Reference, volume 6 book IX, proprietary security in moveable assets and the recent publication of the World Bank Group, Secured Transactions Systems and Collateral Registries, bear witness to the increasing influence of the Guide.

The EBRD Model Law on Secured Transactions (1994) has already been implemented in a number of countries in Eastern Europe, and the Core Principles for a Secured Transactions Law (1997) has also guided legal reform in several countries. And last but certainly not least, the Convention on International

Interests in Mobile Equipment (Cape Town, 2001) is a remarkable success already by any standard. Of particular importance is the Protocol to the Convention on International Interests in Mobile Equipment on Matters specific to Aircraft Equipment (Cape Town, 2001), which has given the world its first asset-based international registry that is based on notice (rather than document) filing and results in the perfection (rather than in the creation) of an interest.

The discussion in the book is very practical, analytical and thorough. To take an example, Dr. Akseli's criticism of the view that is trying to discount all these international instruments on the grounds that they have been unduly influenced by Article 9 of the Uniform Commercial Code, is very justified.

The first and most important question that one should raise with regard to a legislative text is whether it addresses the concrete practical problems it is supposed to address in an effective and balanced way. In the case of a trade law text, this essentially means whether the text facilitates national and international trade while taking into account the interests of all stakeholders in a balanced way without, of course, violating the integrity of the national legal system.

The functional approach to secured transactions is one of the key characteristics of Article 9 UCC (which is itself the result of an enormous comparative law and harmonisation effort, and constitutes a departure from common law), but all these texts adopt it because there is no other way to rationalise secured transactions laws at the national level and harmonise secured transactions laws at the international level. Notice filing for perfection purposes may also come from Article 9 UCC, but again no other way has been suggested so far for an efficient registry system that can provide an objective way for ordering priorities of security interests, including interests serving security purposes (for example, retention-of-title or financial lease interests).

Equally justified is Dr. Akseli's criticism of the view that these international instruments may somehow threaten the integrity of national legal systems, propagate a virus or constitute unsuitable legal transplants. Conventions are the best instrument for the cross-border recognition of security interests, a result that in itself may promote the extension of credit against assets that are likely to cross national borders. In addition, the principles developed by the EBRD and the Guide developed by UNCITRAL provide legislators with sufficient flexibility to address secured transactions law issues in a focused way, taking into account the needs and the legal tradition of every country.

To mention another example demonstrating the thorough analysis of issues in this book, Dr. Akseli is absolutely right that good old asset-based lending did not cause the financial crisis; the violation of its fundamental principles caused it and, of course, the lack of proper control by the supervisory authorities. It is time to return to the principles of asset-based lending to provide markets with the necessary liquidity to grow their way out of this unprecedented financial (and not only) crisis.

Another example of the analytical nature of the book is the structure of the materials. After the first introductory chapters, the book discusses scope and party autonomy, creation, third-party effectiveness and priority of a security interest, acquisition financing and applicable law, following the order in which a legislator would have to address these matters in the law. The fact that the book does not discuss security interests in securities and intellectual property or enforcement and insolvency law issues does not reduce its value and is understandable. Securities and intellectual property raise a whole set of different issues that would justify the writing of a second book. The same applies to enforcement and insolvency law issues, a discussion of which would justify the writing of a third book.

On a personal note, for the benefit of those who may find it strange that a Greek lawyer writes the foreword of a book of a Turkish lawyer, I would like to mention that, in my view, the cup of the historical relations between our two peoples is more than half full; and the interests that bring us together today are stronger than those that may set us apart. This is why the legacy of our two great leaders, Venizelos and Atatürk, is one of peace and friendship. In line with this tradition and in view of the merits of this book, it is an honour and a pleasure for me to write the prologue and wish that the book may have a great journey.

Spiros V. Bazinas*

* Senior Legal Officer, International Trade Law Division, Office of Legal Affairs, United Nations. The International Trade Law Division of the United Nations Office of Legal Affairs serves as the Secretariat of the United Nations Commission on International Trade Law (UNCITRAL). The views expressed are the personal views of the author and do not reflect the views of the United Nations or UNCITRAL.

Acknowledgements

Some of the contents related to anti-assignment clauses of Chapter 4 were originally published in *Journal of Business Law*. I would like to thank the editors and Sweet & Maxwell for granting permission to reproduce some portions of N. Orkun Akseli (2009) 'Contractual Prohibitions and Assignment of Receivables: An English and UN perspective', *JBL*, 650–78.

I would also like to thank Professor Roderick A. Macdonald (McGill University) and acknowledge his permission to cite his paper, 'A Model Law on Secured Transactions: A Representation of Structure? An object of imitation? A type or Design?' presented at The UNCITRAL Third Colloquium on Secured Transactions (1–3 March 2010, Vienna) in the Introduction to this book.

Table of cases

USA

Australia

Netherlands

Table of Conventions, Instruments and Statutes

List of abbreviations

Ala. L. Rev	Alabama Law Review
Am. J. Comp. L.	American Journal of Comparative Law
Am. J. Int'l L.	American Journal of International Law
Am. U. Int'l L. Rev	American University International Law Review
Ariz. J. Int'l & Comp. L.	Arizona Journal of International and Comparative Law
BJIBFL	Butterworths Journal of International Banking and Financial Law
Brook. J. Int'l L.	Brooklyn Journal of International Law
Bus. Law.	Business Lawyer
C.L.J.	Cambridge Law Journal
Cal. L. Rev	California Law Review
Canadian Bus. L.J.	Canadian Business Law Journal
CfiLR	Company, Finance and Insolvency Law Review
Co. Law.	Company Lawyer
Colum. J. Transnat'l L.	Columbia Journal of Transnational Law
Com. L.J.	Commercial Law Journal
Conv.	Conveyancer
Cornell L. Rev.	Cornell Law Review
Dick. L. Rev.	Dickinson Law Review
Duke J. Comp. & Int'l L.	Duke Journal of Comparative and International Law
E.C.F.L.R.	European Company and Financial Law Review
E.J.C.L.	Electronic Journal of Comparative Law
E.R.P.L.	European Review of Private Law
Fla. St. U. J. Transnat'l L. & Pol.	Florida State University Journal of Transnational Law and Policy
I.C.L.Q.	International and Comparative Law Quarterly
IBLJ	International Business Law Journal

Int'l Law.	International Lawyer
J. L. & Com.	Journal of Law and Commerce
J.C.L.	Journal of Comparative Law
J.I.B.L.	Journal of International Banking Law
J.I.B.L.R.	Journal of International Banking Law Review
L. & Bus. Rev. Am.	Law and Business Review of Americas
L.F.M.R.	Law and Financial Markets Review
L.M.C.L.Q.	Lloyds Maritime and Commercial Law Quarterly
L.Q.R.	Law Quarterly Review
La. L. Rev.	Louisiana Law Review
M.L.R.	Modern Law Review
McGill L.J.	Mcgill Law Journal
Melbourne J. Int'l L.	Melbourne Journal of International Law
Mich. L. Rev.	Michigan Law Review
Mon. L.R.	Monash Law Review
N.C.J. Int'l L. & Com. Reg.	North Carolina Journal of International Law and Commercial Regulation
NAFTA: L. & Bus. Rev. Am.	NAFTA: Law and Business review of Americas
O.J.L.S.	Oxford Journal of Legal Studies
Parker Sch. J.E.Eur.L.	Parker School Journal of Eastern European Law
Penn St. Int'l L. Rev.	Pennsylvania State International Law Review
San Diego Int'l L.J.	San Diego International Law Journal
Tex. Int'l L. J.	Texas International Law Journal
Tul. L. Rev.	Tulane Law Review
U. Miami Inter-Am. L. Rev.	University of Miami Inter-American Law Review
U. Pa. J. Int'l Econ. L.	University of Pennsylvania Journal of International Economic Law
U. Pa. L. Rev.	University of Pennsylvania Law Review
UCC L.J.	Uniform Commercial Code Law Journal
Unif. L. Rev.	Uniform Law Review
Va. J. Int'l L.	Virginia Journal of International Law
Va. L. Rev.	Virginian Law Review
VJ	Vindabona Journal of International Commercial Law and Arbitration
Yale L. J.	Yale Law Journal

Introduction

> 'A [security] . . . is for the benefit of both parties; of the debtor because it enables him to borrow more easily; and of the creditor because he has the better security for repayment . . .'[1]

0.1 General

Since the 1970s, the philosophical tenor of secured transactions law has been embodied in an increasing variety of international conventions and instruments. Many of them draw on the assumption that harmonised modernisation of the law of credit and security lowers the cost of credit by creating predictability for international lenders. The problem merits serious consideration. First, taking security for financiers and granting security in return for a loan for small and medium-sized enterprises (SMEs) to expand their businesses by accessing low-cost credit are considered globally critical. Arguably, the majority of world trade relies on credit supplied by banks and other financial institutions to SMEs that comprise 97 percent of businesses and 50 percent of employment globally.[2] Second, with the market interdependency as a result of the so-called globalisation, secured credit is now internationalised by virtue of international conventions and instruments. Internationalisation of secured transactions law may have some other influential political aspects, including more foreign investment or financial aid, in return for transplanting certain laws. Be that as it may, as a result of these two characteristics, the law of international secured transactions provides an optimal lens through which to examine how different international conventions and instruments confront key policy issues.

International conventions and other instruments covered by this book demonstrate that the ability to give adequate security influences not only the cost of credit but also, in some cases, whether credit will be available at all. International instruments, among other features, promote the granting and taking of low-cost credit

1 3.14.4, *The Institutes of Justinian*, 5th edn (1913), J.B. Moyle (trans.). Oxford: Clarendon, p. 132.

2 http://www.ifc.org/ifcext/media.nsf/AttachmentsByTitle/AM09_SME/$FILE/AM09_SME.pdf (last accessed 10 April 2010).

by creating certainty with regards to the status of the asset (for example through registration), by increasing the types of assets to be used as collateral (all assets and obligations), by allowing the creation of security with minimum restrictions and documentation, and by establishing certainty in creditors' priority status. What is meant by low-cost credit is that the risk premium, maintenance, monitoring and transaction costs are not reflected in the interest rate. The difficulties posed by inadequate security laws are intensely felt in countries that are probably most in need of international credit for developing their infrastructures and economies. These are called 'transition economies', which, for various reasons, tend to have secured credit laws that fall below the expectations of international banks and financiers. With the so-called credit crunch (caused by reckless speculation in the housing market by financial institutions with little equity capital and the abusive practice of securitisation of mortgages and other financial instruments with inadequate appreciation of the risks involved as well as the misleading directions of rating agencies[3]), the same argument now equally applies to SMEs and all other types of businesses in developed economies as well.[4] In order to build a market-oriented economy and a lender friendly system, clear and efficient law on secured transactions is crucial. Complementing these observations, empirical studies have illustrated that modernisation of secured credit laws through harmonised rules is a sign to increased credit extensions.[5]

Harmonised modernisation of secured transactions law is one of the most significant methods of overcoming difficulties posed by businesses in accessing low-cost credit. In this context, civil law jurisdictions are generally in need of reform; and the home jurisdictions of the main financial markets and thus, indirectly, the exporters of reform are all common law. This raises cultural, even historical issues.[6] The political sensitivity of the area was also illustrated recently by the antagonistic reception given to the Law Commission's reform proposals, which drew on a UCC Article 9 type of secured transactions regime.[7]

3 Hurst, T. (2009) 'The Role of Credit Rating Agencies in the Current Worldwide Financial Crisis', *Comp. Law*, 61.

4 The UK is the sixth largest economy with 2,645,593 millions of US dollars of gross domestic product according to World Bank ranking for 2008. http://siteresources.worldbank.org/DATASTATISTICS/Resources/GDP.pdf (last accessed September 2009). However, according to Federation of Small and Medium Sized Businesses statistics, small businesses in the UK have serious problems in access to credit. http://www.fsb.org.uk/ Report on *Number Crunching the Credit Crunch* (last accessed September 2009). The liquidity gap in trade finance globally caused by shortage of credit has reached an estimate of US$25bn as of November 2008. '*Lamy warns trade finance situation "deteriorating"*', WTO News, 12 November 2008.

5 Haselmann, R., Pistor, K. and Vig, V. (2006) 'How Law Affects Lending', *Columbia Law and Economics Working Paper No. 285*. Haselmann *et al.* took transition economies as an example and examined the effects of modernisation in secured credit laws and especially the introduction of non-possessory security and the registration system.

6 *See* Ch. 2.

7 Law Commission Consultation Paper No. 176.

There is a commercial necessity in harmonising the law of secured transactions at the international level. The globalisation of financial markets must be supplemented by the globalisation of law in this area. Ulrich Drobnig, in his seminal report[8] in 1977, recommended three available methods of implementation, which included uniform law conventions, model laws, and recommendations. However, he was not optimistic about the possible success of these methods including the recommendations.[9] Indeed, earlier harmonisation efforts mainly in the form of law reforms or conventions have not succeeded in practice, due to political problems, lack of comprehensiveness[10] and lack of understanding the host country's legal and economic systems.[11] One of the main problems in traditional harmonisation methods (such as conventions), apart from lack of comprehensiveness, is the difficulty experienced in the ratification process.[12] In order to overcome problems inherent in the ratification and implementation process, drafters of instruments often prefer to keep the number of instruments of ratification, acceptance, approval or accession necessary to enter a convention into force, at the possible lowest level.[13] Professor Gabriel rightly argues that soft law[14]

8 Report of the Secretary General: Study on Security Interests (A/CN.9/131 and Annex), reprinted in: 8 *Yearbook of the United Nations Commission on International Trade Law*, (1977), p. 171.

9 Ibid. 218, where he reported that '[m]ere recommendations, even if emanating from an international organisation of the highest repute, will not command sufficient moral or other support for adoption by any sizeable number of states'.

10 E.g. the UNIDROIT Convention on International Factoring lacks features such as priority and formal validity.

11 For a critical view, *see* Mistelis, L. (2000) 'Regulatory Aspects: Globalization, Harmonization, Legal Transplants and Law Reform–Some Fundamental Observations', 34 *International Law*, 1055. The same thing is argued for Latin American countries where, for instance in Argentina since the 1990s, there have been three reform attempts, all of which failed including texts prepared by the Centre for Economic Analysis of Law, Central Bank of Argentina and the National Centre for Inter-American Trade Law. *See* Mistelis, L. (1998) 'The EBRD Model Law on Secured Transactions and Its Impact on Collateral Law Reform in Central and Eastern Europe and the former Soviet Union', 5 *Parker Sch. J.E.Eur.L.*, 455, 459 and fn 13. From the transplants argument perspective, *see* Wälde, T. and Gunderson, J. (1994) 'Legislative Reforms in Transition Economies: Western Transplants: A Shortcut to Social Economy Status', 43 *I.C.L.Q.*, 345. But cf. a new secured transactions law was adopted by Mexico in 2000 which introduced non-possessory security interests, a centralised registration system, and self-help remedies. Sheppard, H.E. (2001) 'Overcoming Apathetic Internationalism to Generate Hemispheric Benefits: An Analysis of and Arguments for Recent Secured Transactions Law in Mexico', 10 *Fla. St. U. J. Transnational L. & Pol.*, 133.

12 Dahan, F. and McCormack, G. (2002) 'International Influences and the Polish Law on Secured Transactions: Harmonisation, Unification or What?', *Unif. L. Rev.*, 713, 714–15.

13 E.g. Receivables Convention requires five and the Cape Town entered into force with three. *But* cf. Drobnig in 1977 reported that:

> [i]t would probably be difficult to obtain sufficient government support for an international conference dealing with the relatively technical topic of security interests; and even if the text of an international instrument could be agreed upon, national parliaments would probably be slow and perhaps even reluctant to ratify such a text. Op. cit. (f'note 8), p. 218.

14 'Soft law' is defined as '. . . instruments of normative nature with no legally binding force and which are applied only through voluntary acceptance.' *See* Bonell, M.J. (2005) 'Soft Law and Party Autonomy: The case of the UNIDROIT Principles', 51 *Loy. L. Rev.*, 229.

may mitigate difficulties of harmonisation, which may occur due to the limited mandate given to drafters of instrument, differences of legal traditions, differences of scope of the laws to be harmonised, and the lack of flexibility in achieving harmonisation through treaties or conventions.[15]

From another angle, this problem may have links to legitimacy of organisations and the rules prepared or expressed by them. As the tendency of private rule-making gains pace, concerns regarding legitimacy are raised. Legitimacy, in that sense, attributes effectiveness and powerfulness to the international organisation and the legal instrument prepared by that organisation.[16] The promotion and success of international instruments often require legitimacy of international organisations. Legitimacy is, however, a subjective term. What is legitimate for a Member State may not be considered as legitimate by another State, which prefers to have stronger influence within an international organisation. Arguably, influence in an international organisation leads, in the medium- to long-term, to economic and legal benefits. One of the methods to overcome arguments suggesting lack of legitimacy and of persuasiveness is to incorporate divergent views and be as inclusive as possible.[17] That is to include as many jurisdictions, cultures, experts and relevant industries as possible. Particularly in relation to the working methods of UNCITRAL, some Member States have raised concerns.[18] However, these concerns are harmful to harmonisation efforts. The working methods of UNCITRAL are transparent and clearly set out on their website.[19] One has to be rather more critical to the intentions of those Member States that raise concerns. The more international organisations are transparent, the harder for certain Member States to achieve their political and economic ambitions or agendas in the work of international organisations. Thus they raise concerns as to the legitimacy of working methods to blur the successful work achieved by international

15 Gabriel, H.D. (2009) 'The Advantages of Soft Law in International Commercial Law: The Role of UNIDROIT, UNCITRAL and the Hague Conference', 34 *Brook. J. Int'l L.*, 655, 660 *et seq.* Particularly on this latter challenge, Professor Gabriel argues that conventions are prepared to reflect the legal traditions of adopting States and thus it is necessary to reconcile divergent legal traditions, whereas in soft law instruments it is unnecessary to harmonise an entire area of law but, through selective borrowing, best results may be achieved. Ibid., at 663.

16 In assessing legitimacy, Professor Black and Mr Rouch suggest four criteria: Democratic, Constitutional, Functional or performance-based legitimacy, and Values and objectives-based criteria. *See* Black, J. and Rouch, D. (2008) 'The Development of the Global Markets as Rule-makers: Engagement and Legitimacy', 2 *L.F.M.R.*, 218, 225. For discussion of legitimacy related to UNCITRAL, *see* Kelly, C.R. (2009) 'The Politics of International Economic Law: Legitimacy and the UNCITRAL Working Methods', *Brooklyn Law School Legal Studies Research Papers Working Paper Series No. 140.*

17 For these views, *see generally* Block-Lieb, S. and Halliday, T. (2006) 'Legitimation and Global Lawmaking', *Fordham Law Legal Studies Research Paper No. 952492* (December).

18 France, in particular, has aired her concerns, A/CN.9/635 and A/CN.9/660. These concerns may be summarised as the blurring nature of the role of non-member state entities such as NGOs and the ambiguity of the meaning of consensus the method with which UNCITRAL takes its decisions. *But* cf. the response of the United States A/CN.9/639.

19 http://www.uncitral.org/uncitral/en/about/methods.html (last accessed 10 May 2010).

organisations. It is believed that these concerns diminish the power of other States and the efforts of international organisations who work effectively in the pursuit of international harmonisation and facilitation of credit.

As large numbers of institutions and organisations are involved in the harmonisation process, one of the significant problems is the coordination of these efforts to achieve ratification, domestic implementation and promotion of international instruments[20] (that is, raising awareness at the local practical level, the significance that these instruments are introducing). These are linked to the policies of nations that operate 'wait-and-see' policies. Professor Goode explains this point succinctly as follows:

> The treaty collections are littered with Conventions that have never come into force, for want of the number of required ratifications, or have been eschewed by the major trading States. There are several reasons for this: failure to establish from potential interest groups at the outset that there is a serious problem, which the proposed Convention will help to resolve; hostility from powerful pressure groups; lack of sufficient interest of, or pressure on, Governments to induce them to burden still further an already over-crowded legislative timetable; mutual hold-backs, each State waiting to see what others will do, so that in the end none of them does anything.[21]

Another problem mainly experienced in law reforms is the reluctance of finance and legal sectors to adapt themselves to change for the better.[22] However, more recently, realistic steps have been taken in harmonising the law of secured transactions and associated areas at global and regional levels where international formulating agencies as well as regional organisations have made attempts to harmonise secured credit laws by using Model Laws[23] or Legislative Guides.[24] Particularly,

20 Faria, J.A.E. (2009) 'Future Directions of Legal Harmonisation and Law Reform: Stormy Seas or Prosperous Voyage?', *Unif. L. Rev.*, 5, 21 *et seq.*

21 Goode, R. (1997) 'International Restatements of Contract and English Contract Law', *Unif. L. Rev.*, 231, 232.

22 For example, in England there have been significant but unsuccessful attempts on the reform of secured credit laws. Crowther Committee Report on Consumer Credit (Cmnd 4596, 1971); A Review of Security Interests in Property (Diamond Commission, 1989); Law Commission Report on Company Security Interests No. 296 (August 2005). E.g. Davies, I. (1988) 'The Reform of Personal Property Security Law: Can Article 9 of the US UCC be a Precedent?', 37 *I.C.L.Q.*, 465; Davies, I. (2004) 'The Reform of English Personal Property Security Law: Functionalism and Article 9 of the Uniform Commercial Code', 24 *Legal Studies*, 295, 299; McCormack, G. (2003) 'Quasi-Securities and the Law Commission Consultation Paper on Security Interests – A Brave New World', *L.M.C.L.Q.*, 80; McCormack, G. (2005) 'The Law Commission Consultative Report on Company Security Interests: An Irreverent Riposte', 68 *M.L.R.*, 286.

23 E.g. EBRD Model Law on Secured Transactions.

24 E.g. UNCITRAL Legislative Guide on Secured Transactions. The Guide supplemented by the Receivables Convention as the former, to the extent it applies to assignment of receivables, is based on the principles of the latter.

conceiving legislative guides is a feasible method to harmonise secured transactions law, which is a field where there is clear divergence (concepts deeply rooted to historical issues) between civil and common law systems. In that context, the Legislative Guide on Secured Transactions as a significant instrument prepared with significant efforts is the only feasible method to achieve harmonisation in secured transactions. Furthermore, the topic is not free of politics. It is arguable that conventions can only achieve harmonisation on limited areas and may be considered as an imposition of a particular legal system. Similar arguments apply equally to model laws whose provisions explaining policy decisions may not be as precise and explicit as the recommendations of the Legislative Guide. Thus there is no need for another instrument, at least for now, to explain something that explains it politically and legally well and in a soft manner.[25] Although it is argued that the development of the law of secured transactions is dependent on soft law instruments supplemented by specific and binding conventions,[26] arguably, conventions present two extremities: (a) isolation of international formulating agencies from national institutions and the private sector, and (b) national resistance to conventions that are considered as global impositions by financial institutions and the legal community. The best method to mitigate these extremes is to produce legislative guides that provide flexibility for national legislators in adopting the recommendations, and ensure inclusive representation.[27] In that context, some of these organisations have adopted a piecemeal approach where only certain areas of secured transactions law is to be harmonised by international instruments.[28] Some attempted an overall model law for transition economies and, indeed, may be a model for the European Union's efforts on harmonisation of security interests[29] for intra-community trade, and some of them adopted a comprehensive regime.[30] These efforts have been justified with the general move to achieve consistency in regulation, given fresh impetus with the recent financial crisis created through abusive practices of financing techniques such as securitisation. Basel II

25 For a similar perspective, *see* e.g. Macdonald, R. (2010) 'A Model Law on Secured Transactions: A representation of structure? An object of imitation? A type or design?' available at http://www.uncitral.org/pdf/english/colloquia/3rdSecTrans/Roderick_Macdonald_Edited-ML.pdf (last accessed 24 March 2010).

26 For a similar view, *see* Gabriel, op. cit. (f'note 15), at 672; Kronke, H. (2005) 'Methodical Freedom and Organizational Constraints in the Development of Transnational Commercial Law', 51 *Loy. L. Rev.* 287, 293–4.

27 Block-Lieb and Halliday, op. cit. (f'note 17), at 72.

28 E.g. UN Convention on the Assignment of Receivables in International Trade; UNIDROIT Convention on International Interests in Mobile Equipment.

29 On this, *see* e.g. McCormack, G. (2008) 'The CFR and Credit Securities: A Suitable Case for Treatment?' *WG Hart Legal Workshop Paper* (24 June); Sigman, H.C. and Kieninger, E.M. (2007) *Cross Border Security over Tangibles*, Munich: Sellier, pp. 34 *et seq.*

30 E.g. UNCITRAL Legislative Guide on Secured Transactions. On the methods of harmonisation, *see* Akseli, O. (2008) 'On the Methods of International Harmonisation of Secured Transactions Law', in C.B. Andersen and U.G. Schroeter (eds) *Sharing International Commercial Law across National Boundaries: Festschrift for Albert H. Kritzer on the Occasion of his Eightieth Birthday*. London: Wildy, Simmonds & Hill, p. 1.

requirements urge financial institutions to clarify and make transparent their supervision and legal structures in order to support credit and security.[31] International instruments do not create rules where no laws existed in that area before, but attempt to find common points of domestic secured transactions laws on which a harmonised text can be prepared. The exception to this is the UNIDROIT Convention on International Interests in Mobile Equipment, where the concept of international interest has been introduced for the first time, which is one of the innovative features of the Convention (the other being the dual instrument structure, that is, the Convention and its various protocols). One of the main reasons for not being able to easily create original rules in secured transactions law is the fact that secured transactions law is deeply linked with traditional domestic rules of property law, law of contracts, and insolvency law, and it is complex to create a new rule that is acceptable by all jurisdictions without altering well-established national rules.[32]

0.2 International instruments

0.2.1 UNIDROIT Convention on International Factoring

UNIDROIT commenced its work on factoring in 1974 and the Factoring Convention was adopted by 59 nations in 1988 at a diplomatic conference held in Ottawa. It was prepared with the aim to remove barriers in international factoring transactions.[33] Notwithstanding its shortcomings,[34] it is considered to be the first step towards eventual harmonisation in the assignment of receivables.[35] It has a limited scope as it only applies to factoring contracts arising out of international sale of goods contracts (international factoring). For that, the place of business of the assignor and the debtor must be in different contracting States. Thus internationality of receivables is a key issue in the applicability. Further, for applicability, the assignor, assignee and debtor must all be located in a contracting State, or the law governing the assignment or the underlying contract must be the law of a contracting State. The Convention also indicates the duties of a factor. Thus the factor needs to perform at least two functions of a factor among the four

31 *See* Ch. 2. For discussion of international financial lawmaking, *see* Alexander, K. (2009) 'Global Financial Standards Setting, the G10 Committees and International Economic Law' 34 *Brook. J. Int'l L.*, 861, 865 *et seq.*

32 For more discussion, *see* Ch. 2. However, some authors argue that there should be 'preventive unification'; *see* Hermann, G. (2001) 'The Role of UNCITRAL' in I. Fletcher, M. Cremona and L. Mistelis (eds) *Foundations and Perspectives of International Trade Law*. London: Sweet & Maxwell, pp. 28, 32. Preventive unification is the creation of something new where no laws exist in the first place.

33 UNIDROIT Study LVIII-Doc.1 (1976).

34 E.g. Lack of priority provisions and formal validity of assignment/factoring contract. The Factoring Convention covers only factoring transactions where the original transaction is a sales or services transaction that limits the scope of applicability.

35 Alexander, M.R. (1989) 'Towards Unification and Predictability: The International Factoring Convention', 27 *Colum. J. Transnat'l L.*, 353.

mentioned (financing for the assignor, or maintaining accounts, or collecting receivables, or protection against default).

It is a landmark document demonstrating that it is possible to reach an international consensus on certain legal issues related to international receivables financing. However, as one commentator has stated, 'one theory put forward in explanation of that failure is that [the Factoring Convention] attempted to define substantive laws that were deemed too intrusive by various member states'.[36] The Convention applies only in notification factoring where the debtor is notified of the assignment.

0.2.2 UN Convention on the Assignment of Receivables in International Trade

Upon the insufficiently ambitious nature of the Factoring Convention, the investigations into the need for comprehensive international legal rules on receivables financing commenced in 1992 by UNCITRAL. UNCITRAL held a Congress[37] in 1992 and responded to the number of suggestions[38] made there with two reports prepared in 1993 and 1995.[39] These reports identified certain legal problems in receivables financing, and concluded that it would be both desirable and feasible to develop a set of uniform rules in order to remove obstacles before the international receivables financing.[40] It is arguable that this activity in the early 1990s proves that the Factoring Convention is less ambitious, given the fact that, by then, it was only a recently-finalised instrument. It was observed that:

> the diversity of national laws and the lack of standard transnational rules creates significant additional expenditure, delays and uncertainty [in] many international business transactions . . . [and] parties may be dissuaded from using receivables financing at all and are then forced to rely on . . . more expensive arrangements, such as overdraft facilities, letters of credit or export guarantees.[41]

Upon consideration of these reports, UNCITRAL embarked upon the preparation of an instrument specifically related to a pressing need in international commercial law: the development of a modern set of rules that will assist facilitation of

36 Carsella, M.B. (1998) 'UNCITRAL: First Step in the Globalization of Asset-based Lending', 54 *The Secured Lender*, 108 *et seq*. In 2010, the Factoring Convention was in force in only seven nations (France, Germany, Hungary, Italy, Latvia, Nigeria and Ukraine).

37 *Uniform Commercial Law in the Twenty-First Century*.

38 *Uniform Commercial Law in the Twenty-First Century: Proceedings of the Congress of the United Nations Commission on International Trade Law*, New York: UN, (1995), at 127, 156–7, 159, 251 and 271.

39 *See* A/CN.9/378/Add.3; A/CN.9/412.

40 A/CN.9/412.

41 *See* 'UN investigates receivables financing', *International Trade Finance*, June 3, 1994; 213 ABI/INFORM Global, at 4 *et seq*.

access to low-cost credit. The Receivables Convention was finalised in 2001, after almost a decade of careful and detailed work. It is a sophisticated and potentially far-reaching instrument with innovative and modern features, including a conflict-of-laws approach to priority issues and an optional annex comprising three different rules for priority based on: registration influenced by UCC Article 9 type legislation; time of the contract of assignment influenced by civil law systems' approach; and the time of the notification of assignment influenced by a seminal decision in English law: *Dearle v Hall*.[42] Its applicability is far broader than the Factoring Convention, where the former deals with a broad array of receivables, unlike the latter which deals only with certain types of receivables (those arising out of sale of goods contracts) and only international factoring. The Receivables Convention serves for the modernisation of domestic assignment laws of countries, as well as a set of rules for harmonisation and predictability of rules in cross-border assignment of receivables transactions. The main aim is to overcome the restrictions that limit the flow of cross-border credit and placed on the types of assets that can be used as collateral to obtain credit. Therefore, availability of credit and capital at more affordable rates may be achieved in cross-border trade. Receivables financing is a significant financing technique in modern secured transactions regimes, but in developing economies there are severe restrictions on its use.

So far three States have become signatories of it and one State has ratified it.[43] However, recently, North American nations have been jointly working towards the adoption, which should be regarded as a leading step to international harmonisation[44] and it is believed that other nations will follow suit. The Receivables Convention has a wide scope of applicability and applies not only to assignment of receivables but also to financing practices such as securitisation and project finance. Key policy issues such as effectiveness of assignments made notwithstanding anti-assignment clauses, recognition of assignments of future, bulk and partial

42 (1828) 3 Russ I.

43 Liberia has ratified, and Luxembourg, the USA and Madagascar have signed the Receivables Convention.

44 In 2005 the National Conference of Commissioners on Uniform State Laws initiated a project with the Uniform Law Conference of Canada and Uniform Law Centre of Mexico to harmonise the domestic laws in North America to conform to the rules of the Receivables Convention in order to benefit from the provisions of the Convention in cross-border receivables financing among the three countries. *See* http://www.law.upenn.edu/bll/archives/ulc/aor/2007june_amreport.htm (last accessed March 2010). The adoption of the Receivables Convention has also been recommended in Canada: *see* http://www.ulcc.ca/en/cls/STATUS%20OF%20UNIFORM%20ACTS%20CHART%20August%2029%202008.pdf and http://www.ulcc.ca/en/us/Assignment_Receivables_International_Trade_En.pdf (last accessed March 2010). In the United States the self-execution method of implementation may be chosen. *See* http://www.uncitral.org/pdf/english/colloquia/3rdSecTrans/Ed_Smith_Implementation.pdf (last accessed 6 April 2010). For recommendation for implementation of the Convention in Canada, *see* Deschamps, M. 'United Nations Convention on the Assignment of Receivables in International Trade Implementation in Canada', http://www.uncitral.org/pdf/english/colloquia/3rdSecTrans/Deschamps_Implementation_Edited.pdf (last accessed 6 April 2010).

receivables, wide scope of applicability, clear and predictable priority rules, principle of debtor protection, and the preservation of rights of defence and set-off of the debtor are some of the important features of the Receivables Convention.

0.2.3 The EBRD Model Law on Secured Transactions

Almost at the same time, in April 1992, during the EBRD's first annual meeting, a round-table discussion on "Creditors' Rights and Secured Transactions in Central and Eastern Europe" was led by the Office of the General Counsel. As a consequence of that discussion and a request by central European academics and practitioners, the EBRD commenced a project on a Model Law on Secured Transactions. After deliberations during the first three annual meetings, the Model Law was adopted in 1994.[45] The Model Law is the product of wide consultations and its Secured Transactions Project is sponsored by the UK Know-How Fund, and the initial production of the Model Law was sponsored by the Japan–Europe Cooperation Fund. The EBRD is a financial organisation established to assist transition economies towards a market-oriented economy, and promotes private-sector development and facilitates investment in transition economies. The EBRD was aware of the critical role of facilitation of credit in transition economies through predictable and modern rules, and that clear rules would attract lenders to lower their costs as well as give assurance on the repayment of loans. The objective of the Model Law was that the absence of effective security and enforcement systems in those States could increase the borrowing costs of credit. Particularly in transition economies, limitations placed on the types of assets that could be used as collateral critically restrict the access to credit. This, in turn, prevents the use of many modern financing techniques (most importantly securitisation and project financing) commonly used in modern economies that assist economic growth. Thus a Model Law is to act as a model for transition economies with the aim to facilitate access to credit and investment where the EBRD operates.[46] The Model Law is not intended to be a detailed set of legislation to be adopted by the transition economies, but it merely serves as a model for those countries to use it in their reforms.[47] It reflects principles from both Common and Civil Law systems for Central and Eastern European countries whose legal systems are based on Civil law concepts. It was prepared to fulfil four objectives.

45 Simpson, J.L. and Röver, J-H.M. (1994) 'Model Law on Secured Transactions completed', *Law in Transition*, 1–2 (Spring); Simpson, J. and Menze, J. (2000) 'Ten Years of Secured Transactions Reform', *Law in Transition Part 2*, 20, at 21 (Autumn).

46 *See generally* Röver, J-H.M. (2007) *Secured Lending in Eastern Europe: Comparative Law of Secured Transactions and the EBRD Model Law*. Oxford: Oxford University Press, p. 69. Recently, the EBRD commenced operations for investment in Turkey, which has been a founding shareholder of the EBRD since 1991. The Bank assesses certain areas of commercial law, including secured transactions that are critical in attracting foreign investment. *See* Nussbaumer, M. and Barut, Ö. (2009) 'Assessing Turkey's Commercial Laws: An EBRD Perspective', *Law in Transition*, 60 (Spring).

47 Model Law, at V; *see also* Simpson, J.L. and Röver, J.-H.M. (1997) 'General Principles of a Modern Secured Transactions Law', *NAFTA: L. & Bus. Rev. Am.*, 73.

Firstly, the Model Law illustrates the main components of a modern, secured transactions regime looking at the issue of legal reform objectively. The Model Law is less comprehensive than the Guide, which has built its recommendations partly on the Model Law and also other instruments. Some authors argue that the Model Law and Core Principles are less prescriptive than the Guide and may act as a reference point for Common Frame of Reference.[48] The situation of former Central and Eastern European States confirms that there is a direct relationship between a modern and predictable legal structure and the approach of the foreign investor.[49] Secondly, it also is a point of reference and checklist on how a modern, secured transactions rule should be as the Model Law intends to be a model for national legislations. Thirdly, the Model Law also fulfils the expectations of international lenders and investors by setting out clear, modern and predictable rules for legal reform on secured transactions. This particular aspect was defined by Dahan and Simpson as follows:

> Clearly, the Model Law was drafted by an international financial organisation which is also a commercial bank that applies sound banking and investment principles in all its operations. When signing a deal, the Bank pays particular attention to the security package and seeks to take security over property according to modern financial practice.[50]

Finally, the Model Law also acts as a harmonisation instrument with its modern approach for transition economies.[51] The Model Law was followed by the Core Principles in 1997, when it became evident that the Model Law was helpful in legal reform activities but philosophically core principles were needed to establish the culture rather than translating the Model Law into national languages.[52] The Model Law has been criticised, mainly by American scholars,[53] on the basis of not

48 *See generally* McCormack, G. (2008) 'The CFR and Credit Securities: A Suitable Case for Treatment?' in A. Vaquer (ed.) *European Private Law beyond the Common Frame of Reference: Essays in Honour of Reinhard Zimmermann*, Groningen: Europa Law Publishers, pp. 99, 126.

49 *See* Gray, C.W. and Jarosz, W.W. (1995) 'Law and the Regulation of Foreign Direct Investment: The Experience from Central and Eastern Europe' 33 *Colum. J. Transnat'l L.*, 1.

50 Dahan, F. and Simpson, J. (2004) 'The European Bank for Reconstruction and Development's Secured Transactions Project: a model law and ten core principles for a modern secured transactions law in countries of Central and Eastern Europe (and elsewhere!)' in E.M. Kieninger (ed.) *Security Rights in Movable Property in European Private Law*, Cambridge: Cambridge University Press, pp. 98, 100.

51 For these four objectives, *see* Dahan and Simpson, ibid., pp. 99–101.

52 Dahan and Simpson, ibid, pp. 101–102.

53 *See* e.g. Cohen, N.B. (1998) 'Harmonizing the Law Governing Secured Credit: The Next Frontier', 33 *Tex. Int'l L. J.*, 173, 184; Spanogle, J. (1998) 'A Functional Analysis of the EBRD Model Law on Secured Transactions' in J. Norton and M. Andenas (eds) *Emerging Financial Markets and Secured Transactions*. The Hague: Kluwer, pp. 157, 171–3; Sigman, H. (1998) 'The case for Worldwide Reform of the Law Governing Secured Transactions in Movable Property' in J. Ziegel (ed.) *New Developments in International Commercial and Consumer Law*. Oxford: Hart, p. 229.

having similar concepts to that of the UCC Article 9, requiring registration for the creation of charge as opposed to using it for notice purposes and granting super priority to the unpaid vendor's charge under Article 9.[54] In an assessment work and empirical study conducted by the EBRD in 2004, it was found that the assessment of secured transactions regimes of transition economies was not positive.[55] It was suggested that reform of legal rules should be followed by practical and institutional implementation and confirmed that, if institutions involved in secured transactions function well, relatively advanced market economies will have more effective legal frameworks.[56] The EBRD legal experts provide guidelines as to how law reform should be carried out. This includes drafting of the law by local lawyers, resistance to importation of foreign law concepts, understanding the local legal tradition, and being impartial.[57] As the primary purpose of secured transactions is economic, the goal is to achieve legal efficiency, which may be defined by reference to maximising economic benefit, simplicity, speed, cost, certainty, and fit-to-context.[58] The last referenced criteria, 'fit-to-context', is 'the most elusive'[59] of all as it involves adaptation of the adopted rules to the economic, legal and social context that the host country offers.[60] That can only be achieved if the proposed rules do not heavily draw on the principles of one particular system, but should be 'perceived as legitimate [by reflecting] the needs and expectations of the various stakeholders; and a consensus must develop on the need for the reforms, the form and the timing and method of their implementation'.[61] The Model Law seems to achieve this, as mentioned before, by reflecting civil and common law concepts and principles, and by some prominent commentators suggestion as a starting point and example for harmonisation and reform activities.[62]

54 However, McCormack and Dahan suggest that the protection granted by Model Law Article 9 to the unpaid vendor's charge is limited compared to reservation of title clauses under English law. *See* McCormack, G. and Dahan, F. (1999) 'The EBRD Model Law on Secured Transactions: Comparisons and Convergence', *CfiLR*, 65, 75.

55 Dahan, F. and Simpson, J. (2009) 'Legal Efficiency for Secured Transactions Reform: Bridging the Gap between Economic Analysis and Legal Reasoning', 27 *Penn St. Int'l L. Rev.*, 623, 624 *et seq.*

56 Dahan, F., Kutenicova, E. and Simpson, J. (2004) 'Enforcing Secured Transactions in Central and Eastern Europe: An Empirical Study', *Law in Transition* (Spring), 4, 16.

57 *See* Dahan and Simpson, op. cit. (f'note 55), at 629–31.

58 *See* Dahan, F. and Simpson, J. (2008) 'Legal Efficiency of Secured Transactions Reform: Bridging the Gap between Economic Analysis and Legal Reasoning' in F. Dahan and J. Simpson (eds) *Secured Transactions Reform and Access to Credit*. Cheltenham: Edward Elgar, pp. 132–6.

59 Ibid., at 135.

60 *See* Ch. 2 for the *transplantation* argument where adoption of rules is not sufficient; but legal, social and economic infrastructure along with doctrinal commentaries, case law and precedents need to be adopted and digested as well.

61 *See* Tata, V. 'The Role of Multilaterals in the Promotion of Modern Securities Law', *Comments at the Congress to Celebrate the 40th Annual Session of UNCITRAL*, Vienna 9–12 July 2007.

62 *See generally* McCormack, op. cit. (f'note 48).

0.2.4 UNIDROIT Convention on International Interests in Mobile Equipment

While the Factoring Convention received very little acceptance from the industry, the UNIDROIT Convention on International Interests in Mobile Equipment ('the Cape Town Convention') is a successful instrument breaking new ground by establishing a substantive law regime for asset-based financing.[63] Following the UNIDROIT Convention on International Financial Leasing and its philosophy that allows the enforceability of the lessor's rights against third parties, this led UNIDROIT to commence a work on international interests in mobile equipment after a proposal by the Governing Council. The rationale for this initiative was that the traditional rule of *lex rei sitae* applicable to the validity, priority and enforceability of security rights over high value mobile equipment was not suitable.[64] The Convention aims to establish an international regime in order to overcome difficulties arising from the lack of recognition of creation, enforcement, registry and priority of security interests, and interests held by chargees, conditional sellers and lessors of aircraft equipment, railway rolling stock and space objects in cross-border transactions.[65] The object is that party autonomy and private enforcement increases the borrower's access to capital markets.[66] The importance of asset-based lending and leasing, as well as the significance of predictability in the law governing these financing patterns achieved through harmonised rules and facilitation of credit, is indisputable in the aircraft and other mobile equipment industry. The industry's sheer size, and the volume of transactions for the period between 2008 and 2027, illustrate that the number of new aircraft has been estimated at 29,400 and the market value of transactions has been estimated at over US$3.2 trillion.[67] The idea of drafting a Convention on

63 E.g. Davies, I. (2003) 'The New Lex Mercatoria: International Interests in Mobile Equipment', 52 *I.C.L.Q.*, 151; Goode, R. (2002) 'The Cape Town Convention on International Interests in Mobile Equipment: A Driving Force for International Asset-Based Financing', *Unif. L. Rev.*, 3.

64 Stanford, M. (2002) 'From Ottawa to Cape Town: UNIDROIT's Role in the Modernisation of the Law Governing Leasing and the Taking of Security' in I. Davies (ed.) *Security Interests in Mobile Equipment*. Aldershot: Ashgate, pp. 397, 424–5.

65 Cuming, R.C.C. (2000) '"Hot Issues" in the Development of the (Draft) Convention on International Interests in Mobile Equipment and the (Draft) Aircraft Equipment Protocol', 34 *Int'l Law*, 1093, 1095.

66 Kozuka, S. (2007) 'The Economic Implications of Uniformity in Law' *Unif. L. Rev.* 683, 689.

67 The Boeing Company (2008) *Current Market Outlook 2008–2027*. Seattle: The Boeing Company, p. 28. Airbus Industrie (2008) *Global Market Forecast 2007–2026*, p. 5. Airbus Industrie forecasts 24,262 aircraft worth US$2.8 trillion. It is interesting to note that similar data provided by Lorne Clark and Jeffrey Wool in 1999, based on the Boeing Company's 1998 Current Market Outlook, estimated this number as US$1,200 billion (US$1.2 trillion). This is a clear illustration that the figure, despite a number of critical incidents including terrorism threat, SARS and the invasion of Iraq, has almost tripled itself. *See* Clark, L. and Wool, J. (1999) 'A Report on the Development of the Proposed UNIDROIT Convention on International Interests in Mobile Equipment as Applied to Aircraft Equipment', 31 *UCC L.J.*, 389, 390; Wool, J. (1999) 'The Next Generation of International Aviation Finance Law: An Overview of the Proposed UNIDROIT Convention on International Interests in Mobile Equipment as applied to Aircraft Equipment', 20 *U. Pa. J. Int'l Econ. L.*, 499, fn. 22.

this area was initiated at the UNIDROIT Governing Council's 67th session in 1988 following a proposal. This was followed by a study by Professor Cuming, titled *International Regulation of Aspects of Security Interests in Mobile Equipment*,[68] upon which a questionnaire was designed and circulated to business and financial circles. This was followed by the constitution of a working group of experts in 1992.[69] During the preparation of the Convention and the protocols, close cooperation with international organisations such as the International Air Transport Association (IATA) and ICAO, as well as the unprecedented relationship with the industry, was maintained.[70] The economic impact study conducted by Insead and New York University with regard to the likely economic impact of the Cape Town Convention has clearly positive effects on the philosophy of rules.[71] As a result of this study, key objectives such as clear and transparent priority provisions, enforcement of rights against collateral and the enforceability of rights in bankruptcy were set.[72] A number of groups including Aircraft, Registration, Insolvency, Public International Law Working Groups and International Registry Task Force were established.

One of the critical phases during the drafting of the Cape Town Convention was the creation of a dual instrument approach. While the original idea was to produce a single text setting both general rules common to all equipment types encompassed under the Convention and special rules specific to each equipment, in 1996 the Aircraft Working Group suggested an independent move considering the urgent needs of the aircraft industry that was ready to finance new generation aircraft through the Convention's innovative rules.[73] After a joint recommendation by the Aircraft Working Group and the IATA,[74] and discussions as to whether a unitary but extremely detailed regulation or convention/protocol type

68 UNIDROIT Study LXXII-Doc.1 (1989) where, inter alia, Professor Cumming discussed the inadequacy of *lex rei sitae/lex situs* rule in the case of security interests over mobile equipment.

69 UNIDROIT Study LXXII-Doc.2 (1989); Goode, R. (1998) 'Transcending the Boundaries of Earth and Space: The Preliminary Draft UNIDROIT Convention on International Interests in Mobile Equipment', *Unif. L. Rev.* 52; Gopalan, S. (2003) 'Securing Mobile Assets: The Cape Town Convention and Its Aircraft Protocol', 29 *N.C.J. Int'l L. & Com. Reg.*, 59; Gopalan, S. (2003) 'Harmonization of Commercial Law: Lessons from the Cape Town Convention on International Interests in Mobile Equipment', 9 *L. & Bus. Rev. Am.*, 255.

70 Gopalan, ibid., p 270.

71 For the economic impact assessment, *see* Saunders, A. and Walter, I. (1998) 'Proposed UNIDROIT Convention on International Interests in Mobile Equipment as Applicable to Aircraft Equipment through the Aircraft Equipment Protocol: Economic Impact Assessment'; for a more recent impact study, *see* Saunders, A., Srinivasan, A. and Walter, I. (2006) 'Innovation in International Law and Global Finance: Estimating the Financial Impact of the Cape Town Convention', *NYU Working Paper No.* FIN-06-037.

72 UNIDROIT DC9/DEP-Doc. 8, 2 *et seq.* (June 2010).

73 Sundahl, M.J. (2006) 'The "Cape Town Approach": A New Method of Making International Law', 44 *Colum. J. Transnat'l L.* 339, 350–51; Davies, op. cit. (f'note 63), pp. 163–5.

74 UNIDROIT Study LXXII-Doc.32. Recommending that base convention should be accompanied by equipment-specific protocols and when these protocols enter into force, the base convention is incorporated automatically.

of non-unitary approach would be appropriate, a consensus was reached where there would be a base convention, which would be accompanied by protocols and followed by a consolidated text to make rules more comprehensible.[75] Finally, after almost a decade of careful and detailed work, the Convention and its Aircraft Equipment Protocol were adopted in a Diplomatic Conference held in Cape Town in 2001, which entered into force on 1 April 2004 and is in force in 36 countries.[76] The aircraft protocol entered into force on 1 March 2006 in 31 countries.[77] In 2007, the Railway Rolling Stock Protocol was adopted in Luxembourg. The Convention also has a third protocol on Space Objects, which has not yet been adopted.[78] The clear interest of the United States in implementing this Convention and its protocols may mean that other nations follow suit fairly swiftly. Arguably, the Convention is one of the most successful, original and innovative international secured transactions instruments. The concept of *international interest*[79] on receivables related to high-value mobile equipment and its registration into the International Registry of Mobile Assets are important features of the Cape Town Convention. The registration is maintained through an online registry where international interests are recognised and protected and the priority is determined on a first-to-file basis by registering the interest using the manufacturer's serial number.[80] The registration serves as a notice to third parties, thereby effectiveness of the security interest towards third parties is achieved.[81]

The Receivables Convention, Factoring Convention and the Cape Town Convention aim to create harmonised rules in certain areas of secured transactions law. Although there has been criticism towards a piecemeal approach to harmonisation of secured transactions, harmonising certain aspects of secured transactions will, in the long term, assist overall harmonisation of secured transactions law.[82]

75 UNIDROIT CGE/Int.Int./3-Report, para. 2, p. 1; *see also* Cuming, R.C.C. op. cit. (f'note 65), pp. 1100–1.

76 http://www.unidroit.org/english/implement/i-2001-convention.pdf (last accessed 20 June 2010). The USA ratified the Convention and the Aircraft Protocol and both are in force. The UK has signed both instruments but not ratified yet.

77 http://www.unidroit.org/english/implement/i-2001-aircraftprotocol.pdf (last accessed 20 June 2010).

78 However, the Space Objects Protocol is under development (Study LXXII J). It is interesting to note that a suggestion was made in relation to the use of satellites as collateral in 1992. *See* Proceedings, op. cit. (f'note 38), at 271.

79 'International Interests' include security rights arising under security agreements, lease and conditional sale agreements.

80 www.internationalregistry.aero (last accessed 4 June 2010).

81 From 1 March 2006 (the date of acceptance of registration of security interests), nearly 200,000 registrations have been made in relation to 55,000 objects (aircraft, spare engines and helicopters). *International Registry of International Interests in Aircraft Equipment Third Annual Statistical Report*, 1 January 2008–31 December 2008 (29 January 2010); *see also* UNIDROIT DC9/DEP-Doc. 8, 4 (29 January 2010).

82 *See* Bazinas, S. (1998) 'An International Regime for Receivables Financing: UNCITRAL's Contribution', 8 *Duke J. Comp. & Int'l L.*, 315, 318 and fn 11.

0.2.5 UNCITRAL Legislative Guide on Secured Transactions

In 2000, UNCITRAL embarked upon a far-reaching and sophisticated legislative text aimed to modernise domestic laws. The project was postponed in the late 1970s.[83] Following the thirty-third and thirty-fourth sessions of UNCITRAL in 2000 and 2001, two reports[84] were considered upon which it was decided that a work on security interests in goods involved in commercial activity would be critical given the significant impact of secured credit law in economic growth.[85] Following a colloquium in 2002,[86] it was decided that the form of the work should be a legislative guide[87] that has a flexible nature as opposed to a convention or a model law. The Guide was adopted on 14 December 2007 in the resumed fortieth Commission session[88] upon approval in principle in the thirty-ninth session in 2006.[89] It works in tandem with the Receivables Convention and builds upon various secured transactions instruments.[90]

The legislative reform that the Guide intends will affect both developed and emerging economies. In that sense, the recommendations of the Guide target the modernisation of emerging markets' secured transactions legislations in which inefficient rules often prevent facilitation of secured credit, as well as developed nations with inefficient secured credit laws and those with relatively efficient secured transactions regimes. The Guide acts as a 'blueprint for States wishing to modernise their secured transactions regimes'.[91] The intention of the Guide is 'to be useful to States that do not currently have efficient and effective secured transactions laws, [and] States that already have workable laws but wish to modernize these laws and harmonize them with the laws of other States'.[92] It is not a convention or model law, and its recommendations assist national legislators to enact secured transactions reform. Modernisation through adoption and

83 Bazinas, S. (1998) 'UNCITRAL's work in the field of secured transactions' *in* Norton and Andenas (eds) op. cit. (f'note 53), p. 211.
84 A/CN.9/475 and A/CN.9/496.
85 A/56/17, paras 351–359.
86 A/CN.9/WG.VI/WP.3.
87 A/57/17, paras 202–204.
88 A/CN.9/631, Add. 1–11 (A/62/17, Part I); A/CN.9/631/Add.1–3, A/CN.9/637, Add. 1–8 (A/62/17, Part II).
89 A/61/17 para. 13 and A/CN.9/WG.VI/WP.21/Add. 3.
90 Guide, para. 12, at 3–4. One may argue that the Guide seems to have adopted a 'pyramidal incrementalism', the definition of which can be provided as an instrument building explicitly or implicitly on prior instruments produced by other organisations and the subsequent instrument takes a pyramidal form by having a global consensus. *See* Block-Lieb, S. and Halliday, T.C. (2007) 'Incrementalisms in Global Lawmaking', 32 *Brook. J. Int'l L.*, 851, 900.
91 Kohn, R.M. (2007) 'Promoting the Implementation of the United Nations Convention on the Assignment of Receivables in International Trade and the UNCITRAL Legislative Guide on Secured Transactions', *Comments at the Congress to Celebrate the 40th Annual Session of UNCITRAL*, Vienna 9–12 July.
92 Guide, para. 1, at 1.

implementation of the recommendations will eventually lead to harmonisation of secured transactions regimes. The Guide indicates that the legal regime it envisages is a purely domestic regime. However, as the secured transactions involve parties and assets from different States, the domestic regime it envisages will go far towards, and be accepted as, a cross-border regime.

For the facilitation of credit the Guide suggests that 'secured transactions laws should be structured to enable businesses to maximize the extent to which they can utilize the value inherent in their movable assets to obtain credit'.[93] This is certainly crucial because, in times of financial crisis, individuals as well as businesses have no, or very limited access to, finance as financial institutions are reluctant to lend. This is possibly because of the insufficiency of protection provided by archaic property laws, which often do not recognise anything but immovable and, not very often, movable property as collateral.[94] The rationale of preparing a guide rather than a model law was that the preparation of a model law would not provide the same impact,[95] because the Guide had a more flexible approach through its recommendations rather than a model law or a convention. The Guide reflects clear and predictable rules, as well as the practical truth that secured lending reduces the risk of non-payment and lowers the cost of credit. The Guide recognises that facilitation of credit through clear and predictable rules can only be achieved by 'the relevant infrastructure, judiciary and enforcement mechanisms'.[96] A comprehensive and functional approach to security for facilitated credit is also adopted.[97] The Guide in that sense reflects the philosophy of the UCC Article 9 rather than English law. It is also argued that the Guide's principles reflect the common law approach to credit and security rather than civil law. The particularly problematic title-based devices, the regulation of which varies dramatically among countries, have been dealt with in an innovative method. The Guide contains a unitary and non-unitary approach to acquisition financing devices, thus appearing to be more acceptable to those countries that treat title-based devices as security interest and those that treat them distinct from security interests.[98]

93 Guide, para. 8, at 2.

94 The World Bank has conducted empirical research on the perception of financiers in recognising certain types of collateral. *See* Safavian, M. (2004) 'Firm level evidence on collateral and access to finance' in F. Dahan and J. Simpson (eds), op. cit. (f'note 58), p. 110.

95 *See generally* Bazinas, S. (2006) 'Modernising and Harmonising Secured Credit Law: The Example of the UNCITRAL Draft Legislative Guide on Secured Transactions, Part 1', *BJIBFL* 20; *see generally* Bazinas, S. (2004) 'UNCITRAL's Work in the Field of Secured Transactions', 36 *UCC.L.J.*, 67.

96 *See* Bazinas, S. ibid, at 20. For a similar view in relation to the Model Law and its impact, *see* Dahan, F. and Simpson, J. (2004) 'Secured Transactions in Central and Eastern Europe: European Bank for Reconstruction and Development (EBRD) Assessment', 36 *UCC L.J.*, 77, 101.

97 Ch. 3.

98 Ch. 7.

0.3 Purpose, scope and structure of the book

Harmonisation, as a key concept, is necessary for the facilitation of credit. International conventions and instruments, one way or the other, aim to achieve harmonisation and modernisation of domestic, as well as cross-border, secured transactions laws in order to facilitate access to low-cost credit. Secured transactions, once in the realm of domestic law, are now internationalised by those activities – and hence the title of this book. The following analysis will illustrate how facilitation of credit may be ensured through the main features of international secured transactions instruments. Although some may argue that the Guide aims to modernise only domestic laws, still it certainly will have an impact on international transactions once enacted as secured transactions reform.

The main focus of the book is the analysis of significant international secured transactions law instruments. In that context, the scope of analyses will cover:

(a) the Receivables Convention, which provides substantive and conflict-of-laws rules governing assignment of receivables, whether outright or for security;
(b) the Factoring Convention, which provides rules for relationship among factor, creditor and debtor in the assignment of receivables only arising from international sale of goods;
(c) the Cape Town Convention, which addresses creation, effectiveness against third parties, priority and enforcement of rights created or provided by security interests, retention-of-title and lease of mobile equipment (aircraft, railway rolling stock, space objects) that is in detail governed by protocols;
(d) the Guide, which provides a comprehensive set of rules governing creation, effectiveness against third parties, priority and enforcement of security interests in movables and outright transfer of receivables; and
(e) the Model Law, which addresses creation, effectiveness against third parties, priority and enforcement of a single security right for emerging and transition economies.[99]

The significant impact of this work lies in rationalising the legislative efforts of international standard-setting bodies and multilateral financing organisations and explaining the key principles underlying those efforts to the stakeholders – particularly the emerging economies in Europe and elsewhere. The overarching idea that the monograph will promote is that the future and potential implementation of at least some of the international instruments can only be properly understood and appreciated if the importance and impact of central tenets of these international instruments are appraised. The resulting overview of international secured transactions instruments aims to provide a more theoretically rigorous analytical appraisal of underlying principles, and how these principles are applied to essential features of the modern secured transactions regime envisaged

99 For background details and further information on those instruments, *see* Ch. 2.

by international instruments. The recurrent theme is the argument about facilitation of credit by making the law in this area more predictable.[100] The book compares and contrasts international instruments by distilling their unifying principles and weaving in a discussion with two important jurisdictions (that is, England and the US) on key issues to identify and illustrate problems. The rationale of choosing these two jurisdictions is that they have: firstly, developed financial markets; and secondly, modern rules on secured transactions that are used as a catalyst (in the case of the UCC Article 9) that inspired law revisions in a number of jurisdictions, including Canada and New Zealand; and thirdly, the comparison will provide a useful explanation and example for emerging markets, of how modern and well-established systems facilitate access to lower cost credit by having predictable rules. In addition, this book contests claims that the Guide and the Receivables Convention have an American tone. The book submits that, if particularly these international instruments have been influenced by the UCC Article 9, this argument is fortuitous, as this claim lacks full theoretical and practical support.

The analysis in this book is confined to transactions that create security interests over movable assets. It was thought that the extension of the discussion to security interests in intellectual property would extend the scope unnecessarily.[101] Hence, the exclusion of the very recent draft supplement to the UNICTRAL Guide on Secured Transactions, dealing with security rights in intellectual property. Furthermore, the book does not analyse the UNIDROIT Convention on Substantive Rules for Intermediated Securities, the Hague Convention on the Law Applicable to Certain Rights in respect of Securities Held with an Intermediary,[102] or the EU Financial Collateral Directive; as these are more related to financial market transactions and inclusion of these transactions would have been outside the ambit of the work. The book does not analyse the rights and obligations of parties and third parties, or enforcement and insolvency issues. Rights and obligations of parties and third parties are mainly governed by the law chosen between parties, and the rules envisaged by international instruments are almost always the same. Thus in this book it is thought to be more appropriate to deal with the more pressing issues in financing such as, but not limited to, creation, third-party effectiveness and priority of security interests. Again, enforcement policies are national prerogatives, they depend on national laws, and there

100 This is a critical matter and mentioned in the Preambles of the Receivables Convention (paras 3 and 5), Cape Town Convention (paras 1–2), Guide recommendation 1 and the Model Law introduction para. 1.

101 The Guide itself as it stands currently does not apply to security rights over intellectual property, hence the work on supplement for security rights in intellectual property. See Guide, para. 33, at 39.

102 Recently, there have been suggestions on possible future work on security rights in directly held securities to be considered by UNCITRAL. *See* Kohn, R. 'Possible Future Work on Security Rights in Directly Held Securities' http://www.uncitral.org/pdf/english/colloquia/3rdSecTrans/Richard_Kohn_Edited.pdf (last accessed April 2010).

is no international enforcement mechanism in this area – hence exclusion from the scope of this work. It is also clear that secured transactions law cannot be thought separately from the insolvency law, and the Guide rightly includes a chapter on the impact of insolvency on a security right. However, it is thought that inclusion of insolvency would unmanageably enlarge the scope of this work. Finally, the analysis does not attempt to compare and analyse these international instruments on an article by article basis.

1 Secured credit and fundamental principles of international instruments

1.1 Introduction

Taking security is critical and international formulating agencies, as well as multilateral financial organisations, have expressed interest in the topic in the last four decades by taking active part in the preparation and promotion of instruments to harmonise and modernise the law in that area. Taking security is crucial for banks and financiers that prefer to lend with a minimal risk. Security is also important for businesses to expand their investments and economic growth. Fundamental principles of international instruments illustrate the significance of secured credit and access to credit. Certainty and predictability in secured transactions law are two key words (although often used interchangeably) that underlie the fundamental principles.

This chapter will first, define and describe practices covered by international instruments. Second, the significance and rationale of secured lending will be discussed. Third, fundamental principles of international instruments will be examined. Fundamental principles provide an optimal lens through which to examine how law should support access to credit and lower the cost of credit. It is a known fact that security plays a significant role in lending decisions. The recurrent theme is that taking security is important and the law should have means to support taking security for the facilitation of credit and sustainable investment.

1.2 Defining secured transactions, security interests and assignment of receivables

1.2.1 Secured transactions

The term 'secured transactions' can be defined as transactions that create security interests, or it refers to security over property as opposed to a personal security.[1]

1 Personal security is 'the security furnished by a person . . . [as] a personal obligation assumed by a person other than the debtor . . . [p]ersonal security, therefore, is an obligation assumed by a third party as security for the principal debtor's obligation'. *See* Drobnig, U. (2003) 'Present and Future of Real and Personal Security', 5 *E.R.P.L.*, 623, 625. Some of the personal security instruments can be cited as suretyships, stand-by letters of guarantee and binding comfort letters.

Although the Guide indicates that 'there is no universally accepted definition of secured transactions law',[2] it defines 'secured transaction' as a transaction that creates a security right. This term under the Guide also covers outright transfers of a receivable subject to enforcement exception, although outright transfers do not secure the performance of an obligation.[3] Dahan defines secured transactions as follows:

> an agreement – usually accessory to a credit agreement, present or past – which grants the creditor a right relating to property, the purpose of which is to improve the creditor's chance of getting paid or of receiving whatever else the debtor is required to do by way of performance of the contract . . . Such security may be possessory, where the creditor takes the possession of the subject matter of the security, or non-possessory.[4]

In Canada it is more common to address this area of law as 'personal property security' and in England it is more common to refer to 'the law of credit and security'. 'Security over personal property' is the proper basis in this study and it can be defined as a 'property right granted . . . by the principal debtor itself in its own assets; [and] its peculiar feature is the fact that it conveys with respect to the charged assets, a privileged position to the secured creditor'.[5]

A real security can be granted by both the debtor of the secured obligation and a third party who is not personally obliged to the creditor. There can be security over tangibles and intangibles such as book debts.[6] The former can be constituted as a pledge where the creditor holds possession of the tangible collateral,[7] or by the debtor where the collateral is registered in a specialised registry such as a motor vehicles registry and the debtor continues to enjoy possession while granting security, and the latter can be in certain historical forms such as pledge, charge and mortgage or as an assignment. 'Secured credit' can be defined as a type of credit that is granted with security, which may be personal or proprietary.[8] The creditor takes security to reduce the risk of not being paid, and the cost of utilisation of his

2 Guide, para. 2, at 31.

3 Recommendation 3.

4 Dahan, F. (2000) 'Secured Transactions Law in Western Advanced Economies: Exposing Myths', *Law in Transition*, 37, 38 (Autumn).

5 Drobnig, op. cit. (f'note 1), at 625.

6 'Book Debts' are commonly referred to as 'Account Receivables' under UCC Article 9 terminology.

7 The major usage of creditor-held security can be seen in goods in transit represented by bills of lading or similar negotiable documents and also certified securities. Drobnig, op. cit. (f'note 1), 639.

8 Drobnig, U. (1998) 'Secured Credit in International Insolvency Proceedings', 33 *Tex. Int'l L. J.*, 53, 54; *see* Dahan, F. and McCormack, G. (2002) 'International Influences and the Polish Law on Secured Transactions: Harmonisation, Unification or What?', *Unif. L. Rev.*, 713, 716 *et seq.*

money is lower for a secured than for an unsecured credit.[9] It is arguable that secured credit increases the opportunities for lending.

1.2.2 *Security interest*

A 'security interest' is defined in the UCC terminology as 'an interest in personal property or fixtures which secures payment or performance of an obligation'.[10] Under the UCC Article 9 there is unification for all security interests. The so-called 'substance over form' approach provides that the substance of the transaction has more importance than the form, and thus all transactions that serve security functions are classed as security interests notwithstanding their forms.[11] This is clearly echoed in the Comment to the UCC §9–109: 'when a security interest is created, this Article applies regardless of the form of transaction or the name that parties have given to it'.[12] UCC §9–109 expands the scope of coverage of UCC Article 9 to include not only sales of accounts and chattel paper, but also sales of payment intangibles and promissory notes.[13] Under UCC Article 9, transfers of an interest in accounts and chattel paper (whether or not a transfer for security or sale) must be perfected by filing. UCC Article 9 extends to cover sales of accounts only in order to apply notice filing; however, this does not convert the transaction into a security transaction. UCC Article 9 treats assignments by way of security and by way of sale more or less the same for purposes of perfection (that is, filing or registration) and priorities, but differently for enforcement purposes (generally speaking the buyer has no responsibility to return surplus to the seller).

9 Drobnig, ibid., p. 54; for a similar explanation, *see* Carlson, D.G. 'On the Efficiency of Secured Lending', 80 *Va. L. Rev.*, 2179, 2090–1 (1994) stating that '[t]he way security interests increase a creditor's power is clear: they give the secured party a pre-existing lien so that the secured party need not wait for some future judicial event to engender one'.

10 UCC §1–201(37).

11 The scope of applicability of UCC Article 9 is similar to what has been envisaged by the Law Commission. *See* Law Commission Consultation Paper No. 164, *Registration of Security Interests*, para. 1.26. However, the enactment potential of UCC Article 9 type legislation may diminish in England the 'practical utility' of quasi-security interests such as the sale of receivables or retention-of-title. *See* McCormack, G. (2004) *Secured Credit under English and American Law*. Cambridge: Cambridge University Press, p. 72; McCormack, G. (2000) 'Rewriting the English Law of Personal Property Securities and Article 9 of the US Uniform Commercial Code', 24 *Co. Law*, 6. Guide, para. 103, at 56.

12 UCC §9–109, cmt. 2 (2001). UCC Article 9 combines traditional possessory security rights with non-possessory security rights under one security interest. Though there are exceptions from the scope of UCC Article 9.

13 The perfection and priority rules of UCC Article 9 apply to sales of receivables transactions and, therefore, a factor has to file financing statements in order to prevail. Under UCC Article 9, transfers of an interest in accounts and chattel paper (whether or not a transfer for security or a sale transfer) must be perfected by filing. UCC Article 9 extends to cover sales of accounts only in order to apply the filing requirement, and this does not make the transaction a security transaction.

In English legal terminology it is more common to refer to 'charge'.[14] However, due to fragmentation (traditional/quasi-security distinction), there is no general concept of *security interest* as it is understood under UCC Article 9, and it is more appropriate to distinguish as possessory and non-possessory security.[15] Further classification of rights may be made as legal and equitable, possessory and non-possessory, and consensual and non-consensual security.[16] A charge can be used in different ways where it can be a fixed or floating charge if it is used to refer to a specific legal instrument, or it is used to refer to all types of security interests. Under English law, a charge is a right of recourse against property to guarantee the payment of money due or the performance of some other obligation, and is a consensual security right according to which the chargor (debtor) retains possession of the asset used as collateral and established by agreement concluded between the chargor and chargee.[17] A floating charge does not attach to a specific asset, and permits the debtor to continue his ordinary business without the approval of the creditor and collect the debts for his own exclusive use until the occurrence of a future event, which limits the debtor's power to freely dispose of the charged property.[18] Upon occurrence of a future event, the floating charge will be crystallised and converted into a fixed charge. A fixed charge attaches to a specific asset upon either creation of a charge or acquisition of the asset by the company.[19]

English law does not provide a statutory definition of security. In *Re Paramount Airways Ltd.*[20] security was defined as follows: 'security is created where a person (the creditor) obtains rights exercisable against some property in which the debtor

14 For some implications under English law, *Re BCCI (No. 8)* [1998] AC 214; McCormack, G. (1998) 'Charge Backs and Commercial Certainty in the House of Lords', *CfiLR*, 111.

15 Bridge, M., MacDonald, R., Simmonds, R. and Walsh, C. (1999) 'Formalism, Functionalism and Understanding the Law of Secured Transactions', 44 *McGill L.J.*, 567, 634 *et seq.*

16 Mortgages and charges are consensual non-possessory security created by agreement, whereas equitable lien and maritime lien are non-consensual, non-possessory security interests created by operation of law. Pledge and contractual lien are classified as consensual possessory security interests where the possession of the asset is used by the lender by agreement of the debtor, whereas possessory and statutory lien are classified as non-consensual possessory security interests where the possession is granted to the lender not by agreement but by operation of law. *See* e.g. McCormack, G. (2003 '"Quasi-securities" and the Law Commission Consultation paper on security interests: A brave new world', *L.M.C.L.Q.*, 80; Davies, I. (2004) 'The Reform of English Personal Property security law: functionalism and Article 9 of the Uniform Commercial Code', 24 *Legal Studies*, 295; Bridge *et al*, ibid., pp. 634–5.

17 McCormack, G. (2005) 'The Law Commission Consultative Report on Company Security Interests: An Irreverent Riposte', 68 *M.L.R.*, 286, 287 and n. 11; *Swiss Bank Corp. v Lloyds Bank* [1982] A.C. 584, 595.

18 Ferran, E.V. (1988) 'Floating Charges – the Nature of the Security', *C.L.J.*, 213; Gullifer, L. (2003) 'Will the Law Commission sink the floating charge?', *L.M.C.L.Q.*, 125.

19 Gullifer, ibid., at 126. On this matter, *see generally In re Yorkshire Woolcombers Association Ltd.* [1903] 2 Ch 284; *Re Brightlife Ltd.* [1987] Ch 200; *Re Woodroffes (Musical Instruments) Ltd.* [1986] Ch 366 (Chancery Division); *Agnew v Commissioner of Inland Revenue (Re Brumark Investments Ltd.)* [2001] UKPC 28, [2001] 2 AC 710.

20 [1990] BCC 130.

has an interest in order to enforce the discharge of the debtor's obligation to the creditor.'[21] However, this definition is not comprehensive as it does not recognise the fact that security can be granted by a third party. A far-reaching definition is provided by Professor Goode: 'a security interest is a right given to one party in the asset of another party to secure payment or performance by that other party or by a third party.'[22] A security interest is a right *in rem* that can be granted, by the debtor who owns the property, to the creditor who grants credit on a secured basis. Thus, in order to create a security interest, ownership of the property that serves as collateral is crucial and must be acquired either before the creation or the attachment of security interest.[23] In that context, it is not possible to create a security interest by retention-of-title.[24] Under English law there is 'fragmentation',[25] and there are different rules for hire purchase or conditional sale, mortgage, charge and pledge. Mortgage, charge and pledge are traditional forms of security,[26] whereas transactions such as hire purchase and conditional sales are not as a matter of law considered within the categories of security, but they have a similar economic function. Hire-purchase agreements and conditional sales are known as 'quasi-security' or 'title finance' because the debtor does not have the ownership of the property. The Law Commission observed that as the law classified quasi-security interests according to their form and not to their substance and thus, they are not registrable under the Companies Act 2006, unlike a charge, this may cause problems to potential lenders in ascertaining as to whether credit should be given.[27] In practices such as retention of title, the financier retains full title to the

21 Ibid., p. 149. For another definition of 'security', *see Edwards v Flightline Ltd.* [2003] EWCA Civ 63; [2003] 3 All E.R. 1200, [2003] 1 W.L.R. at 1200 where 'security' is defined as:

> an agreement between a debtor and a creditor that the debt owing shall be paid out of a specific fund coming to the debtor, or an order given by a debtor to his creditor upon a person owing money or holding funds belonging to the giver or the order, directing such person to pay such funds to the creditor, will create a valid equitable charge upon such fund, in other words, will operate as an equitable assignment of the debts or fund to which the order refers. An agreement for valuable consideration that a fund shall be applied in a particular way may found an injunction to restrain its application in another way. But if there is nothing more, such a stipulation will not amount to an equitable assignment. It is necessary to find . . . that an obligation has been imposed in favour of the creditor to pay the debt out of the fund.

22 Gullifer, L. (ed.) (2009) *Goode on Legal Problems of Credit and Security*, 4th edn. London: Sweet & Maxwell, p. 11.

23 *Abbey National Building Society v Cann* [1991] 1 AC 56, 92; *see also* Calnan, R. (2006) *Taking Security Law and Practice*. Bristol: Jordans, pp. 235–6.

24 *McEntire v Crossley Brothers Ltd.* [1895] AC 457, 462; *Armour v Thyssen Edelstahlwerke AG* [1991] 2 AC 339 HL, 351–52 where the appellants transferred the ownership of the steel strip under a contract of sale and they were not creating a right of security and not giving security to a creditor; *Clough Mill Ltd. v Martin* [1985] 1 WLR 111, 123.

25 For a similar view, *see* Goode, R. (1998) *Commercial Law in the Next Millennium: The Hamlyn Lectures Forty-Ninth Series*. London: Sweet & Maxwell, p. 64.

26 For the discussion of traditional security interests *see* e.g. McCormack, op. cit. (f'note 11), Ch. 2.

27 Law Commission Consultation Paper No. 176, at 34.

assets rather than being granted a charge over the assets, and if the debtor fails to pay for the assets they can be retained or sold. Although, in theory, law does not consider them as creating a security, in practice they perform security functions and are used by businesses and banks routinely.[28] Earlier law reform efforts observed that a functional approach should be introduced, and that the definition of security interest should include not only traditional security interests but also the quasi-security interests.[29] Specific recommendations made by the Law Commission in relation to registration of security interests have not been included in the Company Law Reform. Arguably the recommendations of the Law Commission were pragmatic, and were aimed at transactional certainty along the UCC Article 9 lines where a particular form of transaction is irrelevant in the resolution of priority conflicts between secured creditors and third parties. These recommendations include replacing the registration system contained in the companies legislation with a more comprehensive system, setting clear and rational rules for priority by determining priority from the date of registration, a new online system of registry for security interests, possibility to register in advance of the transactions and removal of a 21-day time limit for registration, and removing the distinction between fixed and floating charges while retaining the advantages of floating charges. The Law Commission's scheme was also recommended to be extended to quasi-securities where the scheme should provide for filing of sales of receivables and cover title-based devices.[30] One can argue that banks could have benefited highly from the Law Commission's proposals for reform.

The Guide[31] and the Model Law[32] abandon the distinction between traditional and quasi-security interests and introduce single security right in respect of all types of things and rights. The Guide defines security right as a right that secures payment or other obligation regardless of whether the parties have characterised it as a security right. In that context, under the Guide, depending on the approach adopted by a State (unitary or non-unitary approach to acquisition of financing right),[33] security right[34] will either include retention of title or financial lease right, or exclude these. The Model Law has the formalist approach (distinguishing the grant of security from reservation of title transactions where in the latter the

28 For the advantages of quasi-security interests, *see* Law Commission Consultation Paper No. 164, at 164 *et seq*.

29 Diamond, A. (1989) 'A Review of Security Interests in Property'. London: DTI, HMSO, 'Diamond Report', para. 9.3.2.

30 Law Commission Consultation Paper No. 176. Companies Act 2006, Part 25, regulates Company Charges. Quasi Security interests have not been included under this Part and are not registrable.

31 Guide, para. 101 *et seq*., at 55 *et seq*. (except in retention-of-title devices).

32 Model Law Article 1.

33 *See* Ch. 7 *below*.

34 Guide, at 13. Security right is defined as '. . . a property right in a movable asset that is created by agreement and secures payment or other performance of an obligation, regardless of whether the parties have denominated as a security right . . .'.

seller enjoys the ownership rights, whereas the buyer/hirer/lessee only has the possessory rights).[35] The Model Law's single security right is broader than the UCC Article 9 security interest in that it covers all types of rights; nevertheless, it does not adopt the functional approach. In this context, different security devices may be created and retain their legal nature.[36] Thus there are three methods to create a charge (registered charge, unpaid vendor's charge [similar to transfer-of-title and grant of a security back to the seller] and possessory charge).[37] The Model Law uses the term 'charge' as 'the most general and neutral expression in English to cover consensual security rights'.[38] Under English law, 'charge' may be used to denote mortgages and charges *stricto sensu*. It can be argued that the term 'charge' under the Model Law is not strictly the same as what is understood under English law.[39] The Model Law concept of 'charge' also includes 'pledge'. Pledge is used in Civil Law jurisdictions where the possession of the debtor's asset is actually delivered to the creditor for security (possibly kept in a warehouse or with a trustee), though it is also possible to have a non-possessory pledge, which functions like the English concept of 'charge' where the creditor is not given actual possession but security is registered in the special registry denoting the security right over the goods. In that sense there is a similarity with the English term 'charge', but the difference may be experienced in the specificity aspect, where the latter does not require specificity of assets to be charged.[40]

The Receivables Convention does not make any distinction between outright and security transfers of receivables, thus in a way it follows the UCC Article 9 regime.[41] On the other hand, the Cape Town Convention has a pragmatic regime where the international interest encompasses both traditional security interests, while recognising the uniqueness of other devices and leaving the characterisation to the applicable law under Article 5(3) and accommodates retention of title and leasing transactions that perform security functions, along with security interests.

35 Röver, J-H.M. (2007) *Secured Lending in Eastern Europe: Comparative Law of Secured Transactions and the EBRD Model Law*, Oxford: Oxford University Press, p. 72. Professor Röver indicates that '[t]he Model Law has opted for the formal approach'.

36 *See also* Guide, para. 103, at 56, where it is stated that the Model Law 'creates a specific security right that can work [together] with other security devices (such as leasing) and re-characterizes retention-of-title as a security right'.

37 Model Law Articles 6.2 and 8; 6.4 and 10; 6.3 and 9; 5.6.

38 Model Law Article 1.1.

39 In *Re Bond Worth Ltd.* [1980] Ch 228, 250, Slade J. stated that '[t]he . . . difference between . . . "mortgage" [and] "charge", . . . is that a mortgage involves a conveyance of property subject to a right of redemption, whereas a charge conveys nothing and . . . gives the chargee certain rights over the property as security for the loan'.

40 McCormack and Dahan note, however, that in transition economies, pledge is used in a wider sense that is generally understood in English law. *See* McCormack, G. and Dahan, F. (1999) 'The EBRD Model Law on Secured Transactions: Comparisons and Convergence', *CfiLR*, 65, 69; J. Leavy (2007) 'France' in Sigman, H.C. and Kieninger, E.M., '*Cross Border Security over Tangibles*'. Munich: Sellier, pp. 101 *et seq.*

41 *See* Ch. 3.

This is illustrated by 'agreement creating the interest'[42] and 'agreement providing for the interest'.[43] All of these devices are regulated equally for registration and priority purposes, but differently for the application of default remedies. In that context, an international interest is an interest in a uniquely identifiable object and granted by the chargor under a security agreement; vested in a person who is the conditional seller under a title reservation agreement; or vested in a person who is the lessor under a leasing agreement.[44]

1.2.3 Assignment of receivables

Receivables financing[45] is a significant financing technique and sets the background of the Receivables and Factoring Conventions that attempt to harmonise this portion of the law of secured transactions. The Law Commission observed that in practice the majority of company assets take the form of money owed to them under contracts for the sale of goods and services supplied.[46] Companies finance their business by raising money through receivables by either borrowing where they charge the receivables to a financier/lender (assignment by way of security) or selling them (assignment by way of sale, factoring or securitisation) where the financier/assignee purchases receivables (after deducting its interest rate and fees) from the assignor and recovers receivables from the debtor. The latter practice may be with or without recourse (that is, where the assignor may or may not guarantee the assignee that the debtor will pay, and if the debtor defaults the assignor will repurchase or compensate the loss).[47] If the debtor is notified, he may pay receivables to the assignee; alternatively the assignor may continue to collect the payment on behalf of the assignee (non-notification factoring or financing).[48] Although the use of non-notification assignment is advantageous for the assignor as 'an assignment may be viewed as indicating financial or managerial weakness of the assignor',[49] it carries the risk for the assignee that the debtor may pay to the assignor and get a good discharge. In securitisation,[50] the assignor/

42 Cape Town Convention Article 1(jj) defines security interest as 'an interest created by a security agreement'' For the definition of security agreement, *see* Article 1(ii).

43 Cape Town Convention Article 7, where the former indicates the creation of security interest and the latter retention of title and leasing agreements.

44 Cape Town Convention Article 2(2).

45 For a detailed analysis of receivables financing, *see* Oditah, F. (1991) *Legal Aspects of Receivables Financing*. London: Sweet & Maxwell; A/CN.9/397.

46 Law Commission Report No. 296 (2005), para. 4.1.

47 This type of financing practice may also be known as invoice discounting or block discounting (which relates to consumer receivables).

48 Law Commission Report No. 296 (2005), para. 4.3. Examples of non-notification assignment are block and invoice discounting.

49 A/CN.9/397, para. 10, at 5.

50 For different types of securitisation (true sale, synthetic and whole business), *see e.g.* de Vries Robbé, J.J. (2008) *Securitization Law and Practice in the Face of the Credit Crunch*. Alphen aan den Rijn: Kluwer.

originator may continue to collect the payment on behalf of the assignee.[51] In securitisation, receivables are collected, pooled and then assigned by way of sale (true sale)[52] to a specially established company (SPV – Special Purpose Vehicle), which should be bankruptcy-remote from the assignor. The true sale nature of the transaction is critical, because the rating agency's rating, generally speaking, is made on the assumption that in the event of liquidation, the liquidator should not challenge that the transfer was voided or reversed on the grounds that receivables were transferred by way of security or by a disguised sale transaction.[53] The SPV issues to investors securities or commercial paper, which are secured on the receivables, to raise finance in order to purchase the receivables. In the meantime, the originator/assignor continues to collect the receivables.

Factoring, which involves purchase of receivables by the factoring company (after deduction of interest rate and factoring company's fees), is a significant financing technique for SMEs, enabling them to have access to immediate cash flow. The value of receivables, as opposed to the creditworthiness of the SME, is taken into account in financing decisions. In factoring, receivables are financed as opposed to inventory. The company often assumes the risk of non-payment by the debtor.[54] The factor provides a number of services to the assignor (supplier). These include financing the assignor, protection of default, maintaining account or collecting receivables. Forfaiting is similar to factoring; however, it differs in the way where the assignee waives the right recourse to the assignor if the debtor defaults.

In English law, assignment by way of sale (absolute/outright assignment)[55] and by way of security are treated distinctly[56] and the distinction was confirmed by a number of cases;[57] and especially by *Lloyds & Scottish Finance v Cyril Lord Carpet Sales*[58] where the House of Lords held that the transaction constituted a sale and purchase of debts. The courts, while determining as to whether it is a sale or a

51 On securitisation, *see* e.g. Hill, C.A. (1996) 'Securitization: A Low Cost Sweetener For Lemons', 74 *Wash. U.L.Q.*, 1061; Schwarcz, S.L. (2004) 'Securitization Post-Enron', 25 *Cardozo L. Rev.*, 1539, 1540; Frankel, T. (2002) 'The Law of Cross-Border Securitization: Lex Juris', 12 *Duke J. Comp. & Int'l L.* 475; Schwarz, S.L. (1994) 'The Alchemy of Asset Securitization', 1 *Stan. J. L. Bus. & Fin.*, 133.

52 Although it should be noted that securitisation may involve an outright sale plus sub-charge.

53 For recharacterisation risk, *see* Law Commission Consultation Paper No. 164, para. 6.34 *et seq.*

54 Schwarcz, S.L. (1999) 'Towards a Centralized Perfection System for Cross-Border Receivables Financing', 20 *U. Pa. J. Int'l Econ. L.*, 455, 457.

55 Assignment by way of sale may also be known as factoring according to which the assignee, in addition to assignment, provides services such as finance for the supplier, maintenance of accounts (ledgering), collection of the debts, and protection against default in payments by debtors. *See e.g.* Factoring Convention, Article 1(b). If these services are not provided, the relationship will merely be an invoice discounting. There are other types of factoring such as export factoring (right to payment assigned to a foreign factor resident in the debtor's location), import factoring (right to payment assigned to a local factor resident in the assignor's location) or two factor pattern (where export and import factoring merge).

56 E.g. McCormack, G. (2005) *Registration of Company Charges*, 2nd edn. Bristol: Jordans, pp. 99 *et seq.*

57 E.g. *Siebe Gorman & Co Ltd v Barclays Bank Ltd.* [1979] 2 Lloyd's Law Reports 142; *Re Kent and Sussex Sawmills Ltd.* [1947] Ch. 177.

58 [1992] BCLC 609.

security transaction, investigate the substance rather than the form of the transaction.[59] In general terms, English law treats these transactions distinctly in various respects. One of the points of distinction is that s 136 Law of Property Act 1925 sets out that the assignment must be absolute and not purporting to be by way of charge only. However, an assignment by way of sale can still operate by way of security, and whether s 136 applies depends on the absolute nature of the transfer. Put another way, the assignor must transfer the right to payment to the assignee absolutely. If the assignment is by way of security, the assignor retains an equity of redemption because the ownership of the debt has not been transferred. In that respect, for instance, 'with a mortgage the assignee has ownership of the debt transferred subject to the assignor's right of redemption [and] a charge of a debt . . . gives the chargee not ownership of the debt but rather preferential rights thereto'.[60] Another point of distinction is that assignments by way of sale are not required to be registered and 'do[es] not amount to charges, even if the company agrees to repurchase any receivable that is not paid'.[61] The assignment by way of security requires registration under Part 25 of the Companies Act 2006 if the assignor is a company. The Law Commission recommended the extension of registration of security interests to cover the outright sales of receivables, so that whenever a company sells its book debts to a factor, the factor, rather than writing to each debtor, will be able to secure its position by filing in the register.[62] Another point of distinction is that an assignment by way of security, even if it is registered, may be set aside during the company's liquidation process due to the fact that it may be 'a preference, a transaction at an undervalue, an extortionate credit bargain, a floating charge created during the relevant time, or an attempt to defraud creditors',[63] whereas a sale of receivables transaction may not be avoided on the abovementioned grounds except in the fact that the 'discount given to the [assignee] is deemed to be extortionate'.[64] A further point of distinction relates to taxation of sale and security of receivables where the former is subject to stamp duty and VAT, and the latter is exempt from these.[65] A final point of distinction

59 Sealy, L.S. and Hooley, R.J.A. (2003) *Commercial Law Text, Cases and Materials*, 3rd edn. London: Butterworths, pp. 976 *et seq.*; *Welsh Development Agency v Export Finance Co Ltd.* [1992] BCLC 148, CA. The two-step test (whether the transaction is a sham and whether the language used in the transaction is in line with what the parties have done) adopted by English courts is established in *Orion Finance Ltd. v Crown Financial Management Ltd.* [1996] BCC 621. The second step is instrumental in the recharacterisation of fixed charges over book debts as floating charges in seminal cases, e.g. *Agnew v Commissioner of Inland Revenue* [2001] 3 WLR 454; *National Westminster Bank plc v Spectrum Plus Ltd* [2005] 2 AC 680. On these cases, *see* e.g. Berg, A. (2004) 'Charges over Book Debts: Spectrum case in the Court of Appeal', *J.B.L.*, 581; Berg, A. (2006) 'The cuckoo in the nest of corporate insolvency: Some aspects of the Spectrum case', *J.B.L.*, 22.

60 McCormack, op. cit. (f'note 11), at 55.

61 Op. cit. (f'note 46), para. 4.4.

62 Op. cit. (f'note 46), para. 1.12.

63 Sealy and Hooley, op. cit. (f'note 59), 983; Insolvency Act 1986 ss 238–239, 244–5, 423–5.

64 Sealy and Hooley, op. cit. (f'note 59), 983.

65 Ibid.

is that a further creation of security over the receivables may be prohibited, whereas a sale may not fall within the framework of this prohibition. In addition to these distinctions, three further points are also indicated in *Re George Inglefield Ltd*[66] according to which a seller is not entitled to retrieve the asset by paying the money back to the purchase whereas in a mortgage charge situation the mortgagor is entitled to receive the ownership of the property by making the full payment to the mortgagee; if the mortgagee realises the asset for a higher sum, this needs to be accounted to the mortgagor whereas in a sale it is opposite; and, finally, if the asset is realised for a sum insufficient for repayment, the mortgagee is entitled to recover the full amount from the mortgagor whereas in a sale the mortgagee is not entitled to recover the balance from the seller.[67] Therefore, it can be argued that in legal terms there is a fundamental distinction between the assignment by way of sale and security.

1.2.4 Significant financing practices covered by international instruments

International instruments aim to use title for security purposes, too. Title devices are not traditional security interests; however, they serve the same economic purpose, hence equating them to a security interest by addressing them as quasi-security. One of the most significant methods of using title for security purposes is the contractual arrangement, whereby the seller retains title in the tangible assets in order to secure the repayment of the purchase price of the assets. This is known as retention of title (reservation of title) or the *Romalpa*[68] clause. The buyer has the possession and the right to use and maybe dispose of the asset, while the seller keeps the title until full payment. Upon default the seller has the right of repossession on the assets free of any third-party rights. These rights are generally protected by operation of law and sometimes may be extended by contractual arrangements.[69] The retention-of-title financing pattern has variations such as simple clause, current-account clause, extended clause, tracing clause and aggregation clause.[70] Not all jurisdictions accept all of these variations and, particularly, tracing (where the seller acquires ownership in the proceeds) and aggregation (where the original goods are manufactured into another property, thus lose their

66 [1933] Ch 1; [1932] All ER Rep 244.

67 Ibid., 27–8; 256–7.

68 *Aluminium Industrie Vaassen B. V. v Romalpa Aluminium Ltd.* [1976] 1 WLR 676, where it was held that the retention-of-title clause extending to the proceeds of goods subsequently incorporated into other goods was not a registrable charge, and gave the seller the right over both the goods in the buyer's possession and the proceeds of goods resold.

69 However, for example under the Guide, the supplier's reclamation right is subordinate to earlier security right made effective as against third parties (Recommendation 86).

70 Ch. 7 for further discussion in the context of international instruments. *See also* McCormack, G. (1995) *Reservation of Title*, 2nd edn. London: Sweet & Maxwell; McCormack, op. cit. (f'note 11), at 164 *et seq.*

original identity, and the seller acquires ownership of this resulting property) clauses have not received full acceptance.[71] Retention-of-title clauses are not registrable under Companies Act 2006 s 860, nevertheless, some types of retention-of-title practices may fall within the ambit of s 860(7)(f) and (g).[72] Under UCC Article 9, conditional sales or retention-of-title agreements are combined under the functional approach to security. Unlike in England, under UCC Article 9, for third-party effectiveness, filing is required.[73]

Transfer of title may be advantageous for a creditor, and may be used for security purposes,[74] as it is less costly than creating a security right and, in the event of grantor's insolvency, assets are not included in the insolvency estate as the title of the asset is transferred, as opposed to being collateralised where the title stays with the debtor, but encumbered. However, there is divergence of the treatment of transfer of title for security purposes, which may sometimes be treated similarly to security interests or regarded as evasion of normal rules applicable to security interests, and transfer of title thus held to be null and void.[75] The effects of these transactions may either be recognised as an outright transfer, or more similar to a security right where the latter is a preferred approach under the Guide and the jurisdictions with functional approach to security.

Financial lease is a significant financing technique and 'has developed as an alternative to conditional sale and hire purchase'.[76] It is a hire contract with security functions and a quasi-security, according to which the estimated life of the equipment is equal to the period of the lease and often the equipment stays with one lessee compared to the operating leases which do not have security functions; there may be multiple lessees and the period of hire is for the short term.[77] These two types of lease can be distinguished through their function, the length and the registrability of the longer-term lease.[78] Hire purchase is another similar type of transaction, where the lessee under the contractual arrangement is allowed to

71 Guide, para. 95, at 53–4.

72 'Charge on book debts of the company' and 'floating charge on the company's property or undertaking'.

73 Law Commission Consultation Paper No. 164 recommends the registration of retention-of-title agreements. Para. 7.24.

74 Often referred to as *sale with a right of redemption* or *sale with an option to repurchase*. *See* Guide, para. 89, at 52.

75 Guide, para. 89 at 52.

76 Beale, H., Bridge, M., Gullifer, L. and Lomnicka, E. (2007) *The Law of Personal Property Security*. Oxford: Oxford University Press, p. 203.

77 Ibid., at 203; Law Commission Consultation Paper No. 164, para. 6.15. Under the operating lease, the lessee has no right to purchase the asset, which must have a useful life at the end of the lease period.

78 Law Commission Consultation Paper No. 164, paras 7.30 *et seq*. The Law Commission recommended that any lease (operating and finance leases) of one year or more should be within the registration scheme (perfection and priority). Law Commission Consultation Paper No. 176, para. 2.96. Operating leases are not automatically treated as security interests under UCC Article 9. UCC §1–201(37)(a) according to which whether a transaction constitutes a security interest or lease depends on whether the original term of the lease is equal to or greater than the remaining economic life of the goods.

purchase the hired goods after payment of the majority of the purchase price. Under the Guide, the hire-purchase agreement is included within the definition of financial lease right to the extent that one of the following is met: at the end of the lease period the lessee automatically becomes the owner; the lessee acquires ownership paying no more than a nominal price; or the asset has no more than a nominal residual value.[79]

1.3 Significance and rationale of secured lending

1.3.1 Security affords priority

The significance of taking security for a creditor is to obtain priority before other creditors who may have proprietary interest in the debtor's assets, and to secure the repayment of credit in the event of the debtor's insolvency.[80] In other words, the creditor takes security in order to increase its repayment chances in the event of the debtor's insolvency or default in payment.[81] Failure of banks to take security will rank them behind the preferential creditors as well as categorising them as unsecured creditors.[82] Predictability as to whether the security interest effectively protects the lender's financial expectations and interests is paramount during the lending process. The lender's legitimate concern is whether the security interest is enforceable in the event of the debtor's insolvency. This concern is equally applicable to both domestic and cross-border credit transactions. Financiers prefer stronger and effective security rights, which maintain certainty in credit transactions.[83] The lender's lack of confidence in the markets and the judgment of the borrower's creditworthiness may affect the cost of credit. The recent financial

79 Guide, at 9. For further discussion, *see* Chapter 7.

80 *But cf.* Gullifer, op. cit. (f'note 22), at 1, where she argues that security and priority may not be connected, for example for policy reasons sometimes law may allow unsecured creditors to have priority position over the secured creditors (e.g. in winding up, preferential creditors may have priority over floating charge under Insolvency Act 1986 s 175(2)(b) and the secured claims of a director subordinated to the claims of unsecured creditors under Insolvency Act 1986 s 215(4)).

81 Diamond Report, 9–10. For a similar view *see* McCormack, op. cit. (f'note 11), p. 5; Wood, P. (2008) '*Law and Practice of International Finance*'. London: Sweet & Maxwell, p. 250, where Professor Wood argues that one of the advantages of security interests is to protect creditors on insolvency.

82 For a discussion of ranking and preferential status, *see* McCormack, op. cit. (f'note 11), at 5–7.

83 For example, under UCC Article 9, security over bank accounts can be perfected (made effective against third parties) by virtue of control as opposed to registration or filing (UCC§9–312(b) and 314). In England *Re BCCI (No. 8)* [1998] AC 214 is a significant example. Conceptually, the bank owes money to the customer that the customer has deposited. But the question is whether the money owed by the customer is a debt owed to the bank and can be subject to a charge by the bank? The House Lords held that it was possible to create a charge in favour of the bank, thus permitting the enlargement of security taken from borrowing customers. *See* McCormack, G. (2002) 'Security Interests in Deposit Accounts: An Anglo-American Perspective', *Insolvency Lawyer* 7; McCormack, op. cit. (f'note 11), pp. 249 *et seq.* The Guide recommendation 49 recommends third-party effectiveness through either registration or control with respect to the right to payment of funds credited to the bank account.

crisis has proved that lending to borrowers with little creditworthiness and lack of proper supervision, especially over credit transactions, cause financial risks to the medium- and long-term financing.[84] UNCITRAL observed that '[t]he fundamental justification for secured transactions law lies in the premise that the total net wealth of an economy will increase if more secured credit is available as a complement to unsecured credit'.[85] Furthermore, the concept of *pari passu* may be regarded as a threat to lenders where the assets of the insolvent debtor are distributed equally among the creditors.[86] In order to avoid equal footing with the other creditors, or ranking behind certain creditors who are granted preferential status, lenders prefer to take security that enables them to have priority over the claims of unsecured creditors; thereby effects of the *pari passu* principle are diminished.[87] Indeed, the secured creditor bargains for his priority position and that there will be lack of equal negotiation positions between the parties.[88] However, from the unsecured creditor's perspective, taking security creates a disadvantageous position because unsecured creditors receive less in the event of insolvency and this is a violation of the principle.[89]

The argument of priority of the secured creditor over the unsecured creditor as the motivation of taking security may be linked with the debate over efficiency of secured lending. An academic debate, largely confined to the US (triggered by an analysis[90] regarding the efficiency of secured lending), as to whether the granting of

84 *See* e.g. Tomasic, R. (2008) 'Corporate rescue, governance and risk-taking in Northern Rock' (Part 1) and (Part 2), *Company Lawyer* 29(10): 297–303 and 29(11): 330–7. In a recent comprehensive strategy report published on 20 November 2008, the Basel Committee on Banking Supervision announced that it will strenghten the Basel II framework's risk capture, especially against trading book and off-balance-sheet exposures among others. http://www.bis.org/press/p081120.htm.

85 Guide, para. 46, at 19.

86 *But cf.* Mokal, R. (2001) 'Priority as Pathology: The *Pari Passu* Myth', 69 *C.L.J.* 581, 582, arguing that *pari passu* is less important and does not fulfil the functions attributed to it. Goode, R. (2005) *Principles of Corporate Insolvency Law*, 3rd edn. London: Sweet & Maxwell, para. 7.20 stating that:

> [t]he principle of *pari passu* distribution of assets does not apply to the rights of secured creditors, suppliers of goods under [retention-of-title] or creditors for whom the company holds assets on trust. This . . . is not because these are exceptions to the rule but because such assets do not belong to the company and thus do not fall to be distributed among creditors on any basis.

87 Finch, V. (1999) 'Security Insolvency and Risk' 62 *M.L.R.* 633, 634. Finch, V. *Corporate Insolvency Law: Perspectives and Principles*, Cambridge: Cambridge University Press, 2nd ed., 2009, Chapter 15, especially at 631–35.

88 Bridge. M. (1999) 'The Quistclose Trust in a World of Secured Transactions', 12 *O.J.L.S.*, 333, 340–1, discussing the tension between freedom of contract and the mandatory *pari passu* principle.

89 *See generally* Goode, R. (1983) 'Is the Law too Favourable to Secured Creditors?', 8 *Canadian Bus. L.J.*, 53.

90 Jackson, T. and Kronman, A. (1979) 'Secured Financing and Priorities Among Creditors', 88 *Yale L.J.*, 1143.

security in fact lowers the cost of credit still remains.[91] This is partly driven by a political idea that lenders, essentially, have too much power and are over-dominant in insolvencies. One of the main tenets of the UCC Article 9 is that secured creditors have priority over the unsecured creditors;[92] however, according to some commentators its policy justification is not certain.[93] Bebchuk and Fried observe that granting full priority to secured creditors may cause misinterpretation in the contractual arrangements between borrowers and lenders and this will lead to excessive and inefficient use of security interests, 'which reduces the incentive of firms to take adequate precautions and to choose appropriate investments' such as debt or equity.[94] They argue that debtors may have secured and unsecured creditors in the course of their ordinary business, and the latter cannot adjust the terms of their contract in the face of the increased risk that the secured lending may cause.[95] They suggested partial priority where unsecured creditors are given certain portions in the event that the insolvency of the debtor would be more efficient.[96] From different perspectives the efficiency of secured lending has been criticised. On the one hand, secured credit is found to be not economically efficient. On the other hand, granting full priority to secured creditors is found to be politically wrong and unfair as it violates the interests of unsecured creditors.[97] Some

91 Warren, E. (1997) 'Making Policy with Imperfect Information: The Article 9 Full Priority Debates', 82 *Cornell L. Rev.*, 1373; Klee, K.N. (1997) 'Barbarians at the Trough: Riposte in Defense of the Warren Carve-out Proposal', 82 *Cornell L. Rev.*, 1467; LoPucki, L.M. (1997) 'Should the Secured Credit Carve-Out Apply Only in Bankruptcy? A Systems/Strategic Analysis', 82 *Cornell L. Rev.*, 1483; Harris, S.L. and Mooney, C.W. (1997) 'Measuring the Social Costs and Benefits and Identifying the Victims of Subordinating Security Interests in Bankruptcy', 82 *Cornell L. Rev.*, 1349; Bebchuk, L.A. and Fried, J.M. (1997) 'The Uneasy case for the Priority of Secured Claims in Bankruptcy: Further Thoughts and a Reply to Critics', 82 *Cornell L. Rev.* 1279; Scott, R. (1997) 'The Truth about Secured Financing', 82 *Cornell L. Rev.*, 1436, 1437–8; Schwartz, A. (1997) 'Priority Contracts and Priority in Bankruptcy', 82 *Cornell L. Rev.*, 1396.

92 *See* e.g. Woodward, W. (1997) 'The Realist and Secured Credit: Grant Gilmore, Common Law Courts and the Article 9 Reform Process', 82 *Cornell L Rev.*, 1511.

93 *See* e.g. Bebchuk, L.A. and Fried, J.M. (1996) 'The Uneasy Case for the Priority of Secured Claims in Bankruptcy', 105 *Yale L. J.*, 857; LoPucki, L.M. (1994) 'The Unsecured Creditor's Bargain', 80 *Va. L. Rev.*, 1887, 1947 *et seq.* (arguments regarding the justification of subordination of unsecured creditors).

94 Bebchuk and Fried, ibid., at 934.

95 Bebchuk and Fried, ibid., at 863 *et seq.*; Bebchuk, L.A. and Fried, J.M. (1997) 'The Uneasy Case for the Priority of Secured Claims in Bankruptcy: Further Thoughts and a Reply to Critics', 82 *Cornell L. Rev.*, 1279, 1293–4.

96 Bebchuk and Fried op. cit. (f'note 93), at 934. For a criticism of this suggestion *see* McDonnell, J. (1999) 'Is Revised Article 9 a Little Greedy?', 104 *Com. L. J.*, 241, 262 and fn 41.

97 For a discussion on this matter, *see* sources mentioned in op. cit. (f'note 91) and *see* e.g. Scott, R. (1994) 'The Politics of Article 9', 80 *Va. L. Rev.*, 1783; LoPucki, L.M. (1994) 'The Unsecured Creditors Bargain', 80 *Va. L. Rev.*, 1887; Baird, D. (1994) 'Security Interests Reconsidered', 80 *Va. L. Rev.*, 2249; Carlson, D.G. (1994); 'On the Efficiency of Secured Lending', 80 *Va. L. Rev.*, 2179; Kanda, H. and Levmore, S. (1994) 'Explaining Creditor Priorities', 80 *Va. L. Rev.*, 2103; Harris, S.L. and Mooney, C.W. Jr (1994) 'A Property Based Theory of Security Interests: Taking Debtors' Choices Seriously', 80 *Va. L. Rev.*, 2021; Schwartz, A. (1994) 'Taking the Analysis of Security Seriously', 80 *Va. L. Rev.*, 2073.

authors[98] argued that secured creditors should be denied full priority, and thus full use of collateral, by virtue of the creation of a carve-out, to be used for the unsecured creditors of the insolvent debtor.[99] A carve-out proposal has not been taken on board either in the UCC Article 9 revision or by international secured transactions instruments such as the Guide and the Receivables Convention, which omit carve-out provisions. Some others[100] argued the efficiency of secured credit from law and economics perspectives,[101] and concluded that support for secured credit has no economic rationale or at best has been unproven with no social gains. Commentators[102] use the Modigliani and Miller theory[103] to tie the argument of why security is granted by debtors to the rationale of granting security as a source of raising finance. Briefly, the theory assumes that a firm's value cannot be increased by raising finance through borrowing (debt finance), or issuing and selling shares (equity finance), as the firm's value depends on the claims to the firm's cash flow and concludes that capital structure is irrelevant to the value of the firm.[104]

98 *See* e.g. Warren, op. cit. (f'note 91).

99 *See* McDonnell, op. cit. (f'note 96), 242 and fn 5. Professor McDonnell notes Professor Warren's carve-out proposal of no more than 20 per cent of the collateral proceeds to be reserved for unsecured creditors, and the academic support it received notwithstanding being sidelined by the Drafting Committee of Article 9. Similar proposals were made in the UK; *see* Insolvency Law and Practice: Report of the Review Committee (1982) paras 1538 *et seq.* In the US, the principle of full priority can be found under the US Bankruptcy Code; however, there are exceptions to it, notably under Chapter 11, which place restrictions on the enforcement of security rights. *See generally* Baird, D. and Jackson, T. (1984) 'Corporate Reorganisations and the Treatment of Diverse Ownership Interests: A Comment on Adequate Protection of Secured Creditors in Bankruptcy', 51 *U. Ch. L.Rev.*, 97, 112–14; McCormack, G. (2008) *Corporate Rescue Law-An Anglo-American Perspective.* Chelthenham: Edward Elgar, especially Ch. 3.

100 *See* e.g. Schwartz, A. (1989) 'A Theory of Loan Priorities', *J. Legal Studies.* 209; Schwartz, A. (1994) 'Taking the Analysis of Security Seriously', 80 *Va. L. Rev.*, 2073.

101 For a detailed discussion of economic efficiency *see* Cooter, R. and Ulen, T. (2004) *Law and Economics* (International edition: 4th edn). Harlow: Pearson, pp. 48 *et seq.;* Stephen, F.H. (1988) *The Economics of the Law.* Hertfordshire: Harvester Wheatsheaf, pp. 41–63. Law and Economics scholars use two norms in measuring economic efficiency. These are Pareto optimality and the Kaldor–Hicks criterion. According to Pareto optimality, 'an allocation of resources is efficient if it is not possible to reallocate resources in such a way that *at least* one person is better off and no one else is worse off', at 42. In order to be Pareto optimal, a secured credit will be economically efficient if it makes a secured creditor better off without making an unsecured creditor worse off. According to the Kaldor–Hicks criterion, which is an improvement of the Pareto criterion and a criterion of wealth maximisation, a change in the economy should be operated 'if those who are made better off by it *could* so compensate those made worse off by it that the latter would be as well off as before the change and the former still be better off', at 57. In order to meet this criterion, the secured creditor should compensate potential damage to the unsecured creditor.

102 E.g. Schwartz, ibid., at 2079; McCormack, op. cit. (f'note 11), at 24.

103 Modigliani, F. and Miller, M. (1958) 'The Cost of Capital, Corporation Finance and the Theory of Investment', 48 *Am. Econ. Rev.*, 433.

104 *See also* Schwartz, op. cit. (f'note 100) at 2079; McCormack, op. cit. (f'note 11), at 24; Beale, *et al*, op. cit. (f'note 76), at 4; Baird, D. (1997) 'The Importance of Priority', 82 *Cornell L. Rev.*, 1420, 1422, where he argues that allowing priority through granting security does not in fact increase the value of the firm, and when a firm increases its debt, it 'makes its cost of equity cheaper, but at the same time raises its cost of debt by an equal and offsetting amount'.

In the UK, the so-called 'rescue culture' has resulted in secured creditors' entitlements being lost somewhat by recent legislation.[105] The Enterprise Act 2002 introduced protection to unsecured creditors of a company that has gone into liquidation by setting aside a certain proportion of floating charge realisations.[106] According to s 176A of the Insolvency Act 1986, if a floating charge relates to property of a company that has gone into liquidation, administration, provisional liquidation or receivership, then the official in charge shall make a prescribed part (which is 50 per cent of the net property where that property is less than £10,000; if over £10,000, 50 per cent for the £10,000 and 20 per cent for the exceeding part)[107] of the company's property available for the satisfaction of unsecured debts.[108] This provision applies after claims on the same property secured by a fixed charge or preferential debts are satisfied. This also applies if the company's net property is less than the prescribed minimum and the liquidator, administrator or receiver thinks that the cost of making a distribution to unsecured creditors would be disproportionate to the benefits.[109] This rescue culture also resulted in the loss of a qualifying floating charge holder's right to appoint an administrative receiver.[110] Some commentators[111] rightly suggest that the modernisation of corporate rescue legislation will result in the banks taking fixed charges[112] in their lending practices, as opposed to floating charges, in order to strengthen their positions in the event of the debtor's insolvency. Banks have always been in a more favoured position with respect to secured credit and resisting reform.[113] Banks have been taking fixed charges over a fluctuating class of assets and book debts.[114] Professor Bridge indicates that:

105 By virtue of Enterprise Act 2002 s 251, Crown preference (listed in Schedule 6 of the Insolvency Act as debts due to Inland Revenue, Security contributions and Customs and Excise) is now abolished, which provides a benefit for floating charge holders. Before the Enterprise Act 2002 preferential debtors in insolvency of the debtor were used to being paid in advance of floating charge holders. On the other hand, secured creditors will lose some of their entitlements under s 252 of the Act, which is inserted as s 176A of the Insolvency Act.

106 s 252 of the Enterprise Act 2002, as inserted as s 176A of Insolvency Act 1986.

107 Insolvency Act 1986 (Prescribed Part) Order 2003.

108 S 176A Insolvency Act 1986 and Insolvency Act 1986 (Prescribed Part) Order 2003 (SI 2003/2097).

109 S 176A(3).

110 S 72A Insolvency Act 1986.

111 E.g. Finch, V. (2008) 'Corporate Rescue in a World of Debt', *J.B.L.*, 756, 766; Prentice, D. (2004) 'Bargaining in the Shadow of the Enterprise Act 2002', 5 *E.B.O.R.*, 153, 158–9.

112 However, note that *Spectrum Plus Ltd v National Westminster Bank Plc* [2005] UKHL 41; [2005] 3 W.L.R. 58; [2005] B.C.C. 694 decision refined those instances where fixed charge may be taken.

113 E.g. resistance to recent reform efforts of the Law Commission (No. 296) must be noted here.

114 E.g. *Siebe Gorman & Co Ltd. v Barclays Bank Ltd.* [1979] 2 Lloyd's Rep. 142; *In re Keenan Bros Ltd.* [1986] BCLC 242; *Re New Bullas Trading Ltd.* [1994] 1 BCLC 485 (Court of Appeal). However, this case has been overruled by the House of Lords in *Re Spectrum Plus Ltd* [2005] UKHL 41, [2005] 2 AC 680 and held to be wrong by the Privy Council in *Agnew v Commissioner of Inland Revenue (Re Brumark Investments Ltd.)* [2001] UKPC 28; [2001] 2 AC 710. For a criticism of the decision, *see* Goode, R. (1994) 'Charges over Book Debts: A Missed Opportunity', 110 *LQR*, 592.

> banks have a powerful incentive to [take fixed charges over book debts]: it promotes them ahead of preference creditors and it also ensures that the assets covered by a fixed charge are not applied first to the costs of the liquidation of the company as would happen if they were the subject of a floating charge.[115]

Professor McCormack suggests that creditors may also use quasi-security devices such as factoring, retention of title, or sale and lease back.[116] Although fixed charge may be preferred to increase profitability and obtain priority, in *Brumark*[117] Lord Millet refined those instances where a charge over receivables can be characterised as a fixed charge.[118] The critical issue is whether the borrower (security giver) can collect the proceeds of the debt for its own benefit.[119] If the borrower is able to collect and use the proceeds for its own benefit, this will be classed as a floating charge. The nature of the fixed charge required the lender's control over the charged asset, and the proceeds of the debt, either through collection by the lender as an assignee or by the assignor (borrower) who collects them as a trustee for the assignee. However, the former option is incompatible with the assignment of bulk receivables due to high volume of transactions. The latter option is the undisclosed factoring of receivables where the debtor is not notified of the assignment of right to payment and continues to pay to the assignor.[120] In connection with this latter option, McCormack concludes that as 'factoring offers less flexibility' to the contracting parties, it will not be widely used in daily commerce.[121]

As a general proposition, it is arguable that domestic arguments of whether secured credit is efficient, or full priority should be given to secured creditors over

See also McCormack, op. cit. (f'note 11), at 6–7 where he argues, citing comments of Lord Millet in *Brumark* that the tendency of financially-distressed companies is to rely on the Revenue, which prompts banks to prefer taking fixed charges as opposed to floating charges where the latter is ranked behind preferential debts.

115 Bridge, M. (1996) 'How Far is Article 9 Exportable? The English Experience', 27 *Canadian Bus. L. J.*, 196, 216. With respect to the banking sector it has been correctly pinpointed by Bridge that '[i]f England were to adopt an Article 9 statute, [its] hard-won gains would be surrendered for something new whose implications would take some time to be felt', at 221.

116 McCormack, op. cit. (f'note 11), at 36–7. *See also* McCormack, G. (2002) 'The Nature of Security over Receivables', 23 *Co. Law.*, 84. For the comparison of fixed and floating charges *see* e.g. Wood, P. (2002) 'Fixed and Floating Charges', *C.L.J.*, 472.

117 *Agnew v Commissioner of Inland Revenue* [2001] 2 AC 710.

118 [2001] 2 AC 710, at 721.

119 Lord Millett cites *In re Yorkshire Woolcombers Association Ltd.* [1903] 2 Ch 284, 295, and states that the third characteristic of floating charge described by Romer LJ is the crucial point that distinguishes floating from fixed charge. Lord Millett indicates that the existence of a fixed charge makes it impossible for the security giver to ordinarily continue its business without the consent of the charge holder, and ability to do so without consent is inconsistent with the nature of fixed charge, [2001] 2 AC 710, at 719. For a definition of floating charge *see* also *Illingworth v Houldsworth* [1904] AC 355, 358.

120 E.g. *Lloyds and Scottish Finance v Cyril Lord (Carpet Sales) Ltd.* [1992] BCLC 609.

121 McCormack, op. cit. (f'note 11), at 37.

the unsecured creditors, seem to have little importance to the international harmonisation of secured transactions. It is true that unsecured creditors cannot adjust the amount of credit to changes in the risk; however, one can argue that taking security and having full priority in cross-border transactions is a critical feature of borrowing as well as expanding business. Ability to take security is the decisive factor in lending decisions. First, the rationale of international harmonisation of secured transactions law seems to be different from the rationale of the debate in the US. International harmonisation aims to provide predictability in the rules governing secured credit transactions, which in turn facilitates the flow of credit that is critical for SMEs in developing economies, whereas the domestic US debate seems to be a romantic effort to create equality between those creditors who have the power to take security and those who do not. Recent financial crises have clearly illustrated that banks do not extend credit and, even if they do, they prefer full priority in order to make sure that their claims are satisfied in the event of a debtor's insolvency.[122] Predictability of rules is important for international lenders and many of those international instruments have provisions that are creditor friendly.[123] Second, international lenders, mainly of US origin, who are used to the safe havens of UCC Article 9, will refuse to extend credit if they have any doubt that they will be placed second or are lending on an equal footing with other creditors. Third, the US academic debate, briefly provided above, is mainly of interest for domestic US law. Business practices in the US and in other countries differ. The US, as a leading common law jurisdiction, is known to be creditor friendly.[124] Arguments made against the efficiency of security, and in favour of carve-out proposals in the domestic US perspective, seem to somewhat contradict what international instruments are attempting to achieve.[125] For international activities, the target is pro-creditor rules for predictability of secured credit laws and facilitation of credit. Provisions in international instruments generally protect the priority position of secured creditors. Thus the importance of efficiency of the security debate seems to have limited significance for international instruments. What is more important is that carve-outs do more harm to unsecured creditors

122 For the purposes of this argument, one needs to, unfortunately, ignore the reality that crisis in fact has been caused by reckless lending decisions of financial institutions.

123 E.g. the Receivables Convention and the Guide give effectiveness to an assignment made notwithstanding an anti-assignment clause in the original contract. *See* e.g. Akseli, O. (2009) 'Contractual Prohibitions on Assignment of Receivables: An English and UN Perspective', *J.B.L.*, 650; Bazinas, S. (2003) 'Key Policy Issues of the United Nations Convention on the Assignment of Receivables in International Trade', 11 *Tul. J. Int'l & Comp. L.*, 275; Bazinas, S. (2001) 'Lowering the Cost of Credit: the Promise in the Future UNCITRAL Convention on Assignment of Receivables in International Trade', 9 *Tul. J. Int'l & Comp. L.*, 259.

124 *See* e.g. Wood, P.R. (2005) *Maps of World Financial Law*, 5th edn. London: Allen & Overy LLP, pp. 89–105.

125 E.g. Guide, paras 43–4, at 195 with regard to priority of secured creditor over the unsecured creditor. Recommendations 83–84. The Guide also recommends all asset security agreements be permitted. Recommendation 17. Model Law Article 1.1, 'the single security right in respect of all types of things and rights'.

or the so-called non-adjusting creditors. Financiers may raise the cost of credit in order to compensate their potential losses through carve-out amounts. Nothing may be left to unsecured creditors. Thus, notwithstanding the arguments in favour of granting a proportion of the debtor's assets to unsecured creditors or the efficiency of secured credit, it is submitted that secured credit is important and full priority is necessary for secured creditors: first, for predictability in legal rules and, second, to facilitate creditors to grant low-cost credit to small businesses. The recurrent theme, that of criticalness of lending on a secured basis and having full priority in cross-border transactions, maintains its significance more than ever. International harmonisation activities and international instruments demonstrate that fact and, rightly, omit carve-out proposals.

1.3.2 Security affords control

A secured creditor prefers to take security (fixed or floating charges) in order to control the assets of the debtor and events during the insolvency process.[126] Control through security interests over the assets of the debtor in insolvency process is another strategy to maximise the repayment potential of a loan extended to the debtor.[127] When the debtor grants security over the assets, the creditor is in fact given a controlling position over them. The secured creditor monitors and controls any potential misbehaviour of the debtor through security. The creditor may sell the collateral in the event of default and satisfy its claim, and the potential legal reality as such prompts a debtor to make periodical payments. Furthermore, security motivates the lender to pay as soon as possible so that control can be gained back on the asset, because to do otherwise will result in the debtor losing its assets.[128] This is also linked to the next argument where the debtor is not allowed to take risky business decisions.

1.3.3 Security assists expansion of business

For a borrower, taking security increases opportunities to expand business. From the economic point of view the ability to take security leads to economic activity and increases the opportunities for lending. The secured credit reduces the risk of non-payment as the lender will have recourse to the collateral[129] and this will have

126 Goode, op. cit. (f'note 80), 1–2.

127 For further information *see* Scott, R. (1986) 'A Relational Theory of Secured Financing', 86 *Columbia L. Rev.*, 901; Schwartz, A. (1989) 'A Theory of Loan Priorities', *J. Legal Studies*, 209; McCormack, op. cit. (f'note 11), at 7.

128 For unsecured creditors *see* Beale *et al*, op. cit. (f'note 76), at 4, where they indicate that control mechanisms can be employed over unsecured creditors through financial covenants and default clauses, which may be triggered upon default or an insolvency-related event.

129 Drobnig, op. cit. (f'note 8), at 54. This is also reflected in documents such as the Basel Accord 1988 and the EC Capital Adequacy Directive 2006/49, according to which for capital adequacy purposes security has significance and is critical for risk-weighting of capital. Furthermore, the creditor will be allowed to engage in markets directly and raise finance when the collateral is also comprised of investment securities held with a right of use. *See* Goode, op. cit. (f'note 80), 2.

a positive impact in accessing to low-cost credit.[130] The power granted to the secured creditor by the security interest over the collateral, and the limitations in the security agreement, controls the business decisions of the debtor. The debtor in the course of ordinary business cannot be able to take decisions that carry risk.[131] Any risky decision on the collateral will reduce the value of that asset and the secured creditor will not permit 'wealth-reducing transactions'.[132] Wealth-reducing transactions may include excessive dividend payments, excessive borrowing, assets may be diluted, and company managers may borrow money but then divert them for the sole use of the company.[133] UNCITRAL in its comprehensive Guide observed that:

> [s]tudies have shown as the risk of non-payment is reduced, the availability of credit increases and the cost of credit falls. Studies have also shown that in States where lenders perceive the risks associated with transactions to be high, the cost of credit increases as lenders require increased compensation to evaluate and assume the increased risk.[134]

Empirical studies conducted by economists 'demonstrate a strong positive link between the functioning of the financial system and long-run economic growth'.[135] If a legal system presents predictability in secured transactions, lenders will lend more with long maturities and low interest rates.[136] This will have positive reflections on the financial system, which will eventually lead to economic growth and more investments. Similar arguments are illustrated in empirical and financial studies where it is established that legal and financial factors

130 This positive effect may be reflected as reduction of interest rates and lending with long-term maturities, and hence more economic activity by SMEs.

131 *See generally* Schwartz, A. (1997) 'Priority Contracts and Priority in Bankruptcy', 82 *Cornell L. Rev.*, 1396; Mann, R.J. (1997) 'Explaining the Pattern of Secured Credit', 110 *Harvard L. Rev.*, 625, 683, where Mann concludes that secured credit '. . . [enhances] the borrower's ability to give a credible commitment to refrain from excessive future borrowing and by limiting the borrower's ability to engage in conduct that lessens the likelihood of payment'.

132 Triantis, G. (1992) 'Secured Debt Under Conditions of Imperfect Information' 21 *J. Legal Studies*, 225; Armour, J. (2008) 'The Law and Economics Debate About Secured Lending: Lessons For European Lawmaking?' in H. Eidenmüller and E.M. Kieninger (eds) *The Future of Secured Credit in Europe*. E.C.F.L.R., Munich: De Gruyter Recht, 3, at 8.

133 Finch, op. cit. (f'note 87), p. 641.

134 A/CN.9/WG.6/WP.2 at para. 2.

135 Levine, R. (2004) 'Finance and Growth: Theory and Evidence', *National Bureau of Economic Research, Working Paper 10766*, 85.

136 There has been a debate in the US on the correlation between 'long-term loans' and 'security'. On this, *see* Jackson and Kronman, op. cit. (f'note 90), at 1159; Buckley, F.H. (1986) 'The Bankruptcy Priority Puzzle', 72 *Va. L. Rev.*, 1393, 1444; Mooney and Harris, op. cit. (f'note 97), at 2028; Schwartz, A. (1981) 'Security Interests and Bankruptcy Priorities: A Review of Current Theories', 10 *J. Legal Studies*, 1, 13–14.

among others constrain a firm's growth and the effected firms are consistently small ones.[137]

1.3.4 Security and self-help

By taking security, it is possible to satisfy the secured creditor's claim without judicial intervention.[138] This is generally known as the 'self-help remedies'. However, there is divergence in the approach of civil and common-law jurisdictions to the interests of debtors and creditors. The former tends to be debtor- while the latter is creditor-friendly, and self-help remedies may not always be immediately welcomed as a reason to take security. The problem demonstrates itself especially in the non-possessory security interests where the debtor is in possession of the collateral. The secured creditor's aim is to satisfy its claim without further prolonging the enforcement period. In that context, it can be argued that an effective security is the one that is enforceable immediately and at low cost.[139] However, the implications of this may vary in civil and common law jurisdictions, where in the former it is a great concern that the creditor may abuse this power of self-help remedies and that breaches of peace and violence may occur,[140] and in the latter, the creditor is allowed to use this power albeit with limitations.[141] From the international perspective, the Guide recognises the extrajudicial and judicial enforcement procedures, presents an option to the creditors to choose either of these procedures and, to maximise the impact, recommends certain safeguard principles such as acting in good faith and being commercially reasonable and sending a notice of default.

1.3.5 Security and bargain

Taking security is a 'fair exchange for the credit'.[142] In other words, when the lender extends credit upon bargaining, it is only fair that security is taken.

137 Beck, T., Demirguc-Kunt, A. and Maksimovic, V. (2005) 'Financial and Legal Constraints to Firm Growth: Does Size Matter?', 60 *Journal of Finance*, 137.

138 McCormack, op. cit. (f'note 11), at 8–9; Wood, op. cit. (f'note 81), at 250; Beale *et al*, op. cit. (f'note 76), 4.

139 Cranston, R. (1995) 'Credit, Security and Debt Recovery: Law's Role in Reform in Asia and the Pacific, 39 *St. Louis Univ. L. J.*, 759, 781.

140 Mistelis succinctly explains this as follows: 'Civil law systems normally reject self-help disposition on the grounds that it vests creditors with too much power which can often result in abuse of their rights and criminal-like behaviour, such as blackmailing and the use of physical violence.' Mistelis, L. (1998) 'The EBRD Model Law on Secured Transactions and Its impact on Collateral Law Reform in Central and Eastern Europe and the former Soviet Union', 5 *Parker Sch. J.E.Eur.L.*, 455, 473–4.

141 Cranston, ibid., 782; e.g. UCC Article 9–609.

142 Wood, op. cit. (f'note 81), 250; *see also* McCormack, op. cit. (f'note 11), 12. However, McCormack considers this point as one of the reasons why the law permits the taking of security as opposed to reasons for taking security.

This is a contract between the secured creditor and the debtor. From another perspective, immediate liquidity provided by the secured creditor enables the debtor to enlarge his business[143] and thus it is only fair to take security in return for that.

1.3.6 Security and economic growth

Secured credit promotes economic growth.[144] In this perspective, lenders extend credit relying on the protection provided by security. The ability to extend credit is said to promote economic activity. From the cross-border transactions perspective, lenders extend credit if they are certain that the security created in one jurisdiction is recognised in another jurisdiction, and hence the harmonisation of secured transactions law. This is especially true in developing economies whose secured transactions laws are inefficient. A further critical point is that it is assumed that secured credit lowers the cost of credit. This is also the inception point for many international harmonisation activities.[145] International harmonisation creates predictability and is said to lower the cost of credit. This is critical for SMEs in emerging markets in order for them to access low-cost credit. On the other hand, lenders through predictable rules governing secured transactions will have more confidence in the market and may be able to lend with lower interest rates and longer maturities. As the cost of credit is low, it is more convenient and affordable for SMEs to obtain credit to expand their businesses. Empirical studies demonstrate that there is a correlation between the borrower's financial strength and the attraction to secured credit. In that context, Mann analyses that 'borrowers exhibit an increasing tendency toward unsecured debt as their financial strength increases'.[146] Wood comments in the same direction that public companies often borrow on an unsecured basis and they rather use negative pledge clauses in their contracts.[147] The Law Commission has also observed this motive and reported that 'well-established public companies are able to borrow readily on an unsecured basis, but for many smaller enterprises credit can be obtained on significantly better terms ... if the borrower is able to offer security to the lender'.[148] Therefore, typically, SMEs tend

143 For a detailed discussion, *see* McCormack, op. cit. (f'note 11), 12 *et seq.*

144 *See* Ch. 2.

145 E.g. Receivables Convention Preamble, '*Being of the opinion* that the adoption of uniform rules governing the assignment of receivables would promote the availability of capital and credit at more affordable rates . . .'; Guide, at 20; the Cape Town Convention Preamble, 'Aware of the need to acquire and use mobile equipment of high value or particular economic significance and to facilitate the financing of the acquisition and use of such equipment in an efficient manner . . .'.

146 Mann, op. cit. (f'note 131), 674.

147 Wood, op. cit. (f'note 81), 253. Fleisig empirically provides that in the US one-third of credit is unsecured and about two-thirds is secured. Fleisig, H.W. (2008) 'The Economics of Collateral and of Collateral Reform' in F. Dahan and J. Simpson (eds) *Secured Transactions Reform and Access to Credit*. Cheltenham: Edward Elgar, pp. 81, 88.

148 Law Commission Report No. 296 (2005), para. 1.2.

to borrow on a secured basis.[149] This is also supported by empirical studies that suggest that security is mainly used by small businesses that carry risk.[150]

1.4 Fundamental principles of international conventions and instruments

International instruments have been built upon key objectives and essential policies. The previous section has illustrated the importance of secured credit. This section aims to illustrate major objectives on which international instruments are based and the philosophy of harmonisation in achieving them. This will be followed up in the following chapters by illustrating how these objectives are reflected under international instruments by making references to essential policies that a modern secured transactions regime must possess.

Key policies encompass principles that illustrate the philosophy of facilitation of credit with which a secured transactions regime must be in harmony. In other words, they strategise how credit can be facilitated under various aspects of secured transactions law. Facilitation of credit is the rationale of all international initiatives, which can be described, within the framework of harmonisation, as enabling lenders and borrowers to operate in a legal environment where both parties to a loan transaction can ascertain the consequences of their transaction, and thus the lender does not include the risk premium in the interest rate and lend with longer maturities.[151] High interest rates and short-term maturities deter borrowers from expanding their businesses. International instruments aim to reduce the cost of credit in cross-border credit transactions, and modernise domestic laws by providing harmonised and predictable rules that are beneficial for both parties to a loan transaction.[152] Particular areas of concern that lead international instruments to facilitate credit can be gathered into a number of areas. These are a functional approach to security interests and promotion of non-possessory security interests, ability to use all assets and obligations, efficient creation of security interests, third-party effectiveness, clear priority and conflict-of-laws rules.

149 For the difficulties of obtaining secured credit, *see* Federation of Small Businesses http://www.fsb.org.uk/ Report on Number Crunching the Credit Crunch.

150 Armour, in Eidenmüller and Kieninger (eds), op. cit. (f'note 131), at 9; Lasfer, M.A. (2000) 'Debt Structure, Agency Costs and Firm's Size: An Empirical Investigation', *Working Paper*. London: Cass Business School, at 18. Lasfer concludes that small firms hold more secured and less unsecured debt than larger companies.

151 According to CEAL's findings, well-known small businesses in Latin American countries pay about 6–8 per cent higher than the government borrowing rate for unsecured or secured loans, whereas others pay as much as 12–24 per cent. On the other hand, in the US small businesses pay an interest premium, which ranges between 2 and 10 per cent. This is a clear indication of difficulties in accessing low-cost credit in developing countries. Fleisig, H. and de la Pena, N. (2002) 'SMEs and Collateral', *CEAL Issues Brief No 3*. de la Pena, N. 'Challenges in Implementing Secured Transactions Reform in Latin America' in F. Dahan and J. Simpson (eds) op. cit. (f'note 147), 236, at 241, where Latin American businesses are faced with high interest rates.

152 *See* e.g. the Preamble of the Receivables Convention.

Harmonised law, by being applicable in contracting States, is said to increase access to lower cost credit, to reduce legal conflicts in international or regional cross-border transactions, to promote economic activity and foreign investment.[153] There is a correlation between the facilitation of credit and lowering the cost of credit, in the way that facilitated credit by harmonized and predictable rules reduces the cost of credit for SMEs by minimizing the risk of the secured creditor for not getting paid as the local rules may be ineffective. International instruments recognise the fact that taking security is important and contain rules that complement the fundamental justification of secured transactions law.[154] These rules have been derived from key principles that surround the philosophy of these instruments. At the same time, key policies are linked with interpretation rules according to which international instruments must be interpreted.[155] Arguably key policies of international instruments are more or less the same.[156]

1.4.1 Promotion of low-cost credit

The most significant policy is the promotion of low-cost credit by facilitating access to secured credit. Arguably this is the very reason why international instruments are prepared. If secured credit is available at a reasonable cost, the debtors, creditors and the economy can benefit. Predictable and clear rules are necessary where parties can establish certainty about the consequence of their transaction. International instruments achieve this principle with their clear rules aimed to facilitate the access to low-cost credit in cross-border assignments, loan transactions for specific equipment, and to create a model for countries to modernise their domestic credit and security laws. One of the concerns in promotion of low-cost credit is that domestic laws are generally fragmented or poor, thus they do not achieve the necessary protection for secured creditors to lower their interest rates and lend with high maturities. Under the Cape Town Convention, facilitation of

153 An observation made by the US delegation on the Receivables Convention was as follows:

> The benefits of global economics and trade have not yet been fully realized in many states, and the absence of adequate international commercial finance and credit in this important area is one of the obstacles for achievement of these goals. The [Receivables] Convention can substantially cover that gap and thus benefit countries at all levels of economic development and in all regions. The development of modern commercial finance law relating to the assignment of receivables through the . . . Convention and the ability to generate credit from capital markets through such laws offer an important opportunity to address these goals. . . . The combination of these techniques in the . . . Convention is aimed at assuring the necessary level of commercial certainty, which is critical to the willingness of capital markets to extend credit to areas previously underserved.

A/CN.9/472/Add.3, at 3 *Comments by Governments and International Organizations*.

154 *See* op. cit. (f'note 85) and the accompanying text thereof.

155 E.g. Receivables Convention Art 7(1); Factoring Convention Art 4(1); Cape Town Convention Art 5(1).

156 As the Guide clearly indicates, its work is based on the policies and works of, inter alia, the Model Law and Core Principles, the Receivables Convention and the Cape Town Convention, at 3–4.

credit is a key objective where creditors are intended to be given greater confidence in credit extension decisions that will reduce borrowing costs and enable debtors to access low-cost credit.[157] In both the Receivables and the Factoring Conventions, this policy is reflected in provisions that provide greater predictability in cross-border assignment transactions.[158] The Model Law intends to establish a basic system on which more sophisticated rules can be developed.[159] It has a permissive attitude towards the secured transactions regime. A similar approach is reflected under the Guide's comprehensive scope, which develops on different initiatives, inter alia the Model Law.

1.4.2 Ability to use all assets and obligations and non-possessory security

International instruments, mainly the Receivables Convention,[160] Model Law (Part I) and the Guide,[161] promote the encumbrance of all types of assets and obligations. This can be present or future, conditional or unconditional and tangible or intangible.[162] Furthermore, a modern secured transactions regime must balance the interests of lenders and sellers. The Guide and the Model Law adopt a comprehensive approach, which incorporates all types of assets, rights and people.[163] This is linked to the integrated and functional approach according to which all transactions that serve for security purposes should be considered as secured transactions.[164] The critical point in this policy is that debtors in need of liquidity

157 *See generally* Goode, R. (2008) Convention on International Interests in Mobile Equipment and Protocol Thereto on Matters Specific to Aircraft Equipment Official Commentary. Rome: UNIDROIT, at 14.

158 *See also* the Preamble of the Receivables Conventions where adoption of uniform rules would promote the availability of capital and credit at more affordable rates and facilitate international trade; para. 5. The Factoring Convention's Preamble also indicates the importance of international factoring in the development of international trade and that uniform rules would enable facilitation of international factoring.

159 Introduction, at v.

160 E.g. Article 8 Effectiveness of Assignments.

161 Para. 44, at 21.

162 Under English and American Laws it is possible to take non-possessory security over all types of assets of the debtor including future and present and have a registration system for such rights. *See generally* Chs 3–6.

163 Guide, paras 50 and 61, at 20 and 22–3; the Model Law, at vi. For general principles of modern system, *see* Simpson, J.L. and Röver, J-H.M. (1998) 'General Principles of Modern Secured Transactions Law' in J.J. Norton and M. Andenas (eds) *Emerging Financial Markets and Secured Transactions*. The Hague: Kluwer, pp. 143, 148 *et seq.*

164 Guide, para. 62, at 23. This approach reflects the UCC Article 9 legislation where all transactions that serve security functions are deemed to be secured transactions, but this does not turn them into a security transaction, and they are treated more or less the same for purposes of perfection (i.e. filing or registration) and priorities, but differently for enforcement purposes. For a discussion of this point, *see* Bridge, *et al.*, op. cit. (f'note 15), 580 *et seq.* With regards to acquisition financing devices, *see* Ch. 7.

must be allowed to use the full value of their assets. Some jurisdictions do not permit the assignment of future and bulk receivables due to the requirement of specificity. Non-possessory security interests are not recognised. There are distinct rules applicable to traditional and quasi-security interests in unreformed secured transactions regimes. The approach of international instruments allows parties to overcome difficulties inherent in these areas and modernise their regimes to access credit by using whatever economically valuable asset they have as collateral. The Cape Town Convention facilitates the creation of an international security interest on uniquely identifiable groups of objects such as aircraft engines, airframes, helicopters, railway rolling stock and space assets.[165] The Model Law also permits the ability to use all assets as collateral. The Model Law, however, prefers a formal rather than a functional approach and presents different charges (registered, possessory, unpaid vendors charges and an enterprise charge).[166]

The validation of non-possessory security interests in all types of assets is critical.[167] The main advantage of non-possessory security interest is that it permits the debtor to continue the operation of its business without giving up the possession while the creditor has, on paper, a right *in rem* over the collateral. Non-possessory security interests are widely used in common law jurisdictions whereas their usage is more restricted in civil law jurisdictions. Often, this is for historical reasons such as the fear that this type of security right may violate equality between debtors, some of whom gave possessory security right and lost control over it, whereas the others still have the possession through non-possessory security right and that non-possessory security rights create false wealth by allowing the debtor to use the collateral and this may not be discovered by the other potential creditors. However, with the globalisation of trade it is necessary to take security over future and intangible assets. While it is possible to take security such as a pledge over tangibles (where there is actual transfer of possession), the same cannot be practically possible for the future and intangible assets. While in some countries it is possible to register the security right over a tangible in a registry, but possession may be kept by the debtor and this is addressed as non-possessory publicised pledge[168] performing the functions of common law concept of charge, in the others, there is a clear distinction between pledge and non-possessory security right.[169] Nevertheless, non-possessory security right is a significant feature of modern secured transactions regimes. The pragmatic value of non-possessory security rights can be obtained by

165 Art 2.

166 Röver, op. cit. (f'note 35), 72.

167 *See generally* Chs 2, 4–5; Guide, para. 53, at 21.

168 For instance, in France 'non-possessory publicised pledge over any tangible movable' is possible (French Civil Code art 2333); for more information, *see* Ancel, M.E. 'Recent Reform in France: The Renaissance of a Civilian Collateral Regime?' in F. Dahan and J. Simpson (eds), op. cit. (f'note 147), 259, at 264.

169 For instance, under English law *Pledge* and *Charge* denote different concepts as pledge requires actual or constructive possession. For the definition of 'pledge' in English law, *Official Assignee of Madras v Mercantile Bank of India Ltd.* [1935] AC 53, 58–59.

publicity achieved through a general security rights registry. The Cape Town Convention under Chapter IV and V deals with issues of registration. As a key policy, the Cape Town Convention aims to give priority through clear and simple rules to registered international interests over subsequently-registered international interests and unregistered interests. The Receivables Convention suggests the establishment of a registration system under Optional Annex Article 3, even though States preserve their priority regimes and do not opt into one of the options recommended in the Annex (Article 42(4)). The Guide and the Model Law also suggest the creation of a registration system similar to the UCC Article 9 notice filing method. The purpose of reference to registration under the Model Law is to publicise the charge and the information to be registered is limited.[170]

An important concern that underpins the ability to use all assets as collateral and create a non-possessory security interest is the significance of party autonomy in the proprietary aspects of security. Party autonomy is the freedom of parties to choose those rules that will apply to their contract. The fact that most countries strictly specify a list of secured transactions that parties may conclude in their civil or commercial codes,[171] limits innovative financing techniques. In some of these legislations non-possessory security interests cannot be used or are sometimes frowned upon.[172] Both the Model Law and the Guide support maximum contractual flexibility for the parties to arrange their secured transactions. With globalisation, parties have specific needs to protect their financial interests and the law should positively respond to that by permitting parties to structure secured transactions according to their needs, while respecting other important legislation.[173] The Receivables and the Factoring Conventions have comprehensive party autonomy provisions allowing parties to either derogate entirely from the Convention (as in the case of the Factoring Convention) or, more appropriately, derogation from or variation by agreement of certain provisions (as in the case of the Receivables Convention). In both Conventions the party autonomy concept is designed as a key principle.[174] It is also one of the underlying principles of the Cape Town Convention, according to which high value cross-border transactions 'should be respected and enforced'.[175] The other underlying principle of the Cape

170 Röver, op. cit. (f'note 35), at 73.

171 This is known as the '*numerus clausus*' principle under Civil Law jurisdictions which limits the parties' freedom to enter into contracts to those secured transactions enumerated in the legislation. One can link the party autonomy argument with freedom of contract. McCormack suggests that '[i]f the law, on a prospective basis, forbade the taking of [non-possessory security] then priority over other creditors is not something that a . . . creditor could lawfully have exacted as the price of its loan'. Op. cit. (f'note 11), 13.

172 Mistelis, op. cit. (f'note 140), at 469, where he states that '[a] major defect . . . of secured transactions in many countries is that it is . . . impossible to use non-possessory security rights'; *see also* Claps, G.A.M. and McDonnell, J.B. (2002) 'Secured Credit and Insolvency Law in Argentina and the US: Gaining Insight from a Comparative Perspective', 30 *Ga. J. Int'l & Comp. L.*, 393, 396.

173 Guide, para. 57, at 21–2.

174 Factoring Convention Article 3 and the Receivables Convention Article 6.

175 Goode, op. cit. (f'note 157), at 18.

Town Convention is sensitivity to national legal cultures. According to this principle, contracting States are allowed to make declarations to opt in or out of provisions, as well as to exclude wholly, or partially select, provisions of the Convention such as interim remedies.[176] Interpretation of international instruments' provisions must be made in accordance with the object and purpose as set forth in their preamble, and regard is to be had to their international character and to the need for the promotion of uniformity and observance of good faith.

1.4.3 Efficient rules for creation of security interests

Creation of security interests is a main concern that is acutely experienced in cross-border credit transactions. The international lender prefers to know whether the security created in one jurisdiction will be valid in another jurisdiction. This is particularly important if the debtor's law is inefficient in protecting the financial interests of the secured creditor. In that context, the creation of security rights in a simple and efficient manner, while distinguishing the effectiveness of a security right between the parties from third-party effectiveness, is critical.[177] Unreformed regimes do not draw a distinction between the effectiveness as between the parties and third-party effectiveness, whereas modern secured transactions regimes separate creation from third-party effectiveness. The significance is that creation of a security right as between the parties allows the creditor to enforce the security right against the debtor, and may be used as an unperfected security interest effective against unsecured non-insolvency creditors,[178] whereas the additional step (registration, possession, etc.) for opposability permits the creditor to enforce the security right against third parties.

A security interest created in one jurisdiction should also be recognisable in another jurisdiction and a single security right in respect of all types of things and rights may have the necessary value to achieve this. International lenders are generally wary to the possibility of a security interest created in one jurisdiction and not recognised in the other. That possibility may jeopardise the chances of recouping their loan, thus their interest rates are kept at a higher level. If transaction costs for creation of security rights and formalities are minimised, and a single security right for all kinds of encumbered asset is introduced, there is a possibility to promote low-cost credit. Creation of security rights in future assets and the extension of security into proceeds are crucial and also reflected in the instruments.[179] The Model Law is based on the principle of 'minimum restrictions' where

176 Goode, op. cit. (f'note 157), at 18.

177 *See* Chs 4–5. E.g. Guide, para. 65, at 24; the Receivables Convention Articles 8–10 deal with effectiveness as between the parties and Articles 22–23 and 26–32 deal with effectiveness as against third parties; the Cape Town Convention Chapter II Article 7 deals with effectiveness between parties and Chapter VIII deals with effectiveness as against third parties.

178 Gullifer, op. cit. (f'note 22), at 64.

179 E.g. under the Receivables Convention, as long as the proceeds are identifiable (Article 24(2)) under Article 14, the assignee has a contractual right to proceeds. Guide, para. 64, at 23.

formalities for the creation of security rights are kept to a minimum and single security right is enabled.[180] There is no distinction between the traditional and quasi-security interests under the Model Law.[181] The Model Law contains a broad enterprise charge (Article 5.6) and allows the appointment of a charge administrator,[182] and adopts the common law approach of creation of security rights over a pool of assets. However, for the creation of security rights a single step of creation of security rights is adopted, which includes third-party effectiveness of security interest as opposed to the attachment plus perfection duo as can be found under common law secured transactions regimes.[183] The Guide recognises the simple and efficient manner of creation of security rights.[184] The Receivables Convention has a pragmatic approach to the effectiveness of an assignment by setting aside contractual and statutory limitations on the assignment of receivables (such as assignment future and bulk receivables under Articles 8 and 9) and leaving the form of assignment to the law applicable outside the Convention. The applicable law outside the Convention may be ascertained by the autonomous choice-of-law rules contained in Chapter V. It is important to note that the form of assignment is a condition of priority under Article 22 and 5(g).[185] In addition, an efficient and clear manner of transfer of security rights with minimal requirements (such as a security) follows the assigned receivable without the necessity of a new act of transfer being adopted (Article 10), and contractual limitations are set aside. The Factoring Convention under Articles 5 to 7 enables simple and efficient transfer of rights by setting aside contractual prohibitions,[186] and allows the assignment of future and bulk receivables and rights without the need for a new act of transfer. One of the key objectives of the Cape Town Convention is to facilitate the acquisition and financing of certain high-value mobile equipment by enabling the creation of an 'international interest', which will be recognised by all Contracting States.[187] Probably one of the most innovative features of the Cape Town Convention is the introduction of the concept of 'international interest' to the legal literature. An international interest will be deemed as an interest, in addition to satisfying conditions under Articles 2 and 7, when there is a security, retention of title, or leasing agreements between the parties. However, the Cape Town Convention does not characterise whether an agreement is a security,

180 Model Law, at vi and Part 2 Creation of a Charge.

181 Though there is a distinction between *registered charges* and *possessory charges*, there is also an *unpaid vendor's charge*.

182 Article 25. Röver, op. cit. (f'note 35), at 72–3. There seems to be similarity with the English law; however, English law does not allow the floating charge holders to appoint an administrator receiver in accordance with the Enterprise Act 2002 s 250.

183 Röver, op. cit. (f'note 35), 73.

184 Guide, para. 51, at 20 and Chapter II.

185 However, note that if notification of the debtor is required for the effectiveness of the assignment as between the assignor and the assignee, Article 14(1) is set aside. *See* Chs 4 and 6.

186 However, note that Factoring Convention Article 6 has exceptions allowing anti-assignment clauses to be effective thus limiting the effectiveness of assignment.

187 Goode, op. cit. (f'note 157), at 14.

retention-of-title or leasing agreement and this is left to the substantive law applicable outside the Convention.[188]

1.4.4 Predictable rules for third-party effectiveness

Establishing public knowledge, thus creating predictability and achieving third-party effectiveness, is critical.[189] This policy is instrumental in lowering the cost of credit since the costs of searching previous creditors are reduced by simplifying and making the system transparent. Policies of informing the public are broadly classified into three types.[190] First, civil law systems' method of *numerus clausus* enumerates secured transactions that parties can enter into;[191] however, it limits the possibility of creating a security agreement that will fulfil a specific commercial need. Nevertheless, parties are aware of the particularities of the specific secured transaction defined in the code. A second method to inform the public is the constructive notice where the third party may succeed in outranking the non-possessory security right holder, if the third party at a low cost cannot discover the earlier right.[192] Professor Spanogle, in assessing whether it costs a lot to create an enforceable charge in order to be able to maintain that the law is effective to induce a potential secured creditor to give value for the collateral, argues that for non-possessory security interests a constructive notice concept must be applied, as opposed to actual notice, so that it 'imputes knowledge of a public filing to all the world, including subsequent creditors whether they have actual knowledge of it or not'.[193] The third method is the publicity of existence of non-possessory security rights through registration in a general public registry. The nature of non-possessory security rights, which allows the debtor to possess the collateral while the creditor holds security over it in return for credit extended to the debtor, requires registration, because it is extremely difficult for other secured creditors and third parties to be able to determine other rights on the same asset of the debtor. The rationale is to clarify to potential creditors of the debtor of the amount they can claim in the event of the debtor's insolvency (that is, whether the debtor has given any other security to others and how much),[194] and to avoid any

188 Goode, op. cit. (f'note 157), at 169.

189 Chs 5–6.

190 Armour, in Eidenmüller and Kieninger (eds), op. cit. (f'note 132), 25 *et seq.*

191 Professor Bridge argues that English law adopts the Civil Law notion of *numerus clausus* (citing *Re Cosslett (Contractors) Ltd* [1997] Ch 23); as a counter-argument it is arguable that it seems the creation of security rights under English law is more flexible than it is under Civil Law systems, and under English law there is no list of security rights in comparison to the codified nature of Civil Law security rights. *See* Bridge, M. (2002) 'The English Law of Real Security', 4 *E.R.P.L.*, 483, 486. *See* Ch. 3 for further discussion of *numerus clausus*.

192 Armour, in Eidenmüller and Kieninger (eds), op. cit. (f'note 132), at 26.

193 Spanogle, J.A. 'A Functional Analysis of the EBRD Model Law on Secured Transactions', in Norton and Andenas (eds) op. cit. (f'note 163), 157, 160.

194 *See* M. Bridge, 'The Scope and Limits of Security Interests', in H. Eidenmüller and E.M. Kieninger (eds) op. cit. 132, 181, at 186 (citing *Smith (Administrator of Cosslett (Contractors) Ltd) v Bridgend County Borough Council* [2002] 1 AC 336, at [19].)

misleading decisions that may arise due to disguise of secured credit.[195] The advantage of registration vis-à-vis other policies is doubled with the extensive use of the internet. Thus it has received broad acceptance in international instruments. While the Model Law,[196] Guide,[197] the Cape Town Convention[198] and the Receivables Convention[199] achieve public knowledge through the registration requirements and address this matter as one of their key objectives,[200] the Factoring Convention lacks this vital aspect of secured transactions regime. These instruments require the establishment of a general security rights registry that will create transparency and notify third parties. Registration is an essential element of modern secured transactions regimes, which functionalises those principles such as utility of non-possessory security rights and certainty for creditors. There seems to be tension between the European jurisdictions and North American jurisdictions in the way that the former do not have a similar secured transactions and registration system that exists in the latter.[201] There have been firm critics of the registration system, especially as it is currently set out under the Receivables Convention and the Guide.[202] However, one can dispute that the arguments of those critics ignore the interests and concerns of international lenders regarding certainty. Examples of charges under the Companies Act 2006 and registration requirement thereof are forwarded, but there is no mention of the assignment of receivables by way of sale and the problem that may be caused by lack of registration under English law.[203] Whereas, notwithstanding the substance of the transaction, if all transactions performing security are registered, there will be relative certainty. One can clearly state that registration has been adopted in national[204] and international legislative texts (such as Model Law (Part 2),

195 Bridge, ibid., at 186 and n 19 (citing the seminal Company Law case *Salomon v A Salomon & Co. Ltd.* [1897] AC 22).

196 This is a key feature of the Model Law and it is dealt with under Articles 6(2), 7, 8(3), 11 and 33–35.

197 This is dealt with extensively under Guide Part III.

198 Chapter IV, The International Registry System. This is a key principle under the Cape Town Convention where transparency is achieved through registration and notice is given to third parties. Registration covers interest of a chargee under a security agreement, of a conditional seller and lessor under a conditional sale and lease agreements.

199 Article 42(4) and Annex section II.

200 E.g. The Cape Town Convention and its protocols are designed to achieve predictability through registration and this is one of the five key objectives, '. . . to establish an electronic international registry for the registration of international interests which will give notice of their existence to third parties . . . enable the creditor to preserve its priority against subsequently registered interests and against unregistered interests and the debtor's insolvency administrator'. Goode, op. cit. (f'note 157), at 14.

201 *See* e.g. Kieninger, E-M. (2004) 'Evaluation: A Common Core? Convergences, Subsisting Differences and Possible Ways for Harmonisation' in E-M. Kieninger (ed.), *Security Rights in Movable Property in European Private Law*. Cambridge: Cambridge University Press, pp. 647, 670.

202 E.g. Flessner, A. and Verhagen, H. (2006) *Assignment in European Private International Law*. Munich: Sellier, pp. 55–57 and 71 *et seq*.

203 Under English law, factoring agreements are not registered. Law Commission Report No. 296 has recommended that these should also be registered, paras 4.19–4.25.

204 *See* e.g. Canadian PPSA, UCC Article 9 and New Zealand PPSA.

the Cape Town Convention, the Receivables Convention (Article 42(4) and Annex section II) and the Guide), and its importance was noted by the Law Commission.[205]

1.4.5 Clear priority rules for competing creditors

Clear and predictable priority rules will have the impact of reducing the cost of credit in transactions. Creditors and international lenders must be able to ascertain their priority position in advance of the conclusion of the security agreement. This will have impact in the reduction of transaction and credit costs included in the calculation of interest rates. Priority should be determinable either through registration, or by the order of registration, or by achieving third-party effectiveness through other means. Different priority rules applicable to lenders and sellers create uncertainty and reduce the value of collateral. Different priority rules apply to secured creditors and sellers retaining title. Under the Guide, through a unitary and non-unitary approach to acquisition financing devices there seems to be more predictability as in all cases priority and third-party effectiveness are unified.[206] Under the Receivables Convention all priority rules are connected to the law of the assignor's state as the single and most predictable factor in any given assignment transaction.[207] This is complemented by the recommendations made under the Guide,[208] which have been prepared to modernise domestic secured transactions regimes in line with the Receivables Convention. One of the underlying principles of the Cape Town Convention is the necessity to attain predictability through concise and clear priority rules.[209] A similar underlying philosophy can also be found in the Model Law where a concise and clear priority rule is in place.[210] This is also supplemented by the Core Principles, which recommend the establishment of clear rules governing competing rights. However, the Factoring Convention did not provide any solution on priority issues.

1.4.6 Harmonised conflict-of-laws rules in secured transactions

Harmonisation of conflict-of-laws rules to the extent that they are related to secured transactions law is important.[211] The Receivables Convention achieved a harmonised approach to certain issues such as the priorities and formal validity of

205 Law Commission Report No. 296 para. 2.30, where it is indicated that priority by date of registration will be involved in any EU Directive or regulation as it is also recommended in the Model Law. However, the Law Commission has refrained from focusing on conflict of laws issues related to this area, para. 3.248.

206 Particularly, *see* Chs 6–7.

207 Articles 22 and 30.

208 Part V, recommendations 76–109.

209 Op. cit. (f'note 157), at 8.

210 Article 17.

211 Ch. 8.

assignment of receivables through conflict-of-laws rules. The ineluctable nature of intangibles and the divergent approach of civil and common law jurisdictions make it necessary to regulate certain aspects of secured transactions through conflict of laws. Furthermore, the insufficiency of the *lex situs* rule in determining the applicable law involving intangibles makes it necessary to apply the law of the grantor's (assignor) State. A similar argument also applies for mobile equipment effectively covered by the Cape Town Convention, which rejects the *lex situs* rule and introduces an international interest concept that may be created in accordance with the rules of the Convention, and perfected globally by registration in an international registry. It is submitted that conflict-of-laws rules in the above instruments will create predictability and certainty in cross-border secured transactions, despite criticism towards them.[212]

1.5 Conclusion

Taking security is critical. Recognition of security devices and establishing a comprehensive system are necessary for both facilitation of credit and increased economic activity. Lending decisions have been adversely affected due to the recent financial crisis. This is partly due to secured transactions laws that do not endorse security efficiently, or lack predictability. It is arguable that lending decisions are made taking into account whether the lender has the ability to take security. Fragmented systems of secured transactions increase the cost of credit and uncertainty. Although there are arguments that aim to illustrate the limited effectiveness of secured credit and full priority, the pace of international activities in establishing modernisation and harmonisation in secured transactions law proves that secured credit is important globally. Particularly, domestic law arguments that aim to limit priority status to secured creditors will seem to fail to receive acceptance, given the perspective of international instruments, which often articulate the significance of priority to secured creditors and express rules accordingly. Arguably a clear priority status and the ability to take efficient security will make an instrument more acceptable by the financial sector.

The prospects of success of international secured transactions law instruments are positive. They clearly respond to particular concerns in international finance transactions. International instruments provide a structure for an ideal regime that will enable individuals and SMEs as well as large organisations and smaller banks to access low and affordable credit. Fundamental principles upon which the international instruments are based, aim to facilitate credit in the face of financial crisis by establishing a robust secured transactions system. Establishing an efficient method of creation of security interests, and third-party effectiveness supported by a predictable system of priorities, is critical in reducing the cost of credit. These

212 The criticism is particularly towards the law of the assignor's State connecting factor. *See* e.g. Flessner and Verhagen, op. cit. (f'note 202).

must be complemented by the ability to use all assets and obligations in order to utilise the full economic value to obtain credit. It is arguable that this may be achieved by adopting a comprehensive and functional approach to security. Even then, there may well be issues whether a transaction falls within the ambit of functional definition and this may be the case, particularly in finance leases, retention-of-title clauses and sales of receivables.[213]

The Cape Town Convention establishes a successful system that can be illustrated by the number of ratifications.[214] The philosophy of the Cape Town Convention in establishing the international interest and the international registry is significant in reducing the cost of credit and establishing predictability in high-value mobile equipment. Furthermore, leaving characterisation as to what a particular transaction may be (whether a security interest or a title device) is also critical in producing an important international text. The Guide and the Model Law provide significant sets of rules aiming at modernised harmonisation of domestic secured transactions laws. They can serve as a starting point for domestic law reforms. The Receivables Convention, in establishing a sophisticated and potentially far-reaching set of rules on the assignment of receivables, seems to receive acceptance from the North American jurisdictions. The work of UNCITRAL on secured transactions in creating an ideal set of rules will seem to continue.[215] A legislative text on registration of security interests, arguably, will be timely and appropriate, because the registration system provides transparency, and international instruments utilise the registration system. Obviously, from another angle there needs to be scholarly debate as to whether which instrument best fits the needs of regional organisations[216] and nations, but this is in the nature of competition.

213 Sales of receivables do not secure payment or performance of an obligation; nevertheless, they are included in the Guide within the framework of functional approach to security (Recommendation 3). Similarly, finance leases may be used both for security and non-security reasons and the former, in that sense, falls within the ambit of functional definition. *See also* Law Commission Consultation Paper No. 164, at 190 *et seq.*

214 Thirty-five States have ratified the Cape Town Convention. http://www.unidroit.org/english/implement/i-2001-convention.pdf (last accessed April 2010).

215 *See* A/CN.9/670, paras 124–126. Future work may involve preparation of a model law drawing on the recommendations of the Guide, or a legislative guide on registration of security interests (A/63/17, paras 313, 314 and 318). The Commission also decided that a future work should be undertaken on certain types of securities not covered by the Guide (A/62/17, part I, para. 160). These are particularly directly-held securities, as opposed to indirectly-held, which are adequately covered by UNIDROIT's recent Convention on Intermediated Securities. For a colloquium on secured transactions (A/63/17, para. 319) held 1st–3rd March 2010 in Vienna, *see* http://www.uncitral.org/pdf/english/colloquia/3rdSecTrans/Outline.pdf (last accessed 25 February 2010).

216 For example, the debate on European Security Interest and as to whether the Guide is compatible with the EU Member States' secured transactions regimes, *see generally* H. Eidenmüller and E.M. Kieninger (eds) op. cit. (f'note 1323).

2 Harmonisation of secured transactions law in context

2.1 Introduction

There is a commercial necessity in harmonising secured transactions law. Secured transactions law is at the core of commercial law, and at the crossroads of the law of contracts, consumer law and the law of property, which are deeply rooted in the traditional domestic rules of legal cultures.[1] Traditional roots of secured transactions law are considered to be the resistance point in international harmonisation activities. With the globalisation of financial markets and the increased pace of market interdependency, it is financially necessary and critical to harmonise laws governing secured transactions at the international level to allow businesses to have access to low-cost credit. The ability to take security over movables in addition to immovables is critical. The issue has particular importance for SMEs operating in emerging markets.[2] Amid the recent financial crisis, the same argument equally applies to SMEs in developed economies that are in need of immediate liquidity.[3] The issue was one of the main debating points during the G20 Summit

1 For a similar affirmation, *see* Dahan, F. (2000) 'Secured Transactions Law in Western Advanced Economies: Exposing Myths', *Law in Transition*, 37, 39 (Autumn); Cuming, R.C.C. (1997) 'The Internationalization of Secured Financing Law: The Spreading Influence of the Concepts UCC, Article 9 and its Progeny' in R. Cranston (ed) *Making Commercial Law Essays in Honour of Roy Goode*, Oxford: Clarendon, 499, arguing that the law of secured transactions '. . . is perceived as embodying cultural attitudes and public policy choices that vary greatly among states . . .'.

2 For a detailed analysis and empirical study on whether the financial strength of the borrower has any impact on the decision of secured credit, *see* Mann, R. (1997) 'Explaining the Pattern of Secured Credit', 110 *Harv. L. Rev.*, 625. According to Mann, when the financial power of a borrowing company increases, secured credit becomes less attractive, hence the argument that small and medium-sized businesses need more secured credit than the large businesses that may borrow on an unsecured basis. *See* at 674.

3 For problems in access to credit *see* Federation of Small Businesses http://www.fsb.org.uk/ *Number Crunching the Credit Crunch*. According to this report small businesses suffer from 'hikes from interest rates for loans and overdrafts; poor treatment despite good credit histories; behavioural inconsistencies from strategic to branch level; the imposition of facility fees; reneging on promised finance'. The report also states that there are 4.7 million small businesses in the UK, which employ 13.5 million people. Small businesses employ 58 per cent of the private sector workforce in the UK and contribute more than half of the UK turnover.

held in London in 2009.[4] For financial institutions, within the framework of prudent and effective financial regulation, Basel II requirements[5] insist on a clear and predictable legal structure to support effective flow of credit. On the one hand, harmonised modernisation of secured transactions laws provides facilitated access to low-cost credit for borrowers while, on the other hand, the same phenomenon increases the confidence of lenders, as certainty and predictability maintained by harmonised rules will result in the reduction of interest rates.[6] The lender will not be including the risk premium in the interest rate calculation[7] and is able to lend with long maturities. Therefore, facilitation of credit can be achieved through harmonised rules and harmonisation is the foremost key policy issue.

Fundamental reasons for harmonisation of secured transactions law include facilitation of credit by predictable and modern rules applied in harmony in contracting states, improving cross-border trade by reducing the cost of credit, and thus enabling SMEs to access low-cost credit. Divergence in national secured transactions laws complicates cross-border trade and obstructs businesses who wish to have access to low-cost credit.[8] In that context, it is critical to harmonise secured transactions laws at the international level by including all legal cultures and to achieve modern, harmonised and predictable rules for secured credit transactions.

This chapter is organised as follows. In part two, harmonisation and similar terms within the framework of secured transactions will be discussed. In particular, the significance of harmonisation will be advocated. In part three, the historical backdrop of harmonisation with particular reference to international harmonisation and secured transactions law will be explored. In part four, the rationale of international harmonisation of secured transactions law and the relevant key policy issues will be explored. In that context, the chapter will

4 Recent problems in lending stemming from the financial crisis had been tackled by the G20 Finance Ministers and a communiqué was prepared setting out a number of strategies including restoring global growth and strengthening the financial system to be put into action. *G20 Finance Ministers' and Central Bank Governors' Communiqué*, 14 March 2009.

5 *See* Basel Committee on Banking Supervision, International Convergence of Capital Measurement and Capital Standards; *see especially* Part 2 (IV) and (VI) (Bank for International Settlements, June 2004).

6 For a similar view, *see* Kozolchyk, B. (2009) 'Modernization of Commercial Law: International Uniformity and Economic Development', 34 *Brook. J. Int'l L.*, 709, 718–19 arguing financial institutions '. . . had ample lending capital at their disposal, yet very few were willing to lend to small businesses unless their owners were very well known to the banks and could supply their "personal" signatures and "good" real estate mortgages as collateral'.

7 McCormack, G. (2007) 'The UNCITRAL Legislative Guide on Secured Transactions Functionalism and Form' in B. Foëx, L. Thévenoz, and S.V. Bazinas (eds) *Réforme des sûretés mobilières. Les enseignements du Guide législatif de la CNUDCI/Reforming secured transactions. The UNCITRAL legislative guide as an inspiration*. Genève-Zurich-Bâle: Schulthess, p. 214.

8 For example, in 1992 during the Uniform Commercial Law Congress it was indicated that American lenders were reluctant to lend to non-American borrowers where receivables were used as collateral due to risk in collection that stemmed from differences in legal systems. *See, Uniform Commercial Law in the Twenty-First Century: Proceedings of the Congress of the United Nations Commission on International Trade Law*. New York: UN, at 156 (1995).

demonstrate the rationale of harmonisation and advocate harmonisation through adoption of international secured transactions instruments. Conclusions will be in part five.

2.2 Defining harmonisation in the context of secured transactions

Broadly speaking, harmonisation has been the basic tenor of recent international standard setting activities on various aspects of private law. In the context of international activities on secured transactions the intention is certainly to harmonise the law. Some authors suggest that there are other metaphors such as transplantation[9] and 'viral propagation' used to promote global rules on secured transactions.[10] However, it is submitted that harmonisation is an umbrella term and used to cover particularly the 'viral propagation' metaphor. First, it is argued that legal transplantation, which rarely works,[11] is a method of legal reform. It is the importation of the law of a State to another State, the success of which requires simultaneous importation and digestion of precedents, case law, doctrinal commentaries and education material, which then need to be followed up by continuous reform in the light of the donor State's reform of that particular law. This is simply because the donor State develops its legal order internally, and builds the legal order on its business practices and ethics with which its population is generally familiar. On the other hand, the host State that adopts the legal order needs to structure its business understanding and practices according to the adopted legal order so that the transplant works.[12] But, of course, the main issue is that, prior to

9 For harmonisation and transplantation, *see* e.g. Ancel, M. (1976) 'From the Unification of Law to its Harmonisation', 51 *Tul. L. Rev.*, 108, 114–17; Watson, A. (1976) 'Legal Transplants and Law Reform', 92 *LQR*, 79; Watson, A. (1974) *Legal Transplants: An Approach to Comparative Law*. Edinburgh: Scottish Academic Press, at 30 *et seq.*, explaining various types of reception, e.g. imposed reception, solicited reception, infiltration, penetration, etc.

10 *See* e.g. Macdonald, R.A. (2009) 'Three Metaphors of Norm Migration in International Context', 34 *Brook. J. Int'l L.*, 603. Professor Macdonald suggests that there are three metaphors; namely: harmonisation, transplantation and viral propagation.

11 Kronke, H. (2008) 'Why Transplants Rarely work – Why Convergence is Insufficient in Commercial Law – Methodical Changes in Paradigm in the Harmonisation of Commercial Law' http://www.law.qmul.ac.uk/events/docs/London_February_2008_Kronke.ppt#1 (last accessed October 2009). Professor Kronke correctly states two types of successful transplantation: (1) through imperialism; and (2) through invitation or shared values/ideology. Doubtful transplantation examples are those attempted by invited or solicited scholars. It can be argued that the transplantation mechanism particularly succeeded in Turkey where the Swiss Civil and Obligation Codes were transplanted. Örücü, E. (2000) 'Critical Comparative Law: Considering Paradoxes for Legal Systems in Transition', 4.1 *E.J.C.L.* http://www.ejcl.org/41/art41–1.html (last visited October 2009), where she argues that the reception of laws was a radically reformist approach to tear up the foundations of the old legal system and to build a new one on the basis of the relationship of people and not on the religious values or customs and thus the reform was a significant example of 'social engineering through law'.

12 *See* Berkowitz, D., Pistor, K. and Richard, J-F. (2001) 'Economic Development: Legality and the Transplant Effect', *William Davidson Working Paper No. 410*, at 3 *et seq.* (September).

adoption or transplantation, the appropriate choice needs to be made. In the current economic climate and the financial crisis, it can be argued that the choice is generally made external to the host State. However, knowledge of legal and economic systems of the host and adapting the donor State's rules accordingly carry significant value in the success of transplantation.[13] Particularly in secured transactions, similar economic development, social and administrative infrastructure levels are necessary for considerable success. In other words, using the well-known 'exportability of UCC Article 9' example, unless a country has similar business practices, well-developed social and market infrastructure and a financial level such as the United States has, transplantation or exportation of UCC Article 9 theory cannot create workable results. Second, when critically reviewed, 'viral propagation', as used by commentators[14] to connote the function of the Guide, seems to underrate the real nature of the Guide. Propagation of global norms happens in a number of ways. Some scholars address this as 'isomorphism' or 'convergence'.[15] According to DiMaggio and Powell, isomorphic change (convergence) occurs either through political influence (*coercive isomorphism*) or by responses to uncertainty (*mimetic isomorphism*), or stems from professionalisation (*normative isomorphism*).[16] Coercive isomorphism occurs when political pressures require a reform.[17] Mimetic isomorphism is similar to legal transplantation and occurs when a system is modelled upon another in order to overcome uncertainty.[18] Finally, the normative isomorphism is where professionals define and determine the rules or laws as appropriate.[19]

In the light of these, it can be argued that the Guide, or indeed any other international secured transactions instruments, are not propagating viruses but they are an attempt to harmonise and modernise the law of secured transactions. The Guide may contain traces of UCC Article 9 and, certainly, some Canadian provinces' personal property security act theories that have been influenced by their American counterpart.[20] But this is certainly normal because, arguably, these are the States that promote harmonisation and eventual uniformity on secured transactions law. The Guide considers the views of different legal cultures. During the

13 For more discussion on this *see* Walsh, C. (2000) 'The 'Law' in Law and Development', *Law in Transition*, 7, 12 (Autumn).

14 *See* e.g. Macdonald, op. cit. (f'note 10), at 635 *et seq.*

15 *See* e.g. DiMaggio, P.J. and Powell, W.W. (1983) 'The Iron Cage Revisited: Institutional Isomorphism and Collective Rationality in Organizational Fields', 48 *American Sociological Review*, 147; Halliday, T. and Carruthers, B. (2009) *Bankrupt: Global Lawmaking and Systematic Financial Crisis*. Stanford, CA: Stanford University Press, p. xxiii.

16 DiMaggio and Powell, ibid., at 150 *et seq.*

17 Halliday and Carruthers exemplified this with the reform of laws as a condition of credit by the IMF. *See* ibid., at xxiii and 173–4.

18 It can be argued that the adoption of the Swiss Civil and Obligations Codes, doctrines, scholarly writings and judicial precedents by Turkey in 1926 seems to explain this concept.

19 Halliday and Carruthers, ibid., at xxiii; DiMaggio and Powell, ibid., at 152 *et seq.*

20 E.g. the Ontario PPSA, which takes the functional approach under s 2, *see* McCormack, G. (2002) 'Personal Property Security Law Reform in England and Canada', *J.B.L.*, 113, 120 *et seq.*

deliberations, all delegations', including interest groups', views were considered equally.[21] Thus an argument that suggests that the Guide propagates global norms based on UCC Article 9 must be critically considered.[22] In any case, every international instrument is prone to be influenced by several legal cultures, and maintains an optimal balance if it can in order to be adopted by States. The rules of the Guide and the Cape Town Convention, for instance, are precise formulations, because of the input by the interest groups, e.g. industry representatives as well as the technical and academic representatives.

Notwithstanding legal transplant and viral propagation arguments, it is submitted that the aim of international instruments is to harmonise the law rather than propagating legal cultures to other States, or transplanting rules without setting the right infrastructure. There have been critics of harmonisation in general too.[23] Those critics[24] argued that harmonisation had a utopian nature, lacked coherence, and presented inconsistency through international instruments.[25] Furthermore, the same critics argued that harmonisation might straitjacket countries into stark uniformity by virtue of the mandatory application of instruments that were difficult to amend.[26] Some other commentators criticised the harmonisation process as the product of interest and lobbying groups, thus serving their interests.[27] There are counter-arguments to these objections.[28] First, it can be submitted that the critics misinterpret uniformity and harmonisation, and fail to realise the significance of international harmonisation in an era of globalised financial markets. Although both terms and codification are used interchangeably, they do not mean the same concept. Harmonisation is the preliminary

21 For discussions on legitimacy, *see above* Introduction.

22 For instance, prominent scholars Halliday and Carruthers in the preface of their recent acclaimed book briefly compare the position of delegations in IMF and UNCITRAL by using the US as a metaphor and it seems that the possibility of a delegation in the UNCITRAL to be powerfully influential is less than it is in the IMF. Because in the former there are other delegations and all are equal, whereas in the latter, the financial contribution amount is critical on whose influence will have a decisive effect on the decision-making process and the outcomes. *See* Halliday and Carruthers, op. cit. (f'note 15), at xxii–xxiii.

23 *See* e.g. Hobhouse, J.S. (1990) *International Conventions and Commercial Law: The Pursuit of Uniformity*, 106 *L.Q.R.*, 531; Wheatley, D. (1990) 'Why I oppose the Wind of Change?', *The Times*, 27 March; Stephan, P.B. (1999) 'The Futility of Unification and Harmonization in International Commercial Law', 39 *Va. J. Int'l L.*, 743, 788 *et seq.*; Gretton, G. (1998) 'Mixed Systems: Scotland' *in* J. Norton and M. Andenas (eds) *Emerging Financial Markets and Secured Transactions*. The Hague: Kluwer, pp. 279, 282.

24 Hobhouse, ibid.; Wheatley, ibid.

25 *See* e.g. Hobhouse, ibid., at 533; for a similar argument, *see generally* Walt, S. (1999) 'Novelty and the Risks of Uniform Sales Law', 39 *Va. J. Int'l L.*, 671.

26 Hobhouse, ibid., 533–35.

27 *See* e.g. generally Schwartz, A. and Scott, R. 9 (1995) 'The Political Economy of Private Legislatures', 143 *U. Pa. L. Rev.*

28 *See* e.g. Steyn, J. (1994) 'A Kind of Esperanto' in P. Birks (ed.) *The Frontiers of Liability* Vol. 2. Oxford: Oxford University Press, p. 11; *see also* Goode, R. (1990) 'Why Compromise Makes Sense', *The Times*, 22 May.

step before eventual uniformity. As a general proposition, it can be argued that adoption of an international instrument may create harmony but uniformity can be achieved by uniform interpretation[29] and application of an international instrument.[30] Harmonisation leaves an opportunity for experimentation, whereas uniformity does not.[31] Codification must be used in a sensitive manner in the international arena. For instance, in the context of the harmonisation of private law within the EU, the phrase 'Civil Code' and the thought of codifying European Private Law have attracted criticism.[32] To common lawyers, unlike civil lawyers, a Code may symbolise a civil law system, straitjacket rules, and concepts with which common law jurisdictions may not be familiar. Further criticism is based on concepts linked to constitutional, economic and cultural issues. Codification is generally the main feature of civil law regimes.[33] It contains both harmonisation and unification. For instance, in the US, commercial law rules are contained in the Uniform Commercial Code, though the UCC is not, strictly speaking, a uniform code,[34] but rather is a harmonised set of model rules. Moreover, codification has a different meaning in civil law systems, where the codified rules are not considered as model, but rather strictly applied, uniform rules, which are systemised and illustrate the intervention of the state on private contractual relationships.[35] In that sense, one can argue that in the UCC pattern there is harmonisation and in the civil code pattern, there is unification. Second, harmonisation of laws provides more benefits than divergence of laws. Some of these benefits are reduction of costs in cross-border transactions and legal disputes by virtue of maintained predictability and, within the realm of secured credit law, access to low-cost credit. Third, international instruments do not have mandatory applicability. Mandatory application requirements may easily turn an international instrument into a

29 On uniform manner of interpretation, *see* ibid.; Ferrari, F. (2001) 'Applying the CISG in a truly uniform manner: Tribunale di Vigevano (Italy), 12 July 2000', *Unif. L. Rev.*, 203.

30 Most international instruments have provisions dealing with interpretation, ibid.; Receivables Convention, Article 7; Factoring Convention, Article 4; Cape Town Convention, Article 5.

31 Some authors regard uniformity as an 'imposition of one legal model on all jurisdictions' through indirect influence. Zamora, S. (1995) 'NAFTA and the Harmonization of Domestic Legal Systems: The Side Effects of Free Trade', 12 *Ariz. J. Int'l & Comp. L.*, 401, 405.

32 *See* ibid.; Legrand, P. (2006) 'Antivonbar', 1 *J.C.L.*, 1; Legrand, P. (1997) 'Against a European Civil Code', 60 *M.L.R.*, 44; Legrand, P. (2002) 'On the Unbearable Localness of the Law: Academic Fallacies and Unseasonable Observations', *E.R.P.L.*, 61; Ogus, A. (1999) 'Competition Between National Legal Systems: A Contribution of Economic Analysis to Comparative Law', 48 *I.C.L.Q.*, 405; Weatherill, S. (2004) 'Why Object to Harmonization of Private Law by the EC?', *E.R.P.L.*, 633; Beale, H. 'Finding the Remaining Traps' in S. Grundman and J. Stuyck (eds) (2002) *Academic Green Paper on European Contract Law*. The Hague: Kluwer, pp. 67, 70.

33 French, German and Swiss codification movements are notable activities of the nineteenth century.

34 Hyland, R. (2004) 'The American Experience: Restatements, the UCC, Uniform Laws and Transnational Coordination' in A. Hartkamp and E. Hondius (eds) *Towards a European Civil Code*, 3rd edn. The Hague: Kluwer, p. 59, at 63.

35 Gennaioli, N. and Perotti, E. (2007) 'Codification, Access to Justice and Contractual Innovation', *Oxford Financial Research Centre Law and Finance Seminars*, at 2.

non-starter. Each instrument defines its scope and applicability. In addition, there are well-established rules of party autonomy, and parties may derogate from the provisions of instruments or exclude them as a whole.[36] Finally, international instruments for the harmonisation of secured transactions law, or in general, are not the product of interest groups. It is natural that interest groups and the private sector should be included to achieve more productive results. This is also necessary to create practical instruments rather than theoretical ones, which will not be useful in enhancing the harmonisation process or in solving problems to which the instrument is directed.

In this context, while there are diverse views on the definition of harmonisation,[37] within the framework of secured transactions law it can be defined as an international (for example, under the auspices of UNCITRAL or UNIDROIT) or regional (for example, under the auspices of the EU) process where the laws of countries, to the extent they are related to secured credit, are approximated with each other by certain legislative instruments (such as conventions, model laws and legislative guides) or methods (such as legal reforms)[38] for the purposes of modernisation of rules governing secured transactions and reduction of the cost of credit necessary for SMEs.

2.3 Historical backdrop

As a general proposition, it can be submitted that contemporary international harmonisation activities of secured transactions laws are modern reflections of the nineteenth-century national codifications. The rationale of international harmonisation activities demonstrates similarities to those codifications as well as the preparation philosophy of UCC Article 9. Transactional certainty and promotion of economic activity are the main points of reference for both the codification and

36 E.g. Receivables Convention Article 6; Factoring Convention Article 3; Cape Town Convention Article 15. *See* Chapter 3.

37 Mistelis, L. (2001) 'Is Harmonisation a Necessary Evil? The Future of Harmonisation and New Sources of International Trade Law' in I. Fletcher, M. Cremona and L. Mistelis (eds) *Foundations And Perspectives of International Trade Law*. London: Sweet & Maxwell, pp. 3, 4; Leebron, D.W. (1996) 'Claims for Harmonization: A Theoretical Framework', 27 *Canadian Bus. L. J.*, 63, 66; Ziegel, J. 'Harmonization of Private Laws in Federal Systems of Government: Canada, the USA and Australia' in R. Cranston (ed) op. cit. (f'note 1), 131, 133; Glenn, H.P. (2003) 'Harmony of Laws in the Americas', 34 *U. Miami Inter-Am. L. Rev.*, 223, 246; Zamora, S. ibid., 403; Boodman, M. (1991) 'The Myth of Harmonization of Laws', 39 *Am. J. Comp. L.*, 699, 707; Gopalan, S. (2004) 'The Creation of International Commercial Law: Sovereignty Felled?', 5 *San Diego Int'l L.J.*, 267, 276; Gopalan, S. (2004) 'New Trends in the Making of International Commercial Law', 23 *J. L. & Com.*, 117, 120 *et. seq.*

38 On the methods of harmonisation of secured transactions, *see* ibid., Macdonald, R. (2007) 'Unitary Law Reform, Pluralistic Law Resubstance: Illuminating Legal Change', 67 *La. L. Rev.*, 1114, 1145 *et seq.*, particularly discussing secured transactions law reform; Macdonald, R. op. cit. (f'note 10); Akseli, O. (2008) 'On the Methods of International Harmonisation of Secured Transactions Law' in C.B. Andersen and U.G. Schroeter (eds) *Sharing International Commercial Law across National Boundaries: Festschrift for Albert H. Kritzer on the Occasion of his Eightieth Birthday*. London: Wildy, Simmonds & Hill, pp. 1–12.

international harmonisation movement. The nineteenth-century codification movement served successfully for the creation of nation States, and as a general proposition by promoting their domestic trade and economic powers. This movement has gone through a redaction in time and can be used as an inspiration and inception point for international harmonisation that is a consequence of globalisation. In that sense, international harmonisation of secured transactions aims to create harmonised and modern rules, which are acutely needed to respond appropriately to the problems experienced in cross-border commercial transactions. Thus, contemporary harmonisation activities target transactional certainty and economic growth as well as eventual uniformity.[39]

In England, the evolution of the law of credit and security relates to the financial markets' and financial institutions' desire to achieve certainty in taking security over almost all types of assets of debtors (i.e. giving credit with minimal risk), which is why the law is flexible in the sense that it permits almost anything to be taken as security. However, as the law is not codified, this results in legal interpretation of security interests where a number of concepts are used together. Thus, unsatisfactory results or relative certainty may appear.[40]

It is worth briefly looking at the codification movement in nineteenth-century Europe, which aimed at predictability as well as unification of national laws. Creation of a code that contains commercial and civil matters involves a states's history and culture.[41] In Germany the codification process began in 1814 and the Civil Code was enacted at the end of the nineteenth century.[42] The rationale was the facilitation of the 'emergence of an undivided German nation'.[43] The German codification stemmed from the necessity of legal and transactional certainty[44] for lawyers[45] at a time when 'ever-growing economic interdependencies amongst the respective regions [reflected] a desire to stop divergent regional private law from

39 For the economic efficiency arguments related to harmonisation and unification activities *see generally* Ribstein, L.E. and Kobayashi, B.H. (1996) 'An Economic Analysis of Uniform States Laws', 25 *J. Legal Studies*, 131.

40 On these points *see generally* Chiu, I.H-Y. (2006) 'The Legal Fabrication of Security Interests in the United Kingdom', 31 *N.C.Int'l L. & Com. Reg.*, 703, 707 *et seq.*

41 *See generally* Collins, H. (1995) 'European Private Law and Cultural Identity of States', *E.R.P.L.*, 353.

42 The German BGB (*Bürgerliches Gesetzbuch*) was finalised in 1896 but entered into force in 1900.

43 Views of Anton Thibaut were opposed by Friedrich Carl von Savigny who argued 'the necessity of establishing "an organically progressive legal scholarship which may be common to the whole nation"'. *See* Zimmerman, R. 'Roman Law and the Harmonisation of Private Law in Europe' op. cit. (f'note 34), Hartkamp and Hondius (eds) op. cit., 21, at 23; Zimmermann, R. (2004) *Roman Law, Contemporary Law, European Law: The Civilian Tradition Today*. Oxford: Oxford University Press, pp. 14–15.

44 John, M. (1989) *Politics and the Law in Late Nineteenth-Century Germany: The origins of the Civil Code*. Oxford: Clarendon, p. 4, where he states that

> '[t]he decades after 1848 saw a growing desire for "legal certainty" – a notion which had a range of meanings in the German context . . . [L]egal certainty had Weberian connotations of calculability and predictability in economic activity; a citizen could only make rational decisions about his best course of action if he could predict with reasonable certainty the future application of the law.'

45 Zweigert, K. and Kötz, H. (1998) *An Introduction to Comparative Law*, 3rd edn. Oxford: Oxford University Press, p. 144.

slowing down interregional economic activity'.[46] In France the Code Civil was prepared by a group of practitioners[47] and 'intended to establish uniform law, not new law'.[48] Following the French Revolution, the provisions of the Code Civil reflected the interests of all stakeholders and was based on the idea of society and citizens.[49] The Code considered sociological, political and economic conditions of the early nineteenth century. It was a legislation prepared with the aim of creating legal certainty to protect all parties to a security agreement.[50]

Arguably, the philosophy and the historical conditions surrounding the preparation of UCC Article 9 present similarities to the contemporary international harmonisation efforts. UCC Article 9 aims at transactional certainty. In the latter half of the nineteenth century, codification[51] and harmonisation efforts in the US did not generate successful results because of resistance from legal practitioners.[52] There was a fragmented system. The Uniform Trust Receipts Act was approved in 1933. It contained similar concepts to those of UCC Article 9, particularly the notice filing. Harmonisation efforts for a comprehensive set of rules for secured transactions were commenced under the auspices of the National Conference of Commissioners on Uniform State Laws (NCCUSL)[53] and the American Law Institute (ALI) in the early 1940s.[54] There was necessity for harmonisation that would create transactional certainty and that would enable facilitation of economic growth.[55] The balance between transactional certainty through a comprehensive set of rules and a functional and pragmatic Code[56] was established by Karl

46 Kanning, A.J. (2007) 'The Emergence of a European Private Law: Lessons from 19th Century Germany', 27 *O.J.L.S.*, 193, 207.

47 The French *Code Civil* entered into force in 1804. Watson, A. (1981) *The Making of the Civil Law*. Cambridge, MA: Harvard University Press, pp. 113–14.

48 Zimmermann, op. cit. (f'note 43), 3.

49 *See generally* Ancel, M.E. (2008) 'Recent Reform in France: The Renaissance of a civilian collateral regime?' in F. Dahan and J. Simpson (eds) *Secured Transactions Reform and Access to Credit*. London: Edward Elgar, pp. 259 *et seq.*; Zweigert and Kötz, ibid., at 86.

50 The French law of credit and security has gone through a significant reform recently enabling taking non-possessory security. Ancel, ibid., at 260–61.

51 Here, a brief distinction must be made. The UCC is not a Code in the Civil Law sense where the latter type is more comprehensive than the Common Law type where the general principles of law and equity are still applicable unless excluded by the Code. *See* Hyland, op. cit. (f'note 34), 59, 63.

52 Cook, C.M. (1981) *The American Codification Movement: A Study of Antebellum Legal Reform*. Westport, CA: Greenwood, p. 201.

53 http://www.nccusl.org/ (last accessed 30 December 2008).

54 White, J.J. and Summers, R.S. (2000) *Uniform Commercial Code*, 5th edn. Eagan, MN: West, pp. 3 *et seq.*

55 For a similar view *see* Kripke, H. (1985) 'Law and Economics: Measuring the Economic Efficiency of Commercial Law in a Vacuum of Fact', 133 *U. Pa. L. Rev.*, 929, 931. *See generally* Schnader, W.A. (1967) 'A Short History of the Preparation and Enactment of the Uniform Commercial Code', 22 *U. Miami L. Rev.*, 1; Llewellyn, K. (1957) 'Why We Need the Uniform Commercial Code', 10 *U. Fla. L. Rev.*, 367.

56 Bridge, M.G., MacDonald, R., Simmonds, R. and Walsh, C. (1999) 'Formalism, Functionalism and Understanding the Law of Secured Transactions', 44 *McGill L. J.*, 567, 573 where it is stated that 'Article 9's philosophy is to reject conventional proprietary conceptualism in favour of pure functionalism'.

Llewellyn. UCC Article 9 takes into account American business practices and 'builds upon pre-existing social norms'.[57] Transactional certainty and modernisation of secured transactions regimes were achieved by creating a unitary security interest and by limiting the parties to debtors and secured creditors.[58] A single-notice filing system was established for each state in order to achieve transparency and public information. Registration is also a fundamental aspect of Article 9. Security interests can be created on any type of transaction and asset. A secured creditor is allowed to have priority to the debtor's assets, even though the debtor possesses and uses the assets. Rules for determining priority are straightforward when compared to English law.[59] Different styles of personal property have been merged into a single system. The goal of the drafters was a pragmatic one that provides a secured creditor with 'an interest in personal property that would permit [him] to look to the property as a source of compensation should the obligation not be performed'.[60] The significance of these is that a law, by being predictable and 'specifically designed to evolve with changing conditions',[61] could facilitate the growth of an economy if a response to legal problems is aimed for and the existing business practices are incorporated.

2.4 International harmonisation

International harmonisation of secured transactions laws has been continuing since the early twentieth century. Some of the early examples of harmonisation of security interests include: a uniform conditional sales act enacted by Norway, Sweden and Denmark between 1915 and 1917; the 1939 and 1951 UNIDROIT

57 Cooter, R. (1997) 'Normative Failure Theory of Law', 82 *Cornell L. Rev.*, 947, 948. Scott, R. (1994) 'The Politics of Article 9', 80 *Va. L. Rev.*, 1783, 1850, where Professor Scott states that:

> . . Article 9 regulates asset-based financers, a paradigmatic example of well-organized and cohesive interests, the process is susceptible to disproportionate influence by a single active interest group representing particular financial interests . . . [and suggests that] the law revision process [tends] to propose rules that are both transactionally efficient and distributionally favourable to the dominating interests.

58 Winship, P. (2001) 'The Legal Framework to Secure Loans in the United States: A Comprehensive System for Creating Security Interests', *CEAL Issues Brief, No. 2* (April); *see also* Winship, P. 'Selected Security Interests in the United States' in Norton and Andenas (eds) op. cit. (f'note 23), 267.

59 *See* ibid.; McCormack, G. (2004) *Secured Credit under English and American Law*. Cambridge: Cambridge University Press, pp. 70 *et seq.*; Goode, R. (1996) 'The Exodus of the Floating Charge' in D. Feldman and F. Meisel (eds) *Corporate and Commercial Law: Modern Developments*. London: Lloyds of London Press, pp. 202–3 who argued that unitary security interests coupled with unified rules of attachment, perfection and priority are necessary features in the fragmented system of English commercial law.

60 Cuming, in R. Cranston (ed.), op. cit. (f'note 1), 505.

61 Beck, T., Demirguc-Kunt, A. and Levine, R. (2002) 'Law and Finance: Why Does Legal Origin Matter?', *Policy Research Working Paper No 2904*. Washington, DC:World Bank, p. 4.

Draft provisions on the impact of retention of title in the sale of certain goods; provisions regarding the effect of bankruptcy of reservation of title in the sale of goods in the draft EEC Bankruptcy Convention of 1970; and model reservation of title clauses contained in several General Conditions elaborated by the UN Economic Commission for Europe.[62]

Harmonisation of secured transactions laws gained impetus from the early 1970s, especially with the efforts of two influential international formulating organisations, namely UNCITRAL and UNIDROIT. Apart from these, the Hague Conferences,[63] the European Bank for Reconstruction and Development (EBRD),[64] the World Bank,[65] the European Union (EU),[66] the Organization of American States (OAS)[67] and International Civil Aviation Organization (ICAO)[68] have also taken part in the harmonisation efforts.[69] The interest of international and regional organisations, as well as the multilateral financing organisations in the harmonisation process, demonstrates that secured lending is critical. The international community attributes significant value to the modernisation and harmonisation of secured credit for the following four reasons. First,

62 UNIDROIT Study LXXII – Doc. 1, p.20 *et seq.*; Report of the Secretary General: Study on Security Interests (A/CN.9/131 and Annex), reprinted in: Yearbook of the United Nations Commission on International Trade Law, Vol. 8 (1977), 171, 209 *et seq.*; Burman, H.S. (2003) 'The Commercial Challenge in Modernizing Secured Transactions Law', *Unif. L. Rev.*, 347, 348–9.

63 Convention on the Law Applicable to certain Rights in Respect of Securities Held with an Intermediary.

64 E.g. Mistelis, L. (1998) 'The EBRD Model Law on Secured Transactions and Its impact on Collateral Law Reform in Central and Eastern Europe and the former Soviet Union', 5 *Parker Sch. J.E.Eur.L.*, 455; McCormack, G. and Dahan, F. (1999) 'The EBRD Model Law on Secured Transactions: Comparisons and Convergence', *CfiLR*, 65 *et seq.*

65 World Bank Working Group Paper on 'Building Effective Insolvency Systems: Debtor-Creditor Regimes' (1999 and 2001); World Bank Principles and Guidelines for Effective Insolvency and Creditor Rights Systems (2005); The International Finance Corporation (World Bank) Secured Transactions Systems and Collateral Registries (January 2010).

66 EC Directive on Financial Collateral Arrangements; EC Council Regulation on Insolvency Proceedings.

67 *Model Inter-American Law on Secured Transactions* can be found in (2002) *Unif. L. Rev.*, 262 *et seq.*; Kozolchyk, B. and Wilson, J. (2002) 'The Organization of American States: The New Model Inter-American Law on Secured Transactions', *Unif. L. Rev.*, 69 *et seq.*

68 1948 Geneva Convention on the International Recognition of Rights in Aircraft. The Convention has 87 Contracting states and applies to security interests in aircraft. The Geneva Convention is superseded by the Cape Town Convention Aircraft Protocol Article XXIII as it relates to aircraft objects. *See* Thorne (2006) 'Goodbye, P. Geneva "48", Hello Cape Town, "01"', *BJIBFL*, 439; Weber, L. and Espinola, S. (1999) 'The Development of a New Convention Relating to International Interests in Mobile Equipment, in Particular Aircraft Equipment: A Joint ICAO-UNIDROIT Project', *Unif. L. Rev.*, 463.

69 Other notable law reform initiatives are the American Bar Association/Central and Eastern European Law Initiatives Project (ABA/CEELI) to provide assistance to former Soviet Republics; the University of Maryland Institutional Reform and the Informal Sector (IRIS) Project to provide substantive and technical assistance to nations modernising their secured transactions laws; German Government's technical assistance to former Yugoslavian and central European countries.

modernisation and harmonisation support economic growth. Second, modern secured transactions systems improve financial stability, thus robustness in the face of financial crises is enabled. Third, convergence of diverse legal systems enables the facilitation of globalisation in various fields but particularly commerce. Finally, in an era of information technology and revolutionary technological developments and e-commerce, modern legal texts on secured transactions address new problems in financing transactions, thus legal uncertainties and unnecessary transaction and litigation costs may be avoided.[70] The globalisation of markets, increasing cross-border transaction costs and the diversity of rules on secured credit have justified the efforts of international harmonisation of secured transactions law.

2.4.1 The need for international harmonisation and difficulties

2.4.1.1 Rationale

The rationale of the harmonisation of secured transactions laws is to overcome the divergence and difficulties inherent in domestic and cross-border security agreements, and to modernise the law through harmonisation in order to facilitate the access to low-cost credit. If the rules envisaged in the international instruments are implemented, and provided that there is compatible infrastructure or a potential to establish that infrastructure, the outcome will potentially lead to economic development and an increase in cross-border flow of trade and credit.

There is divergence in the way national systems govern their secured transactions laws. Cohen argues that the diversity of laws causes 'uncertainty and transaction costs that lower the expected value of a transaction to the creditor'.[71] The divergence is also an indirect obstacle to the harmonisation process as it limits the facilitation of credit, which is the very reason for harmonisation. Harmonisation may be achieved by eliminating divergent aspects of secured transactions law,[72] thus transactional certainty by making the law in this area more efficient, modern and predictable for contracting parties may succeed. If there is no harmonisation there may be uncertainty, which can mean in this context 'credit at a high cost, less or no credit, depending on whether the risk can be reasonably estimated'.[73] Transactional certainty via clear and predictable rules enables the lender

70 For these four reasons, *see* Tata, V. (2007) 'The Role of Multilaterals in the Promotion of Modern Securities Law', *Comments at the Congress to Celebrate the 40th Annual Session of UNCITRAL*, at 2, Vienna 9–12 July; *see also* below for discussion of these four points in more detail.

71 Cohen, N.B. (1998) 'Harmonizing the Law Governing Secured Credit: The Next Frontier', 33 *Tex. Int'l L., J.* 173, 176.

72 For a different conceptual approach *see* Hermann, G. 'The Role of UNCITRAL' in I. Fletcher *et al*, op. cit. (f'note 37), 28, 32. He suggests 'preventive unification' to unify an area of law that none of the nations has ever done and this will enable sound and acceptable unification.

73 Bazinas, S. (2006) 'Modernising and Harmonising Secured Credit Law: The Example of the UNCITRAL Draft Legislative Guide on Secured Transactions Part 1', 1 *JIBFL*, 20.

to ascertain the consequences of the credit transaction. In that context, harmonised rules as applied in Contracting States will have a positive effect in reducing the cost of credit in the sense that the lender will not be forced to search domestic law or translate it, thus inclusion of a risk premium in the calculation of interest rate may be avoided. Unless there is a contrary agreement between the contractual parties, as the applicable substantive law in both the lender's and the borrower's countries will be the same by virtue of adopting the same convention, Model Law or the Guide, certainty will be maintained. Certainty as to the consequences of the credit transaction will have the effect of reducing the risk that is included in the calculation of the interest rate in order to cover speculative or possible future losses, which may occur due to the application of inefficient rules. Transactional certainty through internationally harmonised rules may have the effect of injecting confidence to the lenders who consider the market to be a volatile place following the collapse of prominent investment banks in 2008. Reflection of these losses in the calculation of interest rate limits borrowing, and increases the cost of credit; hence the restriction of access to low-cost credit. It can also be argued that granting access to low-cost credit is also important for social equality and economic growth.

2.4.1.2 Divergent laws and complexities

Divergence of national legal regimes on secured transactions law is based on 'property concepts, some of which are peculiar to particular families of law'.[74] In the broader perspective, divergence stems from the proprietary effects of security, which can be found in the philosophy that surrounds security interests,[75] deeply rooted concepts and certain policy decisions. This increases the cost of credit because, first, conflict-of-laws rules are not harmonised and seem to be almost impossible to be harmonised and thus there is unpredictability as to which legal regime will apply to the security agreement. Even if there is relative harmony in conflict-of-laws rules, the importance of, for instance, the use of intangibles as collateral in cross-border transactions makes the operation of *lex situs* impossible. However, conflict-of-laws rules may be used to harmonise certain proprietary problems such as priority of competing claims or the formal validity of assignments[76] by reference to the law of the assignor's State. This has been opposed continuously by scholars from civil-law jurisdictions and some interest groups in common-law jurisdictions.[77] Second, administrative costs such as searching and

74 Cuming, R.C.C. op. cit. (f'note 1), 499; van Erp, S. (2003) 'Civil and Common Property Law: Caveat Comparator – The Value of Legal Historical – Comparative Analysis', *E.R.P.L.*, 394–411; *see also* ***2.3 Historical backdrop***.

75 Goode, R. (1998) 'Security in Cross Border Transactions', 33 *Tex. Int'l L. J.*, 47, 48.

76 Under the Receivables Convention formal validity is a condition to priority.

77 *See* ibid., Financial Markets Law Committee, Issue 121 – European Commission Final Proposal for a Regulation on the law Applicable to Contractual Obligations ('Rome I'), April 2006 and October 2006; Flessner, A. and Verhagen, H. (2006) *Assignment in European Private International Law*. Munich: Sellier; Verhagen, R. (2006) 'Assignment in Commission's Rome I Proposal', *L.M.C.L.Q.*, 270.

learning the applicable law may be high. This endorses the need to have overall harmonised rules on secured transactions or at least in certain aspects of it. Finally, the applicable law may have inefficient rules that may affect investment decisions, as the rules may not protect the interests of financiers[78] or may only accept certain assets such as immovables as collateral.

In practice, divergence is acutely felt in the fundamental aspects of secured transactions law. These include: the creation of security interests and their types as well as the type of assets over which security interests can be created; functionalism of a unitary security interest over the collateral; effectiveness of a security right towards third parties; effective priority regime securing the position of the secured creditor and reducing search costs; and an efficient enforcement mechanism upon default of debtor.[79] Modern secured transactions regimes tend to recognise security over any type of assets of the debtor,[80] and this has been reflected in the international instruments.[81] On the other hand, generally speaking, in unreformed secured transactions regimes, security created over immovable and movable assets seems to be a more acceptable form of collateral; however, generally, they must exist at the time of the security agreement and, due to the principle of specificity, must be specified.[82]

Types of security to be taken over the assets are more flexible and liberal in common law jurisdictions. The principle of party autonomy, which is one of the key principles of international instruments, allows parties to tailor their contract and to apply the type of security that will best achieve the end result. On the other hand, in other jurisdictions security interests that can be created are specified in commercial or civil codes or in specialised legislation, and parties are not allowed to create their own securities beyond the ones listed in the code by a contractual arrangement, thereby lack of comprehensive scope may be observed. Specification of security interests in codes reflects the *numerus clausus* principle. These security interests correspond to certain types of assets, for example mortgage for immovables and pledge for movables. As there is a list of security interests in the law that can be taken, sometimes these security interests do not match what may be understood in common law jurisdictions. For instance,

78 On these points, *see generally* Cohen, N.B. (1999) 'Internationalizing the Law of Secured Credit: Perspectives from the U.S. Experience', 20 *U. Pa. J. Int'l Econ. L.*, 423, 432.

79 Report, op. cit. (f'note 62), 180 *et seq.; see also* Buxbaum, H.L. (2003) 'Unification of the Law Governing Secured Transactions: Progress and Prospects for Reform' 1/2 *Unif. L. Rev.*, 322.

80 Such as immovable or movable, tangible or intangible, future or present and bulk or individual.

81 Ibid., Guide, Model Law, Factoring and Receivables Conventions all recognise the fact that security interest can be created over any type of assets and recognise the effectiveness of, for instance, the assignment of future and bulk receivables. *See also* Guide, para. 50, at 20 where the Guide takes the view that the debtors should be allowed to use the full value inherent in their assets to support credit.

82 For instance, a charge over a business must specify those assets whereas in common law jurisdictions, for example in England, the charge need not specify each item. *See* Wood, P. (2008) *Law and Practice of International Finance*. London: Sweet & Maxwell, pp. 257–8.

a non-possessory pledge may sound unusual to a common lawyer, because both a non-possessory security interest and pledge denote different concepts. However, a non-possessory pledge was known by Roman lawyers and, broadly speaking, for a civil lawyer it may mean a security interest where the debtor keeps possession of the collateral upon creation of a proprietary right over the collateral to secure the obligation to a creditor without actually delivering possession of the collateral to the creditor and publicising it by registration.[83] One critical difference between the civil and common law systems is 'the significance of possession as a determinant of property rights'.[84] Possessory security interests seem to be more acceptable in civil law jurisdictions.[85] Pledge, a possessory security interest, is a significant example according to which the creditor must actually possess the collateral for the creation and third-party effectiveness of the security and, consequently, for the extension of credit. It is a crucial security device in those countries where intangibles are often not considered as acceptable collateral.[86] However, with the emergence and increased use of financing techniques, the feasibility of pledge cannot be justified except in certain tangible assets such as negotiable instruments. The existence of a unitary security interest concept, especially in some of the common law jurisdictions, creates a functional approach to security. Under UCC Article 9, the unitary security interest encompasses all devices that perform security functions,[87] which includes, apart from traditional security devices, factoring of debts, retention of title transactions in the sale of goods, and possessory and non-possessory security interests. Possession is also accepted as a means of perfecting a security interest.[88] A functional approach to security rights does not seem to exist in European Union member States.[89]

83 Zwalve, W. (2004) 'A Labyrinth of Creditors: A Short Introduction to the History of Security Interests in Goods' in E-M. Kieninger (ed.) *Security Rights in Movable Property in European Private Law*. Cambridge: Cambridge University Press, p. 38; for the reform in France and the adoption of a non-possessory pledge *see* Ansaloni, G. (2009) 'Reflection on the Implementation of a Floating Security Interest over Tangible Property in French Law (Study of the New Non-Possessory Pledge)', *IBLJ*, 35; Guide, para. 51, at 43 where traditional pledge and grantor-possessed pledge contrasted.

84 Goode, R. (1993) 'Reflections of the Harmonization of Commercial Law' in R. Cranston and R. Goode (eds) *Commercial and Consumer Law National and International Dimensions*. Oxford: Clarendon, p. 3, at 12.

85 However, for reform in civil law jurisdictions to enable assignment of future receivables, *see* Flessner and Verhagen, op. cit. (f'note 77), 6–7; for reform in France *see* Ancel, op. cit. (f'note 49).

86 For an empirical study on the use of immovables and movables as opposed to intangibles as collateral *see* Safavian, M. (2008) 'Firm level evidence on collateral and access to finance' in F. Dahan and J. Simpson (eds) *Secured Transactions Reform and Access to Credit*. Cheltenham: Edward Elgar, p. 110. However, note that pledge is also used in other meanings such as non-possessory pledge in some transition countries and that encompasses the English term of *charge*. *See* Chapter 1.

87 UCC Article 1–201(37) definition of Security Interest; also *see* UCC Article 9–202 for the title to collateral immaterial; UCC Article 9–102(61) Payment intangible.

88 UCC §9–313.

89 Kieninger, E-M. 'Evaluation: a common core? Convergences, subsisting differences and possible ways for harmonisation' *in* Kieninger (ed) op. cit. (f'note 83), 647, 648–9.

The rights in the collateral and in its proceeds as against third parties arise out of the proprietary effects of the security, and the differences in that respect mean that the harmonisation process may suffer certain obstacles. In some traditional civil law jurisdictions, non-possessory security rights have not been preferred on the grounds that permitting the debtor to possess the collateral while protecting the creditors' claims is considered 'immoral and misleading'.[90] In modern common law secured transactions regimes, personal property security, either tangible or intangible, is publicised by virtue of filing; whereas, in civil law systems, registration of security for the purposes of priority and third-party effectiveness is not, in principle,[91] required.[92] Therefore, in civil law jurisdictions arguably 'security over movables [is often] limited to possessory security',[93] which allows publicity of security often by way of possession. Protection of security over intangibles may not be efficiently provided in the latter. If security interests, particularly non-possessory ones, are registered, notice is given to third parties; claims of false wealth may be avoided.

The recognition of security and minimal formalities that enable the creditor to take and create security without being limited by burdensome conditions[94] are critical differences. In civil law jurisdictions, in the case of assignment of bulk receivables, specificity is required which individualises the collateral. In common law jurisdictions, the conditions of taking security on present, bulk and future assets are less burdensome and the specificity requirement does not exist. This is a particularly crucial matter in securitisation transactions. Notification of the debtor in assignment of receivables as a requirement of formal validity as well as priority is also another important difference that is deeply rooted in civil law jurisdictions.[95] In certain jurisdictions, due to the requirement of notification for the

90 Moglia-Claps, G.A. and McDonnell, J.B. (2002) 'Secured Credit and Insolvency Law in Argentina and the US: Gaining Insight from a Comparative Perspective', 30 *Ga. J. Int'l & Comp. L.*, 393, 396; Hausmann, J. (1996) 'The Value of Public-Notice Filing Under Uniform Commercial Code Article 9: A Comparison with the German Legal System of Securities in Personal Property', 25 *Ga. J. Int'l & Comp. L.*, 427, 452 *et seq. But cf, generally* Ancel, op. cit. (f'note 49), 264 (describing the reform in France and introduction of non-possessory pledge, registration system and possibility to secure future debts).

91 In civil law jurisdictions there are some exceptions, for example, registration may serve as *inter partes* and third-party effectiveness requirement in the case of retention-of-title transactions. *See* e.g. Swiss Civil Code Arts 715–716 and Turkish Civil Code Article 764.

92 *See e.g.* Haag, H. and Peglow, O. (2008) 'Germany' in W. Johnston (ed) *Security over Receivables: An International Handbook.* Oxford: Oxford, p. 193, at 206.

93 Wood, P.R. 'World-Wide Security-Classification of Legal Jurisdictions' in Norton and Andenas (eds) op. cit. (f'note 23), 39, at 43.

94 Such as the necessity of authentication of document by a notary public or notification of debtor. On these and other examples *see* DiLuigi, M.C. (2008) 'Divergence of Security and Property Law in the European Union: The Need for Action', *J.B.L.*, 526.

95 However, the archaic *Dearle v Hall* rule in England may be considered as an obstacle in obtaining priority in the assignment of bulk receivables. For a discussion of bulk assignments and priority issues, *see* Oditah, F. 'Recurrent Issues in Receivables Financing' in Armour, J. and Payne, J. (2009) *Rationality in Company Law Essays in Honour of DD Prentice.* Oxford: Hart, p. 321.

effectiveness of assignment as against the third parties and the debtor, it is required that the debtor must be known before the assignment, and this hinders the effectiveness of assignments of bulk and future receivables. Obtaining priority through clear and transparent rules is crucial in a modern legislation. Priority conflicts in jurisdictions that adopted a UCC Article 9 type of legislation is generally achieved through the first-secured party to file, or perfection by control or filing. In England, the distinction between legal and equitable charges and the ranking of secured and unsecured creditors as well as competition of floating and fixed charges coupled with the Enterprise Act 2002 provisions present a rather complex structure of priorities as compared to UCC Article 9 legislation. On the enforcement end, common law jurisdictions have a flexible approach to enforcing security interests, in case of default of the debtor, by allowing self-help remedies, thus reducing the cost involved in the enforcement process, whereas in other jurisdictions the same flexibility may not be shared in the same degree.

One particular obstacle before harmonisation is the interrelation of insolvency and secured transactions,[96] as insolvency law is the basis of the latter.[97] As insolvency rules widely differ, in any reform effort, the compatibility of the rules of insolvency and secured transactions laws must be maintained.[98] Another complexity arises out of the policies of States that try to achieve technical and economic benefits from harmonisation.[99] For their own policy reasons, certain States tend not to favour harmonisation, but prefer the imposition of their legal systems on model laws or international conventions, and therefore try to achieve in one organisation what they cannot achieve in another. This political aspect of harmonisation leads to overlaps in international efforts. The same argument applies equally to regional harmonisation efforts. It can be argued that uncoordinated emergence of regional harmonisation activities is one of the most threatening issues before international harmonisation activities. International harmonisation activities take place mainly under the auspices of UNCITRAL and UNIDROIT,[100] where legal cultures from different economic and geographical backgrounds are represented. Unless there is coordination between international and regional efforts there will be an overlap and loss of time. Potential overlap of efforts may be felt in the security interests area between the work of UNCITRAL and academic projects conducted under the EU.[101] From another

96 For the relationship between insolvency law and secured transactions, *see* A/CN.9/496, para. 23 *et seq.*

97 Wood, P.R. 'Comparative Financial Law: A Classification of the World's Jurisdictions' in R. Cranston (ed.), op. cit. (f'note 1), 31, at 35.

98 For a similar affirmation *see* Cuming, op. cit. (f'note 1), 499.

99 Buxbaum, op. cit. (f'note 79), 325.

100 Though The Hague Conferences were actively involved in international harmonisation activities and the EU has been involved for its own domestic purposes in harmonisation activities.

101 *E.g.* the Draft Common Frame of Reference security interests work. For an in-depth comparison of compatibility of European Security Interests with the international activities *see* Eidenmüller, H. and Kieninger, E.M. (eds) (2008) *The Future of Secured Credit in Europe*. E.C.F.L.R., Munich: De Gruyter Recht.

perspective even though, for instance, European jurisdictions tribute to international harmonisation activities, it seems that a regionalised version of international instruments is still preferred or insisted upon. This may undermine international harmonisation by being an example to other regional organisations preparing their own versions, which may create, in the long term, disharmony, and cause loss of time and efforts. Recently, there has been a debate regarding the creation of a European Security Right through a Community regulation issued pursuant to EC Treaty Article 308 or a European Model Law.[102] It has been suggested that the Guide should be analysed from the European viewpoint in order to assess its compatibility as to whether it should be adopted as it stands or with certain refinements, and only after that can it be decided whether a new European model is needed.[103] One can agree with this suggestion and argue that if there is a need for a European model, this should follow international agencies' initiatives in order to be parallel to the international efforts rather than re-creating instruments. Finally, in an era of globalised markets, regional aspirations and persistence on regionalism should be abandoned and all efforts must be harmonised with global activities. Operating a wait-and-see policy and complaining about a lack of sufficient input opportunity provided for regional organisations (for instance, due to non-member status) during international formulating agency activities, does not seem to be particularly helpful. For instance, in the EU there is divergence of legal systems as well as economic status. Rather than trying to create a new instrument by departing from the philosophy of the Guide, EU members could work around the existing international instruments and create a good practice example.[104]

102 *See* ibid.; Sigman, H.C. and Kieninger, E.M. (eds) (2007) *Cross-Border Security over Tangibles*. Munich: Sellier, pp. 34 *et seq*. The European Security Right is said to be supplemental to national laws. But for a discussion of possible structures of European Security Right *see* Kieninger, in Kieninger (ed), op. cit. (f'note 83), 665 *et seq*.; Rutgers, J.W. 'Secured Credit and the Internal Market: The Fundamental Freedoms and the EU's Mandate for Legislation' available at SSRN: http://ssrn.com/abstract=1099893 (last accessed March 2009).

103 Beale, H. 'The Future of Secured Credit in Europe: Concluding Remarks' in Eidenmüller and Kieninger, op. cit. (f'note 101), at 396.

104 Some commentators criticise the modern features of the Receivables Convention and the Guide such as the law of the assignor's location and the formal validity of an assignment. The same commentators also argue that the Guide diverts from the law of the assignor's State rule for a good number of specialised financial transactions and this concedes the weakness of the rule. When one critically reviews this argument, it can be realised that receivables financing can only work properly and be harmonised when the priority issues and the formal validity are connected to the law of the assignor's State, which is the single and predictable law in a multifaceted contract. *See* ibid.; Flessner, A. 'Security Interests in Receivables – A European Perspective' in Eidenmüller and Kieninger, op. cit. (f'note 101), 336. *But cf.* Beale, op. cit. (f'note 103), 396, fn 116, commenting on Professor Flessner's argument.

2.4.2 Grounds for harmonisation to overcome divergent approaches

The wide range of differences was established by Ulrich Drobnig's report,[105] which was prepared upon the request of UNCITRAL in 1970.[106] This report suggested that the harmonisation of secured transactions laws was difficult due to their great divergence. The report reflected that national laws vary widely with respect to fundamental aspects of security interests, and that was where difficulty in harmonisation was experienced. Following the Drobnig Report, UNCITRAL considered two reports, one of which related to the national systems on security interests,[107] suggesting the preparation of international personal property security rules covering domestic and international transactions, and the other related to the UCC.[108] A study on the feasibility of uniform rules on security interests was prepared;[109] however, UNCITRAL postponed its work on security interests and the assignment of receivables until the 1990s,[110] both due to the fact that there were wide differences that were serious obstacles to harmonisation and to wait for the outcome of the work on retention of title by the EC and on factoring by UNIDROIT.[111]

The critical and inevitable question is why are there attempts to harmonise the law on secured transactions now? In the 1960s and 1970s, the general view among most legal scholars was that, due to wide differences in secured transactions laws and their relationship with insolvency laws, it was impossible to harmonise the law in this area.[112] Also, until the early 1990s, there has been a great reluctance to extend the harmonisation process to property rights, and one of the main reasons for this was the reluctance of States to incorporate the provisions of conventions impacting on national insolvency laws into their legal systems. This point has been one of the main obstacles that the harmonisation process posed in the context of secured transactions. However, from the 1990s there has been a movement towards the harmonisation of secured transactions laws at both regional and international levels. The potential impact of harmonisation in promoting cross-border trade and economic growth by eliminating barriers has been realised.[113] Therefore, within the last two decades 'with the accelerating pace of market interdependency . . . the importance of a sound legal regime for security interests in personal property, both

105 Report, op. cit. (f'note 62), 171; for a recent general report *see* Drobnig, U. (2003) 'Present and Future of Real and Personal Security', *E.R.P.L.*, 623–660, where he concludes 'to be convinced of the true necessity of a filing system'.

106 UNCITRAL Report on Third Session (1970), A/8017, paras 139–145 (I Yearbook, p. 144).

107 A/CN.9/130.

108 A/CN.9/132.

109 A/32/17, para. 37 (1977).

110 A/35/17, paras 26–28 (1980).

111 *See* idem, at para. 27.

112 *See above* Drobnig Report and relevant considerations.

113 Gopalan, S. (2003) 'Transnational Commercial Law: The Way Forward', 18 *Am. U. Int'l L. Rev.*, 803, 805 *et seq.*

for domestic and cross-border transactions'[114] has been recognised. There are a number of significant grounds for the harmonisation of secured transactions laws. They are all interconnected.

2.4.2.1 Harmonisation is a necessary tool for facilitation of credit and lowering the cost of credit

In order to facilitate access to low-cost credit, secured transactions laws must be predictable, free from complexity and modern. All international instruments reflect the fact that taking security lowers the cost of credit, and this can be achieved through predictable and clear rules that are harmonised and applied in a harmonious way in the Contracting States. If a country's secured transactions law has these characteristics, financiers can extend credit at a lower cost to enterprises in that State. Otherwise, risk inherent in the unreformed laws may create adverse effects to SMEs in their access to low-cost credit. There are widely different laws that govern secured transactions; cross-border commerce is growing rapidly and, in the absence of harmonised legislation on secured transactions, parties will continue to lose their profit and interest in cross-border transactions. In other words, if States harmonise their secured transactions laws on the international level just like the US did in the 1950s, then a businessman located in an emerging market State may obtain credit at a lower cost, and an investor or financier from a developed State will be certain about the results of its transaction in that emerging market State. The businessman in the emerging market State may sell his right to payment at a lower-cost credit, and invest the amount of money that it will receive from the developed market financier in different transactions. Basically, this chain of transactions facilitates both credit and cross-border trade, as legal rules applicable to these transactions will be predictable. To put it simply, the financier will foresee the results of the transaction and not conduct research on the details of the secured transactions laws of the emerging country and, therefore, credit at the lowest possible rate will be extended. For instance, one of the reasons why the Factoring Convention was prepared was that factoring companies were less willing to assume the legal and financial risks linked with international factoring because of uncertainties in national laws and the absence of a predictable uniform set of rules.[115]

Security itself lowers the cost of credit, as 'secured loans attract a lower interest payment than unsecured loans'.[116] The rationale of this view is simple. The secured creditor bargains and pays for the priority position and it is only fair to

114 Goode, R. (2002) 'Harmonised Modernisation of the Law Governing Secured Transactions, Outline' Vol. 7 in 'Worldwide Harmonisation of Private Law and Regional Economic Integration', Congress for the Celebration of 75th Anniversary of UNIDROIT, Rome.

115 *See generally* UNIDROIT Study LVIII- Doc. 1 (1976).

116 McCormack, G. (2003) 'The Priority of Secured Credit: an Anglo-American Perspective', *J.B.L.*, 389, 402; McCormack, G. (2002) 'The Nature of Security over Receivables', 23 *Co. Law.*, 84, 85.

allow the secured creditor to retain the benefits of their original bargain by receiving an equivalent value for their collateral in bankruptcy.[117] The low-cost credit may be accomplished by reducing the lender's risk of being unpaid through harmonised modernisation of secured transactions law. An efficient and modern law of secured transactions will enable the lender to exclude its risk premium in the interest rate calculation.[118] The Centre for Economic Analysis of Law (CEAL) observed in 2002, in relation to microenterprises in Latin America, that they pay high interest rates for relatively smaller loans with short-term maturities than do North American microenterprises.[119]

Appropriate legal reforms under the auspices of international instruments will create harmonisation in secured transactions laws. Facilitation of credit is the very reason for harmonisation and harmonisation of secured transactions laws is said to drive economic growth.[120] The ability to take security gives confidence to lenders, and this has the result of increasing the economic activity as 'security [facilitates] extensions of credit that creditors otherwise would not make, and debtors can use the credit extended to create wealth'.[121] In addition, law reforms are supported and sometimes pressurised[122] in emerging markets by international

117 Jackson, T. and Scott, R. (1989) 'On the Nature of Bankruptcy: an Essay on Bankruptcy Sharing and the Creditors' Bargain', 75 *Va. L. Rev.*, 155, 161.

118 McCormack, op. cit. (f'note 7).

119 Fleisig, H. and de la Pena, N. (2002) 'Microenterprises and Collateral'. *CEAL Issue Brief No. 2*; Fleisig, H. and De la Pena, N. (1997) 'Peru: How Problems in the Framework for Secured Transactions Limit Access to Credit', 3 *NAFTA: L. & Bus. Rev. Am.*, 33. Recently, Mexico, Peru and Guatemala have adopted the OAS Inter-American Model Law on Secured Transactions to modernise their secured transactions laws. *See* Kozolchyk, op. cit. (f'note 6), at 726 *et seq.* However, it can be argued that the adoption of the Model Law should be accompanied by a meaningful constitution of legal infrastructure. Lasfer, M.A. (2000) 'Debt Structure, Agency Costs and Firm's Size: An Empirical Investigation', *Working Paper*. London: Cass Business School, at 14, where the empirical studies illustrate that 68 per cent of small companies' debt is short-term and only 32 per cent is payable in more than one year, while 64 per cent of the larger companies' debt is long-term.

120 *See also* Levine, R. (2004) 'Finance and Growth: Theory and Evidence', *NBER Working Paper 10766*, at 85. For the observations of the US delegation during the negotiations of the Receivables Convention, *see* Chapter 1, fn 152; *see* A/CN.9/472/Add.3, at 3 Compilation of Comments by Governments and International Organizations; *see* Murphy, S.D. (ed.) (2004) 'U.S. Signing of UNCITRAL Convention on Assignment of Receivables', 98 *Am. J. Int'l L.*, 368, 369. *See also* Machoka, P.M. (2006) 'Towards Financial Sector Development – The Role of the UNCITRAL Guide on Secured Transactions', 21 *J.I.B.L.R.*, 529, 529.

121 Harris, S.L. and Mooney, C.W. (1997) 'Measuring the Social Costs and Benefits and Identifying the Victims of Subordinating Security Interests in Bankruptcy', 82 *Cornell L. Rev.*, 1349, 1350.

122 Goode, R. (2003) 'Harmonised Modernisation of the Law Governing Secured Transactions: General-Sectorial, Global-Regional', *Unif. L. Rev.*, 341, 342; *see also* www.natlaw.com/pubs/sfproj.htm (accessed in January 2009) where the World Bank's assistance to Mexico in attracting investment is noted.

organisations in return for credit.[123] In this connection, 'in the case of less developed countries, pressure has come from international organisations such as the World Bank to reform the legal regime [of secured transactions]'.[124] The World Bank in its Working Paper, *Building Effective Insolvency Systems: Debtor–Creditor Regimes*,[125] suggested modernisation of secured credit laws in order to facilitate extension of credit and the availability of efficient default remedies. The rationale of this suggestion is that lack of modern and efficient default remedies in economically less-developed States may pose a risk if the loans provided by the World Bank are subjected to these local laws. In that case, there is the risk of uncertainty, for example as to the validity of the agreements, or sometimes the public sector may argue that there is inconsistency with the local law.[126] Therefore, it is arguable that the conditions of financial support require modernisation of corporate law and making progress on the modernisation and reform of secured credit laws.[127] In that context, the World Bank in *Principles for Effective Insolvency and Creditors' Rights Systems* concentrates on establishing an efficient and reliable system of creditors' 'rights and insolvency. In that context, the Principles have been formulated 'to assist countries in their efforts to evaluate and improve core aspects of their commercial law systems that are fundamental to a sound investment climate and to promote commerce and economic growth'.[128] The Group also highlighted the need for an institutional infrastructure and international cooperation.[129]

123 *See* sources op. cit. (f'note 64). *See* Garro, A. 'Difficulties in Obtaining Secured Lending in Latin America: Why Law Reform Really Matters?' in Norton and Andenas (eds) op. cit. (f'note 23), 251, 256 *et seq.*; Mistelis, L. (2000) 'Regulatory Aspects: Globalization, Harmonization, Legal Transplants, and Law Reform – Some Fundamental Observations', 34 *Int'l Law.*, 1055, 1063 *et seq.* Berkowitz, D., Pistor, K. and Richard, J.-F. (2003) 'The Transplant Effect', 51 *Am. J. Comp. L.*, 163, 164, where it was stated that 'newly designed model laws for secured transactions marketed the value of Western law to their counterparts in the East, backing their campaign to transplant their home legal system with financial aid promises and/or the prospect of joining the European Union'; Ajani, G. (1995) 'By Chance and Prestige: Legal transplants in Russia and Eastern Europe', 43 *Am. J. Comp. L.*, 93, 110 *et seq.*

124 Goode, op. cit. (f'note 114), at 7–8; Goode, op. cit. (f'note 122), 342.

125 www.worldbank.org/ifa/ipg_eng.pdf (last accessed September 2009); for a revised version *see* www.worldbank.org/ifa/FINAL-ICRPrinciples-March2009.pdf (last accessed September 2009); *see also* Johnson, G. (2000) 'Towards International Standards on Insolvency: The Catalytic Role of the World Bank', *Law in Transition* (Spring), 69 *et seq.*

126 Head, J.W. (1996) 'Evolution of the Governing Law for Loan Agreements of the World Bank and Other Multilateral Development Banks', 90 *Am. J. Int'l L.*, 214, 217.

127 There seems to be a close relationship with the current policy of international financing institutions and Professor Drobnig's recommendations in 1977 where he reported with regard to the possibility of developing a model law in this area as follows: 'Perhaps moral persuasion or intellectual insight into the virtues of the model rules will move some states to adopt them. Others may need persuasion by more effective means such as *the insistence on the part of international financing institutions*' (emphasis added), Report, op. cit. (f'note 105), 218.

128 The World Bank Principles for Effective Insolvency and Creditor Rights Systems, 2005, at 2.

129 *See generally* Report of World Bank Working Group on Debtor–Creditor Rights, 1999.

2.4.2.2 *Reduction of legal conflicts and costs in international transactions*

Harmonisation is necessary in order to reduce legal conflicts and risks, and increase predictability[130] in cross-border security transactions.[131] Thereby, the flow of cross-border trade and investment opportunities in the emerging markets can be increased. Legal systems must be responsive to the needs of financial and commercial transactions and the business community. In that connection, it is no longer feasible to insist on the traditional legal rules or to persist with the diversity of national laws. Legal conflicts in cross-border security transactions mainly arise out of the diversity and complexity of national laws, and these legal conflicts increase the cost of transactions unnecessarily[132] as the parties have to do research on the possible outcomes of the transaction that they want to conclude, and on the laws of the State to which the other party belongs to or where it has its place of business. The existing international legal regime relating to the creation,

130 With regard to the Receivables Convention, the Association of the Bar of the City of New York Committee on Foreign and Comparative Law states the following:

> First, transactions which were previously uneconomical may now be feasible, making credit available to some borrowers which had previously been unable to obtain it. Second, even transactions which would have been economical under the old regime will involve less risk, thus freeing capital for additional transactions.

See 57 *The Record* (Fall, 2002), 454–67, 466 (New York: Association of the Bar of the City of New York); with respect to international trade in general, *see* von Ziegler, A. (2000) 'Particularities of the Harmonisation and Unification of International Law of Trade and Commerce' in J. Basedow (ed) *Private Law in the International Arena-Liber Amicorum Kurt Siehr.* The Hague: T.M.C. Asser Press, pp. 875, 879 *et seq.*, stating that '[t]rade presupposes unified rules which make the transaction and any potential problems predictable (i.e. calculable)'; Miller, G.P. (1997) 'The Legal-Economic Analysis of Comparative Civil Procedure', 45 *Am. J. Comp. L.*, 905, 917, arguing that harmonisation reduces transaction costs, 'since the parties to international legal transactions might have a somewhat better sense of the risks and costs of litigation they face in a harmonized system than they do in a diverse one'; *but* cf. Hobhouse, op. cit. (f'note 23), at 532–533, acknowledges the needs of a commercial man regarding accuracy and promptness, but does not engage the fact that in order to achieve this goal, harmonisation and international instruments are necessary, and further states that conventions are not creating certainty and harmony. One cannot concur with the latter opinion.

131 For reduction of costs in cross-border transactions other than harmonisation, *see generally* Schwarcz, S.L. (1998) 'The Universal Language of Cross border Finance', 8 *Duke J. Comp. & Int'l L.*, 235 *et seq.*

132 For the advantages of harmonisation in the reduction of high transaction costs *see* Wool, J. (1997) 'Rethinking the Notion of Uniformity in the Drafting of International Commercial Law: A Preliminary Proposal for the Development of a Policy Based Unification Model', *Unif. L. Rev.*, 46, 47 *et seq.*; Wool, J. (1999) 'The Case for a Commercial Orientation to the Proposed UNIDROIT Convention as Applied to Aircraft Equipment', *Unif. L. Rev.*, 289, 291–2; Cohen, op. cit. (f'note 71), 177 discussing the increase of transaction costs as one of the effects of disharmony. Freedman, P.L. and Click, R.W. (2006) 'Banks That Don't Lend? Unlocking Credit to Spur Growth in Developing Countries', 24 *Development Policy Review*, 279, 290, stating that '[s]ubstantial deficiencies in the legal and regulatory environment in developing countries constitute the primary reason for the low degree of credit extended to the private sector'.

perfection and priority of a security interest is based on, and governed by, the law of the collateral's location, and one can argue that this approach is inadequate to meet the needs of modern international financing transactions, and that reliance on private international law rules, in an era of an increased volume of complex international transactions, may lead the practitioner to undesirable results.[133]

Application of the law of the collateral's location requires research and compliance with different requirements, especially when the transaction involves collateral located in multiple jurisdictions. This is costly and expensive, and certainly undesirable, for the party that tries to secure a loan with a company that has places of business in different jurisdictions. If the collateral is movable property, it may move across borders and this will create unnecessary cost and difficulty in finding the applicable law. In particular, the issue is associated with the problem 'whether and how a security interest created in the [first state] can be reperfected in the [other state]'.[134] The law governing rights on movable property is the law of the place where the movable is situated (*lex situs*), and when a property crosses borders it will have to be subject to a new law due to this principle. The traditional principle does not provide a solution to cross-border transactions and is not conducive to intangible property. This leads one to the point as to 'whether a security interest acquired in the first state has an extra-territorial effect outside its jurisdictional boundaries, even though the security interest . . . would be invalid'.[135] Difficulty in establishing effective priorities is evident. The Guide, and the Receivables Convention, introduces the application of the law of the assignor's State to the creation, third-party effectiveness and priority in intangible assets. The Cape Town Convention also proposes a very innovative concept of international interest, where the third-party effectiveness and priority of an interest is maintained through registration in the international registry. In that context, a party attempting to secure a loan would not need to do research on each and every jurisdiction that the movable collateral may move to.

Another complexity is that sometimes the applicable law is not identifiable because of the difference of interpretation of location by national laws. As an intangible, book debts may have numerous locations. One may notice that the application of the law of the place where the collateral is located is not useful and may lead to uncertainties. Therefore, despite the criticisms from prominent commentators,[136] one can argue that solving the problem through conflict of laws would create certainty and reduce legal conflicts.

133 Goode, op. cit. (f'note 75), at 49 where he states that the application of conflict of laws rules to an international transaction 'is inherently unsatisfactory, for it results in the application to an international transaction of a law designed primarily for domestic transactions'.

134 Goode, op. cit. (f'note 75), 49.

135 Gopalan, S. (2003) 'Harmonization of Commercial Law: Lessons from the Cape Town Convention on International Interests in Mobile Equipment', 9 *L. & Bus. Rev. Am.*, 255, 257.

136 E.g. Flessner, op. cit. (f'notes 77 and 104).

In international transactions when parties subject their contract to a foreign law, it is generally expensive and time-consuming to prove the content of foreign law in courts. Documents must be translated into the language of the forum. Relevant details of the applicable law must be found. Furthermore, parties enter into a client–attorney relationship in the country of the forum in order to have representation before the court. If there is a harmonised text, parties will be able to read the applicable law for their contract in their own language and will not need to depend on the knowledge of the local lawyers in different jurisdictions where they do business, if that jurisdiction is a party to the particular instrument.[137] Therefore, consequences of non-harmonisation can be costly, risky and time-consuming. Whereas, if there is a harmonised text translated into several languages or into the languages of the Contracting States and applied in a harmonised manner initially, it will be more accessible for all the parties.

In unreformed secured transactions regimes, access to credit information is limited as there is no registration system, or at least the registration system is not transparent and efficient; yet this is a key issue for certainty and predictability. Registration has been recommended by both the Receivables Convention[138] and the Guide[139] and it is an important feature of the Model Law[140] and the Cape Town Convention.[141] Furthermore, problems with respect to enforcement reduce the confidence of creditors in the legal system that governs the law of the place where the investment is made. Such problems include issues with court process where satisfaction of creditors' claims is unnecessarily prolonged by delays, costs, interference or favouring debtors. Insufficient priority rules, such as the creditor in possession of collateral, do not provide efficient protection to creditors, especially for intangibles. For instance, in order to facilitate assignment of future and bulk receivables, both of which are important elements under a securitisation pattern, a general description of current and future assets should be sufficient – rather than the necessity of identifying each receivable, especially in the assignment of future bulk receivables.[142] These are important features of both the Receivables Convention (Article 8) and the Guide (Recommendation 24).

137 Goode, R. (2001) 'Insularity or Leadership? The Role of the United Kingdom in the Harmonization of Commercial Law', 50 *I.C.L.Q.*, 751, 752–753.

138 *See* Article 42(4).

139 *See* A/CN.9/631, Guide Part VI, Recommendations 54–75.

140 Model Law Articles 33–35.

141 International Registry of Mobile Assets is established under the supervision of the ICAO. Cuming, R.C.C. (2006) 'The International Registry for interests in Aircraft–An Overview of its Structure', *Unif. L. Rev.*, 18.

142 For some of the problems in unreformed secured transactions laws *see* 'Financial Sector Perspective: Financial Sector's Response to Adequate and Inadequate Secured Transactions Framework' at 21, Presentation made at the International Workshop on Collateral Reform and Access to Credit on 8–9 June 2006. London: EBRD.

2.4.2.3 Harmonised modernisation of secured transactions laws for economic growth and increased foreign investment

There is a causal link between appropriate legal reforms and economic growth. UNCITRAL observed that:

> an effective and predictable legal framework had both short- and long-term macroeconomic benefits. In the short term . . . when countries faced crises in their financial sector, an effective and predictable legal framework is necessary, in particular in terms of enforcement of financial claims, to assist banks and other financial institutions in controlling the deterioration of their claims through quick enforcement mechanisms and to facilitate corporate restructuring by providing a vehicle that would create incentives for interim financing. In the longer term, a flexible and effective legal framework for security rights could serve as a useful tool to increase economic growth [and] without access to affordable credit, economic growth, competitiveness and international trade could not be fostered [as] enterprises [would be] prevented from expanding to meet their full potential.[143]

Lack of creditor confidence may prevent the economic growth of a country, for the reason that financiers will provide credit with higher interest rates in order to compensate for their potential losses from debtor default.[144] Lack of creditor confidence can also be explained by the fact that debtors may sometimes fraudulently transfer assets (*actio pauliana*) when they are close to bankruptcy and, naturally, the creditors can take no action against them. In this context, the only possibility that the creditors have, in order to protect their interests, is to 'restrict their lending . . . in the absence of a functional security system, [as] they cannot prevent a borrower on the verge of failure from liquidating its assets and transferring the proceeds to its owners or related parties'.[145]

Through facilitation of credit and harmonised rules poverty may be reduced because SMEs as well as individual borrowers will be able to access low-cost credit.[146] This has been complemented by studies that suggest that financial development

143 A/CN.9/512, para. 4

144 Kilborn, J. (1996) 'Securing Russia's Future: A Plea for Reform in Russian Secured Transactions Law', 95 *Mich. L. Rev.*, 255, 257; for a similar view, *see* Cuming, R.C.C. 'Modernizing the Secured Financing and Lease Financing Laws of Developing Nations, with Particular Focus on the West Bank and Gaza' in J.S. Ziegel and S. Lerner (eds) (1998) 'New Developments in International Commercial and Consumer Law', *Proceedings of the 8th Biennial Conference of the International Academy of Commercial and Consumer Law*, Oxford: Hart, pp. 183, 184; for the problems and challenges of Central European States in adapting new laws *see* Rajski, J. 'The Challenge of Adapting Law to Market Economies in Post Communist Central European Countries' in Ziegel and Lerner (eds) ibid., 383 *et seq.*

145 Bebchuk, L.A. and Fried, J.M. (1997) 'The Uneasy Case for the Priority of Secured Claims in Bankruptcy: Further Thoughts and Reply to Critics', 82 *Cornell L. Rev.*, 1279, 1330.

146 Kozolchyk, B. (2007) 'Secured Lending and Its Poverty Reduction Effect'. 42 *Texas Int'l L. J.*, 727; *see generally* de la Pena, N. (1999) 'Reforming the Legal Framework for Security Interests in Mobile Equipment', *Unif. L. Rev.*, 347.

reduces obstacles to the expansion of business and income inequality.[147] Furthermore, empirical findings support the fact that active stock markets and well-developed legal systems are crucial in the facilitation of credit.[148]

Modernisation of secured transactions 'would expand credit availability for moveable property and lower the interest rate'.[149] Naturally, every nation needs to modernise its laws to allow its companies to compete at the international level. Two forces have been given as examples that make the modernisation of secured transactions law inevitable for those economies that wish to remain competitive in the global market. These are market-driven – which can be explained as low-cost products, services and low inflation rate – and the other is regulatory forces – which can be explained as an imposition of standards of capitalisation and transparency of information regarding the lender's assets, which means registration.[150] From another aspect, appropriate legal reforms affect economic growth positively.[151] For instance, some industries such as airlines or suppliers of high technology equipment are generally dependent on external financing[152] such as receivables financing. External finance sources would prefer to extend credit to companies that are established in the States that have advanced secured transactions laws in order to protect their interests. External funding sources would prefer not to pose difficulties of enforcement and other associated issues in security interests arising out of less modernised laws. In those countries where secured transactions laws 'do not provide [creditors] with the assurance of meaningful enforcement rights and a transparent priority system, credit in that area may . . . be either expensive or unavailable'.[153] Unreformed

147 Freedman and Click, op. cit. (f'note 132), at 280–1.

148 Demirguc-Kunt, A. and Maksimovic, V. (1998) 'Law, Finance and Firm Growth', 53 *J. Finance*, 2107; Beck, T., Demirguc-Kunt, A., Laeven, L. and Levine, R. (2004) 'Finance, Firm Size and Growth', *NBER Working Paper No. 10983*.

149 Fleisig, H. 'Economic Functions of Security in a Market Economy' in Norton and Andenas op. cit. (f'note 23), 15, 35; Fleisig, H. 'The economics of collateral and of collateral reform' in F. Dahan and J. Simpson (eds) op. cit. (f'note 49), 81, at 88 where he argues that movable property is important for production and growth.

150 Kozolchyk and Wilson, op. cit. (f'note 67), 69.

151 Saunders, A., Srinivasan, A., Walter, I. and Wool, J. (1999) 'The Economic Implications of International Secured Transactions Law Reform: A Case Study', 20 *U. Pa. J. Int'l Econ. L.*, 309, 310–1, where they state that appropriate legal reforms affect economic growth 'by lowering the cost of credit and increasing the availability of financing as well as promoting economic restructuring'; *but* cf. Garro, A. (1990) 'The Reform and Harmonization of Personal Property Security Law in Latin America', 59 *Revista Juridica Universidad de Puerto Rico*, 1, 4, where Garro argues that:

> [i]t would be unrealistic to expect that a modernization and harmonization of personal property security law will solve the problems associated with the lack of finance capital and the slow growth of credit [and] it would be unrealistic to view security devices as the most important form of protection in a credit transaction.

152 Saunders *et al.* ibid., at 330–1 where the argument is that high-value equipment such as aircraft is sold and exported by means of export credit financing by countries who manufacture these equipment. Export credit financing is regulated by the OECD in the member states: *see* www.oecd.org (last accessed December 2008).

153 Buxbaum, op. cit. (f'note 79), 324.

secured transactions laws cannot adequately meet the needs of the modern business community, unless reform enables flexible rules and acceptance of all types of property as collateral. No financier would prefer to risk credit in the case where the collateral moves to another state and the existing interest in this collateral is not recognised due to differences in the secured transactions laws.[154] Naturally, a foreign investor or a financier, for instance, would like to protect his interests when investing in or extending credit to another country and, therefore, would only invest or extend credit at a lower cost, if the national law of that country governing secured transactions is a modern one. Lowering the cost of credit or the facilitation of credit can only be achieved if the legal formalities are minimised and contractual flexibility is maximised. Furthermore, modernisation initiatives, provided that they are adopted, are advantageous for the increased flow of foreign investment to developing States, since a foreign investor would prefer to invest in a country where it thinks that there is stability, certainty and predictability in the law.[155]

Facilitation of credit is possible if domestic rules are made predictable and user-friendly.[156] Empirical studies have illustrated correlation between the predictability of law and lending practices. In connection with this, strengthening of creditors' rights has utmost importance in the facilitation of credit as strong creditor rights increase the willingness of a financier to lend.[157] Findings of Haselmann *et al.* also support the fact that predictability in law and strong creditor rights mainly affect foreign banks positively, and this in turn stimulates foreign investment.[158]

UNCITRAL, during the preparation of the Guide, had observed the following:

> Studies have shown that as the risk of non-payment is reduced, the availability of credit increases and the cost of credit falls. Studies have also shown that States where lenders perceive the risks associated with transactions to be high,

154 Schilling, T. (1985) 'Some European Decisions on Non-Possessory Security Rights in Private International Law', 34 *I.C.L.Q.*, 87, 95 *et seq.; see also* Kohn, R.M. (2007) 'Promoting the Implementation of the United Nations Convention on the Assignment of Receivables in International Trade and the UNCITRAL Legislative Guide on Secured Transactions', *Comments at the Congress to Celebrate the 40th Annual Session of UNCITRAL*, Vienna 9–12 July, p. 2, indicating that credit providers' 'willingness to extend secured credit to businesses in a given country will depend . . . on whether the laws of that State are conducive to obtaining security rights in collateral that can be created and enforced, in an efficient and predictable way'.

155 For a similar view *see* Model Law, at v where it was stated: '[i]f there is a law on secured transactions which . . . [gives] practical protection and remedies in the case of non-payment of a debt then security can become a major part of the investment decision, both for local and international investors.'

156 This can be supported by an observation made by Dahan and Simpson where they remark that '[t]he laws of Central and Eastern Europe are changing and this could lead to a reversal of position with their countries having an economic advantage over their Western neighbours in the market for secured credit.' Dahan, F. and Simpson, J. 'The European Bank for Reconstruction and Development's Secured Transactions Project: A Model Law and Ten Core Principles for a Modern Secured Transactions Law in Countries of Central and Eastern Europe (and Elsewhere!)' in Kieninger (ed), op. cit. (f'note 83), 98, 113.

157 Haselmann, R., Pistor, K. and Vig, V. (2006) 'How Law Affects Lending', *Columbia Law and Economics Working Paper No 285*, 4.

158 Ibid., 4.

> the cost of credit increases as lenders require increased compensation to evaluate and assume the increased risk.[159]

Arguably, the interest of the World Bank and the International Finance Corporation (IFC) in international harmonisation can be linked to the importance of harmonised rules for economic growth, access to finance, and financial investment.[160] The IFC does not lend directly to SMEs in developing nations but rather its investment clients do, and hence may be the pressure to modernise the law of secured credit in those countries.[161] From another angle, the Export–Import Bank of the US in January 2003[162] offered a reduction of one-third of the exposure fee for buyers of US large commercial aircraft established in countries that adopt, ratify and implement the Cape Town Convention. The goal of the offer is to facilitate credit and reduce the risk in cross-border asset-based aircraft financing through harmonised rules that will 'lead to less aircraft-related debt for governments, lower financing costs and enhanced access to funding for airlines, and ticket price savings for passengers'.[163]

2.4.2.4 Importance of intangible property as collateral

Borrowers and lenders enter into high-value credit transactions on a consistent basis. Goode[164] and Buxbaum[165] argue that private parties may find intangible property advantageous, rather than tangible or immovable property, in order to secure their interests, because creation of a security is more flexible through intangible property. Goode argues that intangible property acts as the most valuable collateral and has advantages over tangible property.[166] Without an adequate system on security interests, States may be deprived of the opportunity to access low-cost credit. Collateral has clear significance in the private sector's access to low-cost credit.[167] In some developed countries the use of intangibles and

159 A/CN.9/WG.6/WP.2 para. 2.

160 Fleisig, H., Safavian, M. and de la Pena, N. (2006) *Reforming Collateral Laws to Expand Access to Finance*. Washington, DC: The World Bank, p. xi.

161 www.ifc.org/ifcext/about.nsf/content/About_IFC_Financing (accessed October 2009).

162 'Ex-Im Bank offers One-Third reduction of its exposure fee on export financing for US large commercialaircraft': www.exim.gov/pressrelease.cfm/6F76B4BA-1032-5B0F-BDC2F28463DF4239/ (accessed October 2009).

163 *See* ibid.

164 Gullifer, L. (ed.) (2009) *Goode on Legal Problems of Credit and Security*, 4th edn., London: Sweet & Maxwell, pp. 2–3.

165 Buxbaum, op. cit. (f'note 79), at 324.

166 Gullifer (ed.), ibid., 95:

> [i]ntangible property is today the most valuable object of security for the financier, and pure intangibles possess several advantages over tangible assets. They are not susceptible to physical loss, damage or deterioration; they can be stored on and transferred by computer and turned over in huge volumes without constraints of size or physical delivery requirements; and they may be notionally shifted from one country to another at the press of a button (*footnote omitted*).

167 Fleisig, et al., op. cit. (f'note 160), 1 *et seq.*

movables is more attractive, whereas in economically less-developed countries the use of immovables as collateral is more attractive or more acceptable by financiers.[168] It has been observed that 'in most countries, *intangible capital* is the largest share of total wealth'.[169] Between 2001 and 2005, the World Bank in its Enterprise Surveys, conducted in 60 low- and middle-income countries, established that 22 per cent of company assets are land and buildings, 34 per cent accounts receivables, and 44 per cent machinery; nevertheless, as collateral only 9 per cent accounts receivables, 18 per cent machinery, and 73 per cent lands and buildings are accepted.[170] This is a clear indication that in unreformed secured transaction law regimes there is strong confidence in tangible and immovable assets. However, within the framework of an effective and efficient secured transactions regime this may be regarded as an inadequate system that fails to promote secured credit.[171] The economic impracticality of pledge of movables has been observed by UNCITRAL[172] and economists.[173] Complementing this finding, other empirical studies demonstrate the need to introduce non-possessory security in order to facilitate the availability of credit.[174] In other words, if the scope of security is expanded by virtue of the modernisation of law through law reform, unlimited ability to use any types of assets as collateral, better creditor and predictable priority rights, then SMEs in developing economies may have facilitated access to finance as this will stimulate lending practices of banks.[175] Limitation on the ability to provide receivables or inventory as collateral has been illustrated in the World Bank's studies.[176] Moreover, similar studies have also illustrated that the legal origin has an impact upon the availability of credit as well as creditor protection, and common law jurisdictions have more tendency to lending and creditor

168 *See generally e.g.* Safavian, op. cit. (f'note 86); Simavi, S. (2007) 'Making Finance Work for Africa: The Collateral Debate', *World Bank PDP Forum*; 'Vietnam Increasing Access to Credit through Collateral (Secured Transactions) Reform' (IFC/MPDF); 'Reforming Collateral Laws and Registries: International Best Practices and the Case of China' (FIAS/IFC PEP China, March 2007).

169 *Where is the Wealth of Nations? Measuring Capital for the 21st Century* (2006), 87 available at http://siteresources.worldbank.org/INTEEI/214578-1110886258964/20748034/All.pdf (last accessed February 2010).

170 Safavian, M., Fleisig, H. and Steinbuks, J. (2006) 'Unlocking Dead Capital' *Viewpoint*, Note Number 307 (March), at 2 and Figure 3.

171 For the key objectives of an effective and efficient secured transactions regime, *see* A/CN.9/631 recommendation 1.

172 Guide, paras 57 and 62, at 44 and 46.

173 Fleisig, op. cit. (f'note 149), Dahan and Simpson (eds), at 90 arguing that movable assets cannot effectively serve in unreformed economies as collateral; *see also* Fleisig, H. (1999) 'The Proposed UNIDROIT Convention on Mobile Equipment: Economic Consequences and Issues', *Unif. L. Rev.*, 253, 256.

174 Armour, J. 'The Law and Economics Debate About Secured Lending: Lessons For European Lawmaking?' in H. Eidenmüller and E.M. Kieninger (eds) op. cit. (f'note 101), 3, at 14–19.

175 *See generally* Haselmann et al., op. cit. (f'note 157); Safavian, M. and Sharma, S. (2007) 'When do Creditor Rights Work?', *Policy Research Working Paper No 4296.*

176 For further information, *see generally* World Bank (2004) 'Doing Business in 2004: Understanding Regulation', Washington, DC: Oxford University Press for the WB and IFC.

protection than the civil law jurisdictions have.[177] These empirical studies clearly demonstrate the fact that facilitation of credit and access to low-cost credit are acutely needed in emerging markets. This can only be achieved through international instruments aiming to create harmonised modernisation of secured transactions laws.

2.5 Conclusion

Harmonised modernisation of secured transactions laws is critical both for emerging and developed economies. Arguably, harmonisation is a means to achieve facilitation of credit. It aims at establishing certainty and predictability in the rules that govern secured transactions, which may eventually lead to financiers providing low-cost credit without the need to include the risk premium in the interest rates. Access to low-cost credit is an acutely-felt problem, particularly in emerging markets. It has particular significance for small and medium-sized businesses. Empirical studies have illustrated that emerging markets are in need of immediate liquidity where the use of receivables or other intangibles as collateral is not necessarily accepted by finance institutions. However, the same argument seems to be equally applicable, amidst the credit crisis, to developed economies. It is believed that the harmonised and predictable rules will assist small and medium-sized businesses, as well as the large enterprises, to be able to access affordable credit globally.

International secured transactions law instruments have critical roles in the process of establishing certain and predictable rules that aim for access to affordable credit. International harmonisation efforts are more realistic now than they used to be. There seems to be more convergence than divergence. With the integration of industrial stakeholders in the harmonisation process, particularly in the case of the Cape Town Convention, instruments have become more conducive to achieving the end result of harmonisation for the facilitation of credit.[178] Legal reform cannot only be achieved by adopting rules, but this should be followed by the establishment of relevant infrastructure. It should also be noted that realistically some of the instruments will only be helpful in emerging nations for the benefit of emerging and developed nations. In other words, instruments that fail to meet the expectations of the industry by not providing essential solutions to commercial problems may only be helpful as an inception point for a further reform.

177 *See generally* Beck, T., Demirguc-Kunt, A. and Levine, R. (2004) 'Law and Firms' Access to Finance', *Policy Research Working Paper No 3194*; Beck *et al*, op. cit. (f'note 61).

178 For the integration of industry and other stakeholders in the process, *see* e.g. Gopalan, S. (2008) 'A Demandeur-Centric Approach to Regime Design in Transnational Commercial Law', 39 *Georgetown J. Int'l L.*, 327.

3 Scope of applicability and party autonomy

3.1 Introduction

The purpose of this chapter is to consider some fundamental general provisions of international instruments and to extract the general principles and ingredients of these provisions. Provisions regulating the scope of application of international instruments provide an optimal lens to generally assess their fundamental policies and key objectives. International secured transactions instruments are related to each other and their link is carefully regulated so that they do not overlap. Party autonomy is a key concept under the instruments. The particular issue with the party autonomy is that there should be limits to it, to the extent that it deals with proprietary aspects of secured transactions. It is perfectly normal to fall back to party autonomy as it reflects contractual freedom. However, as long as the issue at hand affects third parties who are not party to the contract, party autonomy should be restricted. International instruments ensure that balance, by embodying principles that agreements cannot affect the rights of any person that is not a party to that agreement.[1]

3.2 Scope of application

Facilitation of credit requires clear and predictable rules. For this, applicability of an instrument must be carefully defined. Adoption of comprehensive and functional approaches may assist debtors and creditors. The scope of application and, particularly for conventions, internationality draws the framework, such as how far an instrument is applicable and whether it is applicable to domestic transactions; hence the internationality issues. Comprehensive and functional approaches aim to fulfil the major objectives by simplifying the applicable rules of secured credit while making them efficient and consistent. They also lift unnecessary limitations over the use of types of collateral, the people who can grant and take security, and the types of transactions and obligations. The applicability has substantive and territorial dimensions.

1 E.g. Receivables Convention Article 6; Guide, Recommendation 10.

3.2.1 Substantive dimension

Substantive scope of application refers to the applicability of an instrument to substantive matters; such as to what type of assets, interests or transactions an instrument applies, as opposed to temporal, territorial or procedural applicability, which refers to when, where and how an instrument applies.

3.2.1.1 Comprehensive and functional approach

Multiplicity of security devices and their definitions cause complexity in cross-border transactions. This has effects over the creation, perfection, priority and enforceability of security taken, or intended to be taken, over the collateral in cross-border transactions.[2] Most international instruments often tend to adopt a functional and comprehensive approach that any transaction that serves security functions should be considered to be a secured transaction and regulated by the same rules.[3] The rationale for this move is quite clear: simplicity, legal predictability and reduction of legal risk rather than fragmentation and multiplicity of transactions that have similar economic functions are instrumental in the facilitation of credit. Functional approach, in general terms, may be defined as an approach to security in which all transactions having similar economic functions, where the payment of a loan or a performance of an obligation is aimed, are treated as secured interests regardless of whether or not they are traditional security interests. In this sense, under a functional approach a conditional buyer or a lessee will be considered as owner, and the seller or the lessor's title will be limited to a security interest, thus title-based devices become equivalent to purchase-money security interest.[4] The Model Law adopts a formalist approach by distinguishing grant of security from the retention of title where the buyer has a possessory interest, whereas the seller retains ownership rights.[5] The Cape Town Convention adopts a functional approach, in the sense that it is not important how a particular State conceptualises a particular transaction, but how it achieves legal predictability by reducing the risk involved in cross-border secured transactions involving mobile equipment. However, there is a nuance here. The functional approach that the Cape Town Convention embodies is neither

2 For a brief commentary on a unitary (comprehensive) approach, *see* Kieninger, E.M. (2008) 'The Scope and Limits of Security Interests–Commentary' in H. Eidenmüller and E.M. Kieninger (eds) *The Future of Secured Credit in Europe*. E.C.F.L.R., Munich: De Gruyter Recht, pp. 215, 216–17.

3 Guide, Recommendations 2 and 8 and, in relation to title finance, Recommendation 9. The Guide adopts a functional approach that is defined as a method according to which secured transactions law 'applies to all contractually created rights in movable assets that secure the payment or other performance of an obligation . . .'. Guide, Statement of Purpose – Chapter I: Receivables Convention Article 2(a).

4 For a similar definition, *see* Gullifer, L. (ed.) (2008) *Goode on Legal Problems of Credit and Security*. London: Sweet & Maxwell, p. 4; for some criticism and detailed treatment of the subject, *see* e.g. Bridge, M. 'The Scope and Limits of Security Interests', in Eidenmüller and Kieninger (eds) op. cit. (f'note 2), 180, 193–5.

5 Röver, J-H. (2007) *Secured Lending in Eastern Europe: Comparative Law of Secured Transactions and the EBRD Model Law*. Oxford: Oxford University Press, p. 72.

exactly the same as UCC Article 9 (i.e. all transactions embodied under the international interest are not characterised as a security interest and the Convention, in any case, does not characterise the transaction) nor the Guide. While the Cape Town Convention retains the separate categories of security interest (charge), conditional sale and lease, their proprietary nature is kept separate but equal, according to which, save remedies, their distinctiveness in national laws is abolished by virtue of the Convention's first-to-file priority approach.[6] Put simply, States have the freedom to apply the functional equivalence by virtue of applying their own legal concepts and terminology. Conversely, under the Guide, the title retention devices are within the general definition of security rights. The international interest under the Cape Town Convention covers both the traditional security interests (Article 2(2)(a)), and interest retained by a conditional seller or a lessor (Article 2(2)(b) and (c)). The international interest does not originate from or depend upon a national law and has proprietary nature.[7] However, the Convention does not define what constitutes proprietary characterisation of the interest and transactions. The distinction between civil and common law approaches in this matter[8] makes it imperative that the proprietary nature of the interest, and whether or not an international interest exists, will depend on the national law. Characterisation of transactions poses certain issues for those jurisdictions that adopt a functional approach, as the types of agreements under the Convention are identified separately. Characterisation of interests and transactions under the Cape Town Convention is left to the applicable law determined by the Forum State's conflict-of-law rules.[9] The question whether an interest falls within the Convention is determined by the Convention itself, and if the interest falls under the definition of security interest, conditional sale or lease, the applicable law will determine whether this interest needs to be recharacterised.[10]

6 Bridge, M. in Eidenmüller and Kieninger (eds) op. cit. (f'note 2), 193; Cuming, R. (2002) 'The Characterisation of Interests and Transactions under the Convention of International Interests in Mobile Equipment, 2001' in I. Davies (ed.) *Security Interests in Mobile Equipment*. Aldershot: Ashgate, pp. 377, 389.

7 For the substantive sphere of application of the Cape Town Convention, *see* Stanford, M. (2002) 'From Ottawa to Cape Town: UNIDROIT's Role in the Modernisation of the Law Governing Leasing and the Taking of Security' in I. Davies (ed.) *Security Interests in Mobile Equipment*. Aldershot: Ashgate, pp. 397, 431–4.

8 For example, in the case of leasing, common law jurisdictions treat the right of a lessee differently than the civil law jurisdictions do. Where in the former a lessee has a special property right according to which, in a long-term lease, it is possible that the lessee may charge the leased asset, whereas in the latter a lessee has a possessory right that does not have the interest that makes it possible to charge the leased property. Cuming, ibid., 386; Bridge, ibid., 193, arguing it is not possible for a lessee under the Convention to encumber assets to the extent of its rights under the lease. *See also* Chapter 1.

9 Cape Town Convention Article 2(4), 5(2), (3). It should be noted that characterisation of transactions, whether it is a security or a title device, mainly relates to default remedies. *See* Goode, R. (2008) *Convention on International Interests in Mobile Equipment and Protocol thereto on Matters Specific to Aircraft Equipment: Official Commentary*, rev. edn. Rome: UNIDROIT, para. 2.36; *but* cf. Cuming, ibid., 391, where Professor Cuming argues that 'issues of characterisation are best determined under the law of the location of the chargor, lessees or buyer as the case may be, at the time the international interest comes into existence.'

10 Goode, ibid., para. 2.36.

It is commented that, as Cape Town Convention Article 7 requires simple conditions to constitute international interests, it is most likely that an interest created under the national law will also qualify as an international interest.[11] An interest created in line with Article 7 will be enforceable in any contracting state whether or not it constitutes a national security interest.[12]

The rationale of a comprehensive and functional approach is that if States structure their secured transactions regimes as comprehensively as possible, encompassing both companies and individuals, without interfering with the consumer protection rules, and apply to all assets[13] and obligations as well as contractually creating all property rights to secure a payment or performance of an obligation,[14] the cost of credit may be reduced.[15] Proceeds should also be encompassed within the framework of the security right. This approach serves for certainty and predictability in the rules governing assignment of receivables, title finance devices, and other possessory and non-possessory security interests. Historically, the rationale of this tendency, especially for cross-border transactions, is the absence of a comprehensive and suitable legal regime from which businesses can enjoy in accordance with their commercial needs, and borrow and lend without being hindered by unnecessary limitations.[16] The pre-UCC Article 9 law did not recognise a comprehensive approach to security rights.[17] Prohibition of, or reluctance to use, certain types of assets,[18] or lack of certain types of security devices, led States to adopt techniques that were *ad hoc*, complex, often inconsistent and inefficient, giving more importance to form rather than the substance or the function that the transaction serves for.[19] On the other hand, some others,[20] realising the advantages of transactional certainty and its importance in reducing the costs of credit, adopted a comprehensive and functional approach.[21]

11 Goode, ibid., para. 4.68.

12 Wool, J. (1999) 'The Next Generation of International Aviation Finance Law: An Overview of the Proposed UNIDROIT Convention on International Interests in Mobile Equipment as Applied to Aircraft Equipment', 20 *U. Pa. J. Int'l Econ. L.*, 499, 517.

13 *See* e.g. Recommendation 17 '. . . [a security right] may also encumber all assets of a grantor . . .'.

14 Guide, Recommendation 2(a)–(d).

15 E.g. Guide, Recommendation 1.

16 See Guide, paras 101–2, at 55–6.

17 The pre-UCC Article 9 US law did not recognise the English equivalent of floating charge and the debtor could not create security on after-acquired property. *See* e.g. *Zartman v First National Bank of Waterloo* (1907) 189 NY 267; *Benedict v Ratner* (1925) 268 US 353. However, the UCC Article 9 drafters considering the wisdom in comprehensive approach prepared Article 9. On this matter, *see* Gilmore, G. (1968) 'Security Law, Formalism and Article 9', 47 *Nebraska L. Rev.*, 659, 672 *et seq.*

18 On this matter for an empirical study, *see* Safavian, M. (2008) 'Firm level evidence on collateral and access to finance' in F. Dahan and J. Simpson (eds) *Secured Transactions Reform and Access to Credit.* Cheltenham: Edward Elgar, pp. 110, 118.

19 *See generally* Guide, para. 44 at 18–9.

20 Notably the American UCC Article 9, New Zealand Personal Property Securities Act 1999 and the common law provinces of Canada (Quebec, a civil law province, declined to adopt the UCC Article 9 type of functional approach to secured transactions).

21 *See* Chapter 2 where the rationale for harmonising the secured transactions law in the USA is explained as mainly to provide transactional certainty in trade across States in line with the practitioners' desire, and to promote economic growth.

A functional approach has attracted academic attention in England[22] and been compared to formalism of the English law in reform proposals.[23] The model and philosophy of UCC Article 9 have become an inspiration to law reform efforts and been examined by prominent scholars.[24] The Guide has a comprehensive approach in that it applies to a wide range of persons and assets that serve as security. It encourages in the comprehensive approach,[25] which equally applies to legal and natural persons, but consumer protection legislation is not affected. As the Guide's rationale is mainly to promote secured credit, having different rules applicable to different types of persons runs against this rationale.[26] The Receivables Convention also opts into the functional approach in that, for example, the term assignment does not make any distinction between assignment by way of sale and security.[27]

3.2.1.2 Significance: advantages and disadvantages

First, a functional approach to security interest should not be regarded as diminishing the significance of different types of transactions. Rather a functional approach clearly reduces the number of rules, while simplifying them. This has the advantage of creating consistent and effective rules, particularly for non-possessory security interests that are used less in unreformed legal systems, particularly due to problems of enforcement.[28] Second, the approach integrates a possessory security right, which is often the centre of lending practices in unreformed secured transactions regimes,[29] under a comprehensive set of rules. Thus

22 E.g. McCormack, G. (2007) 'The UNCITRAL Legislative Guide on Secured Transactions-Functionalism and Form' in B. Foex, L. Thevenoz and S. Bazinas (eds) *Reforming Secured Transactions* Geneva: Schulthess, pp.43–62; McCormack, G. (2003) '"Quasi-Securities" and the Law Commission Consultation Paper on Security Interests – A Brave New World', *L.M.C.L.Q.*, 80; Davies, I. (2004) 'The Reform of English Personal Property Security Law: Functionalism and Article Nine of the Uniform Commercial Code', 24 *Legal Studies*, 295; Bridge, M. 'Form, Substance and Innovation in Personal Property Security Law' *J.B.L.* 1; Bridge, M., Macdonald, R., Simmonds, R. and Walsh, C. (1999) 'Formalism, Functionalism and Understanding the Law of Secured Transactions', 44 *McGill L.J.*, 567.

23 E.g. Report of the Committee on Consumer Credit (Cmnd 4596, 1971); Insolvency Law and Practice (Cmnd 8558, 1982); A Review of Security Interests in Property; Registration of Company Charges: Property other than Land (Consultation Paper No.164, 2002); Company Security Interests (Consultation Paper, No.176, 2004); Law Commission Company Security Interests (No. 296, 2005).

24 E.g. Bridge, M. (1996) 'How Far is Article 9 Exportable? The English Experience', 27 *Canadian Bus. L.J.*, 196; McCormack, G. (2002) 'Personal Property Security Law Reform in England and Canada', *J.B.L.*, 113.

25 Recommendation 1. Promotion of secured credit, utilisation of full value in broad range of assets transactions, obtaining credit in simple and efficient manner, validation of non-possessory security rights, clear and predictability rules, etc.

26 Guide, para. 52, 20, Recommendation 1.

27 Article 2(a).

28 For these advantages see generally Guide, paras 105–106, at 56–7.

29 *See* e.g. Engelhardt, T. and Regitz, B. 'The State of Nature and Lending in an Unreformed Environment: Experience from Early Transition Countries' in Dahan and Simpson (eds) op. cit. (f'note 17), 141, at 153–4.

non-possessory and possessory security rights are merged under one scheme, which enables parties to a financing pattern to be certain about their rights and obligations. Furthermore, the above two points are critical in reforming the law to be applicable to all rights that secured payment in movable assets contractually created, irrespective of the form of the transaction, to the parties to that contract, and irrespective of the type of obligation whether present or future, specific or bulk. The UCC's philosophy of unitary security interest reflects the significance of substance of the transaction over its form.[30] Both traditional and quasi-security rights often serve the same economic purpose.[31] Thus, this approach assists easy access to, and application of, the secured transactions regime's rules.[32] Some authors argue a unitary approach may be implemented without incorporating certain transactions (notably the retention of title), thus not combining it with the functional approach and governing these transactions by their specific rules despite their economic function.[33] Third, the functional approach assists stakeholders to understand the rules underlying secured transactions rather than having then to deal with fragmented rules, which often may not be accessible.

In the centre of these advantages is the significance of notice filing, which is a critical matter for potential creditors and lenders who are forced to make a lending decision. The inherent problem of ostensible ownership in non-possessory security interest is avoided.[34] As the possession of the asset is left with the debtor, it may mislead potential creditors as to the true ownership of the asset, which has already been encumbered by the secured creditor. Integrating these two security rights in the same scheme, and subjecting them to notice requirement, may serve as a cost-reducing element.[35] Some commentators criticised the functional approach, the conceptual context[36] of which evolved from UCC Article 9, as being too generalist, over-inclusive and blurring the distinction between different types of transactions.[37]

30 UCC§9–109(a): 'Except as otherwise provided . . . this article applies to: (1) a transactions regardless of its form, that creates a security interest in personal property or fixtures by contract . . .'.

31 E.g. UCC§1–201(37) security interest securing payment or performance of an obligation.

32 *Cf.* Gullifer, L. (2005) 'Quasi-Security Interests: Functionalism and the Incidents of Security' in I. Davies (ed.) *Issues in International Commercial Law* Aldershot: Ashgate, pp. 3, 7 *et seq.*, arguing that this simplification argument needs to be clarified as to what interests and transactions are similar and this is a choice of policy. Law Commission Report, No 176, para. 2.83, which indicates that the law's treatment of quasi-security rights is as to form and not to the substance. *See generally* Guide, para. 105, at 56.

33 E.g. Kieninger, op. cit. (f'note 2), at 217; for some policy justifications, *see* Gullifer, ibid., 7 *et seq.*

34 Although there are critics of justification of registration on the basis to avoid ostensible ownership, *see* Mooney, C. (1988) 'The Mystery and Myth of "Ostensible Ownership" and Article 9 filing: a critique of the proposals to extend filing requirements to leases', 39 *Ala. L. Rev.*, 683; Gullifer, ibid., 7 *et seq.* There are supporters too, e.g. Goode, R. (1984) 'The Modernisation of Personal Property Security Law', 100 *M.L.R.*, 234.

35 On the significance of notice, *see* Baird, D.G. (1983) 'Notice Filing and the Problem of Ostensible Ownership', 12 *J. Legal Studies*, 53. For discussion on effectiveness against third parties, *see* Chapter 5.

36 *See* e.g. Gilmore, G. (1981) 'The Good Faith Purchase Idea and the UCC: Confessions of a Repentant Draftsman', 15 *Ga. L. Rev.*, 605; McCormack, G. (2003) '"Quasi-Securities" and the Law Commission Consultation Paper on Security Interests – A Brave New World', *L.M.C.L.Q.*, 80.

37 Davies, op. cit. (f'note 21), at 300.

While this may be true, it is arguable that, at least for cross-border transactions, there is no need to have different types of transactions, and a formalist approach complicates an area of law which is already complex and specialist. There may be denial of ownership of seller or lessor in title devices[38] and inclusion of transactions that are not within the meaning of security per se. In an international setting, however, where different rules govern distinct transactions, which, in essence, aim to secure payment or performance of an obligation, it may be reasonable to define all those transactions under one single definition. It is true that that may blur the definition of some transactions, and they may lose their true identities by being assimilated or reduced into a security interest. Another optimal way to achieve the functionality is the same approach taken by the Cape Town Convention; by recognising the distinctive nature of transactions while embodying them in a uniform system of registration and priority rules. In a cross-border transaction, what parties need is whether they can create an enforceable security right that is recognised in other jurisdictions that secures the claim, has opposability against third parties, and whether they have priority. Non-possessory security rights are not recognised in some jurisdictions and there is no need to risk commercial interests. Further, possessory security rights are ineffective when modern financing patterns and commercial needs are concerned. The law should be generalist to be accessible and predictable for parties. Incorporating title-finance devices[39] in the functional approach may facilitate the protection of sellers, and create transparent rules for buyers so they can reuse their collateral to obtain further credit through other means.[40] The rationale is that, as title retention devices are not registrable in those jurisdictions (for example England), potential lenders may not be certain as to whether the asset that is used as collateral to obtain credit has been owned by the debtor.[41] From another perspective, contractual arrangements that serve security functions could be incorporated into a comprehensive system that serves to avoid unnecessary conflicts of priority between different types of creditors.[42] If there is a title retention arrangement between the debtor/buyer and a seller, and concluded after the time of credit arrangement that involves a charge of future asset, the asset will not be owned by the debtor but by the seller. This may not be known to the lender due to the exemption

38 Bridge, in Eidenmüller and Kieninger (eds), op. cit. (fnote 2), 195–6.

39 For further discussion on retention of title devices, *see* Chapter 7. For policy justifications of inclusion of retention of title within a functional scheme, *see* Guide, paras 92–100, at 53 *et seq.*

40 *See* e.g. Law Commission Report, No. 296, para. 21, p xiv, where the rationale of inclusion of title retention devices is explained as the protection of purchasers.

41 The Law Commission Consultation Paper No 176 observed that it would be advantageous to have a registration scheme and thus include the title retention devices within the scheme of registration for the purposes of perfection and priority, para. 2.130. Similar recommendations as to registrability were made by the Cork Committee (Insolvency Law and Practice (1982) Cmnd 6556, para. 1639). The Diamond and Crowther Committees also recommended the treatment of all devices that perform security functions as a traditional security interest. *See also* Law Commission Consultation Paper No 164, para. 7.1 *et seq.*

42 Guide, para. 105, at 56. These different types of creditors could be companies and individuals, security interest holders and quasi-security interest holders.

of title finance devices from registration. The lender either has to trust the debtor's representation or make extensive investigations as to whether there is any other security device on the asset. In both cases the cost of credit may increase. As security cannot be taken on an asset that is not owned at the time of the creation of security interest by the debtor[43] there will be uncertainty. This may cause either rejection of extension of credit to the detriment of the debtor/grantor, or extension of credit but with uncertain results as to who has better priority status. Generally, this is to the detriment of the lender because the debtor has not had any title over the goods so that it can charge it. Title retention devices enjoy super-priority status. Professor Bridge indicates that the effectiveness of English charge is limited by the particular rules that govern title-based transactions.[44] Title retention, and other title finance arrangements in the absence of a functional approach, may hinder the effectiveness of creation of security rights over future assets as the seller will often have better priority rights.[45] Thus there seems to have been commercial necessity that title finance devices should be registrable and included within a functional approach, even though different rules apply for enforcement purposes.[46] In England, the Law Commission's proposal to include title-retention devices under a scheme of a single set of rules, where the priority is determined through registration by virtue of an electronic notice-filing system, has not been widely supported.[47] Finally, as the rules for different security devices are integrated, continuous law reform to align statutory rules to practical reality is avoided.[48]

Conversely, disadvantages of a functional and integrated approach mainly relate to difficulties in re-characterisation of title finance transactions as security interests, which may or may not be welcomed by some jurisdictions that prefer to keep them as quasi-security interests. Moreover, this approach may require the legislation to be gathered under a single scheme, as well as educationally requiring the change of a philosophical understanding of equality of creditors. This is because the secured creditor generally will have, under this scheme, priority over the others. Linked with this argument, it is also presented that the spread of

43 *Abbey National Building Society v Cann* [1991] 1 AC 56, 92.

44 Bridge, op. cit. (f'note 6), 192.

45 Under English law title financiers have super-priority status against chargees. Title finance devices are not registrable and despite the fact that a lender may take charge over the debtor's future assets (*Tailby v Official Receiver* (1888) 13 App. Cas. 523 and *Holroyd v Marshall* (1861) 10 HLC 191), the subsequent title financier may have better priority status. *See also* Law Commission Report No 296.

46 Law Commission Consultation Paper No 176, para. 2.83, at 34; Guide, Recommendations 8 and 9; *but* cf. Law Commission Report No. 296, para. 21.

47 Law Commission Report No 296, para. 21, at xiv. Three points of concern have been raised. First, whether title-retention devices should be registered, thus a public notice is given; second, whether the same remedies on default should apply (i.e. whether after default any surplus should be returned to the debtor); and third, the need to protect the buyers and subsequent lenders according to which a bona fide purchaser of assets under retention of title or secured creditor has no title. Law Commission Report No 296, paras 1.62–64, at 19. For more discussion, *see* Chapter 7.

48 *See also* Bridge, op. cit. (f'note 6), at 181.

secured credit will be the general principle, which is a diversion from the traditional rule of security over specific obligation, asset, parties and right.[49]

It is arguable that the merits of functional and comprehensive approaches philosophically outweigh the disadvantages. Some of the disadvantages cited include the requirement of re-characterisation of certain transactions as secured transaction, expanding the understanding on security rights that it should be interpreted expansively, spreading the secured credit in order to overcome limitations (which is not always permitted in certain unreformed secured transactions regimes), and a unitary legislation that covers all secured transactions, which may require unpicking the rules spread between civil and commercial and other specialised codes (which may mainly be found in Civil Law jurisdictions).[50] Comprehensiveness of the scope of a secured transactions regime is a vital fundamental policy in the facilitation of credit, and particularly adopted by the Guide[51] as a fundamental policy to achieve key objectives. It may be interpreted as a method that defines the limits of a modern secured transactions regime that encompasses all types of assets that may be used as collateral by the widest possible array of people (companies and individuals) with the widest types of obligations and transactions.[52] There should not be, in principle, any limitations to the scope of the secured transactions regime; however, if there are limits or exceptions, these should be clearly set out in the law.[53] These two critical approaches, attached to modern secured credit regimes, facilitate access to credit for a borrower by providing predictable rules, as a lender need not examine the details of creation of, or obtaining priority over, divergent security devices, especially in cross-border transactions, because the secured transactions regime in both parties' jurisdictions will recognise a comprehensive security right. From the comprehensive perspective, English law, like UCC Article 9, permits the creation of security rights in all types of assets (through floating charge) and obligations (present or future, and specific or general).

3.2.1.3 International instruments

The Guide mainly deals with consensual security rights as opposed to non-consensual security rights (interests created by operation of law or court decisions), whereas the latter are only dealt with under the priority Chapter V[54] with a view

49 For the disadvantages see Guide, para. 108, at 57.

50 Ibid.

51 Guide, para. 61, at 23; Recommendation 1.

52 One of the critical issues in taking security is that often individuals are not allowed to take security or indeed they are treated differently from the companies if they are granting security. *See* Guide, para. 10, at 43. In England, for instance, companies and individuals are treated differently if they are granting security. Companies are subject to the Companies Act 2006 Part 25, s 860 *et seq.* and individuals on the other hand are subject to the Bills of Sale Act 1878 and Bills of Sale Act (1878) Amendment Act 1882. For complications on this matter, *see* Bridge, M. (2007) 'England and Wales' in H. Sigman and E.M. Kieninger (eds) *Cross-Border Security over Tangibles*. Munich: Sellier, pp. 125 *et seq.*

53 Guide, para. 44, 41–2; Recommendation 7.

54 Recommendations 83–84.

to modernise secured transactions regimes, and to promote facilitated access to low-cost credit.[55] It has adopted a functional and comprehensive approach. It recommends that the law should cover all rights in movable assets that are created by agreement, and secure the payment or other performance of an obligation regardless of the form of the transaction or the name attributed to it by the parties, and that all persons, types of obligations and transactions and assets should create a secured transactions regime.[56]

A functional and integrated approach is also adopted by the Receivables Convention, in order to ensure certainty in the assignment of receivables, by including outright and security transfers of receivables and creation of security rights in receivables.[57] Certain basic terms have been defined and exclusions and limitations in the Convention's applicability have been set out. The applicability is based on the terms *assignment* and *receivables*. These two terms broaden the scope of applicability and have been defined by encompassing the debtor, the assignor and the assignee in Article 2(a). Defining these terms in the text provides certainty and predictability by conceptualising the aim they serve.[58] A similar practice of defining terms and concepts in a lengthy fashion can be found in the Guide and the Cape Town Convention.[59] The term *assignment* under the Receivables Convention includes outright sales of receivables, assignments for security, creation of security rights in receivables, contractual subrogation and pledge transactions.[60] It is arguable that, as the procedure for collection of a receivable (not the enforcement) by an assignee or a pledgee is identical, it is more appropriate to subject assignment to the same rules.[61] The Receivables Convention excludes unilateral assignments and transfers by operation of law such as statutory subrogation.[62] Under the Guide the term *assignment* similarly covers both outright transfers and transfers for security purposes.[63] As the Guide adopts a functional and comprehensive approach, the term *security right* embodies the right of the assignee in an outright transfer of a receivable. The term does not cover, under the non-unitary approach to acquisition financing, retention of title and financial lease right.[64]

55 Guide, para. 3, 32 *et seq.*; Recommendation 2(d).

56 Guide, paras 110–11, at 57–8. Recommendation 8, first sentence.

57 Bazinas, S. (2008) 'UNCITRAL' in W. Johnston (ed) *Security over Receivables: An International Handbook*. Oxford: Oxford University Press, pp. 601, 603.

58 For the significance of defining terminology in the text, *see* McDonnell, J. (1995) 'Dialogue and Definition in Commercial Law', 89 *Nw. U.L. Rev.* 623.

59 E.g. Guide, pp 32–40, and the Cape Town Convention article 1.

60 Bazinas, S. (2002) 'UNCITRAL's Contribution to the Unification of Receivables Financing Law: The United Nations Convention on the Assignment of Receivables in International Trade', *Unif. L. Rev.*, 49, 51.

61 Guide, para. 103, 100; Recommendation 3.

62 Bazinas, ibid., at 51; however, not all forms of subrogation will necessarily be by operation of law and it depends on intention; *see also generally* Mitchell, C. (2007) *Subrogation: Law and Practice*. Oxford: Oxford University Press.

63 Guide, at 6; Recommendation 3.

64 Guide, at 13.

Under the non-unitary approach, these two latter terms are governed by different rules specifically dealing with them.

The Receivables Convention applies to assignment of trade receivables arising out of agreement between the parties as opposed to those arising by operation of law. It is arguable that there is a similarity between the Receivables Convention and the Guide and UCC Article 9, where they all adopt a functional and integrated approach by making it possible to take security on all types of assets and having no distinction between outright transfers and transfers for security. The significance of this point in relation to the Receivables Convention and the Guide, to the extent the latter applies to receivables financing, is that a functional approach eliminates distinctions that unnecessarily apply to transfers by way of sale and security.[65] In most financing transactions, the parties are often unsure whether the transaction is a sale or a security. Elimination of distinction does not convert an outright sale of receivables into a security interest. Distinct treatment of transfer and security leads parties to use different methods to enjoy a more advantageous regime, which in turn obstructs transparency and predictability.[66] This increases transaction costs as well as having the danger of the sale being re-characterised as security, which means that traditional financing techniques such as factoring may disappear. Furthermore, securitisation as a financing technique is put under risk where the transfer of receivables needs to be in the form of sale, as opposed to security, in order for the special purpose vehicle to be bankruptcy remote. As the distinction between them appears to be different only in the enforcement process, it is logical and creates certainty to incorporate them under a unitary concept. The assignee and the pledgee have the identical ability to collect payment of a receivable, and this tends to lead to the applicability of similar rules to outright assignment and assignment for security purposes.[67] When these financing patterns are governed by the same rules on the creation, third-party effectiveness and priority, except the enforcement of an outright assignment that illustrates difference, there seems to be certainty in the secured transactions law. This certainty can be illustrated as the determination of the nature of an assignment (whether pure assignment or assignment for security purposes), having third-party effectiveness, and having the same priority rules govern all financing patterns that involve assignment of receivables.[68]

This point has divergent effects in English law where the assignment is distinguishable for the purposes of formal validity, perfection and priority. The fragmentation also prevents the compatibility of this concept.[69] Professor McCormack suggests that 'the English [personal property security law] is pragmatic though the

65 Chapter 1 for examples under English Law.

66 Walsh, C. 'Security Interests in Receivables' in Eidenmüller and Kieninger (eds), op. cit. (f'note 2), 321, at 323.

67 *See* e.g. Receivables Convention Article 2 and Guide, Recommendation 3.

68 Guide, para. 103, at 92.

69 *See above* Chapter 1.

overall tendency is to be facilitative and enabling'.[70] The Law Commission recommended the registration of other types of quasi-security interests such as sales of receivables.[71] The Guide has a similar philosophy and recommended the inclusion of outright sale of receivables in the scope.[72] Although outright sale of receivables does not serve security functions, the effect of inclusion of outright sale of receivables within the framework of the Guide, other instruments and reform reports, reflects the desire to gather issues of creation, third-party effectiveness and priority under a unitary system.[73] Including outright sale and transfer for security of receivables under the same rules does not distinguish these two or transform one into the other but, first, subjects them to the same rules on creation, perfection and priority (determined according to the date of filing), but distinctly in relation to enforcement.[74] Secondly, it avoids any unnecessary re-characterisation that may result in a sale being re-characterised as security and harm financing practices such as factoring and securitisation.[75]

The significance of the Guide and the Receivables Convention's approach is that both adopt the comprehensive approach to secured transactions and assignment of receivables, with the ideology that the regime will be more efficient and effective in lowering the cost of credit. The Model Law applies to all types of property[76] and 'loans which secure business credits'.[77] Under the Model Law a natural person can give security for business transactions and not for consumer transactions. The Model Law is mainly for businesses as opposed to consumers, and thus consumer transactions should not be included into the secured transactions regime and, rather, would be more appropriately incorporated into the consumer protection legislation.[78] However, the Model Law does not seem to cover other asset-based financing methods such as financial leasing and factoring.[79] Furthermore,

70 McCormack, G. (2004) *Secure Credit under English and American Law.* Cambridge: Cambridge University Press, p. 1.

71 Law Commission Report No. 296, paras 2.34–39.

72 Guide, Recommendation 3.

73 *See generally* Guide, para. 30, at 38.

74 Recommendation 167, according to which enforcement provisions will not be in general applicable to outright sale of receivables.

75 See above and Guide, para. 31, at 38–9.

76 Model Law Article 5.2.

77 Model Law Article 2, first sentence. McCormack, G. and Dahan, F. (1999) 'The EBRD Model Law on Secured Transactions: Comparisons and Convergence', *CfiLR*, 65, 67. The rationale of this limitation was that as the consumer protection regimes were underdeveloped, encompassing them through security rights at a later time would be desirable.

78 Simpson, J.L. and Röver, J-H.M. (1994) 'Model Law on Secured Transactions Completed', *Law in Transition*, at 1 (Spring) where it is argued that 'it would have been inappropriate and counterproductive to extend the scope of the model to cover other areas'; Röver, op. cit. (f'note 5), at 77.

79 However, this has been regarded as a serious limitation for lenders that lend on the basis of inventory or accounts financing where the lender may have no protection as against the lessee or the unregistered unpaid vendor or to third parties who purchased the receivables through factoring. *See* Spanogle, J.A. (1998) 'A Functional Analysis of the EBRD Model Law on Secured Transactions' in J.J. Norton and M. Andenas (eds) *Emerging Financial Markets and Secured Transactions.* Kluwer, p. 157, at 171.

the Model Law has separate rules for credit sellers (vendors) and lenders (banks), where credit sellers may have an unpaid vendors' charge or possessory charge and lenders may have a registered charge.[80] The Model Law permits the creation of a unitary security interest, which is called the *charge*. The term *charge* is not as comprehensive as UCC Article 9 or the Guide's security interest (hence exclusion of assignment of receivables and finance leases). However, it has been pointed out that the Model Law's charge is not synonymous with the charge under English law.[81] It is, however, arguable that the enterprise charge is similar to the English floating charge concept. The Model Law's approach to security rights is similar to the Guide's, in that a specific security interest can be created 'that can work [together] with other security devices and re-characterizes retention of title as a security right'.[82] However, the Model Law adopts a formal approach and distinguishes a number of charges.[83] The Model Law does not re-characterise retention of title as a security interest even though it creates a specific security interest to work parallel to other security devices.[84]

The Factoring Convention substantively applies to international factoring of international receivables arising out of sales contracts.[85] The fact that the Factoring Convention applies only to international receivables arising from international sales contracts limits its applicability severely. It does not have a comprehensive scope. The rationale for limiting the applicability to international factoring contracts was an attempt to unify international factoring, and it was thought that a limitation as such would attract States to accept the uniform rules on international factoring. Otherwise, States which have well-established domestic rules, that are applicable not only to factoring transactions but also to other commercial transactions, could have been reluctant to accept changes in their domestic laws. Thus domestic laws are not affected; however, the Convention is thought to be an initial model for nations to develop their laws in this area.[86]

The Receivables Convention does not explain the nature of transfer as to whether it is an outright, or a security assignment, transfer. This matter has been left to law applicable outside the Convention.[87] This may be a cause for concern

80 Registered Charge Article 8, Article 9 Unpaid Vendor's Charge, and Article 10 Possessory Charge.

81 Röver, op. cit. (f'note 5), at 76.

82 Guide, para. 103, at 56; *see also* Model Law, at vii, where the Model Law is based around a single security right in respect of all types of things and rights. The Model Law has 'single security right' and 'flexible definition of secured debt and charged property'.

83 Röver, op. cit. (f'note 5), at 72, stating that the Model Law adopts a formal approach.

84 *But* cf. Guide, para. 103, at 56.

85 The Factoring Convention Article 2(1). However, if internationality requirements are met, the Factoring Convention may be applicable to domestic factoring of international receivables.

86 Alexander, M.R. (1989) 'Towards Unification and Predictability: The International Factoring Convention', 27 *Colum. J. Transnt'l L.*, 353, 366; UNIDROIT Study LVIII-Doc.25, at 5–6 (1986); Mestre, F. (1987) 'Explanatory Report on the draft Convention on International Factoring', *Unif. L. Rev.*, 85, 93, para. 10.

87 *Explanatory Note of the UNCITRAL Secretariat on the United Nations Convention on the Assignment of Receivables in International Trade* ('Explanatory Note'). New York: United Nations Publication (2004), 29.

from a harmonisation perspective, as an assignment by way of sale and by way of security are distinct and not all jurisdictions treat them in a unitary manner. Nevertheless, this point may be compensated through the provisions of the Guide and the Model Law. First, the Guide and the Model Law may, in general, complement the Receivables Convention. The Guide and the Model Law are intended for the modernisation of domestic laws; especially because the Guide reflects the principles of both the Model Law and the Receivables Convention,[88] the reference to the domestic law provides harmony. Second, both the Guide and the Model Law provide for single security right over the collateral.[89] Therefore, there will not be any fragmentation in the secured transactions regime. and the domestic law will treat assignments parallel to the Receivables Convention's treatment. Third, the Guide applies to outright transfers of receivables and describes what an outright transfer of receivables is, and treats it under the assignment and security right.[90] The inclusion of outright transfers in the scope of the Guide comes with significant changes in the way that the secured transactions law is understood in many jurisdictions. Even though outright transfers are not considered security interests, their inclusion within the frame of secured transactions presents the problem of enforcement. As receivables are intangibles, therefore different from movable tangible assets, by their nature it is not possible for the creditor to seize and, consequently, to sell or to retain possession for the satisfaction of claim. The outright sale of receivables[91] is included in the functional approach, not because this type of financing technique secures the payment of an obligation but because it is often difficult to distinguish whether a transaction is an assignment by way of sale or security.[92] The Guide recommends the abolition of all types of rights serving security purposes, and the inclusion of them in a unitary notion of security right, with the exception of acquisition financing devices.[93]

The Cape Town Convention applies to the creation of international interest on certain categories of high-value mobile equipment and associated rights.[94] The

88 For instance, Articles 8–10 and 17–23 of the Receivables Convention are reflected in the Guide. The Guide builds on the work of the Model Law. *See* Guide, para.12, at 3.

89 Guide, paras 111–12, at 58, and the Model Law, Article 1.

90 Guide, paras 25–31, at 37–8. Under recommendation 1 the definition of 'assignment' and 'security right' clearly refer to outright transfer of receivables, and even though outright transfer of receivables does not secure the payment of an obligation for convenience the term assignment also covers it. The same equally applies to the definition of security rights, and an outright transfer of receivables is included in the definition of security right. Recommendation 3.

91 Recommendation 3.

92 Bridge *et al.*, op. cit. (fnote 21), at 581–2, n. 46, discussing the difficulties in distinguishing transactions. The Guide takes the view that outright assignment of receivables is included in the scope of applicability (thus rules on creation, third party effectiveness and priority shall apply regardless) on the grounds that it is difficult to determine assignments by way of sale and security, and that the practical mechanisms at both the collection and enforcement of an outright assignment and a security interest are identical. *See* Guide, para. 25, at 37.

93 Guide, para. 110–11, at 58 Recommendation 8, second sentence; Recommendations 8 and 9. For more information, *see* Chapter 7.

94 Cape Town Convention Article 2(1).

Cape Town Convention's scope of applicability is defined by the type of property (aircraft, space objects and railway rolling stocks) that is the subject matter of those transactions that are covered (*e.g.* security interests, leasing and retention-of-title transactions). Under Article 1(a), the term 'assignment' has a similar definition to the Receivables Convention where it refers to a contract which, whether by way of security or otherwise, confers on the assignee associated rights with or without a transfer of the related international interest. The interest as used under the Convention is on specific equipment rather than a class of equipment. The Cape Town Convention does not apply to outright sales, as these do not have a concept of debtor or a proprietary interest involving debtors. However, the Aircraft Protocol Article III extends the registration and priority provisions to apply to outright sales of aircraft. It is possible under the Cape Town Convention to register the sale or prospective sale as the Convention applies to them with the exception of default remedies.[95]

The term *receivable* under the Receivables Convention covers a broad array of receivables and practices. These include trade receivables from sale and supply of goods, loan receivables, consumer receivables and sovereign receivables. Financing techniques such as asset-based financing, securitisation, factoring and project financing are also covered.[96] Receivables arising out of the rights of parties under a negotiable instrument, consumer protection, or real estate law such as rents fall within the scope.[97] Asset-based financing, including purchase-money financing, falls within the frame of the Receivables Convention. However, under Article 4(3)–(5), the Receivables Convention cannot affect the rights of certain parties to the assignment of such receivables. Disputes between the assignee and a person with a right over the property related to receivables arising out of immovable property will be referred to the law of the state where the immovable property is located.[98] Under Article 4(1) and (2), certain types of receivables and assignments are excluded.[99] These include, due to lack of a market, assignments made to an individual for his or her personal, family or household purposes, as these fall within the

95 Goode, op. cit. (f'note 9), 86. Aircraft Protocol Article III and Cape Town Convention Article 41.

96 *See* Bazinas, op. cit. (f'note 58), 51. Explanatory Note, op. cit. (f'note 85), para. 10, 30.

97 *But cf.* The Law Commission Report No. 296, which seems to define receivables in a narrower fashion where only monetary obligations (whether or not they have been earned by performance arising from goods or services supplied, energy services supplied or brokerage fees) are included. Para. 4.29.

98 Bazinas, S. (2002) 'Multi-Jurisdictional Receivables Financing: UNCITRAL's Impact on Securitization and Cross-Border Perfection', 12 *Duke J. Comp. & Int'l L.*, 365, n.14; *but cf.* Sigman, H. and Smith, E. (2002) 'Toward Facilitating Cross Border Secured Financing and Securitization: An Analysis of the United Nations Convention on the Assignment of Receivables in International Trade', 57 *Bus. Law.*, 727, 735–6. However, immovable property is excluded from the Guide due to requirements of special title registration indexed by asset not by grantor; nevertheless receivables representing proceeds of immovable property are covered as well as security rights in the attachment. Guide, para. 40, 50; Recommendations 21 and 43.

99 There are limitations to the scope of the provision on anti-assignment agreements between the assignor and the debtor as described under Article 9(3), where the article that gives effectiveness to assignments made notwithstanding an anti-assignment clause applies only to assignments of receivables arising under certain contracts. *See* the Receivables Convention Article 9.

framework of an assignment to a consumer.[100] Assignment of certain types of receivables, such as financial receivables, receivables arising under securities,[101] swap transactions and letters of credit are excluded. These receivables have already been sufficiently regulated, hence their exclusion.[102] The Receivables Convention applies to the assignment of receivables from negotiable instruments, but Article 4(3) stipulates that the applicability of the Convention does not affect the rights and obligations of any person under the law governing negotiable instruments. If the transfer of security rights in sale, loan or the holding of, or agreement to, repurchase securities or other financial assets or instruments held with an intermediary, which are listed in Article 4(2)(e), are not negotiable instruments, then they will not be subject to the Convention; rather, they will be, by virtue of Article 4(3), subject to applicable national law. Bazinas notes 'priority issues with respect to securities related receivables will be subject to the law applicable under law outside the Convention'.[103] The priority rule under the Receivables Convention is the law of the assignor's State (Article 22), but in the case of assignment of receivables in negotiable instruments this is not feasible, and the more convenient method to determine priority is to apply the law of the instrument's location as opposed to the location of the holder in due course.

In comparison to the broad array of coverage of the Receivables Convention, the same term under the Factoring Convention only refers to receivables arising out of sales contracts.[104] Under the Guide, the term *receivables* excludes a right to payment under negotiable instrument, an obligation to pay under an independent undertaking, and an obligation of a bank to pay funds credited to a bank account; thus it does not apply to pure outright transfer of these, but applies if the transfer is for security proposes.[105] The rationale of excluding outright sale of negotiable instruments, rights to receive proceeds under an independent undertaking, and

100 Assignment of consumer receivables is covered by the Convention. *See* Explanatory Note, op. cit. (f'note 85), para. 11, 30.

101 Especially, the Convention excludes, by virtue of Article 4(2)(e), transactions involving the assignment of receivables from securities or other financial assets or instruments held with an intermediary. For more information, *see* A/56/17.

102 Bazinas, op. cit. (f'note 96), 367; for the practices not covered by the UNCITRAL Convention, *see also* Bazinas, S. (2001) 'Lowering the Cost of Credit: The Promise in the Future UNCITRAL Convention on Assignment of Receivables in International Trade', 9 *Tul. J. Int'l & Comp. L.*, 259, 268.

103 Bazinas, op. cit. (f'note 96), n.13; Bazinas, op. cit. (f'note 58), 52. *See* Chapter 8.

104 *See generally* Goode, R. (1988) 'Conclusions of the Leasing and Factoring Conventions–II', *J.B.L.*, 510; Ferrari, F. (1997) 'The International Sphere of Application of the 1988 Ottawa Convention on International Factoring', 31 *Int'l Law.*, 41; Ferrari, F. (1999) 'The International Sphere of Application of the 1988 Ottawa Convention on International Factoring', *IBLJ*, 895; Reisman, A. (1988) 'The International Factoring Convention', 44 *The Secured Lender*, 26; Goode, R. (1984) 'Uniform Law on International Factoring' in *Unification and Comparative Law in Theory and Practice: Contributions in Honour of Jean Georges Sauveplanne.* Deventer: Kluwer, p. 91; Alexander, M.R. (1989) 'Towards Unification and Predictability: The International Factoring Convention', 27 *Colum. J. Transnt'l L.*, 353.

105 Guide, para. 26, 37.

rights to payment of funds credited to a bank account from the scope is to establish harmony in priority issues as these require different priority rules. Under the Guide, a security and outright transfer of receivables will be registered and the priority will be determined in accordance with the date of registration. If the same priority rules apply, in a priority competition between an outright transfer of receivables and a right to payment under negotiable instrument or right to proceeds or funds credited to a bank account, outright transfer will not have better priority as against the others, because the priority for negotiable instruments will be obtained through possession and in the others through control.[106] Thus the Guide has separate rules for these[107] and does not include them under the outright sale of receivables stipulated under recommendation 3. However, the Guide suggests that outright transfer of negotiable instruments may be included as security right in the secured transactions regime, thus general priority rules apply by giving effectiveness against third parties upon the transfer.[108] The Guide excludes[109] its applicability to aircraft, railway rolling stock and space objects as they fall squarely within the scope of the Cape Town Convention, and any further and distinct regulation would overlap with already well-established rules laid down by the latter.[110] Furthermore, intellectual property,[111] securities,[112] payment rights arising under financial contracts governed by netting agreements, and payment rights arising under foreign exchange transactions are excluded.

3.2.2 Territorial dimension

Territorial applicability refers to a convention's application to international or domestic transactions, hence the importance of determination of internationality. The Receivables Convention applies to international assignment of domestic receivables (international assignment connection) and to domestic assignment of international receivables (international receivable connection) – provided that the assignor is located in a Contracting State at the time of the assignment contract and, exceptionally, to the domestic assignment of domestic receivables.[113] In this context, it applies when there is an international assignment or an international

106 Guide, para. 27, 37.

107 Recommendations 101, 103 and 107. *See* Chapter 7.

108 Guide, para. 29, 38. These priority rules are set out in recommendations 101 and 102; *see also* Chapter 6.

109 Recommendation 4 details the excluded practices and assets from the scope.

110 *See below* ***3.3 The relationship between instruments.***

111 A/CN.9/WG.VI/WP. 42 and A/CN.9/689.

112 There are separate studies under way by UNIDROIT on a Convention on Substantive Rules Regarding Intermediated Securities and the Hague Conference on Private International Law, Convention on the Law Applicable to Certain Rights in Respect of Securities Held with Intermediary.

113 Receivables Convention Article 1(1)(a) and (b), respectively.

receivable.[114] The connecting factor is the time and location of the assignor. Internationality[115] under the Receivables Convention is expanded by fixing internationality on both the assignment and the receivable,[116] and based on two different approaches designated under Article 3. First, the Convention applies to assignments that are international (an *international assignment* is an assignment where the assignor and the assignee are located in different States, as it relates to the contract of assignment) at the time of the conclusion of the assignment contract and, second, to receivables that are international (an *international receivable* is a receivable where the assignor and the debtor are located in different States, as it relates to the original contract) at the time of the original contract. The international criterion is met when receivables are assigned internationally or the assignment relates to international receivables. It does not, in principle, apply to domestic assignment of domestic receivables. However, there are two exceptions[117] according to which, first, in a chain of assignments, if the Convention has applied previously, then it will continue to apply to domestic assignment of domestic receivables.[118] Second, with an effort to establish a uniform priority regime, the Convention covers all priority issues by being applicable to the conflicts between the domestic and foreign assignee of domestic receivable.[119] In the latter exception, the application of the law of the assignor's State to priority provision is achieved.

The Factoring Convention, on the other hand, determines internationality pursuant to the parties to the contract of sale having their places of business in

114 However, some authors misinterpret the applicability of the UN Convention and argue that it only applies to international assignments. *See* e.g. Steffens, L. (2006) 'The New Rule on the Assignment of Rights in Rome I – The Solution to All our Proprietary Problems? – Determination of the Conflict of Laws Rule in Respect of the Proprietary Aspects of Assignment', 4 *E.R.P.L.*, 543, 545 stating that '. . . the UNCITRAL Convention only applies to international assignment as defined therein . . .'. Other authors also misinterpret the Receivables Convention's priority rule, which is also clearly related to its applicability, stating that it 'has a serious flaw'. One cannot agree with this argument either. For more discussion, *see below* and Chapter 8. Flessner, A. and Verhagen, H. (2006) *Assignment in European Private International Law*. Munich: Sellier, p. 61; Verhagen, H. (2006) 'Assignment in the Commission's "Rome-I proposal"', *L.M.C.L.Q.*, 270.

115 For earlier views on the inclusion of international assignments of domestic receivables, *see* Bazinas, S. (1998) 'An International Legal Regime for Receivables Financing: UNCITRAL's Contribution', 8 *Duke J. Comp. & Int'l L.*, 315, 323 *et seq.*

116 Bazinas, ibid., 324 where the rationale is explained as follows:

> [t]he [rationale] . . . is to cover not only international factoring and discounting transactions (which normally involve international trade receivables assigned in bulk) but also [securitisation] transactions, which may involve a high volume of small amount domestic consumer receivables (a practice of growing importance that is believed to have the potential of giving consumers increased access to lower cost credit) and refinancing transactions which may involve individual large amount receivables.

117 Articles 1(1)(b); 5(m)(i) and 22.

118 A/CN.9/489, para. 38 and paras 19–20. ('[I]f a receivable is domestic, its assignment may come within the ambit of the . . . Convention; if it is international or it is part of a chain of assignments that includes an earlier international assignment.').

119 Explanatory Note, op. cit. (f'note 85), para. 15.

different States, which subjects the applicability to the internationality of receivables. The time for the determination of internationality is the time of the conclusion of the sales contract.[120] The Factoring Convention thus applies to international factoring of international receivables as the internationality, exclusively, depends upon the receivables rather than the factoring contract.[121] That said, the Factoring Convention may still be applicable to domestic factoring of international receivables. If the receivable is international (the applicability requirement) and either the States of the debtor, the assignee and the assignor are Contracting States, or the sales contract and the factoring contract are governed by the law of a Contracting State,[122] then the receivable is assignable between the parties to the factoring contract whose places of business are in the same State, and the Convention will apply to the said factoring contract.[123]

One of the critical aspects of the Receivables Convention is its regulation of *location*[124] that is defined in Article 5(h),[125] and affects both the applicability and priority issues (Article 22). 'Location' is the place of business of a person (the central administration) or, if there is no place of business, the habitual residence of a person. The Convention does not make any distinctions between natural and legal persons, and applying the test as the assignor's central administration thus avoids any complexity.[126] The place of the assignor's business (the centre of administration), from the assignee's perspective, is a predictable connection because it can be discovered by checking the company's documents or the other public documents.[127] In the case of multiple places of business, the Receivables Convention's approach differs from the traditional location rule by referring to the place of central administration when an

120 Mestre, op. cit. (f'note 84), 105, para. 21.

121 Philbrick, W.C. (1994) 'The Use of Factoring in International Commercial Transactions and the Need for the Legal Uniformity as Applied to Factoring Transactions between the United States and Japan', 99 *Com. L.J.*, 141, 155.

122 Article 2(1)(a) and (b). In order to expand the applicability, same Contracting State's law or different Contracting States' laws may be applicable to the sales and the factoring contract. *See* Mestre, op. cit. (f'note 84), 109, para. 22. These two prongs have been identified by Professor Ferrari as the 'direct' and 'indirect' applicability. *See* Ferrari, op. cit. (f'note 102), 52. The indirect applicability also allows the Factoring Convention to be applicable through private international law rules pursuant to Article 2(1)(b). *See* UNIDROIT Study LVIII-Doc. 33, para. 22.

123 Ferrari, F. (2001) 'How to Create One Uniform Contract Law', 5 *VJ*, 3, 11; *but cf.* Reisman, A. (1990) 'The Uniform Commercial Code and the Convention on International Factoring', 22 *UCC.L.J.*, 320, 323.

124 Although the Receivables Convention does not expressly define what needs to be understood by the 'location of the assignor's state', this can clearly be deduced from the second sentence of Article 5(h) which is the *central administration* of the assignor. For more discussion of *location*, *see* Chapter 8.

125 However, some authors argue that the term 'location' or the 'location of the assignor' have not been defined in the Convention. *See* e.g. Steffens, op. cit. (f'note 112), 546.

126 *See also* Kieninger, E.M. and Sigman, H. (2006) 'The Rome-I Proposed Regulation and the Assignment of Receivables', *The European Legal Forum*, Part 1, 3. *But cf.* UCC§ 9–307(b) where there are two types of rules, *see* ibid.

127 Walsh, C. (2001) 'Receivables Financing and the Conflict of Laws: The UNCITRAL Draft Convention on the Assignment of Receivables in International Trade', 106 *Dick. L. Rev.*, 159, 175 *et seq.*

assignee or the assignor has places of business in more than one State, whereas the traditional rule refers to the law of the place which has the closest relationship to the relevant transaction.[128] However, in a cross-border transaction with multiple parties, and where disputes may involve the insolvency of the assignor who may attempt to evade proceedings by establishing itself in more insolvency sympathetic jurisdictions to the detriment of creditors,[129] it is often difficult to ascertain the law of the place with closest relationship; thus the Receivables Convention's approach is a feasible one which intersects the law applicable to priorities and the law of the place of insolvency.[130] If the debtor has multiple places of business in more than one State, the location refers to the place most closely connected to the original contract.[131] The rationale is 'to ensure that the debtor is not surprised by the application of legal rules to which the original contract between the debtor and the assignor has no apparent relationship'.[132] The Receivables Convention applies to contracts made through branch offices if the assignor's central administration is located in a Contracting State. This prevents the application of the law of the State where the branch is located. Put simply, the Receivables Convention may still be applicable even if the assignment is made between the assignee's branch and the assignor's central administration located in the same State.[133] This may be an appropriate starting point for a harmonised application as the law of the assignor's State (where the central administration is located, that is the place of business of the assignor as defined under Article 5(h)) will be applicable to priority disputes.[134]

Location is also linked to the internationality requirement as the main applicability connection. For the Convention to apply, the assignor must be located in a Contracting State at the time of the conclusion of the assignment contract (Article 1(1)(a)) and the debtor must be located in a Contracting State at the time of the conclusion of the original contract (Article 1(3)). The reference to the time of the conclusion of the assignment contract is critical because the law of the assignor's State applies to the formal validity and priority issues, and clarity for the assignee as to which State's law is applicable to these issues is, thus, maintained. This is a predictable connection point and the applicability does not rest on the private international law rules that could have created uncertainty, as the applicability of

128 Explanatory Note, op. cit. (f'note 85), para. 19. The Note suggests that the place of central administration can also be understood ('in other terms, the principal place of business or the main centre of interests'). There seems to be similarity with the UCC in the case of the assignor having multiple places of business if the assignor is an organisation as opposed to an individual. UCC§ 9–307(b)(3) exceptions for 'registered organisations' (1) under UCC§ 9–102(a)(70) and 9–307(e) and (2) under 9–307(c).

129 Walsh, op. cit. (f'note 125), 176.

130 For more discussion of choice-of-law matters *see* Chapter 8.

131 Article 36 allows federal states to make a declaration to apply their own location rules for inter-state disputes.

132 Explanatory Note, op. cit. (f'note 85), para. 19. This rule also reflects the debtor protection principle.

133 Explanatory Note, op. cit. (f'note 85), para. 20. For further discussion on the rule related to the location of banks and their branch offices *see* Chapter 8 .

134 Article 22. *See* Kieninger and Sigman, op. cit. (f'note 124), 4.

the Convention is already broad.[135] The reference to the time of the conclusion of the original contract is critical for the debtor, as this is the time when the debtor becomes a part of the tripartite legal relationship. At the time the original contract is concluded, the debtor will be certain with regard to the law applicable to his legal position. A reference to the time of assignment would not be compatible because the debtor is not a party to the assignment.[136] The international character of an assignment is determined by the location of the assignee and the assignor when they are located in different States at the time of the conclusion of the contract of assignment, and the international character of a receivable is determined by the location of the assignor and the debtor when they are located in different States at the time of the conclusion of the original contract. In relation to Article 1(3), debtor related provisions under Chapter IV section II of the Convention will apply if either the debtor is located in a Contracting State or the law governing the original contract from which the receivables arise is the law of a Contracting State;[137] thus the applicability to a debtor who is not located in a Contracting State is achieved by the latter option. The debtor is protected by both the debtor provisions and the notification requirements of the Convention,[138] and thus needs not be located in a Contracting State that is also valid with regard to the applicability of priority provisions. This is because priority and debtor protection have separate applicability rules,[139] and thus the debtor is protected from being subject to a previously unknown text; but this protection does not hinder the applicability of provisions governing the relationship between the assignee and the assignor. The Convention thus becomes applicable to the relationship between the assignor and the assignee (assignment contract) or the assignee and a competing claimant (priority matters), even if the debtor-related provisions do not apply to the assignment.[140]

There is a distinction between Article 1(3), where territorial scope is an issue, and Article 1(4), where territorial scope is not an issue, in the sense that for the application of Chapter V there is no need for an assignment to be connected to the assignor or the debtor's State.[141] The forum has to be in a Contracting State as Chapter V contains conflict of laws rules and it applies as the conflict of laws rules of the forum. There is no need for any party to be located in a Contracting State. Fulfilling internationality is sufficient. In that sense, Article 1(4) requires internationality as defined in Article 3 to ensure certainty. Location of parties is not an

135 Bazinas, op. cit. (f'note 58), 50; *But cf.* the applicability of the Factoring Convention which is indirectly based on private international law rules (Article 2(1)(b)).

136 Explanatory Note, op. cit. (f'note 85), para. 14, where it was stated that 'a subsequent change does not affect the application of the Convention'.

137 Explanatory Note, op. cit. (f'note 85), para. 17.

138 Receivables Convention Articles 15–21.

139 Priority is governed by the law of the assignor's State and, for the Convention to apply, the assignor needs to be located in a contracting State; whereas for the debtor protection provisions to apply, the debtor need not be located in a contracting State.

140 Explanatory Note, op. cit. (f'note 85), 32, para. 17.

141 Explanatory Note, op. cit. (f'note 85), para. 54, where it is stated that 'The Convention contains a set of conflict of laws rules that may apply independently of any territorial link with a State party to the Convention'.

issue for the application of Chapter V,[142] as internationality is sufficient for the application of conflict-of-laws rules. The application of the Convention may be extended so as to apply its conflict-of-laws rules.[143] Conflict-of-laws provisions contained under Chapter V may be applicable when internationality is met but, due to the assignor being located in a non-contracting State, the Convention may not be directly applicable. Chapter V enables the application of the Convention even if the assignor or the debtor (when a dispute involves debtor's rights and obligations) is located in a non-Contracting State, or the law governing the receivable is not the law of a Contracting State.[144] The reference of Article 1(4) to Chapter V (and naturally to Article 30),[145] enables priority provisions to be applicable to a debtor located in a non-Contracting State. Also, as the priority provisions do not affect the debtor, the provisions of the Convention dealing with priorities should be applicable to a debtor who is not located in a State party to the Convention.

The Cape Town Convention's applicability, according to Article 3, is subject to the location of the debtor[146] in a Contracting State at the time of the agreement creating or providing for the international interest.[147] Under Article 3(2) the location of the creditor is irrelevant so far as the applicability of the Convention is concerned. The fact that the debtor's location is fixed as the connecting fact creates predictability, because the debtor in the sense that is understood under the Cape Town Convention is similar to the assignor in the Receivables Convention (*i.e.* there is one debtor or assignor in those transactions whose location can be established easily). However, the significance of the debtor's location is critical, and Article 4 details the possible locations of the debtor in order to expand the scope of application of the Convention. It can be argued that this approach has significant advantages (in terms of reduction of debate as to which definition of location is better) over the Receivables Convention's definition of location.[148] According to Article 4, a debtor shall be deemed to have been situated in any Contracting State under the law of which it is incorporated or formed; where it has registered office or statutory seat; where it has its centre of administration; or where it has its place of business. The place of business in case of multiple places of business will be the principal place of business, if none it is the habitual

142 Chapter V of the Receivables Convention also has the gap-filling character.

143 A/CN.9/466, 39, para. 146 (where it was stated 'from a legislative point of view, it would not be appropriate to attempt, in essence, to prepare a mini private international law convention within a substantive law convention'); *see* Walsh, op. cit. (f'note 125), 165 *et seq.*

144 Explanatory Note, op. cit. (f'note 85), para. 54. Article 26.

145 Article 30 deals with the law applicable to priority as part of the autonomous conflict-of-laws chapter. However, one should note that Chapter V may be opted out.

146 Cape Town Convention Article 1(j).

147 *Cf.* the difference of applicability between the Cape Town (Article 3) and the Receivables Conventions (Article 3).

148 Article 5(h) place of business of a person or the person's habitual residence; for a detailed discussion of the location under the Receivables Convention, *see* Kieninger and Sigman, op. cit. (f'note 124); for some reservations about *central administration* in relation to SMEs, *see* A/CN.9/472/Add.2, Comments by Factors Chain International, at 9.

residence. The multiplicity of choice in determining the location of the debtor certainly enlarges the scope of the Convention, and makes it more acceptable by reducing the debate on what may constitute the location. The location of the debtor is deemed to be in a Contracting State for the purposes of its applicability in the case of States with territorial units if the debtor is located (as defined under Article 4) in a territorial unit where the Convention applies or if the debtor has a registered office.[149] The applicability of the Convention is extended to those companies who are established under federal law, and the Convention applies to those companies as an extension of the law of the contracting state. In case of doubt as to whether the territorial unit's law is applicable, the State law or the law that is closely connected to the transaction applies.[150] At the time of the conclusion of the agreement that creates an international interest if the debtor is not located in a contracting state, a subsequent move to a contracting state does not trigger the applicability of the Convention.[151] Whereas, if the debtor moves to a non-contracting state after registration of an international interest, the applicability of the Convention continues and is not affected by this move which is particularly important for achieving harmonisation in establishing priority under Article 29(1).[152] This approach is particularly critical because the location of the debtor being in a contracting state is a trigger to the applicability of the Convention and an element in the determination of priority. The applicability of the Convention continues even if the debtor grants security over the same asset and registers in a non-contracting state registry. In this case, the first creditor has the right to have priority through the application of the Convention. Certain concerns were raised in relation to the applicability of the Convention by a court located in a non-contracting state.[153] The applicability of the Convention by a court of a non-contracting state may be possible if the choice-of-law rules lead to the law of a contracting state (hence the applicability of the Convention). Although this may be a feasible solution for contractual remedies, the same argument cannot be easily made for international interests. International interests are over certain equipment and need registration, but if the equipment moves from one state to another the applicable law cannot be immediately established.[154] The inadequacy of the *lex situs* rules has been clearly set out,[155] the particular aim of which is to identify rules applicable to validity and priority issues provided the equipment does not cross borders. It is evident that space objects, aircraft and railway rolling stock do not fit into that criterion and *lex situs* is not a particularly useful method to ascertain applicability. Furthermore, the Convention does not clarify mobility and internationality, which

149 Cape Town Convention Article 52(5)(a).
150 Article 5(4)
151 Article 3(1). Goode, op. cit. (f'note 9), 22.
152 For background information on internationality and priority, *see* UNIDROIT Study LXXII, Doc. 8, at 18 and some concerns indicated in Doc. 10.
153 Unidroit Study LXXII, Doc.10; *Goode*, op. cit. (f'note 9), para. 2.20.
154 Goode, op. cit. (f'note 9), para. 2.20.
155 Unidroit Study LXXII, Doc.1, 26.

enables the applicability of the Convention to domestic transactions, unless States make a declaration opting out of its application to internal transactions, where the creditor and the debtor as well as the equipment are all located in one State.[156] It is arguable that the rationale for inclusion of internal transactions is to avoid inconsistencies that a creditor may face in the event of cross-border movement and to maintain harmony in the application of priority rules.[157] The Aircraft Protocol's applicability provision (Article IV) works along Article 3(1) of the Convention by providing an alternative connecting factor. The connecting factor in that perspective, which enables the applicability of the Convention, is the registration of helicopters or airframes in the domestic aircraft register of a contracting state that is the state of registry and this registration is deemed to have been effectuated back to the time of the agreement.[158] The Convention still applies even if the debtor is located in a contracting state and the registration is made in a non-contracting state. As per aircraft objects, Article IV(2) clarifies the notion of location according to which, even if the parties to a transaction are located in the same state, an airframe is deemed to be located in the state of registry of the aircraft of which it is a part; an aircraft engine is deemed to be located in the state of registry of the aircraft on which it is installed or where it is physically located unless it is installed, and a helicopter is deemed to be located in its state of registry. Thus, Aircraft Protocol clarifies the notion of location where internal transactions are concerned.

3.3 The relationship between instruments

The Receivables Convention, the Factoring Convention, the Guide and the Cape Town Convention have close links by making references to each other. Clear referencing and mapping out the relationship in the instruments are critical, because they reduce any potential overlaps and assist practitioners. It should be noted that the Factoring, the Receivables and the Cape Town Conventions are piecemeal international instruments whereas, particularly, the Guide is a comprehensive text presenting solutions to areas established by these conventions and beyond.

156 Article 50. Goode, op. cit. (f'note 9), 275, where it is stated that this situation will likely occur in railway rolling stock.

157 Article 50(2) states that notwithstanding the possibility of declaring the non-applicability of the Convention to internal transactions, Article 29 (priority of competing interests), among other provisions, shall continue to apply to the internal transaction. Nevertheless, the applicability of Article 50 does not affect the registration and priority rules of the Convention. The relation between the national interest and the international registry in that sense is that by virtue of Articles 8(4), 16 and 9(1), a national interest can be registered in the international registry to give notice of the existence of the national interest (Article 16(1)(d)) thus protection is established as against subsequent claims.

158 Airframes can be defined as the main body of the aircraft excluding its engines. Article I(2)(e) Aircraft Protocol. Article IV(1) has no application to aircraft engines where there is no nationality registration system. Goode, op. cit. (f'note 9), para. 5.25.

The Receivables Convention, by virtue of Article 38(2), prevails over the Factoring Convention. The latter, in Article 15, acknowledges that it will not prevail over any treaty that may be entered into. However, if the Receivables Convention does not apply to the debtor (*i.e.* the debtor is not located in a State party to the Receivables Convention or the law governing the original contract is not the law of a State party to the Convention),[159] then it will not prevail over the Factoring Convention and, therefore, it will not affect the applicability of the Factoring Convention to the rights and obligations of the debtor. The Cape Town Convention makes a clear reference to the Receivables Convention in Article 45 *bis*, stating that it will prevail over the Receivables Convention as it relates to the assignment of receivables which are associated rights related to international interests in aircraft objects, railway rolling stock and space assets. As the Cape Town Convention's priority provisions relating to competing assignments of associated rights have a limited scope, Cape Town's prevalence over the Receivables Convention has limited impact.[160] The Receivables Convention in Article 38(1) confirms that it will not prevail over any international agreement that may be entered into and that governs transactions dealt with by the Receivables Convention.[161] The Receivables Convention deals with the assignment of receivables, and Cape Town with international interest and its assignments. The rationale for this coordination is that the Cape Town Convention applies to both assignments[162] of international interests and associated rights.[163] Although in the Receivables Convention there is no reference to the Guide, the latter makes a clear reference to the former, in that the Guide is built on the principles and work of the Receivables Convention. The relationship between the Receivables Convention and the Guide is crucial. The Guide reflects the principles[164] of the Convention and supplements it on matters referred by the Convention to domestic law[165] as the

159 On the coordination of the applicability of the Convention and the conflict of conventions, *see generally* Ferrari, F. (2003) 'The Relationship between International Uniform Contract Law Conventions', 22 *J.L. & Com.*, 57, 62 *et seq.*; Ferrari, F. (2000) 'The UNCITRAL Draft Convention on Assignment of Receivables Financing: Applicability, General Provisions and the Conflict of Conventions', 1 *Melbourne J. Int'l L.*, 1.

160 Goode, R. (2002) 'The Cape Town Convention on International Interests in Mobile Equipment: A Driving Force for International Asset-Based Financing', *Unif. L. Rev.*, 3, 11.

161 For a discussion as to whether Rome I Regulation should be given supremacy over the Receivables Convention under Article 38(1), *see* Krupski, J. (2007) 'Cross-Border Receivables Financing at the Crossroads of Legal Traditions, Capital Markets, Uniform Law and Modernity', *Unif. L. Rev.*, 57, 65 *et seq.*

162 An assignment may or may not transfer related international interest (Cape Town Convention Article 1(b)); however, for an assignment to be within the scope of the Convention it has to transfer the international interest (Article 32(3)).

163 Cape Town Convention Articles 32(3) and 1(c); *see* Chapter 6.

164 Such as debtor protection, removal of statutory prohibitions, and contractual limitations, on assignment and party autonomy.

165 Such as priority or formal validity issues where the law of the state of assignor applies; *See* Bazinas, S. (2006) 'Modernising and Harmonising Secured Credit Law: The Example of the UNCITRAL Draft Legislative Guide on Secured Transactions, Part 1', *B.J.I.B.F.L.*, 20.

Convention may have effects on domestic law.[166] The Guide maps out its relationship with the Cape Town Convention by limiting the application of the Guide's recommendations. Thus the Guide does not apply to aircraft, space objects and railway rolling stock as far as these are covered by a national legislation or an international agreement to which the State enacting legislation based on the Guide is a party, and the matters covered by this law are addressed in the national law or the international agreement.[167] The Guide clearly makes reference to the Model Law by being built upon and furthering the work set out in the Model Law.[168]

The Cape Town Convention does not exclude the creation of security interests in domestic law. An international interest may be considered as a security interest under the national law.[169] This means that if a country adopts the Model Law or the Guide, a security interest created in accordance with their articles or recommendations will have no adverse affect to the international interest created under the Cape Town Convention. The Guide recognises the priority of registration in the specialised registries, which are asset-based registries, to have priority over registration in the general registry.[170] Professor Goode suggests that an interest under the Cape Town Convention that may be created or provided for under a security, title-retention or leasing agreement will, at the same time, constitute an international interest – thus both the domestic security interest and an international interest will co-exist.[171] However, two critical points are made which reflect the strength of a registered international interest. A registered international interest will have priority over, first, a domestic interest which is not registered and not a right having priority without registration (in accordance with Article 39) and, second, a national interest notice of which is not so registered.[172] The Guide reflects those principles of the Cape Town Convention and, unless aircraft, railway rolling stock and the space objects are covered by national legislation or international agreements to which a State is a party, the Guide shall apply.[173]

One of the novel and innovative features of the Cape Town Convention is its relationship to its protocols.[174] Protocols control the Convention in its application and

166 It is arguable that it applies to domestic assignment of international assignments, and certain issues such as priority and formal validity issues are referred to the applicable domestic law.

167 Guide, para. 32, 48 and Recommendation 4(a). It is indicated that those terms should be understood according to their meanings in the national legislation or the international agreement, thus any overlap or conflict is avoided.

168 Guide, para. 12, at 3.

169 On this matter, *see* Cuming, in Davies (ed.), op. cit. (f'note 6), 384–5.

170 Guide, Chapters III and V.

171 Goode, R. (2001) 'The Unidroit Mobile Equipment Convention' in M. Bridge and R. Stevens *Cross Border Security and Insolvency*. Oxford: Oxford University Press, pp. 225, 234.

172 See Goode, op. cit. (f'note 158), 12–13.

173 Guide, para. 32, at 39. Recommendation 4(a).

174 For the rationale for drafting a base convention and accompanying protocols, *see* Introduction. Professor Sundahl argues that the Cape Town Protocols do not fall into one of the traditional categories of protocols of signature, amendment, optional protocols, or protocols to a framework convention. But they create a new type. Sundahl, M.J. (2006) 'The "Cape Town Approach": A New Method of Making International Law', 44 *Colum. J. Transnat'l L.*, 339, 355; Goode, R. (2001)

commencement as well as the amendment or addition of new provisions to the base Convention. The Convention, acting as a 'base' for all protocols, covers common and fundamental areas to all three industries reflected in the protocols. Details specific to equipment are covered under the Protocols.[175] Articles 6 and 49 of the Cape Town Convention establish this relationship according to which, under Article 6(1), the Convention and the Protocol shall be interpreted as a single instrument and the protocol shall prevail in case of inconsistency;[176] and, under Article 49, the Convention has effect on a particular asset (aircraft, railway rolling stock or satellite) according to the terms of the particular Protocol (Article 49(1)(b)) and once the relevant protocol and the Convention enter into force (Article 49(1)(a)). In case of conflict between the Convention and Protocols, the latter prevail (Article 6(2)). Furthermore, as each Protocol will have different levels of control over the base Convention, a Contracting State to multiple Protocols will have differing obligations. The two-instrument approach provides flexibility and uniformity for specific mobile equipment while producing highly sophisticated instruments where protocols control the Convention. The protocols could be created using fast-track procedures, including establishing a working group by UNIDROIT, circulation of drafts to Contracting States to the Cape Town Convention and, finally, accession through opt-out mechanism.[177]

3.4 Party autonomy

Party autonomy is one of the key principles of international instruments, and a fundamental principle for a modern secured transactions regime. It can simply be defined as the freedom and maximum flexibility of parties to agree on the terms that will govern their contract.[178] Within the context of secured transactions law, party autonomy refers to 'security rights [arising] from an agreement between grantors and secured creditors'.[179] Freedom of contract, according to which the parties are free to tailor their contract consistent with their commercial needs, is crucial. Provided that there are limitations to protect mandatory provisions common to national laws, the principle of party autonomy has a firm economic basis, and creates efficiency in the sense that it reduces transaction costs as the parties are more knowledgeable to assess their commercial needs.[180] It has been argued that

'The Preliminary Draft UNIDROIT Convention on International Interests in Mobile Equipment', *Unif. L. Rev.*, 265, 269–71; Stanford, M. (2002) 'From Ottawa to Cape Town: UNIDROIT's Role in the Modernisation of the Law Governing Leasing and the Taking of Security' in I. Davies (ed.) *Security Interests in Mobile Equipment*, Aldershot: Ashgate, pp. 397, 429–30.

175 UNIDROIT Study LXXIIJ-Docs 13–14.

176 Chinkin, C. and Kessedjian, C. (1999) 'The Legal Relationship between the proposed UNIDROIT Convention and its Equipment-Specific Protocols', *Unif. L. Rev.*, 323, 323–5.

177 For further information, *see* Chinkin and Kessedjian, ibid., 326–7; Cape Town Convention Article 51 Future Protocols. *See also* I. Davies, (2003) 'The New *Lex Mercatoria*: International Interests in Mobile Equipment', 52 *I.C.L.Q.*, 151, 162 *et seq.*

178 E.g. Guide Recommendation 1(i).

179 Guide, para. 114, 59.

180 *See generally* J. Basedow, (2007) 'Lex Mercatoria and the Private International Law of Contracts in Economic Perspective', *Unif. L. Rev.*, 697, 713.

restrictions in the creation and use of security rights should be limited; and parties to a security agreement should be able to define the secured debt, secured assets, their contractual obligations and the rights to transfer those assets.[181] This is necessary in an era of globalised markets. Parties to credit and security transactions have diverse goals which may not necessarily be foreseen by codified rules, because the market is dynamic; whereas codified rules are abstract and general and apply to concrete legal problems, thus often not reflecting the dynamism of markets. As the secured transactions law is in the intersection of property and contract law, the issue becomes more critical. Although under contract law parties are able to draft a contract according to their needs, under property law this is not always possible due to the strictly defined types of security rights. Property law rules generally have a mandatory character. In that context, under the international instruments the purpose of the party autonomy principle is to provide flexibility in the negotiation of security agreements rather than restricting them to a uniform set of rules. This flexibility can be achieved by the minimal use of mandatory rules to achieve transparency and predictability of rights.[182] However, while the mandatory rules need to be applied minimally in order to reflect the party autonomy principle, within the realm of secured transactions there should be certain limitations. Limitations to party autonomy in this context ensure fairness among all parties that are affected by the security agreement. In security agreements, lenders often have stronger bargaining positions, because the creditor, chargee or the assignee has the financial strength whereas the debtor, the chargor/grantor or the assignor is in need of immediate liquidity. Through party autonomy, it is considered that parties are given a wider option to structure their transactions, which in return permits the grantors to have a wider access to low-cost credit.[183] This strong bargaining position is coupled with the proprietary rights involved in credit and security transactions. The fact that security agreements involve proprietary rights may mean that the grantor, the assignor or the debtor may lose ownership in case of default or third parties may be adversely affected. Any change in the already-negotiated or settled terms must involve the consent of all parties and derogation from, or variation by agreement of, the terms or the non-mandatory provisions should bind those who are parties to that agreement and not affect the rights of third parties.[184] This particular aspect that draws the limits of the principle of party autonomy is reflected in the international instruments.

Civil Law regimes generally confine parties to specified security devices corresponding to specific assets which are well defined and detailed in the Codes and contractually, outside the codified rules, new types of devices and rights cannot be

181 Simpson, J.L. and Röver, J-H.M. (1997) 'General Principles of a Modern Secured Transactions Law', 3 *NAFTA: Law and Bus. Rev. Am.*, 73, 81.

182 Guide, para. 115, 59.

183 Guide, para. 117, 59.

184 A/CN.9/WG.VI/WP.27/Add. 1, 19.

created in return for consideration.[185] There is a restrictive approach towards non-possessory security rights.[186] *Numerus clausus* is reflected in Civil Law regimes as a principle underlying property laws and typifies the contents and types of rights that can be created. The principle is 'characteristic of post-feudal civil law systems',[187] and was developed after the French Revolution during the drafting of the French Civil Code in order to confine security devices to a certain number of types.[188] Thus, under Civil Law regimes, contractual freedom on proprietary rights is fairly restricted.[189] On the other hand, under Common Law 'the only restriction on parties' freedom to choose their own law was that the choice had to be bona fide and legal'.[190] It is possible to create security devices and rights contractually without being confined to defined types, and parties are given the freedom to tailor their transactions provided that derogations or variations do not affect third party rights. Under UCC Article 1–102(3), variation by agreement is also generally permitted except as otherwise provided in the UCC, and except that the obligations of good faith, diligence, reasonableness and care may not be disclaimed by agreement. However, parties may by agreement determine the standards as long as these determined standards are not 'manifestly unreasonable'.[191] The UCC clearly supports the modernisation of law and continuation of commercial practices through

185 Dolan, J.F. and Vegter, J.B. (1996) 'A Voluntary Filing System for Secured Financing Transactions in the European Union', 6 *E.R.P.L.*, 195, 206; van Erp, S. (2003) 'A Numerus Quasi-Clausus of Property Rights as a Constitutive Element of a Future European Property Law?', 7 *E.J.C.L.* www.ejcl.org/72/art72-2.html (last accessed 30 June 2010); DiLuigi, M.C. (2008) 'Divergences of Security and Property Law in the European Union: The Need for Action', *J.B.L.*, 526, 530 *et seq.*

186 Garro, A. (1990) 'The Reform and Harmonisation of Personal Property Security Law in Latin America', 59 *Revista Juridica Universidad de Puerto Rico*, 1, 31 *et seq.*

187 Van Erp, op. cit. (f'note 183).

188 Mattei, U. (2000) *Basic Principles of Property Law: A Comparative Legal and Economic Introduction.* Westport, CA: Greenwood, p. 14. Commentators argue, however, that common law systems have recently started to be aware of the *numerus clausus* principle. For the common law reflections of the *numerus clausus* principle, *see* e.g., Hansmann, H.B. and Kraakman, R. (2002) 'Property, Contract and Verification: The *Numerus Clausus* Problem and the Divisibility of Rights', 31 *J. Legal Studies*, 373; Gordley, J. (2000) 'The Common Law in the Twentieth Century: Some Unfinished Business', 88 *Cal. L. Rev.*, 1817; Merrill, T. and Smith, H. (2000) 'Optimal Standardization in the Law of Property: The *Numerus Clausus* Principle', 110 *Yale L. J.*, 1.

189 Professor Bridge argues that '. . . there is consensus that old, artificial restrictions on the grant of security in legal systems will not be retained and that a creditor in principle be free to bargain for as much security as it wants'. Bridge, op. cit. (2000) (f'note 6), 181 and n.1. One can agree with the general philosophy of this statement which is illustrated through (a) *numerus clausus* and (b) the expropriation in part of floating charge holders in favour of preferential creditors and unsecured creditors by the setting aside of a certain percentage for unsecured creditors [s 252 Enterprise Act 2002 and s. 176A Insolvency Act 1986] under the Enterprise Act 2002.

190 Goode, R. (2004) *Commercial Law*, 3rd edn. London: Butterworths, 1099; *see also* Bridge, M. (2001) 'English Conflict Rules for Transfers of Movables: A Contract-Based Approach?' in M. Bridge and R. Stevens (eds) *Cross-Border Security and Insolvency*. Oxford: Oxford University Press, p. 123, 123.

191 The term 'manifestly unreasonable' is also used in the Aircraft Protocol Article IX(3), possibly illustrating UCC Article 9 influence, in relation to modification of default remedies provisions referring to the 'reasonableness of a contractual provision as to the mode of exercise of a remedy', as well as encouragement of reliance on contractual wording. *See also* Goode, op. cit. (f'note 9), at 320.

agreement of parties.[192] Most of the UCC's provisions are not mandatory and their effect may be varied. Professors White and Summers succinctly explain this as '[m]ost commercial law is therefore not in the Code at all but in private agreements'.[193] Similar ideas in relation to the innovativeness of, for instance, English Law and the significance of party autonomy in commercial dealings as being one of the key principles of commercial law was put forward by Professor Goode.[194] However, party autonomy does not exist in proprietary matters where *lex situs* is the governing law. Professor Bridge indicates that '[t]he absence of autonomy in property matters inhibits transactions in that it limits the prospects of avoiding legal risk'.[195]

The Receivables Convention, the Guide, the Cape Town Convention, the Factoring Convention and the Model Law reflect the principle of party autonomy, and expand the collateralisation of assets as a means to promote secured credit, albeit with some limitations, in order to balance the interests of all parties. This, in a way, enables the expansive use of non-possessory security interests which have been made too difficult to be used by secured transactions regimes due to the lack of modern features of a secured transactions regime. It has been suggested that, through party autonomy, parties to a security agreement will achieve more advantageous results and avoid transaction costs in creating security interests than they can by way of enumerated principles.[196] Both the Guide and the Model Law may achieve this expansion of collateralisation of assets through their party autonomy principles.

Party autonomy is a key principle of the Factoring Convention. Article 3 allows derogation from the entire Convention and not from individual provisions. In the early stages of the drafting, although a proposal was made with regard to the mandatory application of the whole Convention,[197] this was rejected and the majority view was that the principle of party autonomy should be beneficial for the success of the Convention as 'many States would . . . [only] be prepared to accept an instrument from whose provisions the parties could derogate'.[198] The Convention allows both the parties to the factoring contract (Article 3(1)(a)) and the underlying contract (Article 3(1)(b)) to be able to derogate from the entire Convention. Exclusion of the Convention as a whole contradicts with the debtor protection and the general aim of predictability and facilitation of credit. First, once the assignor and the assignee derogate from the entire Convention, the debtor as well as the

192 UCC Article 1–102(2)(b).

193 J.J. White and R.S. Summers (2000) *Uniform Commercial Code*, 5th edn. St. Paul, MI: West, p. 8.

194 R. Goode (1988) 'The Codification of Commercial Law', 14 *Mon. L.R.*, 135, 147 *et seq.*

195 Bridge, op. cit. (f'note 188), at 123 (citing *Vita Foods Products Inc v Unus Shipping Co Ltd* [1939] AC 277).

196 Jackson, T. and Kronman, A. (1979) 'Secured Financing and Priorities Among Creditors', 88 *Yale L.J.*, 1143, 1157.

197 Mestre, op. cit. (f'note 84), 111. The rationale of this proposal was that the factoring industry would not be keen on excluding the application of the Convention that was prepared to facilitate international factoring, and exclusion would undermine this objective by granting freedom to the parties to the original contract to choose a different law outside the Convention. UNIDROIT Study LVIII-Doc.33, para. 24.

198 UNIDROIT Study LVIII-Doc.33, para. 24.

third parties will be left with the unknown, manipulated applicable law (most probably the assignee's law) chosen by the assignor and the assignee, and imposed by the assignee as the stronger party in the bargain. Second, if the underlying parties exclude the Convention, even though a notification will be made to the assignee, the assignee will have to make enquiries about the new set of rules that will apply to the contract. This has the risk of increasing the cost of credit. By allowing the parties to the underlying contract to derogate from the entire Convention, the legitimate interests of the debtor, whose position was affected by the assignment, have been recognised.[199] However, unlike derogation by the parties to the factoring contract where the debtor is not notified, in the case of derogation by the parties to the underlying contract the assignee must be notified that the Convention shall not apply to the assignments of future receivables.[200] Third, exclusion as a whole may contradict with the setting aside of contractual prohibitions. The Factoring Convention gives effectiveness to assignments made notwithstanding anti-assignment clauses in the original contract. As the Convention can be excluded by the parties to the underlying contract, this presents the debtor, who may be aware of the consequences of the application of the Factoring Convention in that context, with a critical opportunity to exclude the Convention. If a Contracting State does not make a declaration under Article 18,[201] the debtor will have the risk of dealing with someone other than the original creditor because the anti-assignment clause in an agreement will not be applicable and the assignment will be valid. Due to that risk, when concluding the original contract in order to prevent any potential assignments, the debtor may always prefer to exclude the application of the Convention as a whole, depending on the negotiations with the assignor, thus the Convention's applicability as well as its effect is undermined.

The Receivables Convention considers party autonomy as a key principle. Derogation from, or variation by agreement of, certain provisions is allowed. The assignor, the assignee and the debtor can derogate or vary by agreement from those provisions related to their rights and obligations under Chapter IV. Article 6 acknowledges both the freedom of contract to meet their goals and the participation of the third parties in assignment contracts.[202] The debtor, the assignor and the assignee can benefit from the party autonomy provision provided they do not modify or vary the rights and obligations without the consent of a third party who is not a part of the agreement. This article is modelled on Article 6 of the Convention on Contracts for the International Sale of Goods (CISG).[203] However, unlike Article 6 CISG, the Receivables Convention does not allow parties to vary or derogate from provisions that affect the legal position of third parties. This is critical because the Receivables Convention deals with the proprietary aspects of an

199 UNIDROIT Study LVIII-Doc.33, para. 26.

200 Ibid.

201 Upon declaration, the Factoring Convention's anti-assignment overriding clauses shall be inapplicable in that State.

202 Bazinas, op. cit. (f'note 100), 266 *et seq.*; Bazinas, op. cit. (f'note 96), 374.

203 A/CN.9/489, para. 78.

assignment, and any change affecting the rights and obligations of third parties could frustrate the main objective of the Convention which is the promotion of availability of capital and credit at more affordable rates in cross-border transactions through predictable rules.[204] This sets the first limitation on the party autonomy principle in favour of third parties. Third parties may be anyone who is not a party to either the assignment contract (the debtor) or the underlying contract (the assignee) and, in any case, other creditors. These provisions from which the assignor, the assignee and the debtor can derogate are called 'the default rules'. Their function is to fill gaps[205] left in the assignment contract. Default rules include rights and obligations of the assignor and the assignee, representations, notification and payment, and the right to proceeds.[206] As those provisions on which parties have contractual freedom relate to contractual matters as opposed to proprietary aspects of assignment, they have an 'educative and risk-allocating value'.[207] The assignor has the responsibility to represent[208] as to the assignor's absolute right to assign the receivable, which has not been assigned previously, and the existence of the debtor's defences. However, the assignor and the assignee may agree to shift the risk of such defences to the assignee, but this may have a negative effect on the cost of credit as the assignee would prefer not to have a disadvantage as against the debtor. Depending on the agreement, the assignor may represent the debtor's payability.[209] Often the assignor may be ignorant and overlook notification of the debtor and this may cause risks for the assignee. In order to avoid this possibility, the parties may agree for the assignee to notify the debtor (for the protection of debtor under Article 16(1)) in a language that is reasonably expected to inform him about its contents. For example, an agreement between the assignor and the assignee can be in direct conflict with the debtor protection in the Convention, such that Article 6 sentence two[210] would have to be invoked to override what they had agreed. Thus, in relation to the language example given above, the assignor and the assignee may conclude an agreement that authorises the assignee to give notice in his own language (assuming that this language is different from the debtor's). Within the party autonomy context, under Article 13(1) the assignee may already have notified the debtor and the agreement would be to make it the assignee's sole responsibility. Under Article 14, regulating right to proceeds, the assignee in general has the right to retain proceeds and any agreement between the debtor and the assignor that is inconsistent with the assignee's rights should not adversely affect the assignee.[211] A second limitation on the party autonomy is linked to Article

204 A/CN.9/489, para. 78.
205 These gaps can be filled by Articles 11–14.
206 Articles 11; 12; 13–14, 16–17; 14, 22 respectively.
207 Bazinas, op. cit. (f'note 100), 276.
208 Article 12 (1). For more detailed treatment of debtor's rights and obligations, *see* Chapter 6.
209 Article 12(2).
210 'Such an agreement does not affect the rights of any person who is not a party to the agreement.' This is one of the limitations on the party autonomy provision. *See* Explanatory Note, op. cit. (f'note 85), para. 22.
211 This is due to second sentence of Article 6. For more detailed treatment of Article 14, *see* Chapter 6.

19(2), according to which the debtor and the assignor in the underlying contract may not waive defences of the debtor arising from fraudulent acts of the assignee and the debtor's incapacity. The debtor and the assignor may enter into an agreement not to raise defences and rights of set-off by virtue of Article 19(1) and, for the most part, agreements to waive defences are governed by party autonomy; therefore, Article 19(1) does not establish a limitation on party autonomy.

There may be a conflict between contractual freedom and prohibitions on the assignment of receivables. The Receivables Convention recognises the effectiveness of an assignment made notwithstanding any agreement between the assignor and the debtor. The conflict is whether contractual freedom under Article 6 should be given precedence without hindering international assignment practices. In a typical case, the Convention overrides anti-assignment clauses in the original contract and the debtor is aware that when the Convention applies, the anti-assignment clause will not be effective. Thus, the debtor prefers derogation from, or variation of, certain Convention provisions. However, derogation is not possible from Article 9, which governs overriding contractual prohibitions, because it is not located under the rights and obligations chapter of the Convention and, moreover, the assignee, as a third party, would have been adversely affected by the anti-assignment clause as well as derogation from the Convention's provisions. Finally, Article 22 governing the law applicable to competing rights[212] is a quasi-mandatory clause.[213] That is to say, its application can only be bypassed if it is manifestly contrary to the public policy of the forum State, in which case the mandatory law priority rule of the forum State shall apply.[214] However, under Article 23(2), mandatory rules of a State other than the assignor's State do not have the authority to change the applicability of the law of the assignor's State to priority conflicts. The exception under Article 23(3) stipulates where an insolvency proceeding is in place in a State other than the assignor's State, the forum's priority rules shall apply, thus bypassing the rule in Article 22. Article 22 governs the proprietary aspects of an assignment. It would adversely affect the interests of third parties if the assignor and the assignee were allowed to derogate from this rule. This matter has been debated during the consultation and drafting process of Rome I Regulation.

As in the Receivables Convention, party autonomy is a key principle of the Guide. The Guide recommends States to adopt the principle of party autonomy as the basis of a secured transactions regime.[215] The Guide takes a facilitative rather than formalistic position as a fundamental policy.[216] Therefore, mandatory

212 For further details on priority rule as well as its exceptions, *see* Chapter 6.

213 Some commentators, however, argue that Article 22 has a mandatory application and that the EU should be cautious in its ratification. One cannot concur with this view. But, in fact, Article 22 has no mandatory application and, although Article 6 encompasses Article 22, the latter has exceptions under Articles 23 and 24 that limit its mandatory application. For criticism of Article 22, *see* Flessner, A. 'Security Interests in Receivables–A European Perspective' in Eidenmüller and Kieninger (eds), op. cit. (f'note 2), 347.

214 Receivables Convention Articles 22 and 23; Explanatory Note of the Receivables Convention, 41.

215 Guide, para. 118, at 60.

216 Guide, para. 70, at 25.

rules are kept at the minimum level in order to protect fairness and legitimate interests of third parties.[217] Under recommendation 10, the Guide generally sets out its party autonomy policy which is similar to, but broader than, the Receivables Convention and recommends that the law should provide, with certain exceptions that are clearly defined, that the secured creditor and the grantor or the debtor may derogate from or vary by agreement its provisions relating to their respective rights and obligations.[218] However, in doing that, the parties should not affect the rights of third parties. The exceptions to party autonomy ensure this balance and relate to the creation of security rights,[219] rights and obligations of the parties to a security agreement,[220] enforcement of security rights,[221] acquisition financing unitary and non-unitary options, and choice of law issues. The party autonomy under the creation of security interests applies where it is possible for the parties to agree that the assets will be partially encumbered or encumbered to a certain amount.[222] There is very limited ground in the Guide to operate party autonomy with regard to conflict-of-law issues as the rules apply to proprietary aspects. This is a logical approach, because setting out rules that may regulate the parties' choice-of-law options promotes predictability, which in return facilitates credit. A clear connecting factor, on which parties have no autonomy, promotes certainty and reduces the disparity between the parties' bargaining positions. In that context, party autonomy, within the context of choice-of-law rules, is only permitted under recommendation 216, according to which the grantor and the secured creditor can choose the law applicable to their mutual rights and obligations in their security agreement; and in the absence of this choice, it will be the law governing their security agreement. The purpose of the exception in recommendation 216 is that rights and obligations of parties to a security agreement are contractual aspects, whereas creation, third party effectiveness and priority of competing rights involve proprietary aspects of rights that have the risk of affecting third-party rights.[223] Therefore, an exception may be justified and parties may have autonomy in their rights and obligations.[224] This approach is consistent with Rome I Regulation on the Law Applicable to Contractual Obligations[225] Articles

217 Rights and obligations of parties to a security agreement and third parties, Chapters VI and VII.

218 Guide, Recommendation 10.

219 Recommendations 14–15. Minimum information in Recommendation 14 consists of intention of parties to create a security right, identification of parties and the asset, maximum monetary amount for which the security may be enforced, as well as the description of the secured obligation, and in Recommendation 15 the form of a security agreement may be oral if accompanied by possession, or in writing indicating the intention of the grantor to encumber the asset. For more information, *see* Chapter 4.

220 Recommendations 111–12, Mandatory rules have been kept to a minimum, regulating only matters that are closely related to public policy issues.

221 Recommendations 132–6.

222 Guide, para. 50, at 177.

223 Guide, para. 13, at 386.

224 Guide, paras 11, 12 and 61, at 385–6 and 397.

225 OJ 177, 04/07/2008, pp. 0006–0016, Regulation (EC) No. 593/2008 of the European Parliament and of the Council of 17 June 2008 on the Law Applicable to Contractual Obligations (Rome I).

3 and 4 where parties have the freedom to choose the applicable law and, in the absence of choice of law, the law most closely connected to the security agreement applies. This may be the law of the lender who has the characteristic performance in a security agreement.[226]

Party autonomy is one of the key principles of the Cape Town Convention and its Protocols.[227] The aim is to reflect and respect the intentions of parties to high-volume transactions.[228] Parties should not be confined to enumerated transactions; rather, they should be allowed to create their own transactions that will match their commercial needs, and thus enforceability of aircraft financing documents are enhanced without reducing the need for negotiation of the terms of those documents.[229] Party autonomy in that sense serves as a significant tool to reduce the cost of credit by presenting predictability to both parties to a lending or leasing transaction, but particularly to financiers. For instance, the inclusion of self-help remedies in the Aircraft Protocol is an example of the strength of the party autonomy culture under the Cape Town Convention.[230] It was observed by Professor Cuming that a convention would provide necessary flexibility, fairness and balance in reducing the cost of credit in this area.[231] The principle is referred to in the preamble and interpretation sections of the Convention and embodied in some articles.[232] In that context, the Convention is 'predicated upon a respect for mercantile practice as reflected in contracts and an interpretation of contracts in line with their accepted commercial meanings'.[233] Under the Convention, this is particularly true for choice-of-law clauses and the secured creditor's rights in the case of debtor's insolvency. In the meantime, the Convention protects the interests of the debtor against unreasonable contractual terms and allows Contracting States to opt out of provisions that are against the fundamental policies of that State. This reflects the sensitivity to a national legal cultures principle. Article 15 embodies the general principle of party autonomy with restrictions. The parties have the freedom to derogate from, or vary the effect of, provisions embodied under Chapter III titled 'Default Remedies', except for mandatory provisions on which party autonomy is limited,[234] and it is possible for parties to impose

226 Guide, para. 61, at 397.

227 For the Aircraft Protocol, there is a high degree of party autonomy with limitations in order to protect the interests of the debtor whereby restricting the exercise of remedies in the event of debtor default.

228 As high-value equipment is purchased through export credit financing techniques and this generally involves governments and their agencies, it has been argued that '[a] restriction on the ability of parties to enforce their contractual agreement is often a restriction on the ability of governments to effectuate financing [programmes]'. Wool, op. cit. (f'note 12), 508.

229 *Annex I-Cape Town Papers Series, vol. 1, Contract Practices under the Cape Town Convention* http://www.awg.aero/pdf/Annex5.pdf (last accessed 5 June 2010).

230 Article 8 Remedies of Chargee; Aircraft Protocol Article IX. Article 54(2) allows for opting out of self-help remedies.

231 UNIDROIT Study LXXII-Doc.1, 5.

232 E.g. Cape Town Convention Article 42 on choice of forum.

233 Goode, op. cit. (f'note 9), 149.

234 For some background information, *see* UNIDROIT Study LXXII-Doc.35, 5.

contractual limitations on the exercise of rights under the Convention.[235] Parties' agreement must be in writing. Limitations protect third parties who are not part of the agreement and there are certain limits.[236] Party autonomy applies under Article 11 where parties may agree upon in writing as to the events that constitute a default or, although not included under chapter III, party autonomy is maintained where parties subordinate their rights under Article 29(5) governing priority of competing interests, provided they do not affect other priority rights. On the other hand, party autonomy is considered to be inappropriate in the insolvency context. Under Article 30(3), the effect of rules related to the avoidance of preferences, transfers in fraud of creditors, and insolvency procedure designed to limit the enforcement of security rights in the interests of creditors, have been considered to be inappropriate to be solved by the principle of freedom of contract. If parties have autonomy on matters affecting insolvency procedures, it will cause unforeseen risks for creditors who will be unaware of fraudulent transfers and who are not party to those agreements. In that context, under the Aircraft Protocol Article XI, Contracting States are offered the ability to opt in or out of one of the insolvency remedies.[237] Also, under the Aircraft Protocol Article IV(3), the parties are permitted to exclude by writing the application of remedies on insolvency, and derogate from, or vary by agreement of, the provisions of the Protocol – except Article IX(2)-(4) dealing with exercising remedies. In that sense, parties are not allowed to derogate from, or vary by agreement of, remedies provisions that affect the rights of third parties.

Contractual flexibility is also an underlying principle of the Model Law. It denotes a flexible definition of 'secured debt'[238] and 'charged property'.[239] This is explained in EBRD's Law in Transition:

> [The Model Law] is . . . intended to form a basis from which national legislation for transition countries can be developed, to act as a starting point, indicating through a legal text how the principal components of a secured transactions law can be drafted but allowing for a high degree of flexibility to enable adaptation to local circumstances and to be a reference point which can be turned to for guidance and illustration.[240]

Similar philosophy is reflected in the Core Principles, according to which commercial flexibility should be a core principle and 'as far as possible the parties should be able to adapt security to the needs of their particular transaction'.[241] It

235 For further information, *see* Goode, op. cit. (f'note 9), para. 2.38.

236 Cape Town Convention Articles 8(3), (4), (5), (6), 9(3), 13(2) and 14.

237 These are Aircraft Protocol Article XI Alternative A and B. *See also* Davies, op. cit. (f'note 175), 171–2.

238 Article 4.1.

239 Article 5.1.

240 Simpson, J. and Menze, J. (2000) 'Ten Years of Secured Transactions Reform', *Law in Transition*, Part 2, 20, 21 (Autumn).

241 *See* ibid., at 26. EBRD Core Principles Number 10 envisages this approach.

is clear that the Model Law supports party autonomy with limitations, similar to the other international instruments, to protect the interests of parties who are not a party to an agreement but who may potentially be affected. The approach also avoids over-burdening the parties with mandatory rules that may often be inappropriate to the parties' commercial needs. The Model Law ensures this contractual freedom by permitting a flexible definition of secured debt and charged property as long as the secured debt and the collateral are identifiable at the outset.[242] These can be described either specifically or generally.[243] This enables parties to secure their bulk receivables without having to burden themselves to identify each and every item and describe their secured debts as present and future debts as long as these are identifiable at the outset.[244] The Model Law also permits the change of the secured debt as well as the collateral during the period of the security.

3.5 Conclusion

The scope of applicability, the relationship between the instruments, and party autonomy may be said to establish the backbone of international instruments. The scope of applicability sets substantive and territorial perspectives of an instrument. The unitary and functional approaches to security seem to dominate the Receivables Convention and the Guide, whereas a non-unitary approach finds its place in the Cape Town Convention and the Model Law. The conventions have carefully-designed territorial and substantive applicability provisions so that they do not overlap with each other, and so that their applicability is broad enough to respond to the needs of the relevant area and sector they are directed to. Particularly in relation to the Guide, inclusion of retention-of-title and financial leasing within the functional approach to security may compel certain jurisdictions to amend their systems and establish general security rights registries. Prominent scholars have suggested that security interests should have limits, but at the same time secured credit should not be confined within a narrow conceptual definition.[245] Party autonomy should have restrictions and must not affect the proprietary aspects of a transaction.

242 E.g. under Article 4(2) the secured debt must be determined or in monetary terms determinable.
243 Article 4(3).
244 This is identical to the Receivables Convention's approach under Article 8.
245 Bridge, in Eidenmüller and Kieninger, op. cit. (fnote 4), at 214.

4 Creation of security rights

4.1 Introduction

A simple and efficient manner of creation of security rights is critical in lowering the cost of credit and is known to be one of the key principles of international instruments. Predictable rules on the effectiveness of a security right between the debtor and secured creditor, arguably, will be instrumental to achieve facilitation of credit. As part of this, it is also crucial to recognise the effectiveness of non-possessory security rights in all types of assets.[1] In essence, creation is the process where the security right becomes effective by an agreement between the secured creditor and debtor (grantor) who grants to the former the right to enforce this interest over the assets of the latter in the latter's default.[2] The economic power that the creation of security rights grants over the assets of the debtor is clear: simply, the secured creditor lends, and takes security over the existing or future assets of the borrower by concluding an agreement stipulating post-default rights according to which, in case of default in payments or insolvency of the debtor, the secured creditor will have the right to enforce the security interest to satisfy the claim, thus, in a way, controlling the business decisions of the borrower.

Facilitation of credit requires clear, efficient, simple and functional rules for the creation of security rights. Minimal formalities, a single method for creating security rights and an ability to create security rights over future assets without the need for additional documents are instrumental in the facilitation of credit. The grantor should be able to use the same asset to grant multiple security rights.[3] Unnecessary formalities have adverse effects on the cost of credit. Specification of the time of creation is critical. An efficient creation procedure of security rights must address a number of issues, including who may grant and be the beneficiary of a security right, and what types of assets and obligations may be encumbered and secured by a security right. Unreformed secured transactions regimes exclude certain goods, obligations and transactions. There are restrictions as to who can be a party to a secured transaction. This chapter will explore the issues

1 E.g. Guide, recommendation 1(e).

2 Creation/attachment does not necessarily indicate that the security interest is effective as against third parties. For third-party effectiveness ('perfection') further steps need to be taken. *See* Chapter 5.

experienced in the creation of security interests and how international instruments minimise formalities in order to facilitate access to credit. The concept of international interest and its significance will also be examined.

4.2 Recurrent problems in the creation of security rights

Cross-border transactions endure problems about creation of effective security rights. Particular points of tension, within the context of creation, in unreformed regimes include uncertainty as to who may grant and be the beneficiary of a security right, and what types of assets and obligations may be encumbered and secured by a security right. Harmonised modernisation, aimed at by international instruments, serves as a means to ensure that security rights created in one jurisdiction are recognised in another. Facilitation of credit requires simple and efficient rules, which support the creation of security interests over all types of debtor's assets and obligations. Non-recognition of certain types of security rights or the inability to use assets in unreformed regimes, which may otherwise be acceptable as collateral in modern secured transactions systems, increase the cost of credit and often hinder access to credit. International lenders extend credit when there is predictability that the security right created in the borrower's jurisdiction is valid, perfected, has a priority status and is enforceable. This is a particular concern in unreformed regimes, where rules do not efficiently endorse security.[4] These problems lead lenders to refuse financing or lend with high interest rates in cross-border transactions, as they cannot ascertain whether the security right created is valid and enforceable.[5] Fragmented laws (where different laws apply to movables and receivables or one law applies to companies and the other to individuals, enabling them to give security under different circumstances) and limited applicability of these laws severely limit access to low cost credit. There is doubt that movable or intangible property can be used as collateral. In emerging markets access to low cost credit and the permissibility to use any type of collateral are critical for firms to be able to access low-cost credit. The limit on who can give and take security as well as what type of assets can be used as collateral have negative impact on the economic growth. First, the owners of assets who are unable to utilise them lose the advantages of secured lending. The value of their assets is diminished. Second, fragmented laws increase the cost of credit as parties have to

3 To operate this objective effectively, a registration system notifying third parties is necessary. *See* Chapter 5.

4 E.g. Fleisig H.W. and De la Pena, N. (1997) 'Peru: How Problems in the Framework for Secured Transactions Limit Access to Credit', 3 *NAFTA: Law and Business Review of the Americas* 33, 35–6.

5 De la Pena, N. (1999) 'Reforming the Legal Framework for Security Interests in Mobile Equipment', *Unif. L. Rev.* 347, 349; De la Pena, N. (2008) 'Challenges in Implementing Secured Transactions Reform in Latin America', in F. Dahan and J. Simpson (eds) *Secured Transactions Reform and Access to Credit*. Cheltenham: Edward Elgar, 236, 243.

determine the applicable law and whether this law permits both taking security over a particular asset and certain people to grant security.[6]

The cost of credit may also increase if there is relatively little predictability on certain practices. Inability to create floating security interests sets a financial burden on the borrower as the inventory cannot be collateralised. Furthermore, specificity requirement, according to which information such as collateral, debtor and amount have to be specified before creating a security interest, restrict the ability to create security interest over after-acquired property.[7] Limitations concerning creation of floating security interests over future assets are obstacles to financing. In unreformed regimes, collateralisation of future assets is not permitted, due to the requirements of specific identification, where creation of security in assets acquired, and in changing pools of assets arising after the conclusion of the security agreement, is also not permitted.[8] This is based on the concern that creation of security over a debtor's future assets may cause over-commitment[9] and the perception in some legal systems that property must be protected and the grantor cannot grant to the secured creditor more than what the grantor has or may acquire.[10] Moreover, the idea that only presently existing goods can be pledged, contributes to this restriction. Firms in unreformed regimes may not have sufficient existing assets to enter into further investment and have to offer future assets as collateral in order to obtain credit. In particular, intangibles (for example, receivables or intellectual property rights) are often not accepted as collateral in unreformed regimes.[11] International instruments take the view that taking security over future assets, as long as it does not violate consumer protection legislation, should be possible, and a general description of the encumbered

6 Fleisig, H., Safavian, M. and De la Pena, N. (2006) *Reforming Collateral Laws to Expand Access to Finance*. Washington DC: World Bank, 25 *et seq.* Fragmentation of laws pattern can be found in England where companies are subject to Companies Act 2006 Part 25, s. 860 *et seq.* and individuals are subject to Bills of Sale Act 1878 and Bills of Sale Act (1878) Amendment Act 1882. For further discussion, *see e.g.* Bridge, M. (2002) 'The English Law of Real Security', 4 *E.R.P.L.* 483, 486.

7 Fleisig *et al.* (2006), 29.

8 A/CN.9/WG.VI/WP.3, para. 14.

9 Guide, para. 63, 23.

10 *Nemo dat quod habet* (One cannot give what one has not got). A lessee may create a security right in his right as the lessee and not on the property being leased because the latter will have to be done as a proprietary interest, over which the lessee has no right as he only has contractual right. However, it should be noted that under English law there are exceptions to the rule under common law (e.g. *Dearle v Hall*) and statutes (e.g. Factors Act 1889 s. 9, Hire Purchase Act 1964 s. 27 and Sale of Goods Act 1979 ss. 24–25). *See* Bridge, M. (2002) *Personal Property Law*, 3rd edn. Oxford: Oxford University Press, at 116 *et seq.*; Beale, H., Bridge, M., Gullifer, L. and Lomnicka, E. (2007) *The Law of Personal Property Security*. Oxford: Oxford University Press, 433 *et seq.*

11 For some empirical figures on the non-permissibility of receivables, *see* Safavian, M. 'Firm level evidence on collateral and access to finance', in F. Dahan and J. Simpson (eds) (2008) *Secured Transactions Reform and Access to Credit*. Cheltenham: Edward Elgar, 110, 118, where banks accept as collateral 73 per cent land and buildings, 18 per cent machinery and 9 per cent book debts, whereas among the firms' composition of assets, land and buildings hold only 22 per cent (machinery 44 per cent and book debts 34 per cent).

asset or the obligations should achieve this goal.[12] International instruments also facilitate the use and acceptance of intangibles as collateral.[13]

Continuation of security interests in proceeds is generally not recognised in unreformed regimes. Problems in this area generally meet at a point where it must be determined whether the original security agreement covers proceeds automatically or a specific mention must be made in order to be part of security. The principle of party autonomy, as a key principle of international instruments, and the objective of facilitation of credit lead to the policy that a security right in encumbered assets should automatically extend to the identifiable proceeds without the requirement to indicate previously and explicitly in the security agreement.[14] This also postulates that proceeds and products are to be understood within the key objectives of those international instruments.

In the light of the above, the risk encountered in cross-border transactions is whether the creation of a security right in one country is recognised and enforceable in another. The divergent approach of laws to security means that effectiveness of security rights is not always achieved in cross-border transactions. This has a negative impact on lending decisions. Sometimes the law applicable to the creation of security interests may be different from the law applicable to the other parts of the contract. Complications arising out of application of multiple laws to a lending transaction are apparent. These include disparity in bargaining positions with regard to the applicable law and vulnerability of borrowers in accessing low-cost credit by being subject to unfavourable rules. Divergent rules in national laws and the uncertainty of whether a transaction involves an outright assignment or an assignment for security purposes also pose threats to assignment practices, as often it is not possible to distinguish them from each other. The Receivables Convention and the Guide adopt a trend, where the assignment is subjected to the same rules notwithstanding its character as an outright transfer or transfer for security purposes.[15] Issues regarding the effectiveness of assignments tend to be felt in notification requirement of the debtor or written contract of assignment.

In this context, pragmatic modernisation through harmonisation of secured transactions laws may overcome difficulties in the creation of security rights. Arguably, predictability can be ensured by a single security right in respect of all types of things and rights (comprehensive functional approach)[16] and by the ability to use all assets encumbered and obligations secured by a security agreement. Minimisation of transaction costs (such as removal of notarisation, which may involve high fees) and formalities that otherwise incentivise lenders to keep their interest rates high to recover their conjectured future losses, will complement

12 E.g. Guide, recommendation 13 and 17; Receivables Convention Articles 8(2) and 2(a); Model Law Articles 4.4 and 5.5.

13 E.g. Receivables Convention and the Guide are notable developments in this area.

14 E.g. Guide, recommendation 19; Receivables Convention Articles 5(j), 14 and 24(2); Model Law Article 5.8–5.9.

15 Receivables Convention Article 2 and Guide recommendation 3. The Receivables Convention does not provide for a substantive rule for the formal validity issues and leaves it to the law applicable.

16 For some suggestions on this matter, *see* Fleisig *et al.*, op. cit. (f'note 6), 54 *et seq.*

facilitation of credit. Issues posed in relation to non-recognition of effectiveness of bulk and future receivables, contractual restrictions that hinder the effectiveness of security rights, creation of rights over funds credited to a bank and contractual right to proceeds are critical in the effectiveness of security rights. Thus, lending decisions may be shaped according to how effectively a country's reform activities address these matters.

4.3 Creation of security rights

4.3.1 Relationship and distinction between creation and third-party effectiveness

Effectiveness of security interests, third-party effectiveness, the priority they grant to creditors and enforceability have always been tension points in secured transactions. The creditor's aim is to guarantee that a security interest created in favour of the creditor in one jurisdiction will be recognised in the other, grant priority and, eventually, be enforceable in the event of the debtor's default or insolvency. The creation process, where a security interest in favour of the secured creditor is fixed over the assets of the debtor, grants the creditor rights *in rem* against the debtor. Distinguishing third-party effectiveness and creation of security rights arguably enables grantors to be able to utilise the same asset and its full value by securing it to multiple creditors and remaining in possession, while regulating the priority in an optimal way.

The basic policy issue is whether the creation of a security right is sufficient to establish effectiveness between the parties as well as third-party effectiveness or whether an additional act is needed for third-party effectiveness. Effectiveness between the parties establishes a right *in rem* by separating personal rights from real rights, though it looks like it establishes a contractual right by being only enforceable against the debtor. The third-party effectiveness, or the so-called perfection, is the proprietary aspect that establishes a right *in rem* that is opposable to third parties. There are two main approaches to effectiveness of a security interest.[17] One of the approaches (that is generally adopted in some civil law jurisdictions and some transition economies[18]) views that a security interest is fully effective (both between parties and against third parties) by fulfilling a single step according to which an agreement is concluded and third parties are notified (in receivables), the interest is registered (in ships and aircraft) or the collateral's possession is delivered (as in the case of tangibles). This approach conceptualises the taking of security interest over the grantor's assets and establishing a proprietary right that is enforceable and effective against both the grantor and third parties under an integrated single

17 A third one, the 'hybrid approach', ensures that the security interest is effective against all parties as of the time it is created except against other secured creditors. The disadvantage is that competing claimants are distinguished and different rules apply to different categories, which may cause uncertainty, particularly in cross-border transactions. *See* Guide, paras 1–7, 65–6.

18 *EBRD Publicity of Security Rights Guiding Principles for the Development of a Charges Registry* (2004) at 13 (EBRD Guiding Principles).

method. Thus, there is no need to complete an additional act to make the security interest effective against third parties. Failure to fulfil one of those will render the interest ineffective (as not created), even as between the parties. This will also lead to no third-party effectiveness. A good example is a traditional pledge where, following a pledge agreement, the possession of the asset must actually be transferred, and without the transfer one cannot talk about creation.

The second approach is generally adopted by international instruments and supports the concept that additional steps are necessary for third-party effectiveness, which depends on the nature of the transaction; creation does not necessarily grant rights against third parties[19] and this approach recommends that creation of security interests should be a separate process from third-party effectiveness, which needs to be achieved in addition to concluding the security agreement. Thus, contractual and proprietary aspects are separated. This latter additional process, mainly envisaged as registration under international instruments (with some alternatives in the Guide), makes the security interest opposable to third parties by establishing notice, and sets the priority ranking. Generally, an unregistered security interest continues to be effective against the debtor but not against the creditors or insolvency administrator in the debtor's insolvency. UCC Article 9 type secured transactions regimes and international instruments[20] (and to a certain extent some Eastern European jurisdictions)[21] adopt this two-pronged approach, where an agreement is entered into between parties that creates the security interest and renders it effective as between parties, and a registration in a general security rights registry that renders it effective as against third parties by providing notice of the possible existence of a security interest. In this approach when a security interest is created by an agreement between the parties, the interest, unless it is registered, will have no effect on third parties who acquire rights subsequently on the same asset but will only be effective against the grantor.[22] One of the reasons provided in favour of the use of an additional method for third-party effectiveness is that in the absence of an additional method, mere creation of a security interest may 'result in the creation of a secret security right'.[23] Third parties may not have information on earlier security interest, thus, particularly non-possessory security devices require publicity. The rationale for this approach can be explained as follows: first, it allows the debtor to be able to utilise the same asset by granting security over it to multiple secured creditors and the additional step under the Guide perfectly serves as a priority point; second, as the additional step serves as a means to achieve third-party effectiveness, there seems to be no

19 But cf. Model Law Article 6.2.

20 E.g. Guide, Chapter III; Receivables Convention, effectiveness issues are dealt with under Article 22–23 and 26–32; Cape Town Convention, Chapter VIII.

21 With regards to Romania, *see* Röver, J-H. (2007) *Secured Lending in Eastern Europe: Comparative Law of Secured Transactions and the EBRD Model Law*. Oxford: Oxford University Press, fn. 49, at 73; EBRD Guiding Principles, fn. 9, at 3. In Bulgaria retention-of-title and financial lease must be registered, and in Romania assignment of receivables, conditional sales and financial leases must be registered.

22 However, it may also have an effect on subsequently created but non-registered charges.

23 E.g. Guide, para. 8, at 105 and paras 1–3, at 65.

reason to subject the creation of a security right between the parties to further onerous requirements such as notification (which is not suitable in the case of assignment of future receivables).[24]

The creation of security rights may be called 'attachment' in some legal systems,[25] but does not fully mean creation as it is understood under international instruments.[26] In some systems creation may be a single step action where conclusion of agreement and registration or delivery of possession constitutes creation and third-party effectiveness. In England, the word 'attachment' is not really used by practitioners, who talk more of a security interest being created and then becoming effective against third parties.[27] Under English law a security can either be created through transfer of a property interest, as in the case of mortgage, or by encumbering through registration over the assets, as in the case of charge.[28] Attachment as used under the UCC§9–203(a) and (b), unlike the Guide, which avoids using the term and prefers 'creation of a security right',[29] does not denote creation of rights and obligations *inter partes* as understood under the Guide. Rather, it describes formalities necessary to create enforceable security interest against the debtor and third parties.[30] In other words, the term 'attachment' establishes a property interest on the collateral identified by the parties.[31] Thus, the distinction is that under the Guide, rights and obligations are merely created *inter partes*; for third party effectiveness further requirements need to be fulfilled and the created security right is only effective against the debtor in the absence of registration, whereas under the UCC, once the security interest is attached on a collateral it becomes effective against both the debtor and the third parties. Perfection is a necessary tool for priority, thus without perfection a secured party will not have any priority status against other secured creditors.

24 For a similar argument, *see* Lukas, M. (2008) 'Attachment/Creation of a Security Interest', in H. Eidenmüller and E.M. Kieninger (eds), *The Future of Secured Credit in Europe* E.C.F.L.R. Munich: De Gruyter Recht, 135, 139.

25 UCC§9–203(a).

26 E.g. Receivables Convention, Article 2(a) uses the term 'creation of rights in receivables'; Guide, Chapter II 'Creation of a Security Right'; Cape Town Convention, Chapter II 'Constitution of an International Interest'. *See* Goode, R. (2008) *Convention on International Interests in Mobile Equipment and Protocol Thereto on Matters Specific to Aircraft Equipment Official Commentary – Revised Edition.* Rome: UNIDROIT, 35. For a similar terminology, *see* UCC§9–102(a)(73), which encompasses both security interests and title finance transactions and illustrates a functional approach: '"Security agreement" means an agreement that creates or provides for a security interest'.

27 *See e.g.* Calnan, R. (2006) *Taking Security: Law and Practice.* Bristol: Jordans, 139 *et seq.*; but cf. Gullifer, L. (ed.) (2009) *Goode on Legal Problems of Credit and Security.* London: Sweet & Maxwell, 4th edn., para. 2–02; Law Commission Consultation Paper (No. 176), para. 2.13 *et seq.*

28 Beale *et al.*, op. cit. (f'note 10), para. 20.54 at 707.

29 Guide, recommendation 13. There is also a term called *attachment* under the Guide which does not mean the same as attachment as discussed here.

30 *See also* Veneziano, A. (2008) 'Attachment/Creation of a Security Right', in Eidenmüller and Kieninger (eds), op. cit. (f'note 24), 113, 118.

31 Lawrence, W., Henning, W. and Freyermuth, W. (2004) *Understanding Secured Transactions*, 3rd edn. Lexis Nexis, at 68.

The Guide distinguishes creation from the third-party effectiveness without making a distinction between categories of competing claimants,[32] which is compatible with its fundamental policies of functional and comprehensive regime of secured transactions.[33] Under the Guide, registration in the general security rights registry is not synonymous with the creation of a security right. Notice-filing by itself, without creation, is not sufficient to establish third-party effectiveness.[34] The order of creation and registration becomes significant when a subsequent third party creates and registers a security interest, despite the first creditor registering an earlier security interest that has not yet been created. Even though the subsequent creditor has actual notice, the first registered but not created charge will have no third-party effectiveness.[35] Registration only provides notice of the existence of a possible security interest and does not provide evidence of the creation of a security right, as the security right may be created in the future, and with the possibility of advance registration under the Guide, the secured creditor may register the interest to provide notice to potential creditors.[36] Thus, the creation of a security right will depend on whether the parties have fulfilled the relevant conditions required under the Guide.[37] It is a consequence of the rule that both creation and registration must occur for third-party effectiveness. There is one exception, however, in relation to priority conflicts. Priority among competing secured creditors, whose security interests have third-party effectiveness through registration, will be determined by the order of registration. As a consequence of this rule, in a conflict between two competing secured creditors, one of whom has registered but not created a security interest before and the other who has completed both steps (creation and registration), the first to register the security interest will have priority.[38]

The Model Law requires that registration is a constitutive element of creation of a registered charge (Article 6.2), and thus departs from the Guide's policy. Similarly, for the possessory charge, a charging agreement and the possession of the charged property must be given (Articles 6.4 and 10.1). Possession by itself does not create the charge and the charging instrument must also be concluded. The Receivables Convention follows the Guide's pattern; formal validity of assignment is a condition to priority and left to the applicable law, and registration for a third-party effectiveness mechanism is recommended.[39] The Receivables Convention adopts an approach that distinguishes between two types of effectiveness.[40] The Factoring

32 Guide, para. 65, at 24 and para. 5, at 66.

33 Guide, para. 51, at 20 and para. 65, at 24. The aim is to establish a comprehensive regime to engage in conflicts between all competing claimants as opposed to having different regimes for different competing claimants.

34 Recommendations 29 and 32. *See* Chapter 5.

35 EBRD Guiding Principles, at 13; Guide, para. 39, at 112.

36 Recommendation 33. The same advance registration is also possible under the Receivables Convention and the Cape Town Convention.

37 Recommendations 13–15.

38 Guide, para. 40, at 112.

39 Articles 5(g), 22 and 42(4).

40 *See e.g.* Bazinas, S. (2003) 'Key Policy Issues of the United Nations Convention on the Assignment of Receivables in International Trade', 11 *Tul. J. Int'l & Comp. L.*, 275.

Convention, on the other hand, does not regulate formal validity of assignments. It only sets aside certain contractual and statutory limitations. The Cape Town Convention adopts a similar approach, wherein Article 7 deals with effectiveness between parties and specifies where the agreement creating the interest, or providing for the interest, establishes the international interest. On the other hand, Articles 29–30 deal with the effects of an international interest as against third parties. Therefore, registration and creation of an international interest are clearly distinguished.[41]

4.3.2 Minimum formalities and creation of security rights

Effectiveness of security rights between parties has two important aspects. First, the steps that must be taken to create a security interest and second, the time of effectiveness as between parties. The solution to these issues differs according to the type of assets (such as receivables, negotiable instruments, bank accounts, proceeds) for which a security right is created. International instruments, in general, reflect the significance of minimum formalities in the creation and the single security right. Access to low cost credit requires a predictable, simple and efficient system for creation of security rights. One clear example is the necessity to distinguish creation and third-party effectiveness in order to avoid unnecessary contractual formalities to protect third party rights, which are not required within the framework of effectiveness between parties.[42] If the creation of a security right is achieved in a simple manner, arguably the cost of credit will be lower. As a key objective the Guide supports minimum formalities in the creation of security rights. The Guide's approach is a clear response to the unnecessary requirements that integrate creation and third-party effectiveness.[43] Thus, third party effectiveness requirements (e.g. registration, delivery of possession, control) are not part of the formalities to make a security effective between parties where the latter,[44] under the Guide's comprehensive and functional approach, apply to all types of transactions including outright transfer of receivables and title-based devices. Bazinas argues in relation to the Guide's approach and establishing the concept of priority that debtors will be able to utilise the economic value of their assets while in possession and thus create multiple charges to multiple creditors on the same

41 For further discussion on this matter, *see* Chapter 5.

42 Guide, para. 6, at 66.

43 Chapter II of the Guide regulates formal validity rules for the creation of an effective security right between the debtor and the secured creditor. *Inter partes* effectiveness is also referred to under recommendation 30, where the effectiveness between debtor and secured creditor is clearly distinguished from the effectiveness as against third parties, and a secured right will be deemed effective between parties even if it is not effective against third parties. Chapter III of the Guide regulates effectiveness as against third parties. *Erga omnes* effectiveness is referred to in recommendation 29, according to which third party effectiveness can be achieved if a security right is effectively created and one of the methods under recommendations 32, 34–35 to ensure third-party effectiveness is followed. *See* Guide, paras 5–8, at 104–05. *See below* Chapter 5.

44 Guide, recommendations, 13–28.

assets, and creditors by virtue of a separate effectiveness mechanism will be able to ascertain their priority status before extending credit.[45]

The Receivables Convention removes statutory and contractual limitations on the assignment of receivables (Articles 8–10); other effectiveness matters are left to the applicable law.[46] The form of the contract of assignment, whether the assignment contract should be written or not[47] and whether other particular formalities such as notification of the debtor are required, is left to the law applicable outside the Convention (Article 27). It is arguable that if States adopt the Guide, the law applicable outside the Convention may be the recommendations of the Guide. Under the Guide, the security agreement is created between the grantor and the secured creditor by an agreement,[48] and that agreement must reflect the intention of parties to create a security right, identify parties, describe the secured obligation and the encumbered assets in a reasonable manner and state the maximum monetary amount for which the security right may be enforced.[49] The Guide is flexible and requires the minimum of formalities to create security rights.[50] The form of the security agreement[51] demonstrates flexibility, and even oral agreements may create security rights if the agreement accompanies possession of the asset by the secured creditor. Possession, however, must be public, continuous and unequivocal and it should not be a constructive possession. Otherwise the written agreement must demonstrate the parties' intent to create a security right. The term *creation* also applies to title-retention devices, illustrating a divergence from, for example, the Cape Town Convention Article 7, which talks of an agreement 'creating' for security interests and 'providing for' for title-retention devices and illustrates similarity to the UCC Article 9's notion of security agreement.[52] This is because in retention-of-title and leasing agreements the creditor's interest precedes the agreement providing for international interest and does not derive from

45 Bazinas, S. (2006) 'Modernising and Harmonising Secured Credit Law: The Example of the UNCITRAL Draft Legislative Guide on Secured Transactions, Part 1', *BJIBFL* 20, 21.

46 Receivables Convention Articles 22–23 and 26–32.

47 The term 'writing' is defined under the Receivables Convention Article 5(c); it includes electronic record and clarifies that 'signing' can be in forms other than manual signing. For some comparisons with the UCC, *see* UCC§1–201(46), (39); UCC§9–102(a)(7) and (69). UCC Article 9 requires that a security agreement to be authenticated for the security interest to be enforceable UCC§9–203(a),(b)(3).

48 Recommendation 13.

49 Recommendation 14. The maximum amount requirement assists subordinate lending in the sense that some states require the identification of the maximum amount for which the security interest may be claimed in the encumbered assets and this is particularly critical in securing future obligations, as during the security agreement the amount of obligation is unknown. This limitation on the security interest protects the debtor from over-indebtedness. However, there are also disadvantages to this, by which the maximum amount may lead to limitation of available credit from creditors, which in turn deprives the debtor of the ability to use the full value of his/her assets. *See* Guide, paras 38–48, at 74–7.

50 It is possible to create security rights using electronic communication. *See* Recommendation 11.

51 Recommendation 15.

52 UCC§9–102(a)(73) '"Security agreement" means an agreement that creates or provides for a security interest.'

it. Arguably, under the Cape Town Convention the time of creation of an international interest cannot be before the chargor has the power to dispose the object, which may or may not derive from a proprietary right under the applicable law.[53] The Guide stipulates the time of creation depending on the type of asset, which clarifies doubts with regards to the time of creation of the security right. If at the time of the conclusion of the security agreement the grantor has rights or power to encumber the assets, then it will be deemed that the security right is created at that time; otherwise, in the case of future assets, security right will be deemed to be created at the time when the grantor acquires rights or power to encumber the asset. Thus, in the latter, the security agreement may be entered into before the grantor acquires rights over the property.[54] In that context, in after-acquired property the security 'cannot vest until the [grantor] actually acquires title to specific assets falling within the generic categories of after acquired assets over which security was granted.'[55] Thus, this will be the time when the grantor has rights in the collateral.

Under both the Guide and the Model Law a security right (charge) is a property right (right *in rem*).[56] A right *in rem* allows the holder of that right to enforce it over third parties in addition to the debtor enabling the holder of that right to enforce it in case of debtor's default and to have priority over the unsecured creditors and others in debtor's insolvency. When the security right is created, it is considered to be effective against the grantor (debtor). Under English law security rights are rights *in rem* and enforceable towards third parties, thus fulfilling the basic criteria of a modern secured transactions regime.[57] The UCC Article 9 also adopts a similar approach, where the secured creditor has a proprietary right, thus not full ownership, and the debtor retains the title.

Few formalities are required to create a security interest under English law. The main requirement is that parties must have the intention to create a security interest over an identifiable asset. For a security interest to attach, an agreement between the debtor and the secured creditor must be concluded. The intention must indicate that the agreement creates a security interest and not a contractual right. The intention of parties should also make it clear that the interest should attach immediately or, if the grantor acquires rights in the future, at the occurrence of this event.[58] The collateral must be included in

53 Article 7; see Goode, op. cit. (f'note 26), 175–7; *see also below* Section 4.4 INTERNATIONAL INTERESTS.

54 Recommendation 13. There is some similarity with UCC Article 9 requirements, *see below*.

55 Walsh, C. (2003) 'Super-Priority for Asset Acquisition Financing in Secured Transactions Law: Formalism or Functionalism?', in S. Worthington (ed.) *Commercial Law and Commercial Practice*. Oxford: Hart, 457, at 458.

56 Model Law states that the charge is 'a property right and not merely an obligation', at vi. Under the Guide, '[a] security right . . . is a property right (as opposed to a personal right) in movable assets (as opposed to immovable property) created by agreement (as opposed to statutory or judgment rights) between the grantor and the secured creditor', para. 1, at 74.

57 For a similar argument, *see* McCormack, G. (2004) *Secured Credit under English and American Law*. Cambridge: Cambridge University Press, 46.

58 This reflects the principle in Guide, recommendation 13.

the description in the security agreement. The asset serving as collateral must be identifiable, the debtor must have an interest in the collateral or a power to grant security and the asset must secure an obligation. Additionally, any contractual conditions must be completed and, in the case of pledge, actual or constructive possession must be transferred to the creditor.[59] These conditions reflect similarities with international instruments.[60] The floating charge is created when it attaches to the assets of the debtor and when crystallisation occurs it becomes a fixed charge. Notwithstanding a charge is a fixed or a floating one, it attaches to the assets, however, the difference is that the floating charge permits the debtor to deal with the assets until crystallisation.[61]

The grantor needs to have rights, not necessarily ownership, in the collateral in order for the security interests to be attached under UCC Article 9. This is because requiring ownership of the collateral would have restricted the grantor to be able to utilise full value of the assets by assigning them to multiple creditors. Put another way, if the grantor had transferred the assets outright, the requirement of ownership would have restricted him from creating another security right over the same asset, as there would have been a property right over the asset to establish a security right. This would also have been against the basic of policy priority and perfection under UCC Article 9.[62] The security interest attaches when it becomes enforceable between the creditor and debtor (UCC§9–203). The interest becomes enforceable when an obligation has been created, which will occur when value is given and the grantor has rights in the collateral. The term 'attachment' does not mean *stricto sensu* formal validity that is understood under some of the international instruments. Attachment grants the secured party a property right to foreclose on the collateral upon the default of the debtor. UCC§9–203(b) requires three fundamental steps for the creation of enforceable security interests. In addition to a security agreement,[63] which is a critical condition upon the conclusion of which the security interest attaches, the secured party must give value and the debtor must have rights, or power to transfer rights, in the collateral to the secured creditor. The security agreement must be authenticated[64] by the grantor ('debtor' under the UCC Article 9 terminology) unless the secured party takes possession or control of the asset. The security agreement must describe the collateral. Subject to some exceptions,[65] the security agreement sets out those terms that are effective between the secured party

59 Gullifer, op. cit. (f'note 27), 65 *et seq.*

60 E.g. Guide recommendation 14 has similar requirements. Power to dispose of assets, as in Cape Town Convention Article 7, and identifiability, as required in all instruments, are similar to other instruments. Constructive possession is not permitted under the Guide. For further discussion on this point, *see* Chapter 5.

61 Walsh, op. cit. (f'note 55), 458 and fn. 7.

62 Bridge, M., MacDonald, R., Simmonds, R. and Walsh, C. (1999) 'Formalism, Functionalism and Understanding the Law of Secured Transactions', 44 *McGill L.J.* 567, 585–6 and fn. 59.

63 UCC§9–203(b)(3)

64 UCC §9–102(7). Authentication, in general terms, means to sign or execute or otherwise adopt a symbol or encryption to identify the person and adopt a record.

65 E.g. UCC§9–204(b).

and the debtor, against the purchasers of collateral and against creditors claiming rights over the same collateral.[66] The attachment gives rights to proceeds (UCC§9–203(f) and 9–315) and is regarded as attachment of a security interest in a supporting obligation for the collateral. One of the crucial features of the UCC Article 9 is that the security agreement, like the international instruments,[67] may cover future assets (after-acquired property), where the security agreement attaches only after the debtor obtains rights in the collateral,[68] and this is in line with the party autonomy, where parties may agree to postpone the time of attachment.[69] The security agreement (UCC§9–102(73)), similar to the Cape Town Convention's description of international interest, 'creates or provides for' a security interest, the rationale of which can be attributed to the functional approach of UCC Article 9 to security interest which encompasses all transactions in movables serving for security purposes. Sigman succinctly explains this as follows:

> Debtor grants a security interest to Secured Party in all Debtor's inventory, wherever located, whenever acquired, to secure all of Debtor's present and future obligations, of whatever nature, whenever and however arising, in favor of Secured Party. This will create a security interest not only in Debtor's present and future inventory, but also automatically . . . in all proceeds of whatever nature . . . or evidenced by an instrument . . . or chattel paper . . .[70]

The EBRD Core Principles support effective creation of security interests[71] by indicating that the security right should have proprietary nature, which is why the Model Law's security right is a property right and not merely an obligation.[72] Also the significance of quick, inexpensive and simple creation of security rights and their non-possessory nature are confirmed. This assumption is also assisted by the First Principle, which suggests that the security must not be prohibited in order to increase lending on improved terms. The creation of security is achieved through minimum formalities, upon which the effectively created security right can be effectively asserted to third parties, granting priority to the chargeholder, and continues to be effective during the insolvency of the chargor.[73] These reflect the ideas

66 UCC§9–201.

67 *See e.g.* Guide recommendation 13; Receivables Convention Article 8.

68 UCC§9–203(b)(2) and 204.

69 UCC§9–203(a).

70 Sigman, H. (2004) 'Security in Movables in the United States – Uniform Commercial Code Article 9: A Basis for Comparison' in E-M. Kieninger, (ed.) *Security Rights in Movable Property in European Private Law*. Cambridge: Cambridge, 54, at 64.

71 EBRD Core Principles, Principle 2 recommends the quick, cheap and simple creation of a proprietary non-possessory security right.

72 For more information on the Model Law's security right, *see e.g.* Simpson, J.L. and Röver, J-H.M. (1998) 'General Principles of a Modern Secured Transactions Law', in J. Norton and M. Andenas (eds) *Emerging Financial Markets and Secured Transactions*. The Hague: Kluwer, 143, 145–153.

73 This is equally true in the sense that the costs of taking and maintaining security should be low, according to which high costs of security should not be reflected in the price of credit so that the efficiency of credit is not diminished. This reflects the EBRD Core Principles Sixth Principle. *See generally* Röver, op. cit. (f'note 21), 87.

established in the Guide that stipulate that the law should ensure that the price for creation of security rights should be low; the procedure is simple and effective[74] so that a security right created in one jurisdiction is recognised in the other. The Model Law sets the details of formalities necessary for creation of charge under Part 2. The Model Law has a flexible definition of secured debt and charged property. Parties can define and structure the secured debt and rights that can be secured. A secured debt may be identified specifically or generally (Article 4.3.2), or as conditional or future (Article 4.3.4). The charge may secure one or more debts (Article 4.1). Charged property may be identified specifically or generally (Article 5.5). A charge may cover things and rights that are not owned by the chargor at the time of creation of charge (Articles 5.8 and 6.8). However, Article 6.8 does not apply to an unpaid vendor's charge or possessory charge, as in those cases the ownership needs to be transferred for the charge to be created. The charged property may be identified as all the assets of the enterprise (Article 5.6), which leads to the concept of enterprise charge, drawing on the English floating charge. Following this flexible nature of charge and secured debt under the Model Law, for the creation of a registered or a possessory charge, a charging instrument must be concluded between the chargor and chargeholder, and registration or possession must take place (Articles 6.2 and 6.4). In the case of a possessory charge, the maximum amount secured need not be shown on the charging instrument; nevertheless, it needs to appear in the registration statement. The unpaid vendor's charge is created under Article 9.1, according to which a written agreement must be concluded and there is no need for registration (after six months it may be registered and converted into a registered charge) or delivery of enforcement notice; under Article 17.3 the unpaid vendor's charge has priority over the registered charge. The charging instrument, which must be dated and contain the identity of the chargor, the chargeholder, charged property and the secured debt, is only necessary for registered and possessory charges.

Creation of 'all-assets security' (similar to the English floating charge) over the entire business of a company plays a pivotal role under the Guide.[75] A similar argument also applies to the types of obligations secured by a security right; thus, any type of obligation may be secured by a security right.[76] EBRD Core Principles on Secured Transactions also recommends that security should be available over all types of assets by securing all types of debts and between all types of persons.[77] Under English law, through the floating charge, the assets of the debtor are encumbered by the secured creditor (chargor). However, with the recent changes in the law made by the Enterprise Act 2002, which requires certain percentages of

74 Recommendations 14–15.

75 Recommendation 17: '[A security right] may . . . encumber all assets of a grantor.' The general recommendations of the Guide with regards to creation also apply to receivables discussed under asset specific recommendations and to outright assignment of receivables.

76 Recommendation 16.

77 EBRD Core Principles on Secured Transactions Principle 7.

floating charge realisations to be set aside for unsecured creditors,[78] the Guide differs from English law in the sense that it does not allow carve-outs. The Guide highlights the significance of creation of security over all types of assets, present or future,[79] and the secured obligation may be determined or determinable, future or present and conditional or fluctuating obligations.[80] In the case of future assets, the creation of security rights takes place when the grantor acquires a right in respect of those assets or the power to encumber that property.[81] This combination is followed by the automatic extension of security to identifiable proceeds and to the proceeds of proceeds.[82] The Guide's comprehensive functional approach extends the application of its rules on creation to outright assignments,[83] assignments of future and bulk receivables, security over funds credited to a bank account, over proceeds under an independent undertaking and over negotiable instruments or goods represented by the documents.[84] The ability to secure all available assets of the debtor is critical. The after-acquired property interests (when all the property of the debtor is used as security for a debt, the debtor acquires property, which then becomes part of the security for the debt) may lead to a priority position for the secured creditor. Thus, under UCC Article 9 purchase-money security interests are given priority[85] as they represent new value/money in the debtor's property (the creditor lends money, without which a new material cannot be purchased).

The Receivables Convention leaves formal validity of assignment to the law applicable outside the Convention. The applicable law outside the Convention may be ascertained by the autonomous conflict-of-law rules contained in Chapter V. It is important to note that the form of assignment is a condition of priority under Articles 22 and 5(g). For an assignment to be effective between the assignor and the assignee, notification of the debtor is not necessary.[86] Similarly the formal validity of the contract of assignment between the parties is also governed by the law of assignor's location under Article 27. In addition, Article 10 deals with the efficient and clear manner of transfer of security rights, with minimal requirements where a security is deemed to follow the assigned receivable without the necessity of a new act of transfer, and contractual limitations

78 *See above* Chapter 1 for more discussion of the Enterprise Act 2002. *See e.g.* Gullifer, L. (2008) 'The Reforms of the Enterprise Act 2002 and the Floating Charge as a Security Device', 46 *Can. Bus. L. J.* 399.

79 Recommendations 2(a), 13 and 17.

80 Recommendations 2(c) and 16; Guide, paras 38 *et seq.*, at 74.

81 Recommendation 13.

82 There is a possibility that the parties may agree otherwise. Recommendation 19. UCC §9–205 also allows the security interest to be passed automatically to the proceeds of the original collateral.

83 Guide, para. 25, at 37.

84 Recommendations 13–28, but specifically 23–28.

85 They are perfected upon attachment (automatic perfection) and if a purchase-money security interest is perfected by filing within a certain period (generally before or within 20 days after the debtor receives the collateral), it will have priority over other secured creditors. UCC §9–317(e).

86 Receivables Convention Article 14(1).

are set aside. With regard to the material validity of the assignment between the assignor and assignee, as long as the assignment contract is effective as a contract, the assignment will be considered to be effective.[87] Additionally, under Article 14(1) for the assignment to be effective as between the assignor and the assignee no notification is necessary. However, parties may agree otherwise.

A charge under the Model Law can be created if the chargor is the owner of the charged property, the charge secures the debt and the chargor has the power to grant the charge at the time of creation of charge or at least it is deemed to be created.[88] The Model Law supports minimal formalities for the creation of security rights and is based on the single security right (charge) for all types of things and rights,[89] thus lifting the distinction between traditional security rights (pledges of rights and movables and mortgages).[90] The Model Law contains registered, possessory, unpaid vendor's charges and enterprise charges.[91] A charging instrument is necessary for the creation of a registered and possessory charge (Article 7). However, a charging instrument is not necessary for the unpaid vendor's charge; rather, under Article 9.1 a written retention-of-title agreement between the vendor and the purchaser is necessary, where the vendor retains title or obtains security right over the asset until payment of the purchase price. The charging instrument identifies the chargor and chargeholder, indicates the date, the secured debt and the charged asset, all of which will be indicated in the registration statement. For the registration of charges, under Article 8, a registration statement is required. It seems that without a registration statement a charge (except the unpaid vendor's charge) cannot be created under the Model Law. A registration statement is considered a formal validity condition of a charge. Therefore, unlike the approach under the Guide, under the Model Law, creation of a security is sufficient to establish effectiveness both between parties and against third parties.[92]

4.3.3 Statutory and contractual limitations

Statutory limitations on the assignment of future and bulk receivables, mainly related to the requirements of notification and specificity, are set aside by international instruments[93] and the same has been recommended by law reform bodies.[94] In certain instances, assignments are not effective due to anti-assignment clauses included in the original contracts. Under international instruments, contractual

87 Receivables Convention Articles 2 and 11.

88 Model Law Article 6.5.

89 Model Law Articles 4 and 5.2 enable charging of all secured types of debts and property.

90 Model Law, at vi; Article 1(1) and Part 2 Creation of a Charge.

91 Articles 5.6, 8, 9, 10.

92 *See generally* Röver, op. cit. (f'note 21), 73; *see* op. cit. (f'note 19).

93 Receivables Convention Article 8; Guide recommendation 23; Model Law Article 5.5, 5.8–5.9; Factoring Convention Article 5.

94 Law Commission Report No. 296 (August 2005), paras 4.40 and 6.73.

limitations are set aside to recognise the effectiveness of assignments,[95] in order to facilitate financing practices as well as provide access to credit, without which assignors cannot expand their businesses. Creation of security rights in future assets and the extension of security into proceeds are crucial and are reflected in the instruments.[96] The Guide treats permitting security rights in future assets of a grantor as a fundamental policy.[97]

4.3.3.1 Creation of security right and the assignment of bulk and future receivables

An assignment of bulk receivables is an assignment where bulk receivables are assigned as a mass and not specified individually. A future receivable is a receivable arising from a contract that is concluded after the conclusion of the assignment contract that assigns it. The difference between a conditional right and a future right is that the former is in existence, arising out of an existing contract, and although the right is conditional, its assignability is universally accepted, whereas a future right does not exist and the contract out of which it will arise has not been concluded at the time of its assignment. The assignability of future receivables is not globally recognised.[98] Notification of underlying debtors presents a critical problem in that it provides no means of constituting a security interest on the future receivables of a business, since there is no debtor to notify until the right to payment arises.[99] Notification requirement increases the cost of credit by introducing administrative burden in the assignment of bulk receivables. The requirement of specificity, which derives from the 'doctrine of specificity', prevents assignment of future receivables. According to this doctrine, the property must be identified specifically in order to be transferred either in the form of specification of the debtor or the information on the receivable; the security created over a future property will be deemed as a security for pre-existing debt, which may be treated as voidable preference. Granting security over future receivables may be frowned upon on the grounds that it diminishes the means of income or weakens the funds available to unsecured creditors,[100] who cannot adjust their positions. The concern over assignments of bulk and future receivables is that

95 Receivables Convention Article 9; Guide recommendation 24; Model Law Article 5.4; Factoring Convention Article 6. Also in case law, *see e.g. Caledonia North Sea Ltd v London Bridge Engineering Ltd* [2000] Lloyd's Rep IR 249 (Ct Sn: IH), 267–268, where Lord Rodger of Earlsferry states that '. . . modern legal systems tend to recognise that rights are transferable . . .'.

96 E.g. under the Receivables Convention, as long as the proceeds are identifiable (Article 24(2)) under Article 14, the assignee has a contractual right to proceeds. Guide, para. 64, at 23–4, as fundamental policy security rights extend to proceeds.

97 Guide, para. 63, at 23.

98 Zweigert, K. and Kötz, H. (1998) *An Introduction to Comparative Law*, 3rd edn. Oxford: Clarendon Press, 445 *et seq.*; Wood, P.R. (1998) 'World-Wide Security – Classification of Legal Jurisdictions' in Norton and Andenas (eds), op. cit. (f'note 72), 39, at 40 *et seq.*

99 Serick, R. (1990) *Securities in Movables in German Law: An Outline*. London: Kluwer, 81–82 (arguing that the desire to maintain secrecy is the main reason why pledges of intangibles are not generally used in German financing practice).

100 Wood, P.R. (1995) *Comparative Law of Security and Guarantees*. London: Sweet & Maxwell, 40 *et seq.*

these types of financing practices may have impact 'on the economic freedom of the assignor or related specificity concerns'.[101] The restriction of security over future receivables arises out of 'the desire to prevent future property being caught up as a security for pre-existing debt'.[102] Also, in certain jurisdictions statutory prohibitions on bulk assignments have been justified with the 'concerns about the advantage gained by [large] financing institutions, obtaining a bulk assignment . . . and future receivables from their borrowers, over small suppliers, who are often protected by retention of title arrangements'.[103] The cost of credit is affected by describing each receivable upon its creation, notifying the debtor and overseeing the administrative work to ensure an effective transfer. Administrative costs arise when the assignor and the assignee create new agreements each time a receivable comes into existence.

Under English law, future receivables are assignable in equity[104] but not assignable at law.[105] English law 'regards an unearned debt under an existing contract as an existing debt',[106] as this will be a present right to future income.[107] In order to obtain a legal title of receivables as a result of a statutory assignment, s.136 of the Law of Property Act 1925 must be conformed to after the receivable has come into existence. If an assignment of future receivables is supported by consideration,[108] it may be effective as an agreement to assign in equity if and when the receivable comes into existence,[109] upon which the ownership passes automatically. Receivables may be assigned under factoring practice using the whole turnover agreement, according to which the receivables may be purchased upon providing the consideration necessary to assign the receivables.[110] The doctrine of specificity

101 Bazinas, S. (2002) 'Multi-Jurisdictional Receivables Financing: UNCITRAL's Impact on Securitization and Cross-Border Perfection', 12 *Duke J. Comp. & Int'l L.* 365, 371.

102 Wood, op. cit. (f'note 100), at 41.

103 Bazinas, *ibid.*, at 372.

104 *Legard v. Hodges* (1792) 1 Ves. Junr. 478 (Eng. C.A. 1792); *Tailby v. Official Receiver* (1888) L.R. 13 App. Cas. 523, at 545; *Norman v. Federal Comr of Taxation* (1963) 109 CLR 9, 24 High Court of Australia, where it is explained that '. . . in equity . . . present assignment of something to be acquired in the future is, when made for value, construed as an agreement to assign the thing when it is acquired. . . . The purported assignee thus gets an equitable interest in the property immediately the legal ownership of it is acquired by the assignor, assuming it to have been sufficiently described to be then identifiable.'

105 *Lunn v. Thornton* (1845) 1 C.B. 379.

106 Derham, R. (2003) *The Law of Set-Off*, 3rd edn. Oxford: Oxford University Press, 791.

107 *Shepherd v. Commissioner of Taxation* [1966] A.L.R. 969.

108 Oditah, F. (1991) *Legal Aspects of Receivables Financing*. London: Sweet & Maxwell, 27.

109 Sealy, L.S. and Hooley, R.J.A. (2003) *Commercial Law Text, Cases and Materials*, 3rd edn. London: Butterworths, 908–9; McCormack, G. (1987) 'Fixed Charges on Future Book Debts', *Co. Law.* 3, 6; Treitel, G. (2003) *The Law of Contract*. London: Sweet & Maxwell, 11th edn., 683; Goode, R. (1982) 'Some Aspects of Factoring Law – The Acquisition of Rights in the Receivables', *J.B.L.* 240, 242; Kötz, H. (1991) *International Encyclopaedia of Comparative Law Rights of Third Parties Third Party Beneficiaries and Assignment*. 13–82; *Glegg v. Bromley* [1912] 3 K.B. 474, CA.

110 Sealy and Hooley, *ibid.*, 989–90. Future receivables cannot be assigned under facultative agreements where receivables may be purchased once they come into existence and the transaction becomes an equitable assignment. Therefore, the assignee is not under any duty to purchase the receivables that are not yet in existence and to provide consideration.

has been abolished so far as it prevented security over future receivables by *Holroyd v Marshall*[111] and *Tailby v Official Receiver*.[112] Both cases permitted the generic identification of future receivables, thus making the specificity requirement futile.[113] A new act of transfer is not necessary for the effectiveness of the assignment of future receivables because the security agreement becomes effective between the parties as of the moment of acquisition of the property by the debtor, thus a new act of transfer is not necessary.[114] Under UCC§9–204 a security agreement may create or provide for a security interest in after-acquired property without a supplemental action.[115] This section adopts the principle of the floating lien, which was rejected in the pre-UCC Article 9 era.[116]

Notification requirement on the part of the debtor is also a concern, as the debtor is unknown at the time of the assignment and the assignee may not notify of the assignment to secure priority against other assignees to whom the assignor might have subsequently assigned.[117] *Dearle v Hall*[118] is ineffectual in protecting the priority in the assignment of future receivables until they come into existence.[119] As notification cannot be made until the debt comes into existence, the debtor's equities[120] cannot be prevented from being enforceable as against the assignor. Professor Oditah argues that 'the debt from an executory contract does not arise except subject to the debtor's cross claim [and] . . . the cross claim would have been eligible for equitable set-off'.[121]

Bulk assignment is used 'where the [assignor's] pattern of trade consists of a large number of small debtor accounts but where he does not meet the standards

111 (1861) 10 HLC 191, [1861–1873] All ER Rep 414.

112 (1888) L.R. 13 App. Cas. 523. The future receivable must match the description in the assignment upon coming into existence (at 533).

113 Receivables Convention Article 8(1)(b) also requires identifiability in the case of future receivables at the time of conclusion of original contract.

114 Gullifer, op. cit. (f'note 27), at 7. This is also the regulation under the Guide, Receivables Convention Article 8(2) and Factoring Convention Article 5(b).

115 UCC §9–204, cmt. 2, which states that 'a security interest in after-acquired property is not merely an equitable interest; no further action by the secured party – such as a supplemental agreement covering the new collateral – is required'.

116 Most notably, *Benedict v Ratner* (1925) 268 US 353.

117 *Calisher v. Forbes* (1871–72) L.R. 7 Ch. App. 109; *Johnstone v. Cox* (1880) L.R. 16 Ch.D. 571 *aff.d* (1881) 19 L.R. Ch.D. 17, C.A.

118 (1828) 3 Russ. 1.

119 *Somerset v. Cox* (1865) 33 Beav 634.

120 For various views on whether or not notice of assignment has any effectiveness to crystallise the debtor's equities, *see e.g.* Wood, P. (1989) *English and International Set-off*. London: Sweet & Maxwell, Ch. 16–117; Oditah, op. cit. (f'note 108), at 240; Derham, op. cit. (f'note 106), at 794; *Roxburghe v. Cox* (1881) 17 Ch D 520, 527. Under the Receivables Convention Article 18(2), the debtor may raise rights of set-off available at the time of notification received by the debtor against the assignee. As the future receivables are effective as of the conclusion of original contract this will not be an issue and the assignee is protected from the rights of set-off.

121 Oditah, op. cit. (f'note 108), at 239; *Rother Iron Works Ltd. v. Canterbury Precision Engineers Ltd.* [1974] Q.B. 1, 6. For difficulties in relation to assignment of bulk and future receivables and priority matters, *see e.g.* Oditah, F. (2009) 'Recurrent Issues in Receivables Financing', in J. Armour and J. Payne (eds) *Rationality in Company Law Essays in Honour of DD Prentice*. Oxford: Hart, 321.

of financial standing'.[122] One of the conditions[123] for a security interest to attach, other than by operation of law, is the identifiability of the subject matter. A security interest cannot be created on an asset that cannot be identifiable at the time of the security agreement, or alternatively, cannot be identifiable as subsequently falling within its terms.[124] Until the time of identification the assignee may not have security on these goods. If an unidentified part of a bulk asset is given as security, this will not create a security for the assignee as it is not possible to ascertain which part of this bulk is the subject matter of the security.[125] If there is an unidentified receivable then a security interest in that unidentified intangible cannot be granted, but a part interest in an identified receivable can be granted.[126] Thus, for example, assignment of a certain percentage of a receivable would be effective as a security interest.[127] In this identification specificity is not required. Only the identifiability of the asset, as falling within the terms of the security agreement, would be necessary.[128] UCC§9–108 governs and validates bulk assignments.[129] A sufficient description and reasonable identification of collateral – such as in a specific listing, category, type of collateral defined in the UCC, quantity, computational or allocational formula or procedure, or any other method – is necessary to ascertain whether bulk assignment is effective if the identity of the collateral is objectively determinable.[130] UCC§9–108(a) stipulates that a description will be sufficient, whether or not it is specific, if it reasonably identifies what is described.[131] This is also an illustration of recognising the effectiveness of partial assignments or assignments of undivided interests.[132] A safe harbour rule is provided 'that makes sufficient a description that identifies collateral by category or by a type of collateral defined in the UCC'.[133] In that context, UCC§9–108(b) supplements the rule in UCC§9–108(a). An 'all-assets' supergeneric description of the collateral will not be sufficient to create a security interest under UCC§9–108(c), as it will not be reasonably identifying the collateral.

122 Salinger, F. (2006) *Factoring: The Law and Practice of Invoice Finance*, 4th edn. London: Sweet & Maxwell, at 18–9.

123 Other conditions are security transfer or agreement; debtor's interest or power to dispose; obligation to be secured; fulfilment of contractual conditions for attachment.

124 Gullifer, op. cit. (f'note 27), 68–9.

125 *Re London Wine Co. (Shippers)* (1986) PCC 121.

126 Gullifer, op. cit. (f'note 27), 67–9.

127 E.g. *Brice v. Bannister* (1878) L.R. 3 Q.B.D. 765; *Durham Bros. v. Robertson* [1898] 1 Q.B. 765; *Re Steel Wing Co. Ltd.* [1921] 1 Ch. 349.

128 International instruments followed a similar approach, *see below*.

129 UCC §9–201.

130 UCC §9–108(b)

131 *In re Pickle Logging, Inc.*, 286 B.R. 181 (Bkrtcy. M.D. Ga., 2002); *In re McAllister*, 267 B.R. 614 (Bkrtcy. N.D. Iowa, 2001); *In re Bennett Funding Group, Inc.*, 255 B.R. 616 (N.D.N.Y. 2000).

132 UCC §9–108(b)(5).

133 Sigman, H. and Smith, E. (2002) 'Toward Facilitating Cross-Border Secured Financing and Securitization: An Analysis of the United Nations Convention on the Assignment of Receivables in International Trade', 57 *Bus. Law.* 727, 738 and n.65; UCC §9–108(b)(2)–(3).

International instruments set aside statutory limitations and favour assignability without requiring additional conditions.[134] The Factoring Convention Article 5(a) sets aside statutory limitations that prohibit the effectiveness of assignment of bulk and future receivables on the grounds they have not been specified individually. In relation to future receivables, Article 5(b) provides that a new act of transfer is unnecessary and a provision in a factoring contract will serve as a means to transfer once the future receivables come into existence. The Factoring Convention, unlike the Receivables Convention,[135] recognises the effectiveness of an assignment of future and bulk receivables only as between the parties to a factoring contract. The rationale was 'to avoid any ambiguity as regards the scope of the article in those legal systems where the term 'supplier' [assignor] might be understood . . . [as including] a trustee in bankruptcy carrying on the supplier's business'.[136] As the Factoring Convention does not deal with the question of priorities with respect to the receivables between the assignee and third parties, the scope of Article 5 is 'limited to the validity and enforceability of assignments of [bulk and] future receivables as between the [assignor] and [assignee]'.[137] As the rule operates between the assignee and assignor, it will not bind the debtor unless he has written notice relating to the receivables arising under the original contract, made at or before the time when notice is given. In a contract of assignment, receivables should be described in such terms by the contract and must be identifiable to the contract. The time of identification for existing receivables is the time of conclusion of the contract, and for future receivables it is the time when receivables come into existence. Specification of the moment at which a transfer becomes effective will clarify doubts in those systems, where assignment of bulk and future receivables are not recognised and a new act of transfer is needed.[138] The Factoring Convention does not establish rules regulating the validity of the factoring agreement.[139] Arguably, to the detriment of the Convention, the validity is left to be determined by the applicable law according to the conflict of laws rules of the forum.

The Guide and the Receivables Convention adopt the view, particularly in relation to the assignment of future receivables, that 'as long as the assignor and assignee are in agreement as to the scope of the receivables assigned, no further formality need be imposed in order for the assignment to be effective between

134 E.g. Receivables Convention Article 8, Factoring Convention Article 5, Guide recommendation 23 and Model Law Articles 4.3.2, 4.3.4, 4.4 and 5.5.

135 Receivables Convention Article 8(1), *see below*.

136 Mestre, F. (1987) 'Explanatory Report on the Draft Convention on International Factoring', *Unif. L. Rev.* 85, at 115.

137 UNIDROIT Study LVIII–Doc. 14, para. 30.

138 UNIDROIT Study LVIII–Doc. 33, at 17, para. 30. Similarly, under English Law (*Tailby v. Official Receiver*) specificity is not required, but a description of receivables, which can be identified to the contract with regard to bulk assignments and the assignment of future receivables, is necessary. The same argument applies equally to UCC Article 9.

139 Goode, R. (1987) 'The Legal Aspects of International Factoring', in K.F. Hagenmüller and H.J. Sommer (eds) *Factoring Handbuch National–International*. Frankfurt: Fritz Knapp Verlag, 149, 157.

them'.[140] The Receivables Convention Article 8 and the Guide recommendation 23 set aside statutory limitations that prevent the effectiveness of assignment of bulk and future receivables as well as partial or undivided interests. The rationale is to facilitate receivables financing and enable effectiveness of assignments in a changing pool of receivables, which is the pattern in securitisations.[141] The rationale of restricting these types of assignments is to protect 'the assignor from excessive limitations on its economic activity, addressed by requirements for a specific description of the assigned receivable'.[142] However, specific description requirement, which may be described as the requirement that an assignor specify each and every receivable before assigning them, causes high administrative burden, which negatively affects the cost of credit and sometimes, as in the case of assignment of future receivables, may not be possible. The Receivables Convention defines 'existing' and 'future receivable'.[143] With respect to future receivables, it is argued that when the time of transfer is closer to the time of assignment, more certainty and predictability could be achieved as to rights of the assignee.[144]

The Receivables Convention Article 8(1) and the Guide recommendation 23(a) recognise the effectiveness as between the assignor and the assignee or as against the debtor or as against third parties. Article 8(1) also protects the priority of an assignee by rejecting any rule that denies priority of an assignee just because there is an assignment of bulk and future receivables. An assignment cannot be deemed ineffective as against the assignor, the assignee and the debtor or a third party just because it is an assignment of future receivables or a receivable that is not individually identified at the time of the assignment. The Receivables Convention only requires that these receivables be identifiable as receivables to which the assignment relates. It seems that, in the case of bulk receivables, a specific description of the receivables is not necessary, and description can be general so long as the receivables may be identified to the assignment contract. Article 8(1)(b) also provides for bulk assignments that they should be identifiable at the time of the assignment, if they cannot be identified individually under Article 8(1)(a). For the assignment of future receivables it is necessary that receivables, at the time of the conclusion of the contract from which the receivables arise, be identified as

140 Guide, para. 105, at 92.

141 For the Receivables Convention, *see* Bazinas, S. (1998) 'An International Legal Regime for Receivables Financing: UNCITRAL's Contribution', 8 *Duke J. Comp. & Int'l L.* 315, 329 and n. 69; Markell, B. (2002) 'UNCITRAL's Receivables Convention: The First Step, But not the Last', 12 *Duke J. Comp. & Int'l L.* 401, 403.

142 Bazinas, S. (2001) 'Lowering the Cost of Credit: The Promise in the Future UNCITRAL Convention on Assignment of Receivables in International Trade', 9 *Tul. J. Int'l & Comp. L.* 259, 265.

143 Article 5(b); A/CN.9/489, para. 87. An 'existing receivable' arises upon or before conclusion of the contract of assignment and a 'future receivable' arises after conclusion of the contract of assignment. The Guide has no particular definition for these, however, and defines the term 'receivable' in a similar way to the Receivables Convention Article 2(a), as a right to payment of a monetary obligation, excluding receivables arising from bank deposits, letter of credit and negotiable instruments. Guide, at 32, Receivables Convention Article 4(2)(f)–(g) and 4(3).

144 For a similar assertion, *see* A/CN.9/434, para. 119.

receivables to which the assignment relates. Identification of the exact moment at which the transfer becomes effective clarifies doubts in those legal systems where assignment of bulk and future receivables are not recognised. Effectuating future receivables as of the time of the conclusion of the original contract 'would not compromise the rights of the assignee, since in practice credit was extended at the time when an actual transaction from which receivables might flow was concluded'.[145] The Receivables Convention Article 8(2) and the Guide recommendation 23(b), like English law and UCC Article 9, support the view that a new act of transfer is not necessary for the effectiveness of assignment of future receivables. The rationale is that future receivables arise after the contract of assignment; therefore, there is no need to have a new assignment document covering that receivable. However, parties may agree otherwise. The Receivables Convention Article 10(1) supplements this and provides that a personal or property accessory right securing payment of the assigned receivable is transferred to the assignee without a new act of transfer.

Similarly, the Model Law[146] stipulates that a secure debt may be identified specifically or generally. The secured debt may also be a future receivable and it is sufficient if it is identified in the contract at the time the security agreement is concluded. Security rights may be granted over future assets. Secured debt may be conditional. Model Law Articles 4.3.4 and 4.4 clarify the position that a receivable that will be created after the security agreement will be effective if it is identified, even generally, in the security agreement. The Model Law permits the effectiveness of security between the parties if the security right is concerned with several specific items or categories. The same argument applies to bulk receivables; the charged property need not be listed individually and can be identified individually.[147]

4.3.3.2 Contractual prohibitions over the assignment of receivables and creation of a security right[148]

Principles of free negotiability and the protection of the bona fide purchaser are critical points in so far as free assignability is concerned. These go to the root of freedom and sanctity of contract, which are cornerstones of market-based economies. The principle of free negotiability suggests that financiers should not be restrained from accepting an assignment due to an anti-assignment clause. A prohibition on the assignment of right to payment may be considered 'contrary to public

145 A/CN.9/434, para. 118; A/CN.9/445, paras 224 *et seq.*

146 Article 4.3.2.

147 Articles 5.1 and 5.5.

148 *See e.g.* Goode, R. (2009) 'Contractual prohibitions against assignment', *L.M.C.L.Q.* 300; Akseli, O. (2009) 'Contractual Prohibitions on Assignment of Receivables: An English and UN Perspective', *J.B.L.* 650.

policy as an unacceptable restraint on alienation'.[149] Free assignability is necessary to protect the bona fide purchaser.[150] It is probable that the assignor may finance the business by selling the debts, and an assignment can produce new and immediate finance or cash flow to grant working capital for new business ventures and thus extend the business scope. Hence, it can be argued that free assignability actually fosters risk management, and private law restrictions, as far as possible, should not impede the risk management techniques used to manage a financier's risk exposures (and, indeed, these often have to be used according to international capital standards). Thus, prohibition of assignment should not be imposed upon the creditor.

All receivables are, in principle, assignable unless the assignment is prohibited by agreement, statute or public policy considerations.[151] Free assignability is vital for 'both businesses and consumer affairs, since credit is commonly obtained on the security of insurance policies, hire-purchase contracts and traders' and builders' book debts'.[152] The debtor has a legitimate interest in insisting on an anti-assignment clause, for protection against a change in the creditor and for legal certainty that there will be good discharge upon making payment to the original creditor without having to deal with someone else with whom there is no previous business dealing.[153] To a certain extent, debtors may be protected by law or by a specific provision in a convention.[154] After an anti-assignment clause is overridden, the debtor should be able to claim from the assignor due to breach of contract.[155] The assignor has the benefit of assigning the receivables to a financier, as a source of financing essential for the development of the business may be obtained and the use of anti-assignment clauses may pose a threat to lending practices,[156] to the cost of credit and to the creation of security over a receivable.[157] In order to facilitate the flow of cross-border credit and access to low-cost credit, anti-assignment clauses should be overridden and assignments should be effectuated.

A change of creditor may cause difficulties, statutory prohibitions may prove to be inadequate and the debtor may need protection with a contractual prohibition to which the creditor has agreed that the claim is incapable of transfer without the

149 Gullifer, op cit, (f'note 27), 118; *Tom Shaw & Co., v. Moss Empires Ltd.* (1908) 25 T.L.R. 190. Examples of public policy may include, among others, maintenance and champerty, and public servants' remuneration and tort claims.

150 Gilmore, G. (1954) 'The Commercial Doctrine of Good Faith Purchase', 63 *Yale L.J.* 1057, 1121.

151 A/CN.9/397, para. 20. *Mulkerrins v PricewaterhouseCoopers (a firm)* [2003] UKHL 41; [2003] 1 WLR 1937, para. 13 (benefit of a contract may be assigned to a third party without the consent of the debtor; unless there are contractual prohibitions, however, an assignment under s. 136 of the Law of Property Act 1925 cannot be objected as there is no debtor's consent requirement).

152 Allcock, B. (1983) 'Restrictions on the Assignment of Contractual Rights', 42 *C.L.J.* 328.

153 Mestre, F. (1987) 'Explanatory Report on the Draft Convention on International Factoring', *Unif. L. Rev.* 85, at 117.

154 E.g. the Receivables Convention's debtor protection principle and protection of debtor against assignor under Article 10(3).

155 E.g. Receivables Convention Article 9(2).

156 Goode, R. (1979) 'Inalienable Rights', 42 *M.L.R.* 553, 556.

157 Kötz, H. (1997) *European Contract Law–Volume 1: Formation, Validity, and Content of Contracts, Contract and Third Parties.* Oxford: Clarendon Press, 273.

consent of the debtor.[158] An assignment has contractual and proprietary aspects. A contractual aspect is the relationship between the assignor and the assignee (the assignment contract), while the proprietary aspect is the effect of the assignment on the debtor and third parties such as creditors of the assignor and his trustee in bankruptcy. The prohibition has an effect between the debtor and the assignee and, therefore, a contractual prohibition on an assignment entitles a debtor to refuse to deal with the assignee, disregard the notice of assignment and to continue to pay to the assignor.[159] In this case the debtor may obtain a good discharge. The assignment thus may not be considered as a statutory assignment as indicated under s.136 of the Law of Property Act 1925, the consequence of which requires the assignee to be accompanied by the assignor to sue. This may have adverse effects for the assignee, especially if the assignor is insolvent. In the event of a valid assignment as such, 'the debtor's payment to the [assignor] . . . will give him a good discharge and he will have the same rights of set-off as if the debt had not been subject to the factoring agreement'.[160] In early common law, as with Roman law, personal rights could not be transferred.[161] Courts have recognised the assignability of rights to payment to respond the needs of growing commerce and claims have been made transferable without the consent of the debtor. The prohibition of assignments is inconsistent with modern financing techniques, especially where there is an ongoing business. In the assignment of bulk receivables, 'those engaged in (non-notification) invoice discounting would not even be able to intervene directly with their clients' customers to negotiate a waiver of the no assignment clause'.[162] Under English law anti-assignment clauses are felt to be of critical importance, are increasingly used by large organisations and local authorities as part of their standard terms of trading and are considered to be standard

158 Some recent cases under English law related to the consent of the debtor are *Barbados Trust Co Ltd v Bank of Zambia* [2007] 2 All E.R. (Comm) 445; [2007] EWCA Civ 148; *Hendry v. Chartsearch Ltd.* [1998] C.L.C. 1382, (CA (Civ Div)); *Liverpool City Council v. Walton Group Plc.* [2001] N.P.C. 135, [2002] 1 E.G.L.R. 149, (Ch. D.); *Gan Insurance Co. Ltd. v. Tai Ping Insurance Co. Ltd.* [2001] EWCA Civ 1047, [2001] 2 All E.R. (Comm.) 299. *See also* McKnight, A. (2003) 'Contractual Restrictions on a Creditor's Right to Alienate Debts: Part 2', 18 *J.I.B.L.* 43 *et seq.*, where he argues that the debtor's consent must be sought – if unreasonably refused, an application for a declaration of the effectiveness of the assignment must be made to the court.

159 For this proposition, e.g. *Linden Garden Trust Ltd. v. Lenesta Sludge Disposal Ltd.* [1994] 1 A.C. 85, [1993] 3 All E.R. 417, 432, where it was stated that 'an assignment of contractual rights in breach of a prohibition against such assignment is ineffective to vest the contractual rights in the assignee'.

160 Salinger, op. cit. (f'note 122), 219.

161 The law forbade oppression of the debtor by the assignee and substation of the contract between the debtor and creditor. *See* Zweigert and Kötz, op. cit. (f'note 98), 443; Marshall, O.R. (1950) *The Assignment of Choses in Action*. London: Pitman's Equity Series, 35–9. For a historical overview, *see* McMeel, G. (2004) 'The Modern Law of Assignment: Public Policy and Contractual Restrictions on Transferability', *L.M.C.L.Q.* 483, 488 *et seq.* (arguing that 'debt was 'too personal' to be freely assigned'); Bailey, S.J. (1932) 'Assignment of Debts in England from the Twelfth to the Twentieth Century', 48 *L.Q.R.* 248, 249; Farnsworth, E.A. (1990) *Farnsworth on Contracts*, 2nd edn. New York: Aspen, §11.2, 62; Gilmore, G. (1965) *Security Interests in Personal Property*. Boston: Little, Brown & Co., §7.3, 200.

162 Goode, op. cit. (f'note 156), 556.

conditions of hire purchase agreements.[163] Statutes[164] prohibit the assignment of some rights, as does public policy.[165] Certain contracts, such as contracts of personal service, are, by their nature, non-assignable.[166] UCC Article 9 accepts free assignability.[167]

The rationale for anti-assignment clauses can be summarised as follows. First, despite having received notice of assignment, large organisations, as debtors, may pay by mistake to the assignor and overlook the notice, losing the chance of a good discharge[168] and possibly being compelled to pay for the second time.[169] Second, prohibition arises out of a concern that rights of set-off accruing from the relationship of the assignor and the debtor will be cut off[170] as of the time of notice of an assignment.[171] Under UCC§9–404, all rights that the debtor has against the assignor with regard to the current transaction can be asserted against the assignee. All rights in other matters that the debtor acquires against the assignor before notice can be asserted against the assignee. From the debtor protection perspective, as a result of the assignment, the debtor must not be worse off.[172] In *Linden Gardens Trust Ltd., v Lenesta Sludge Disposals Ltd.,*[173] Lord Browne-Wilkinson noted that one of the main concerns of debtors, in their contractual relationships and in a possible assignment, was the impossibility of relying upon new equities against the assignor after the receipt of notification of assignment.[174] Third, anti-assignment clauses are intended to prevent a debtor having to deal with someone who would have been refused to be contracted with directly in the first place

163 Bridge, op. cit. (f'note 10), 159 and n.42; *United Dominion Trust Ltd., v. Parkway Motors Ltd.*, [1955] 1 W.L.R. 719.

164 E.g. Social Security benefit and child benefits are not assignable; *see* Social Security Administration Act 1992 s.187; Pension Schemes Act 1993 s.159; Pensions Act 1995 s. 91.

165 *Re Mirams* [1891] 1 Q.B. 594; *Methwold v. Walbank* (1750) 2 Ves. Sen. 238 and *Liverpool Corp. v. Wright* (1859) 28 L.J.Ch. 868; *Arbuthnot v. Norton* (1846) 5 Moo PCC 219; for a similar decision in the US, *see e.g. Byers v. Comer* 68 P.2d 671 (Ariz.), *modified*, 70 P.2d 330 (Ariz. 1937); McMeel, op. cit. (f'note 161), at 494 *et seq.*; Worthington, S. (2007) 'The Disappearing Divide between Property and Obligation: The Impact of Aligning Legal Analysis and Commercial Expectation', 42 *Tex. Int'l L. J.* 917, 927–8; Bell, A.P. (1989) *Modern Law or Personal Property in England and Ireland.* London: Butterworths, 380.

166 E.g. *Nokes v. Doncaster Amalgamated Collieries Ltd.* [1940] A.C. 1014.

167 UCC§§9–406(f) and 9–408(d) override restrictions arising out of statutes and rule of law. UCC§9–406(d) provides free alienability of rights to payment and that any agreement between an account debtor and an assignor is ineffective. UCC§9–406(d)(2) and 9–408(a)(2) eliminate all argument that any assignment made notwithstanding an anti-assignment clause nonetheless constitutes breach as between debtor and assignor.

168 McCormack, G. (2000) 'Debts and Non-assignment Clauses', *J.B.L.* 422, 425–6.

169 *Brice v Bannister* (1878) 3 Q.B.D. 569.

170 Goode, R. (2002) 'Assignment Clauses in International Contracts', 3–4 *I.B.L.J.* 389, 396.

171 E.g. *Business Computers Ltd. v. Anglo-African Leasing Ltd.* [1977] 1 WLR 578.

172 That is the rationale for the assignee taking the assignment 'subject to equities' and thus the debtor should have no concerns. *Mulkerrins v PricewaterhouseCoopers (a firm)* [2003] UKHL 41; [2003] 1 WLR 1937, at para. 15; Gilmore, G. (1964) 'The Assignee of Contract Rights and His Precarious Security', 74 *Yale L. J.* 217, 227 *et seq.*

173 [1994] 1 AC 85; [1993] 3 All ER 417.

174 [1993] 3 All ER 417, at 429; [1994] 1 AC 85, at 105.

for perfectly commercial reasons.[175] In *Linden Gardens* Lord Browne-Wilkinson clarified that a contractual prohibition could prevent an assignment as between the assignee and the debtor, but the assignment is still effective as between assignor and assignee.[176] Fourth, transaction costs may increase if the creditor or the debtor changes, 'due to the effect of certain provisions in loan agreements such as increased costs and tax clauses'.[177]

Disputes arising out of anti-assignment clauses may be felt on a number of occasions.[178] First, the anti-assignment clause may be effective as between the assignor and the debtor, but has no effectiveness as against the assignee and the breach only grants the debtor the right to claim damages from the assignor.[179] Conversely, UCC Article 9 does not permit the debtor to claim rights against the assignor in respect of breach of anti-assignment clause.[180] Second, the anti-assignment may effectively prevent the assignor from assigning the right to payment to third parties and, thus, the debtor is not affected and can get a good discharge by paying the assignor. However, the assignor has the right to enter into a contract to assign the fruits of the contract. Arguably the debtor is effectively protected, as any agreement between the assignor and a third party regarding the assignment of the fruits of the contract, after the debtor's payment, cannot realistically affect the debtor or its interests.[181] Third, the anti-assignment clause effectively prohibits the assignor from assigning both the right to payment and its fruits, even after the payment is done. This interpretation clearly excludes the assignor from access to immediate financing and may have adverse financial affects.[182] Although the aim is to protect the debtor, the assignor's prohibition of assigning the fruits of the contract should not be limited. Fourth, the breach of an anti-assignment clause enables the debtor to claim damages and to avoid the

175 *Don King Productions Inc., v. Warren* [1998] 2 All ER 608 (High Court); [1999] 2 All ER 218 (Court of Appeal); [2000] Ch. 291, 319. *Yeandle v. Wynn Realisations Ltd.*, (1995) 47 Con. L. R. 1 (CA (Civ Div)). Tettenborn, A. (1998) 'Trust of Unassignable Agreements', *L.M.C.L.Q.* 498 *et seq.*; Tettenborn, A. (1999) 'Trusts and Unassignable Agreements – Again', *L.M.C.L.Q.* 353 *et seq.*

176 [1994] 1 AC 85, 108. Sealy and Hooley, op. cit. (f'note 109), 943 *et seq.* The decision in *Helstan Securities Ltd. v. Hertfordshire County Council* [1978] 3 All ER 262 (Q.B.D.) is distinguished in *Linden Gardens.*

177 McKnight, A. (2003) *Contractual Prohibitions on a Creditor's Right to Alienate Debts.* 18 *J.I.B.L.* 1, 3.

178 Goode, op. cit. (f'note 156), 554.

179 Receivables Convention Article 9; Guide, recommendation 24.

180 UCC§§9–406(d)(2), 9–407(a)(2) and 9–408(a)(2).

181 *See* McMeel, op. cit. (f'note 161), at 500 (arguing that this interpretation appears to be the path that English law is moving towards, although qualifying that the law is not explicitly moving towards the view that the second interpretation takes). *See also* [1994] 1 AC 85, 105.

182 Professor Goode states that an anti-assignment clause under this interpretation will be 'as a matter of law devoid of effect'. An anti-assignment clause is inserted for the benefit of the debtor and nobody else. Goode, op. cit. (f'note 156), 554–555; McMeel, op. cit. (f'note 161), 500.

contract with the assignor and thus, reduces or extinguishes the assignor's right to payment.[183]

The effectiveness of anti-assignment clauses was recognised in *Helstan Securities Ltd. v Hertfordshire County Council.*[184] It was held that the restriction in the contract precluded the assignment[185] and that the debtor had a defence to the assignee's action; thus, the assignment itself was invalid, and, therefore, ineffective between the assignee and the debtor. The *Helstan* decision also renders the purported assignment ineffective as between the assignor and assignee.[186] However, no assignee would take a financial risk to receive an assignment from a creditor knowing that he would be unpaid due to an anti-assignment clause, which renders the proprietary dimension of the assignment ineffective between the debtor and the assignee, and even further between the assignor and assignee. In any case, what are transferred are the fruits of the contract, not the actual duty of performance. If the assignor is insolvent the assignee may have no rights to the proceeds, which would constitute part of the insolvent assignor's estate,[187] and leaving the assignee without any rights may lead the assignee to lose prevailing rights against the liquidator or trustee in bankruptcy.[188] In lowering the cost of credit and fostering economic development in emerging markets, in transitional economies or even in developed economies by using English law as a catalyst, the law should be predictable. Those are economies that tend to be bulk commodity-producing or large scale manufacturers/exporters, hence the increased need for smooth-operating, low-cost efficacious finance not to be hampered by the exaggerated difficulties that prohibitions on assignments can create for the securitising and factoring of bulk receivables. The Law Commission's report had also recommended that the prohibition of assignment should have no effect against a third party assignee.[189] An assignment made in breach of an anti-assignment clause may grant the assignee 'a valid but unenforceable right of property in the debt'.[190] In the normal way, the priority will be determined in accordance with the *Dearle v Hall* rule. There are

183 Goode, op. cit. (f'note 156), 554. This has been rejected in the Receivables Convention and the Guide, and a breach of an anti-assignment clause by the assignor is not in itself a sufficient reason for the avoidance of the original contract by the debtor, thus restricting the debtor from strengthening his bargaining power. But *cf.* Lord Browne-Wilkinson, who suggested in *Linden Gardens* that interpretations one and four were 'very unlikely to occur'; [1994] 1 AC 85, 104.

184 [1978] 3 All E.R. 262 (Q.B.D.).

185 *Ibid.*, at 266.

186 Gullifer, op. cit. (f'note 27), 117. Professor Goode rightly argues that this part of the decision is incorrect.

187 For a similar statement, *see* Goode, R. (2004) *Commercial Law*, 3rd edn. London: Butterworths, 749 and n. 51 (stating that '[t]he effect of such a prohibition is to limit the factor's title to the proceeds of the assigned debt in the hands of the assignor').

188 Bridge, op. cit. (f'note 10), at 160.

189 Law Commission Report No. 296, paras. 4.40 and 6.73; *Caledonia North Sea Ltd v London Bridge Engineering Ltd* [2000] Lloyd's Rep IR 249 (Ct Sn: IH), 267–268, where Lord Rodger of Earlsferry states that '. . . modern legal systems tend to recognise that rights are transferable . . .'.

190 McCormack, op. cit. (f'note 168), 442.

decisions[191] that support free assignability and ineffectiveness of anti-assignment clauses, where a party who is bound by an earlier assignment to assign its contractual rights cannot escape the assignment by contracting in a later contract on the grounds that there should be a restriction upon assignment in the contract.[192]

The assignee may sue the assignor for breach of assignment contract by failing to obtain the consent of the debtor to the assignment.[193] If the assignor is insolvent and receives payment from the debtor, the assignee must then 'assert a proprietary claim against the assignor in order to take priority over his other creditors'.[194] In this connection, 'the assignee may be able to rely on the assignor's conduct as amounting to a declaration of trust of the proceeds of the debt in favour of the assignee'.[195] An anti-assignment clause does not prevent the assignor from having to account for the fruits of the contract to the assignee once they are received. Thus, an assignor may hold the fruits of a contract on trust for the assignee. It is rightly suggested that an assignee notwithstanding an anti-assignment clause will still be able to claim the fruits of the debt that are already held by the assignor under express trust, or under the constructive trust if there is no express trust.[196] The law attributes tortious liability on the assignee where the assignee, with the knowledge of an anti-assignment clause, induces the assignor to breach that clause.[197] Arguably the assignee should not be held liable on the sole ground of his mere knowledge of the existence of an anti-assignment clause and he must actually induce or facilitate the breach.[198] It is critical to determine how widely defined the term 'facilitate' may be. Level and type of knowledge is vital and there is a great need for clarity. The assignee's inferred knowledge is not enough: his knowledge must be actual knowledge.[199] The UCC does not attribute tortious liability to the assignee.[200]

191 E.g. *Foamcrete v. Thrust Engineering* (21 December 2000) 2000 WL 33122473 (CA), [2002] B.C.C. 221.

192 But *cf.* McKnight, op. cit. (f'note 158), 43 *et seq.* However, the decision was rightly criticised in that it would be largely ineffective against banks that provide future finance but not against factoring companies that purchase existing accounts. Bridge, op. cit. (f'note 10), 162.

193 [1994] 1 A.C. 85, 109–110, *per* Lord Browne-Wilkinson.

194 Sealy and Hooley, op. cit. (f'note 176), at 951.

195 Sealy and Hooley, op. cit. (f'note 176), at 951; *Re Turcan* (1888) 40 Ch D 5; *Barbados Trust Co. v. Bank of Zambia* [2007] EWCA Civ 148, [2007] 1 Lloyd's Rep. 495, where the owner of the debt declared a trust over the receivables in favour of the buyer and the Court of Appeal supported this technique. Turner, P.G. (2008) 'Trusts of Debts of Restricted Assignability', *C.L.J.*, 67, at 23–25; Trukhtanov, A. (2007) 'Trust of a Non-Assignable Contractual Benefit: *Barbados Trust Company v. Bank of Zambia*' 70(5) *M.L.R.*, 848–856.

196 Bridge, op. cit. (f'note 10), at 161–162; *International Factors Ltd. v Rodriguez* [1979] QB 351.

197 McKnight, A. (2002) 'Restrictions on Dealing with Assets in Financing Documents: Their Role, Meaning and Effect' 17 *J.I.B.L.* 193, 198 *et seq.*; McCormack, op. cit. (f'note 57), 231–32.

198 *Merkur Island Shipping Corp., v. Laughton* [1983] 2 A.C. 570, 608; [1983] 2 All E.R. 189; *see* McKnight, *ibid.*, at 200.

199 McCormack, op. cit. (f'note 57), at 232; *Swiss Bank Corp. v. Lloyds Bank Ltd.* [1979] Ch. 548, at 575, [1979] 2 All E.R. 853, (Ch. D.).

200 UCC §9–406 cmt. 5.

The Receivables Convention Article 9 and the Guide recommendation 24 partially invalidate contractual limitations to the assignment of receivables[201] and recognise the effectiveness of an assignment as between the assignor and the assignee and as against the debtor. The Model Law Article 5.4 gives effectiveness to charges made notwithstanding an anti-assignment clause and has exceptions.[202] The approach of unrestricted assignability has the potential to facilitate the flow of credit in cross border transactions.[203] The rule attempts to protect the interests of the debtor and the assignee and overcomes obstacles to the free flow of credit in international markets and transactions so that an assignor can invest further. The assignment made notwithstanding an anti-assignment clause will be effective as against the debtor and third parties such as creditors of the assignor and his trustee in bankruptcy (the proprietary dimension of the assignment). The Receivables Convention and the Guide do not permit contracting states to make a declaration to override the effectiveness of free assignability. A number of approaches have been considered under the Receivables Convention for formulating the effectiveness of assignments.[204] The rationale of the approaches adopted is that if there are no restrictions in receivables financing, credit flow may be facilitated and assignees will be more willing to extend lower cost credit. Consequently, the Receivables Convention gave 'precedence to the interest of the economy as a whole, even at the expense of some inconvenience to the debtor, rather than to protect debtors that have a way of protecting themselves'.[205] A similar rationale equally applies to the Guide's approach on this matter. The possibility of effectuating assignments despite contractual limitations will not adversely affect debtors who already have mechanisms such as defences and rights of set-off under the Receivables Convention[206] and the Guide.[207] Moreover, debtors may sometimes have sufficient bargaining positions and thus, can protect themselves.[208] Furthermore,

201 Recommendation 24(c) applies, as does the Receivables Convention defined under Article 9(3), to trade receivables. This is considered as a limitation to the rule under Article 9(1) and recommendation 24(a).

202 The clause in the contract will be deemed to prohibit the charging of rights: (a) Article 5.4.1, where the charged property is a contractual obligation other than money; and (b) Article 5.4.2, where the charge of a secured debt does not extend to the charge granted by the third party who owes that debt to the chargor. *See* McCormack, G. and Dahan, F. (1998) 'The EBRD Model Law on Secured Transactions: Comparison and Convergence', *CfiLR* 65, 70 and n. 16.

203 Bazinas, S. (1998) 'UNCITRAL's Work in the Field of Secured Transactions', in Norton and Andenas (eds), op. cit. (f'note 72), 211, 216. Anti-assignment is overridden by Article 10(2), which provides for the transfer of a right securing payment of the assigned receivable notwithstanding an anti-assignment clause.

204 A/CN.9/397, para. 22.

205 Bazinas, op. cit. (f'note 101), 373.

206 Receivables Convention Articles 15 *et seq.* deal with the debtor protection principle. Bazinas, S. (2002) 'UNCITRAL's Contribution to the Unification of Receivables Financing Law: The United Nations Convention on the Assignment of Receivables in International Trade', *Unif. L. Rev.*, 49.

207 Guide, recommendation 48.

208 A/CN.9/631/Add.1, para. 230 indicates that debtors (e.g. consumers) may have protection through statutory prohibitions. The Receivables Convention protects consumers and does not override consumer protection legislation (Article 4(4)).

effectiveness of an assignment overriding an anti-assignment clause would not adversely affect small debtors, as 'they do not have the bargaining power to insert anti-assignment clauses in their contracts and . . . would continue paying the same bank account or post office box'.[209]

The Receivables Convention Article 9(2) protects the assignee by providing that assignor's breach of an anti-assignment clause is not in itself a sufficient reason for the debtor to avoid the original contract.[210] The Guide has a similar protection under recommendation 24(b). Thus, in both cases tortious liability of the assignee for potential inducement of the assignor to breach the contract have been avoided. The liability of the assignor for breach of the anti-assignment clause is preserved under the Convention and the Guide;[211] however, the debtor may not terminate the agreement on the grounds of breach of an anti-assignment clause as is provided by Articles 9(2) and 10(3). This approach prevents the debtor avoiding the contract and strengthening his bargaining power.[212] If the debtor is given the right to avoid the contract solely on the ground that the assignment violated the anti-assignment clause, this will affect the cost of credit as the assignor will be threatened with the avoidance of the contract and the loss of a trading partner. This may lead to a point where the assignor will not assign the right to payment and will wait until the due date to be paid by the debtor, when the assignee may be forced to pay compensation on the ground that the anti-assignment clause is breached, which led the debtor to avoid the contract. Arguably the approach adopted by the Receivables Convention and the Guide promotes receivables financing and lowers the cost of credit as it relieves the assignee of an unnecessary burden of having to examine potentially large numbers of underlying contracts especially in the case of assignment of bulk and future receivables.[213]

The assignor may be held liable for breach of contract of anti-assignment, but the right to compensatory damages that the debtor may have under the applicable law has been left outside the Receivables Convention.[214] Any liability that the assignor may have for breach of the original contract has not been eliminated under law applicable outside the Convention. The applicable law may have a compatible regulation in the Guide. This has a positive impact on the cost of credit as 'the risk of the contract being avoided or the assignee being held liable for breach of a contractual limitation on assignment by the assignor could in itself have a negative impact on the cost of credit'.[215] Arguably the assignor may obtain low-cost credit, as the assignee will have no liability for breach of anti-assignment

209 A/CN.9/WG.II/WP.105, para. 83; A/CN.9/489, para. 103.

210 This is considered as a second limitation to the rule in Article 9(1).

211 But cf. the UCC Article 9, op. cit. (f'note 180) and the accompanying text.

212 For a similar view, *see* Bazinas, S. (2003) 'Key Policy Issues of the United Nations Convention on the Assignment of Receivables in International Trade', 11 *Tul. J. Int'l & Comp. L.* 275, 287.

213 A/CN.9/631/Add.1, para. 232.

214 A/CN.9/489, para. 99. As a comparison UCC §§9–406 and 9–408 do not have the same protection for the debtor's rights against the assignor who breaches the anti-assignment clause.

215 *Ibid.*

clause. The approach of the Receivables Convention and the Guide also promote the assignability of future and bulk receivables where, in the event of anti-assignment clauses, an assignee may be required to check the documentation of each receivable in order to ascertain assignability, which may be costly in the assignment of bulk receivables and almost impossible in future receivables.[216] Additionally, recognising the effectiveness of assignments notwithstanding anti-assignment clauses has the potential to enhance the flow of cross border trade and is 'consistent with the market economy principles and the principle against restraints on alienation of property'.[217]

The liability of the assignee to the debtor under the Receivables Convention and the Guide is limited, and they protect the assignee from liability 'under applicable national law for accepting an assignment of the receivable, if the liability would be based solely upon the assignee's knowledge of the contractual anti-assignment term'.[218] A person who is not a party to an agreement between the assignor and the debtor, on the sole ground that he had knowledge of the agreement, is protected under Article 9(2) and recommendation 24(b). In general, the knowledge of the assignee of the anti-assignment clause is irrelevant and the assignee cannot be held liable on the sole ground of his knowledge of it.[219] There must be additional grounds for knowledge in order for the assignee to be held liable as the third party. Knowledge may be relevant in the case of tortious liability of the assignee, such as for malicious interference with advantageous relations.[220] The Receivables Convention Article 18(3) and the Guide recommendation 120(c) do not allow the debtor to make a claim for breach of anti-assignment clause against the assignee by way of set-off so as to defeat the assignee's demand for payment. The rationale is that in order to lower the cost of credit, the interest of the assignee has to be protected against the debtor's defences and right of set-off, where the latter may wish to raise these against the assignee just because the assignor breached the anti-assignment clause. Moreover, the debtor is allowed to hold the assignor liable under certain circumstances for breach.

The Receivables Convention does not override domestic statutes or rules of law restricting assignments, as domestic rules may cover much broader types of receivables, such as wages, maintenance and pensions. Assignment of receivables owed by sovereign debtors is within the scope, but contracting States can make a reservation by virtue of Article 40.[221] Sovereign receivables can be subjected to statutory prohibitions rather than contractual prohibitions. Receivables

216 A/CN.9/489, para. 100.

217 Ibid; Bazinas, op. cit. (f'note 142), 265.

218 Sigman and Smith, op. cit. (f'note 133), 746; Sigman, H. and Smith, E. (2001) 'The Draft UNCITRAL Convention on Assignment of Receivables in International Trade: A Summary of the Key Provisions as Completion Draws Near', 33 *UCC L. J.* 344, 352.

219 This may 'inadvertently result in encouraging the assignee either to avoid a due diligence test or to proceed with such a test and refuse to accept the receivables or accept them at a much lower price'. A/CN.9/470, para. 102.

220 A/CN.9/470, para. 102; A/CN.9/WG.II/WP.105, para. 85.

221 A/CN.9/489 para. 104.

Convention Articles 9 and 40 relate to all debts owed by a state-owned entity. The ground for the reservation is that 'not all [States] have a policy of invalidating the assignment of sovereign receivables by law, but may instead rely on contractual limitations'.[222] In some States there are statutory limitations on assignment, and in others there are none and they simply rely on contractual limitations on assignment.[223] In order to prevent state entities coming under an obligation to pay a party as an assignee[224] in, for example, public procurement contacts,[225] the Receivables Convention aimed to be 'more acceptable to such States [by virtue of Article 40, which] allows them to ensure the effectiveness of such contractual limitations with respect to sovereign debtors by making a declaration'.[226] Under Article 40, a contracting State is permitted to declare whether an assignment of a receivable owed by a governmental debtor in that State will be excluded from the Convention rules that override contractual anti-assignment terms.[227] Contracting States will be able to opt out of the ineffectiveness of anti-assignment clauses in cases where the government itself is the debtor, and Article 9 will have no effect on a sovereign debtor who is located in a contracting State that makes a declaration, and will only be effective against the debtors of the receivables other than sovereign debtors.

The Factoring Convention Article 6(1) has a similar philosophy, where an anti-assignment clause is overridden to give effectiveness to assignments. However, the impact of this provision is diminished by the declaration option provided in Article 6(2), according to which the anti-assignment clause will still be effective against assignees if the debtor is located in a State that declares that it will not be bound by free assignability.[228] This exception is included in order to accommodate the needs of States having a strong policy in favour of upholding anti-assignment clauses.[229] Article 6(3) protects the debtor and holds the assignor liable for breach of any obligation of good faith owed by the assignor to the debtor or in respect of an assignment made in breach of the terms of the contract of sale of goods. The

222 Bazinas, op. cit. (f'note 101), 373. It was also considered that it was necessary to uphold anti-assignment clauses in syndicated credit agreements. A/CN.9/432, para. 117.

223 A/CN.9/489/Add.1, para. 64; A/CN.9/486. In England, for instance, governmental debtors generally rely on contractual rather than statutory prohibitions. If the UK was to ratify the Receivables Convention, under a declaration of Article 40, governmental debtors would not experience problems with the Receivables Convention, Article 9.

224 A/CN.9/455, para. 48.

225 A/CN.9/456, para. 115.

226 A/CN.9/489/Add.1, para. 64.

227 In the USA the Federal Assignment of Claims Act of 1940 forbids assignments of claims against, and contracts with, the U.S. government. *See* Ryan, R.H.Jr. (1999) 'Trade Receivables Purchases' *SD71 ALI-ABA* 305, 355 *et seq.*

228 Factoring Convention Article 6(2) makes a reference to Article 18 according to which the assignment shall not be effective against the debtor, when at the time of the conclusion of the sales contract, the debtor has its place of business in a contracting state that makes declaration which grants a contracting state not to be bound by free assignability. UNIDROIT Study LVIII-Doc. 33, 19.

229 Alexander, M. (1989) 'Note, Towards Unification and Predictability: The International Factoring Convention', 27 *Colum. J. Transnat'l Law*, 353, 371.

good faith owed by the assignor to the debtor is the debtor's belief that the assignor will not assign the right to payment to a third person, and Article 6(3) obliges the assignor with 'an indispensable general duty of good faith . . . towards the debtor for breach of the non-assignability clause contained in the sales contract'.[230] Similarly, the assignor's liability is preserved towards the debtor in respect of breach of original contract. These assist the assignee's position in respect of being paid by the debtor and reject the liability of the assignee towards the debtor. The Factoring Convention does not contain general exceptions to the free assignability of receivables. It does not make any distinction between sovereign and ordinary debtors.

4.3.4 Creation of security interest over bank accounts

A bank account under the Guide is defined as an account maintained by a bank to which funds may be credited. The term is broad and includes either checking or current and savings or time deposit accounts. However, a right against the bank to payment evidenced by a negotiable instrument is not included.[231] The security right is created over the right to payment of funds credited to the bank account and not on the bank account. Right to payment of funds credited to bank accounts presents certain issues. The security right is effective between the grantor and the secured creditor. It is argued that a depositary bank, as the debtor of receivables, is not bound by the assignment or the security right made despite anti-assignment clause or a clause limiting the creation of such a security right. The depository bank's consent is necessary for the recognition of the secured creditor and the obligation arising out of security agreement.[232] A security right over bank accounts is subject to similar formal validity rules envisaged under the Guide.[233]

4.4 International interests

The Cape Town Convention aims to facilitate acquisition and financing of mobile equipment. It enables the creation of a unique concept called an international interest. A new international interest was first envisaged in 1992, was favoured by the Working Group and eventually became the main point of reference of the Convention.[234] The other suggestion was recognition of the validity of a security interest created under the law of another State.[235] However, difficulties with this option were apparent. First, it would have required the recognition of a security interest created in a contracting State in another State, and a right in the

230 Ferrari, F. (1999) 'General Principles and International Uniform Commercial Law Conventions: A Study of the 1980 Vienna Sales Convention and the 1988 Unidroit Conventions on International Factoring and Leasing', 10 *Pace Int'l L. Rev.* 157, at 179.

231 Guide, at. 7.

232 Recommendation 26.

233 Recommendations 13–15.

234 UNIDROIT Study LXXII-Doc.5, para. 8.

235 UNIDROIT Study LXXII-Doc.5, para. 9.

equipment would have had to be characterised by the Convention as a security interest. The types of transactions covered under the concept of international interest vary widely in legal systems. There could have been problems of recognition, based on failure to fulfil formal validity rules or substantive rules in contracting States. Second, this would have involved complicating the already complex area of secured transactions, which is governed differently among legal systems and could have produced unworkable results, such as lack of interest in the Convention and increases in the cost of credit. Third, remedies could have posed problems where the difference between title-based devices and security interest are concerned.[236] Thus, an entirely freestanding international security interest, supported by an international public notice system, was preferred.[237]

An international interest will be deemed as an interest, in addition to satisfying conditions under Articles 2 and 7, when there is a security agreement, retention-of-title or a leasing agreement between the parties; thus, a single security right will be established. A written agreement, identification of the object in the agreement and the power of disposal of chargor, conditional seller or the lessor on the object are required. Additionally, if the agreement is a security agreement the obligation needs to be determinable, but the maximum amount need not be indicated.[238] The concept of '*international interest*' combines the constitution of an interest held by a creditor,[239] which may accommodate traditional security or title-based devices.[240] Thus, the traditional formalist approach is avoided. The international interest should be recognised in any contracting State and is a right *in rem*, giving the right to trace the equipment in the hands of third parties and granting the secured party a right to payment from the proceeds of sale of the equipment in preference to other creditors.[241] Thus, creation of a new concept of international interest is critical and produces results that assist facilitation of credit.

An international interest is described under Article 2, according to which an interest is constituted in writing as prescribed under Article 7 in uniquely identifiable objects, such as airframes, aircraft, railway rolling stock or space objects. The particular reason for unique identifiability is that, as the Convention works around an asset-based rather than a debtor-based registration system, it is necessary to identify the equipment at the outset in the agreement, creating or providing for an international interest, so that this can be registered in the international registry. Article 7 prescribes international interests by agreement creating (used for security interests) or providing for the interests (used for retention-of-title or leasing transactions). An international interest is granted by the chargor under a security

236 UNIDROIT Study LXXII-Doc.6, Add.2, para. 1.

237 UNIDROIT Study LXII-Doc.7, para. 6.

238 But cf. the Guide requires the indication of maximum amount. Op. cit. (f'note 49). In England, charges on aircraft are within the scope of Mortgaging Aircraft Order 1972. SI No. 1268 of 1972.

239 Article 1(o).

240 *See generally* Honnebier, B.P. and Milo, J.M. (2004) 'The Convention of Cape Town: The Creation of International Interests in Mobile Equipment', 12 *E.R.P.L.*, 3.

241 UNIDROIT Study LXII-Doc.5, para. 8.

agreement,[242] or vested in a conditional seller under a retention-of-title agreement or a lessor under a leasing agreement.[243] The international interest holder need not have ownership rights. The creation of an international interest receives its basis or power from the Convention and not from the national law. Thus, upon registration the international interest is granted a priority status over national interest, later registered international interests and unregistered interests, and has opposability in the debtor's insolvency against third parties.[244] An interest constituted through one of these agreements is distinct, albeit covered by the same concept, and cannot fall into the category of the other one. An international interest is created, or provided for, by a written security, retention-of-title or leasing agreement by a debtor located in a contracting State at the time of the conclusion of the agreement or under the aircraft protocol, where the aircraft is registered in a contracting State at the time of conclusion of contract.[245] In the case of retention-of-title and leasing agreements, the creditor's interest precedes the agreement providing for international interest, as it arises out of a contract of sale between the manufacturer and the conditional seller/lessor, hence the phrase '*provides for*' under Article 7.

The Convention applies to a security agreement[246] where a chargor grants, or agrees to grant, to a chargee an interest, which includes an ownership interest in or over an object to secure the performance of present or future obligations of the chargor or a third person. The simple idea behind this definition is that the chargor at the time of the conclusion of the agreement may not have the interest in the object and this permits the creation of an international interest without the necessity of any other action as soon as the interest is acquired. The security agreement creates an *in rem* claim in favour of the chargee, and Article 7, without mentioning the property right in the object, requires the chargor to have the power to dispose of the object.[247]

It seems that the applicable law is granted stronger autonomy on the constitution of international interest. Under the Cape Town Convention, the substantive applicable law determines whether an interest is a security interest or a title-based device for the purposes of applicability of default remedies. The Convention does not characterise the agreement, it only specifies whether the interest falls within one of the categories defined under Article 2(2), which is assisted by a long list of definitions contained under Article 1, which, in turn, prevents parties using national law concepts in interpreting the Convention. Thus, the international interest is autonomous and derives from the Convention.[248] If the interest falls

242 Article 2(2)(a).
243 Article 2(2)(b) and (c).
244 *See* Chapters 5 and 6.
245 Article 7 and Aircraft Protocol.
246 Article 1(ii) and for the security interest 1(jj).
247 Cuming, R. (2002) 'The Characterisation of Interests and Transactions under the Convention of International Interests in Mobile Equipment, 2001', in I. Davies (ed.) *Security Interests in Mobile Equipment*, Aldershot: Ashgate, 377, 383–4.
248 Goode, op. cit. (f'note 26), para. 2.42, at 35.

within one of the categories under Article 2(2) (i.e. an interest arising out of a security agreement or vested under a retention-of-title agreement or leasing agreement), the substantive law applicable outside the Convention will determine whether an agreement is a security agreement, title reservation or leasing agreement. Thus, the status of the interest, mainly for the purposes of the applicability of remedies, is determined by the applicable law. Moreover, the existence and the time of coming into existence of the contract are determined by the applicable law.

The difference between the UCC Article 9 and the Cape Town Convention's international interest is that the former characterises retention-of-title agreements as security interests[249] by rather looking at their functions, whereas the latter treats the proprietary rights that a security interest (charge), retention-of-title and leasing agreement represents 'as separate but equal'.[250] They are treated equally in determination of priorities (first in time rule), but distinctively in the application of remedies.[251] The significance of this can be seen between those legal systems that distinguish security interests and title-based devices and those that do not. Thus, remedies of a defaulting chargor, lessee or buyer are affected under this approach.[252] When considering scope for future reform Professor Bridge argued that the Cape Town Convention's approach of disregarding functionality and combining title-based and traditional security devices under the same framework for priority and publicity, but a different framework for remedies, could be applicable for European efforts to create a harmonised secured transactions law.[253]

The formal requirements of an agreement that creates or provides for an interest is addressed under Article 7, according to which the agreement needs to be in writing, must relate to an object of which the chargor, conditional seller or the lessor has the power to dispose, must identify the object in conformity with the relevant protocol and, in the case of a security agreement, requires the secured obligation to be determinable without the need to state the sum or maximum sum secured. Similar to English law and UCC Article 9, there are few formalities for the creation of international interests. Proceeds, as a narrowly defined notion,[254] cover proceeds arising from total or partial loss or destruction of the object or its confiscation. Proceeds arising from the sale of an object are not covered, as this

249 UCC§1–201(37), 'an interest in personal property or fixtures which secures payment or performance of an obligation'. For a discussion on this matter, *see* Cuming, op. cit. (f'note 247), 388–9.

250 Bridge, M. (2008) 'The Scope and Limits of Security Interests', in Eidenmüller and Kieninger (eds), op. cit. (f'note 24), 180, 193.

251 While default remedies for security agreements are detailed (Articles 8–9), remedies for the conditional seller and lessor are more modest (Article 10) and naturally suggest that the seller or the lessor re-takes possession or control. Further, Article 29(4) contains special priority rules for conditional seller and lessor.

252 If the applicable law characterises the agreement as a security agreement, Article 10, otherwise (title reservation or leasing agreement characterisation) Articles 8 and 9 will be applicable.

253 Bridge, ibid, at 214.

254 Article 1(w) confines applicable proceeds to insurance and other loss-related proceeds and does not extend to general proceeds.

falls within the ambit of the Receivables Convention. As a final point, formal validity of assignment of international interests deserves brief attention. Both the Cape Town Convention and the Aircraft Protocol require the assignment agreement to be in writing, that the object be identified in the agreement and, if it is an assignment by way of security, that the obligations secured by the assignment must be identified.[255]

4.5 Conclusion

Predictable rules in the creation of security rights, arguably, have the value of lowering the cost of credit. Rules must clearly endorse the secured creditor's interest in the collateral. This can be achieved by minimising the requirements to effectuate a security right, granting the ability to utilise full economic value of all assets and obligations of the debtor, distinguishing effectiveness as between the parties from the third-party effectiveness, extending the security right to the proceeds, overriding statutory and contractual limitations that obstruct creation of security rights, and recognising the effectiveness of future and bulk receivables. International instruments generally ensure that there is a distinction between third-party effectiveness and the creation of security rights,[256] thus minimising the requirements for creation of security rights. They also recognise the significance of assignment of bulk and future receivables and the futility of anti-assignment clauses, and remove any limitations adversely affecting these patterns. While in unreformed secured transactions regimes it is not permissible to use all assets and obligations to be secured, modern regimes and international instruments approve the utility of all types of assets. A single security right also has the ability to reduce complexities. What is more striking, perhaps, is the Cape Town Convention's international interest as an innovative concept. International interest embodies both security interests as well as title devices and rather than straight-jacketing contracting States to characterise their title devices into a traditional security interest, it allows them to use them as they are but requires them to register in an international registry and, save exceptions, obtain priority on a first-to-file basis.[257]

255 Article 32(1).

256 Particularly, Cape Town Convention, the Guide and the Receivables Convention.

257 Chapter 6.

5 Effectiveness of security interests against third parties

5.1 Introduction

Third-party effectiveness of security interests (which has similar functions to the UCC Article 9 concept of 'perfection')[1] is the process whereby, following the creation of a security interest (where the security interest becomes effective against the debtor/grantor), the secured creditor takes an additional step (notification, registration, taking possession or control) to make the security interest binding on or effective against third parties (liquidator, administrator and creditors).[2] The additional step, particularly the public notice, prevents potential creditors being adversely affected by the principle of *nemo dat quod non habet*.[3] Methods of achieving third-party effectiveness vary among legal cultures. Broadly, there are two methods: registration and possession. A lesser known method (except in North American jurisdictions or in jurisdictions reflecting UCC Article 9 type secured transactions regime) is control,[4] whereby the collateral, in the form of funds credited to a bank account, investment security or letter of credit rights, is controlled by the secured party through an agreement concluded between the bank and the secured party and particularly effective in the case of debtor default. In comparison with English law,[5] methods for third-party effectiveness under UCC Article 9 provide a broader array of options, where control, automatic perfection, and temporary perfection may be indicated depending on the nature of collateral.

Problems in creating practical and inexpensive publicity methods in order to establish priority among creditors have negative impact on lending decisions. In

1 For a discussion on the difference between perfection and third-party effectiveness, *see* below.

2 Sometimes an additional step to perfect or give effectiveness of a security interest against other creditors or in insolvency is not necessary, as the security interest becomes effective automatically upon creation/attachment.

3 UNIDROIT Study LXXII-Doc. 1, 9 (1989). Under English law, the *nemo dat* principle generally protects the seller/owner if the buyer in possession utilises the goods in possession. There are certain exceptions for conditional sale or hire purchase agreements but there seems to be no exception for leases. However, original owners may be under risk due to lack of generalised registration and publicity. For further information, *see* Beale, H., Bridge, M., Gullifer, L. and Lomnicka, E. (2007) *The Law of Personal Property Security*. Oxford: Oxford University Press, Chapters 5, 7 and 13.

4 UCC §9–314.

5 Possession and registration are the main two methods, but there is also control under the Financial Collateral Directives. *See* f'note 216 and the accompanying text below.

modern secured transactions systems the debtor retains possession, and with the existence of registry the creditor can achieve third-party effectiveness and provide notice. Unreformed secured transactions regimes either have no method to publicise the existence of a security interest, requiring traditional methods of possession by creditor, or their existing methods are impractical, fragmented or too expensive for third parties to be able to do searches (as in the case of paper based registries or excessive fee requirements for registry searches), which in turn increases the cost of credit. In some systems the law requires registration of the security agreement, which is not feasible, and in others there are restrictions as to who can access those registry systems. Arguably the most feasible method to lower the cost of credit is establishing an electronic registration system, which can be accessed with nominal fees and by anyone interested and this registration system should give notice to third parties on the possible existence of the security right over the collateral. This system should be supplemented with alternatives (possession and control) for certain collateral.

This chapter examines third-party effectiveness of security interests. The recurrent theme is that for facilitation of credit, reducing the risk associated with credit and establishing certainty, it is necessary to have clear rules for third-party effectiveness. The additional step has the advantage of informing third parties of proprietary rights over the debtor's assets by avoiding claims of apparent/ostensible ownership and having a positive impact on the lending decisions to the extent that it creates predictability. It is arguable that third-party effectiveness should preferably be registration of security interests but, naturally, there will be alternatives to registration. The particular issue of debate is about the requirement of a general security interests registration system necessary to notify potential creditors. The system is well known in secured transactions regimes that adopt a comprehensive and functional approach to security interests but not so much in others. The significance of this point is that a functional approach, as envisaged in the Guide or the Receivables Convention, will require all security interests to be registered (save for exceptions under the Guide and options provided under the optional annex of the Receivables Convention) for third-party effectiveness. The Cape Town Convention's registration concept contains original features and requires international interest to be registered for public notice and priority purposes. The Model Law underlies the importance of public knowledge and ensures that publicity is achieved by relying on registration for registered charges.[6]

5.2 Rationale for third-party effectiveness

The rationale for an additional procedure for third-party effectiveness is described as providing a 'public notice of the actual or potential existence of a security right in an asset'.[7] As security is important for prevention of risk of non-payment, it seems only

6 EBRD Core Principles on Secured Transactions Principle 8 recommends an effective means of publicising the existence of security rights.

7 Guide, para. 1, at 103. For a similar argument, *see* Stürner, R. (2008) 'Perfection and Priority of Security Rights Commentary', in H. Eidenmüller and E.M. Kieninger (eds) *The Future of Secured Credit in Europe* E.C.F.L.R. Munich: De Gruyter Recht, 166, 168.

logical to establish a system that will provide certainty in ascertaining priority ranking. The creditor may take into possession of or have control over the collateral, in which case certainty may be established, but still third parties must be notified so that no subsequent security interest on the asset can be created. It is generally accepted that there is commonality between methods of achieving third-party effectiveness (notifying public) and obtaining priority status.[8] The additional step to achieve third-party effectiveness in that sense is often used to determine the secured creditor's priority. In that context, ensuring prospective creditors are informed in a cost-effective, transparent and simple manner is instrumental in reducing the cost of credit and critical for prospective creditors to be able to ascertain their priority rankings.

Concerns with respect to apparent ownership, where the debtor keeps possession of property on which there may be a security or ownership right in favour of a third party, have led legislators to take measures to avoid misleading creditors.[9] Particularly, secret security interests may be created over intangibles. In order to avoid false wealth claims it is necessary to establish a publicity system (preferably a registration system but, especially, it is appropriate to publicise any security interest over intangibles through registration). In that context, the additional step, firstly, informs potential secured creditors of the existence of a prior secured creditor who encumbers the grantor's assets; thus, it serves as a public notice. Third-party effectiveness through registration or possession serves as a public notice and potential secured creditors may take lending decisions accordingly. However, unlike possession, registration enables the debtor to be able to utilise the collateral and repay the debt. Furthermore, borrowers may be able to use the same collateral to obtain further loans. Secondly, as the information provided by the additional step alerts 'the grantor's creditors, prospective buyers and other third parties to the potential existence of a security right, there is no need for special rules protecting third parties against the risk posed by hidden [. . .] security rights in the grantor's assets'.[10] Thirdly, the additional procedure may assist the constitution of ranking of priority between secured creditor and competing claimants.[11] In relation to the last two objectives, Dahan and McCormack argue that 'compliance with perfection requirements may act as a measure of reassurance for the secured

8 Gullifer, L. (ed.) (2009) *Goode on Legal Problems of Credit and Security*. London: Sweet & Maxwell, 79.

9 *See* Beale *et al.*, op. cit. (f'note 3), at 323–4. Two of these measures can be found, the first in the doctrine of reputed ownership (introduced by the Bankruptcy Statute of 1623 [21 Jac 1, c 19], which was abolished by the Insolvency Act 1986), and the second, in the requirement of registration of transactions or documents, out of which a security interest arises over the debtor-in-possession property. However, in England the registration requirement does not extend to conditional sale or hire-purchase agreements under which the debtor has possession, but the ownership rests with a third party. The Law Commission Consultation Paper 164 asked whether these transactions should be registrable (para. 7.23), and provisionally agreed that retention of title clauses should be registrable (para. 7.24). Under English law security granted by individuals (absolute bills of sale of security bills) can be registered under the Bills of Sale Act (1878) Amendment Act 1882, and security granted by companies and limited liability partnerships (LLPs) is governed by the Companies Act 2006 part 25, according to which certain charges (s. 860(7)) are registered for effectiveness against other creditors or in insolvency.

10 Guide, para. 1, at 103.

11 For the points that contribute to predictability and certainty, *see* ibid.

lender, as it gives the lender priority over later lenders, secured or unsecured, and also renders the security interest immune from later legal challenge'.[12]

However, achieving third-party effectiveness does not always necessarily grant a priority position (though a security interest that has no third-party effectiveness cannot be asserted to third parties) to a secured creditor against competing claimants, as only the nature and status of rights determine the priority status (i.e. different types of competing security interests must be ranked among themselves).[13] UCC Article 9 treats registration as a requirement for perfection of a security interest created or attached previously, and priority rules are linked to this concept in the same comprehensive integrated registration regime. However, unlike the UCC Article 9, in England the Companies Act 2006 does not contain any priority rules and they are determined by rules outside this legislation. Under the Companies Act 2006 s. 874, failing to register a charge will render the security void in the debtor's insolvency against a liquidator or administrator and a creditor of the company; otherwise an unregistered charge is effective against a company. Put another way, subsequent registered charges will have priority over the earlier unregistered charge. Furthermore, registration is considered as constructive notice to those who would reasonably be expected to search the register[14] and thus grants priority to a legal interest over the equitable one and this has close links to the functioning of *Dearle v Hall.*[15]

The Guide recommends that a security interest that has achieved third-party effectiveness will continue to have third-party effects, even if a right other than the security right on the encumbered asset is transferred.[16] In that context, perfection and priority are two different concepts and perfection is generally, but not always, required to obtain the priority status. The additional step to achieving third-party effectiveness has significance in protecting the priority status of secured creditor as against subsequent secured creditors, debtor's liquidators and insolvency administrators. In certain cases, failing to perfect a security interest will jeopardise the creditor's priority position as against subsequent creditors and purchasers.[17] In the

12 Dahan, F. and McCormack, G. (2002) 'International Influences and the Polish Law on Secured Transactions: Harmonisation, Unification or What?', *Unif. L. Rev.* 713, at 728.

13 Guide, para. 15, at 106. *See also* Chapter 6.

14 Constructive notice does not extend to buyers in the ordinary course of business as this category cannot be expected to search the register; thus, registration is not constructive notice to all the world. Under both the UCC Article 9 and English law buyers in the ordinary course of business are free of both floating charges and fixed charges if they are unaware of the existence of the latter. *See* McCormack, G. (2004) *Secured Credit under English and American Law*. Cambridge: Cambridge University Press, 106–7.

15 Beale, *et al.*, op. cit. (f'note 3), 408 *et seq.*

16 Recommendation 31. There are exceptions to this traditional rule that security right follows the main asset, which are mainly related to priority issues, particularly when the encumbered asset is transferred in the ordinary course of business, the buyer, lessee of the encumbered asset, acquires the rights free of a security right (Recommendations 79–81). *See* Chapter 6 below.

17 E.g. Companies Act 2006 ss. 870 and 874. Non-registration within 21 days will make the charge void against other creditors, liquidator or administrator. Priority between charges is not governed by the order of registration, as a previously created charge that has not been registered may well have priority over the subsequently created charge within a 21 day period. Thus, first-in-time creation will have more significance.

assignment of receivables, when there are subsequent assignees of the same receivable, in order to secure the priority position, it may be necessary for the first assignee to notify the debtor of the assignment so that subsequent assignees cannot overtake the first assignee's priority status by acquiring the legal title without notice.[18]

In jurisdictions that link priority to perfection, where the priority status of creditors is determined by the time of perfection (most generally, this is the time of registration), the additional step for third-party effectiveness is necessary. However, when there is automatic perfection (when the security interest is perfected upon attachment/creation) an additional step to make the security interest effective against third parties is not necessary.[19] In English law, it seems difficult to differentiate perfection from priority.[20] The registration system aims to inform third parties of the existence of a prior proprietary right on the debtor's assets and to assist in determining priority ranking of secured creditors. However, the current English system lacks comprehensiveness where there are different priority and perfection rules. Security interests created by companies and by individuals are governed by different legislations. As there is no general registry system, there may be difficulty in drawing a clear distinction between priority and perfection. Charges that can be registrable under the Companies Act 2006 are limited and outdated.[21] In the case of retention-of-title transactions, which are not registrable in English law, innocent third parties are adversely affected as they have no means to be able to discover these rights.[22]

Although the additional procedure on third-party effectiveness may take various forms (such as transfer of possession in the case of tangibles, registration of notice in a general security rights registry on an intangible or tangible property, or through notification), they are classified generally under three categories. First, under civil law systems the concept of *numerus clausus* provides a type of publicity for the existence of security interests that are enumerated in civil codes, as the parties are restricted in the number of security interests that they can enter into.[23] Second, the 'constructive notice' concept enables the third party to succeed in

18 *Dearle v Hall* (1828) 3 Russ 1.

19 UCC §9–309.

20 For a similar view, *see* Beale *et al.*, op. cit. (f'note 3), at 328.

21 Companies Act 2006 s. 860(7); Law Commission Consultation Paper 164, para. 3.12.

22 Goode, R. (2004) *Commercial Law*, 3rd edn., Butterworths: London, 674.

23 *See* Chapter 3. In relation to security interests, *see* Hansmann, H. and Kraakman, R. (2002) 'Property, Contract and Verification: The Numerus Clausus Problem and the Divisibility of Rights', *John M. Olin Centre for Law, Economics and Business Discussion Paper No. 388*, at 28–30. Professors Hansmann and Kraakman rightly argue that:

> . . . by limiting the types of property rights that can be created even when notice of those rights can be provided through a registry, the law facilitates the formation of other more useful forms of property rights. By this means, the total value of property rights – the value of the rights of the rights created less the user-borne and the non-user-borne costs of the verification rules – is increased.

outranking the non-possessory security right holder, if the third party cannot discover the earlier right at a low cost.[24] The significance of constructive notice is that a subsequent creditor or purchaser cannot claim that a loan has been made in good faith without inspecting registry.[25] Thus, even though subsequent creditors or third parties do not have actual knowledge, constructive notice attributes knowledge of a prior security right on the asset. Third, the publicity of the existence of the non-possessory security interest through registration in a public registry informs the public and potential creditors of the existence of a prior security interest. The rationale of registration is to make it clear to potential creditors of the debtor of the amount they can claim in the event of debtor's insolvency (i.e. whether the debtor has given any other security to others and how much)[26] and to prevent subsequent creditors being misled by a disguised secured credit.[27] The publicity should prevent a subsequent creditor from acquiring rights that have already been subject to a security right that has not been publicised. The registration of security interests as a method to inform third parties and to establish third-party effectiveness has received acceptance in international secured transactions law instruments.[28]

In the context of secured transactions reform, third-party effectiveness raises a number of issues. First, most international secured transactions instruments contain additional methods for third-party effectiveness of security interests. Thus, it is critical to decide whether a security interest that is effective *inter partes* also constitutes third-party effectiveness for the purposes of gaining priority. This involves the critical question of the additional method's role in determining the priority. Second, if it is necessary to effectuate an already created security interest against third parties, third parties need to be identified. Third parties may include secured and unsecured creditors of grantor/assignor, insolvency administrators and subsequent assignees. Third, what types of methods will be sufficient to achieve third-party effectiveness of a security interest needs to be determined.

24 Armour, J. (2008) 'The Law and Economics Debate about Secured Lending: Lessons for European Lawmaking?', in Eidenmüller and Kieninger (eds), op. cit. (f'note 7), 3, at 26. The UCC Article 9 notice registration system does not amount to constructive notice of the financing statement or its contents.

25 Spanogle, J. (1998) 'A Functional Analysis of the EBRD Model Law on Secured Transactions', in J. Norton and M. Andenas (eds) *Emerging Financial Markets and Secured Transactions*. Kluwer, 157, at 160.

26 Bridge, M. (2008) 'The Scope and Limits of Security Interests', in Eidenmüller and Kieninger (eds), op. cit. (f'note 7), 181, at 186; *Smith (Administrator of Cosslett (Contractors) Ltd) v Bridgend County Borough Council* [2002] 1 AC 336, at [19].

27 Bridge, ibid, at 186 and n.19 (citing *Salomon v. A Salomon & Co. Ltd.* [1897] AC 22).

28 Receivables Convention Article 42(4); Cape Town Convention chapters IV and V; Guide, Chapters III and IV; Model Law Part 2, 5 and introduction point 6 (public registration), which states that the 'Model Law achieves publicity mainly by relying on registration of charges at a separate registry'. The Factoring Convention, however, does not include any meaningful regulation on this matter.

This issue particularly involves whether registration is a necessity in determining the priority status of a security interest on intangible property.[29]

5.2.1 Third-party effectiveness and creation[30]

Third-party effectiveness under the Guide will be established after a security interest is created upon completing the relevant steps[31] and one of the methods of third-party effectiveness referred to in recommendations 32, 34 or 35 is fulfilled (recommendations 29 and 32). The Guide explicitly recommends that registration of a notice does not create a security right and is not necessary for the creation of a security right. Thus, a clear distinction is drawn between third-party effectiveness and creation of security rights.[32] A security interest created between the parties will not be adversely affected even if third-party effectiveness is not achieved (Recommendation 30) and an interest can be registered before its creation especially in the case of security agreements covering future assets. As the registration can take place before the creation of security right, if a third party acquires rights in the interim period, third-party effectiveness will depend on whether the security interest is created or not. The third party may acquire the asset free of any subsequent created security interest even though the interest is registered. The impact of this relationship on priority ranking is that priority among secured creditors, whose rights against third parties are made effective by registration, will be determined on the order of registration rather than creation.[33] This is an exception to the rule that third-party effectiveness dates from the time of both creation and registration. In certain cases some assets may need to be registered in special registers, though not necessarily for third-party effectiveness but mainly for preservation of priority ranking, which may be either title registers (land registers) or mortgage registers (aircraft, ship or motor vehicle). The Model Law does not follow the distinction of effectiveness of a security interest between parties and against third parties, and rather accepts the sufficiency of creation of a security right to establish effectiveness both between parties and against third parties.[34] A charging instrument and a registration statement are required for the creation and registration of a charge under the Model Law, except for the unpaid vendor's

29 But cf. e.g. Schäfer, H-B. (2008) 'The Law and Economics Debate About Secured Lending: Lessons for European Lawmaking?', in Eidenmüller and Kieninger (eds), op. cit. (f'note 7), 30, at 35, where it is argued that despite the necessity to register a non-possessed security interest, establishing registers is not necessary and in some civil law jurisdictions (e.g. Germany) priority problems are solved by judge-made rules.

30 For the distinction and further discussion, *see* Chapter 4.

31 These conditions are set out in recommendations 13–15.

32 Recommendation 33.

33 Recommendation 76; *see also* Chapter 6.

34 Röver, J-H. (2007) *Secured Lending in Eastern Europe: Comparative Law of Secured Transactions and the EBRD Model Law*. Oxford: Oxford University Press, at 73, para. 7.23; *see also* Dahan, F. and McCormack, G. (1998) 'The EBRD Model Law on Secured Transactions: Comparisons and Convergence', *CfiLR* 65, 79.

charge.[35] Failure to publicise a charge is also a ground to make that charge ineffective against third parties.[36]

In addition to serving as a public notice to those who search for the existence of an earlier registered interest under the Cape Town Convention, registration also protects the creditor's priority and ensures that the international interest is effective against third parties in the debtor's insolvency. Registration does not necessarily grant protection against the debtor, thus failure to register an international interest in the international registry does not affect the rights of the chargee or lessor against the chargor or lessee.[37] However, failure to register will cause loss of priority status and the interest will not have opposability in the debtor's insolvency. Third-party effectiveness by possession was not accepted under the Cape Town Convention, as in cross-border mobile equipment secured transactions third-party effectiveness would only be feasible by means of registration.[38] Registration of an interest, however, is not an element of creation or validity of that interest.[39] Until the international interest is registered, the created international interest will confer benefits envisaged under the default remedies (Articles 8–10). Thus registration is an additional step, which must be completed upon creation of an interest (an interest effective between parties) in order to have third-party effectiveness under the Cape Town Convention. A registered interest that is not created does not have third-party effectiveness until it is duly created.

The distinction between creation and third-party effectiveness constitutes some further conceptual and definitional issues. In particular, the notion of 'third parties' must be applied and understood in a uniform manner in order to effectuate the security interest to all those interested parties and to establish an efficient public knowledge and priority system. In those jurisdictions where creation of a security interest is sufficient to grant effectiveness to both between parties and against third parties, the security interest is deemed to be effective against the grantor's secured or unsecured creditors and insolvency administrator. In that context, the rationale is 'notice of a security right should matter only to those third parties that take a security right, purchase an encumbered asset or otherwise give value in direct reliance on the grantor's apparently unencumbered title to the asset'.[40] This is because unsecured creditors lend on an unsecured basis, taking the risk of being subordinated by subsequent secured creditors who lend on a

35 Model Law Articles 7 and 8. *See also* Chapter 4.

36 EBRD Guiding Principles, Principle 4.

37 Cape Town Convention Articles 29 and 30(1).

38 UNIDROIT Study LXII-Doc.7, para. 11 (1993), where it is pointed out that '[w]hile there was some support for the idea of it being possible for the international security interests to be perfected by possession, possession was recognised as being of relatively limited use in the case of mobile equipment and it was accordingly acknowledged that perfection would in most cases have to be by registration'. UNIDROIT Study LXII-Doc.5, para. 8 (1992), envisaging an international security interest registered and publicised in an international registration system.

39 Wool, J. (1999) 'The Next Generation of International Aviation Finance Law: An overview of the Proposed Unidroit Convention on International Interests in Mobile Equipment as applied to Aircraft Equipment', 20 *U. Pa. J. Int'l Econ. L.* 499, 540.

40 Guide, para. 10, at 105.

secured basis and, therefore, pay for their priority positions. However, as a counter-argument it can be submitted that an additional step is necessary to establish an efficient and predictable information system that publicises the existence of a security right to the grantor's other creditors, particularly the unsecured ones, and insolvency administrator. First, for unsecured creditors an additional procedure for third-party effectiveness means that they can make their lending decisions in accordance with the information on the registry, rather than the general financial standing of the grantor. Second, the existence of an additional procedure, preferably in the form of registry, prevents fraudulent transfers of property between the insolvent grantor and a preferential creditor. Third, a clear public registration system permits judgment creditors to predict the cost of enforcement and, in the case of insolvency proceedings, the registration system reduces the cost in determining which assets of the grantor are encumbered.[41] On the other hand, as the registration system is a significant part of an efficient secured transactions regime, if there is no meaningful registration system, there may be no, or less, certainty prior to the conclusion of the security agreement between the secured creditor and grantor. It is arguable that certainty has the determinative effect in the cost of credit, according to which the secured creditor may either increase or lower the interest rate, thereby determining the amount of risk premium. Actual knowledge of the existence of a prior security interest may be sufficient to make a security interest effective against a subsequent creditor or buyer. However, without a significant system that assists the proof of existence of a prior security interest, third parties may assume that 'the prior secured creditor has implicitly consented to the risk of its rights being ineffective against third parties'.[42] Even when there is a registration system, when a security interest is not registered in a system that requires creation of security interest between parties and then registration for third-party effectiveness, it is argued that the security interest will be incomplete, and even if a third party has notice of this (actual knowledge), the security interest should not have third-party effectiveness, as it may be difficult to prove knowledge.[43] This may also be the case where there may be multiple incomplete security interests with no third-party effectiveness, in which case priority may be given in the order of creation (i.e. conclusion of security agreement between the parties).[44]

5.2.2 *Difference between third-party effectiveness and perfection*

North American secured credit legislations use the term perfection[45] (which is similar to, but does not necessarily have the same meaning as, third-party

41 For these reasons, *see* Guide, para. 11, at 105.

42 Guide, para. 12, at 106.

43 EBRD Guiding Principles, at 13.

44 Ibid.

45 E.g. UCC Article 9 Part 3 and Ontario Personal Property Security Act Part III. Jurisdictions affected by the UCC Article 9 type of secured transactions regime, such as New Zealand Personal Property Securities Act 1999 Part 4, use the term 'perfection'. In academic/practitioner works this is called 'perfection'. *See e.g.* Beale, *et al.*, op. cit. (f'note 3), 323 *et seq.*, arguing that for a charge to be

effectiveness, used under the Guide) to inform third parties of a prior security interest over the collateral, according to which there is a distinction between creation of a security interest and third-party effectiveness and priority ranking. The term is not defined in the UCC; however, it denotes a security interest becoming effective against third parties in order for the creditor to gain priority (i.e. relatively better rights). Put another way, it refers to the set of requirements that need to be completed in order to obtain priority against third parties including other secured creditors who perfected their security interests and insolvency administrators. The registration requirement aims to notify parties of the existence of an earlier security interest. Under UCC Article 9, perfection is 'a tool of the priority regime'.[46] That is, perfection of security interests leads to priority. However, if an attached security interest is not perfected, an unperfected security interest will still be valid and effective against third parties but it will be subordinated to the perfected one.[47] In contrast, elsewhere, the conclusion of a security agreement between the secured creditor and the grantor, or any other requirement necessary to vest the title in the secured creditor, is sufficient both to make the security interest effective between the secured creditor and grantor and against third parties and to establish priority rankings.[48] However, the divergence in the legal systems' approach in establishing effectiveness as between the parties, third-party effectiveness and ultimately priority ranking, presents significant difficulties for international instruments in formulating a generally acceptable rule.[49]

The Guide does not use the term *perfection* and rather prefers 'effectiveness as against third parties' to promote certainty through the simple method of registration (though it has exceptions and alternatives)[50] and to ascertain priority status of creditors. If no third-party effectiveness is achieved, there will not be any priority contest. As perfection denotes a position for a security interest that gives priority,[51]

effective against another creditor or in insolvency it must be registered, otherwise it is imperfect and thus the usage of perfection is established, at 325. *See also* Goode, op. cit. (f'note 22), 624. For a detailed account of perfection under UCC Article 9, *see* White, J.J. and Summers, R.S. (2000) *Uniform Commercial Code*, 5th edn. St. Paul: West, 757 *et seq.*

46 Sigman, H.C. (2008) 'Perfection and Priority of Security Rights', in Eidenmüller and Kieninger (eds), op. cit. (f'note 7), 143, at 145. *See* Sigman, H.C. and Kieninger, E-M. (2007) 'Introduction', in H.C. Sigman and E-M. Kieninger (eds) *Cross-Border Security over Tangibles*. Munich: Sellier, 1, 37.

47 For similar arguments, *see* Veneziano, A. (2008) 'Attachment/Creation of a Security Right', in Eidenmüller and Kieninger (eds), op. cit. (f'note 7), 113, at 118–19. Under English Law Companies Act 2006 s. 874 failure to register a charge will render the charge ineffective in the insolvency of the debtor (against the liquidator, administrator or the creditors of the company) but the charge will still be effective as against the debtor.

48 *See* Chapter 4.

49 Walsh, C. (2001) 'Receivables Financing and the Conflict of Laws: The UNCITRAL Draft Convention on the Assignment of Receivables in International Trade' 106 *Dick. L. Rev.* 159, 189.

50 Recommendations 32, 34–35.

51 UCC §9-308–UCC §9-316. For arguments on distinction between third-party effectiveness and perfection, *see* Sigman and Kieninger, op. cit. (f'note 46), 37–38, where they criticise the use of 'effectiveness', which presents 'a stark dichotomy'.

it assumes that attachment[52] is completed. Perfection may occur before or after attachment[53] but, for perfection to be completed, attachment must occur. These steps will depend on the nature of the transaction and maybe filing or taking possession by the secured party or another person on behalf of the secured party. Certain types of assets such as investment securities, financial collateral or bank accounts may require control.[54] Perfection has links with the notion of priority, which determines the prevailing effectively created security right, whether or not it is perfected (made effective against third parties).[55] Perfection is not related to the relationship between the secured creditor and the debtor. Rather, it gives public notice of the existence of a security right over the collateral of the debtor, and gives better rights to the secured party in the event of a dispute between the secured party and the third party claimant over the collateral of the debtor. An unperfected security interest (an interest that has no third-party effectiveness), though effective against the debtor, may be subordinated to other secured creditors due to perfected security interest's third-party effectiveness. Nevertheless, unperfected security interests may have priority over other competing claimants.[56] Under the Guide, if a security interest, which is already created and effective between secured creditor and grantor, is not made effective against third parties by one of the methods envisaged, the security interest will have no third-party effects and the creditor will have no priority right. However, the security interest will be effective between the parties (the secured creditor and the grantor).

5.3 Methods of achieving third-party effectiveness

In essence, two significant approaches to achieve third-party effectiveness function to inform third parties of the possible existence of a security right: registration and possession. As a general argument, for facilitation of credit, it is generally accepted that the debtor needs to remain in possession of the asset so that by utilising this asset the creditor is repaid. As the significance of intangible assets is increased and sophisticated methods of financing are used, traditional financing methods, where actual delivery of possession is necessary, seem to be ineffective. Particularly,

52 UCC §9–203(a) and (b). A security interest attaches when it becomes enforceable and enforceability occurs when the debtor has agreed to create a security interest, value has been given and the debtor has rights in the collateral or the power to transfer rights in the collateral to a secured party.

53 UCC §9–308(a), UCC §9–502(d). A financing statement may be filed before the security agreement of attachment.

54 UCC §9–106. Control will also grant priority over an earlier secured creditor who perfected its interest through filing. UCC §9–328.

55 Both under UCC Article 9 and the Guide, a purchase-money security interest (where the seller of collateral takes security to secure the price of the assets sold or a third person, who advances credit to the debtor for the purposes of debtor to acquire rights in the collateral) will subordinate even a perfected security interest. Thus, perfection does not always protect the secured creditor.

56 Sigman and Kieninger (eds), op. cit. (f'note 46), at 37. But cf. the Guide's third-party effectiveness notion.

utility of future assets as collateral and receivables cannot be the subject of pledge.[57] Publicity serves as a means of protection of third parties by avoiding false wealth appearances, determination of priority and protection of grantors against loss of ownership to bona fide third parties.[58] Thus, there is necessity to establish third-party effectiveness by using methods that will create certainty and predictability. In order to establish a modern secured transactions regime, where third-party effectiveness works efficiently, it is necessary to have a general security interests registry, which provides notice to third parties and is supported with alternative methods providing notice, either by taking possession of those collateral, the possession of which need to be actually delivered to the creditor, or control of the collateral.

For receivables there is a separate regime to establish third-party effectiveness. Notification of the debtor about the assignment or the existence of the security interest achieves third-party effectiveness.[59] Notice to the debtor does not publicise the assignment or security interests to a third party but merely requires the debtor to make payment to the assignee/creditor.[60] The priority in successive assignments will be given to the first assignee who notifies first, without the knowledge of the earlier assignment. However, with the sophistication of financial life, notification of debtor is not feasible to match the requirements of financing practices. For example, in the case of assignment of bulk and future receivables, notification of the debtor is burdensome and raises the cost of credit. Additionally, in the case of assignment of future receivables, as the debtor is not known at the time of assignment, notification cannot be effectively made. Moreover, an assignor may not wish to inform the debtor of the assignment, as this may have a negative impact on the assignor's financial standing. If there is an assignment by way of sale the assignee may prefer the assignor to collect on their behalf (this may be in securitisation and in factoring). Notification of debtor cannot provide a similar public notice to that achieved by registration, and requiring the assignee to notify first will complicate transactions and increase the cost of credit. The assignor's creditors will continue to rely on the representations of the assignor. Thus, the requirement of registration in a general registry provides the advantage to assignees and to third parties of evaluating the risk involved with priority rankings and reduces the cost of credit by avoiding unnecessary transaction costs. Notification of the debtor, where registration is the method of achieving third-party effectiveness, is used as an enforcement mechanism, rather than achieving third-party

57 However, if receivables are converted into a negotiable instrument it is possible to pledge the negotiable instrument to have third-party effectiveness.

58 Struycken, T.H.D. (1998) 'The Proprietary Aspects of International Assignment of Debts and the Rome Convention, Article 12', *L.M.C.L.Q.* 345, 355.

59 Under the Receivables Convention notification is not required for the effectiveness of an assignment between assignee and the assignor. *See* Chapter 4.

60 EBRD Publicity of Security Rights Guiding Principles for the Development of a Charges Registry (2004) at 8 (EBRD Guiding Principles).

effectiveness.[61] The Receivables Convention considers formal validity of a contract of assignment as a condition to priority, and the definition of priority encompasses requirements necessary to render the right effective against a competing claimant (another assignee, assignor's creditor or insolvency administrator).[62] Third-party effectiveness of the assignment, like the priority among competing claims, is subject to the law of the assignor's State, and additionally, the optional annex provides a substantive law solution to the issue of third-party effectiveness and priority ranking.[63] Arguably, when States adopt the Guide, under the above rule, the recommendations of the Guide will become the domestic law of the assignor's State, and the Guide's rules on third-party effectiveness will be applicable. The requirement of registration with respect to assignment of receivables is a significant method of solving difficulties regarding priorities in the event that there are competing assignees on the same receivable. Professor McCormack argues that,

> requiring notice to be filed in a public register is a more logically coherent way of sorting out priorities [and] determining the rank of assignments according to the order in which each is publicised by registration would enable the later assignees to work out more efficiently a fair purchase price for the receivables or the legal and operational risks of the transaction as the case may be.[64]

Under English law although registration perfects security by constituting notice to those who can reasonably be expected to search, there is still a necessity to notify the debtor[65] under *Dearle v Hall*.[66] The rationale for notice in the case of successive assignments is to bind subsequent assignees. The priority of the first assignee will be protected if the subsequent assignee is expected to know the existence of the

61 Guide, para. 26, at 109. Professor Walsh argues that notification is also used as a condition of effectiveness of assignment as between the parties. Walsh, C. (2008) 'Security Interests in Receivables', in Eidenmüller and Kieninger (eds), op. cit. (f'note 7), 321, 324.

62 Receivables Convention Article 5(g), '. . . and whether any requirements necessary to render the right effective against a competing claimants have been satisfied'; Articles 5(m) and 22.

63 For priority of competing claims under the Receivables Convention, *see* Chapters 6 and 8.

64 McCormack, G. (2002) 'Personal Property Security Law Reform in England and Canada', *J.B.L.* 113, 132; Walsh, C. (1997) 'Registration, Constructive Notice and the Rule in Dearle v. Hall', 12 *Banking & Finance L.R.* 129.

65 For reasons including enabling the debtor to get good discharge by paying the assignee; to prevent new equities arising as the assignee acquires rights subject to equities at the time of assignment; to prevent modification of the underlying agreement; to secure priority and to benefit from the statutory assignment under the Law of Property Act 1925 s.136(1), where the assignee can sue in his own name. *See* Gullifer, op. cit. (f'note 8), 111–2; Bell, A.P. (1989) *Modern Law of Personal Property in England and Ireland*, London: Butterworths, 361 *et seq.*

66 (1828) 3 Russ. 1. The obsolete nature of *Dearle v Hall* precipitated the Law Commission's recommendations in the Consultative Papers and Report on registration of company security interests that a registration system be created that would operate more effectively within the framework of modern financing practices, and an electronic notice-filing scheme for charges and sales of

prior encumbrance. However, all these requirements in a modern financing world are too complicated. As there is a distinction between a charge and an assignment by way of sale, where the latter is not registrable, it seems questionable whether a factor should have constructive notice of the existence of an earlier registered charge by virtue of *Wilson v Kelland*,[67] which then affects the priority position of the factor under *Dearle v Hall*.[68] Thus, it seems more credit facilitative to require overall registration and link perfection and priority, in line with the Law Commission's recommendations, to the first-in-time registration. This should be in harmony with the Guide's recommendations, which adopt third-party effectiveness over receivables through registration without having any distinction as assignment by way of sale or security and without the need for further notification. A similar argument also applies to the Receivables Convention.

5.3.1 Registration

Registration (filing) is a significant method of establishing third-party effectiveness, which aims to notify the public of the current nature, ownership or any other proprietary interests over the debtor's assets. It is arguably the most efficient method when compared with other methods that establish third-party effectiveness (publicity).[69] Professor Garro points out that '[t]he degree of effectiveness and sophistication of secured credit largely depends on a system of providing public notice of nonpossessory security interests which is comprehensive, simple, efficient and inexpensive'.[70] International instruments accept registration as the most suitable method to achieve third-party effectiveness. There are various methods of registration, including those that make a reference to the type of transaction, the status of the grantor, the identity of the secured creditor or the type of encumbered asset.[71] The Guide links registration or notice filing to the key objective that

receivables should be introduced. Law Commission Company Security Interests Consultation Report (No. 296) at 9 and 108–110 (in relation to sales of receivables by companies, that priority should depend on the date of registration of the financing statement, and that failing to register a sale of receivables at the onset of insolvency should result in non-effectiveness of the sale against administrator or liquidator). In the case of general assignment of receivables by an individual other than a company, registration is a requirement under the Bills of Sale Act 1878 and the Insolvency Act 1986 s. 344 as security bills of sale. Failure to register will render the assignment void in the debtor's bankruptcy against third parties, particularly the trustee in bankruptcy. For an examination of the Report, *see e.g.* McCormack, G. (2005) 'The Law Commission Consultative Report on Company Security Interests: An Irreverent Riposte', 68 *M.L.R.* 286.

67 [1910] 2 Ch. 306, 313, (Ch. D.); *see also* McCormack, G. (1994) *Registration of Company Charges*. London: Sweet & Maxwell, 133, stating that, "[s]ince registration is deemed to constitute notice the holder of the subsequent legal interest will be postponed to the holder of the prior equitable interest"; de Lacy, J. (2001) 'Constructive Notice and Company Charge Registration', *Conv.* 122.

68 For a further discussion, *see* Bridge, in Eidenmüller and Kieninger (eds), op. cit. (f'note 26), at 207.

69 EBRD Guiding Principles, Principle 3.

70 Garro, A.M. (1990) 'The Reform and Harmonization of Personal Property Security Law in Latin America', 59 *Revista Juridica Universidad de Puerto Rico* 1, 57.

71 Guide, para. 29, 110 *et seq.*

underlies the equal treatment of lenders and trade suppliers. As a fundamental policy, the Guide recommends that the secured transactions regime should set out that sellers and lenders that provide credit to enable a buyer to acquire movable assets be treated in the same way.[72]

With the increased significance of receivables as collateral and receivables financing as a critical method of raising finance, establishing third-party effectiveness through registration in a general security rights registry has gained importance. The single registry also has the wisdom of eliminating fragmented registries. A similar argument is also applicable in the case of transactions financing high value mobile equipment. One of the key features of the Cape Town Convention is creating transparency in providing information about the existence of an international interest over high value mobile equipment through the international registration system. This argument also applies to the Guide, where the key objective in establishing a general security interest registry is to enhance certainty and transparency by providing for registration of a notice in a general security rights registry. The creation of a general security interest registry is a key to achieving predictability and facilitation of credit. This is true for intangible assets, particularly for receivables, which are not suitable to be secured or transferred through physical possession (pledge) or for those assets that need to be left in the possession of the debtor who needs to continue business by utilising the assets for repayment. Except in certain cases,[73] registration in a general security rights registry under the Guide provides third-party effectiveness and priority. Priority in this case is determined on the basis of first-to-file.

Notification of third parties through registration, thereby establishing third-party effectiveness, is operational in modern secured transactions systems, whereas in unreformed systems lack of registration, arguably, has a negative effect on the cost of credit. Even when a registration system exists in unreformed systems it is expensive, burdensome and inefficient by being paper-based[74] and requiring the complete transactional document, which suggests that registration is necessary for both creation and third-party effectiveness.[75] Lack, or the inefficiency of, a registration system has the risk of hindering economic development. The main economic argument behind the essential nature of registration is that 'a borrower with collateral, relative to a borrower without, can get nine times more credit relative to cash flow, can have eleven times longer to repay, and will pay an interest rate about half as high'.[76] The registration will encourage the flow of credit by

72 For more detailed discussion, *see* Chapter 7.

73 Under the Guide, certain acquisition financing devices present exceptions, *see* Chapter 7.

74 For some empirical figures where small businesses in Latin America pay higher interest rates than their counterparts in the USA, *see* de la Pena, N. and Fleisig, H. (2002) 'SMEs and Collateral', *CEAL Issues Brief No. 3, October 2002*; Fleisig, H. and de la Pena, N. (1997) 'Peru: How Problems in the Framework for Secured Transactions Limit Access to Credit', 3 *NAFTA Law & Bus. Rev. Am.*, 33, 62 *et seq.*

75 Wilson, J.M. (2007) 'Movable Equipment Financing in Latin America: Application of the OAS Model Law, the Cape Town Convention and the Luxembourg Rail Protocol', *Unif. L. Rev.*, 473, 485.

76 R. Chaves, H. Fleisig and N. De la Pena, 'Secured Transactions Reform: Early Results from Romania' *CEAL Issue Brief September 2004.*

creating predictability and ascertaining priority ranking. It is claimed that creation of a publicity/registration system aims to reduce the risk of non-payment and thus, has an economic reason rather than a legal one.[77]

An efficient system of notifying the public with the necessary amount of information provides possibilities to avoid claims of creditor misleading or ostensible ownership.[78] Secured creditors can establish their status and make lending decisions according to an advance notification system. Registration provides a modern method of ascertaining the order of ranking between competing claimants. As the order of registration will be determined by the date of registration, creditors will be presented with certainty, and the priority of an earlier secured creditor or a person with an acquisition right will not be adversely affected. Perhaps what is more significant about registration is the secured creditor's concern in relation to the availability of debtor's assets in case of insolvency.[79] Lenders depend on clear and transparent information about borrowers, through which they monitor the financial activities of borrowers. The ability to monitor borrowers and their activities in the credit market facilitates the flow of credit. In the absence of a registration system, financiers often rely on borrowers' representations. However, reliable and clear information may often not be possible. Registration, therefore, aims to override the spread of asymmetric information in credit markets by facilitating the allocation of credit.[80] Borrowers, who are aware of the secured creditor's ability to monitor, refrain from repeatedly offering their assets as collateral. Lending decisions, arguably, are made more efficiently.[81]

An efficient registration system must be practical to achieve its public notice function. The Guide sets out detailed registry system recommendations for optimal use and application of third-party effectiveness requirements.[82] The Guide, similar to the UCC Article 9, where a financing statement is filed as opposed to the security agreement itself, recommends a notice registration system, where a debtor based registration system is envisaged, which enables the registration of all present and future registrable transactions entered into by the debtor. The Cape Town Convention and its protocols, the Model Law and the Receivables Convention's optional annex also adopt and support a notice registration system. Notice filing in a general security rights register[83] involves registration of limited

77 EBRD Guiding Principles, at 4.

78 On notice filing, *see e.g.* McCormack, G. (2002) 'Notice filing versus Transactions Filing? A Comparison of the English and US Law of Security Interests', *Insolvency Lawyer*, 166; Baird, D. (1983) 'Notice Filing and the Problem of Ostensible Ownership', 12 *J. Legal Stud.*, 53.

79 *Smith (Administrator of Cosslett (Contractors) Ltd) v Bridgend County Borough Council* [2001] UKHL 58, [2002] 1 AC 336, at [19] (Lord Millett).

80 *See* Lopez-De-Silanes, F. (2008) 'Turning the Key to Credit: Credit Access and Credit Institutions', in F. Dahan and J. Simpson (eds) *Secured Transactions Reform and Access to Credit*. Cheltenham: Edward Elgar, at 6.

81 In England quasi-security interests operate without a registration system (save hire-purchase agreements for motor vehicles).

82 Guide, Chapter IV.

83 Recommendations 32 and 54; *see also* Guide, para. 12, at 151. Receivables Convention Optional Annex Article 4(1).

information (such as identities of parties, description of the encumbered asset, duration of registration and maximum sum of the security)[84] for achieving third-party effectiveness of security rights. Notice registration as opposed to transaction filing has considerable advantages where the former provides reduced administrative and archival burden, and it is sufficient to establish, through entry of basic minimum information rather than the security agreement itself, third-party effectiveness rather than creation of a security right.[85] Transaction filing, unlike notice filing, provides evidence of the specific security interest and device. Notice filing enables setting priority from the date of registration rather than the creation. Notice filing, where the single registration is made in advance of creation, is also essentially beneficial for quasi-security devices, including outright sale of receivables and retention-of-title arrangements, as having to register them as and when they come into existence would be burdensome.[86]

Access to the registered system must be simple and inexpensive. Registration should be made online and searching should be easy.[87] All interested parties and potential creditors should be able to access and search the system.[88] Even in systems where there is registration certain restrictions limit access to information, which results in the lender's inability to decide whether there is a prior interest on the asset. These restrictions in unreformed jurisdictions include limitations on who can inspect the registry, the location (courts and notaries) and the structure of the registry (paper based). On the other hand, in reformed secured transactions regimes registration (either transaction or notice filing) is completed on the internet, which allows anyone to search the information available on the lender, debtor and the collateral. Furthermore, simply providing basic information, thus achieving the notice function, rather than registering the security agreement itself, should be satisfactory.[89] This also ensures that the details of the parties' agreement are kept confidential. Depending on whether all the debtor's assets can be charged, the registration may either be made against the name of the debtor or the collateral. For simplicity reasons, if all the debtor's assets can be charged, registration should be made against the debtor's name.

In addition to general security rights registries, there may be specialised registries that are mainly asset-based, where rights over specific types of assets are

84 Recommendation 57; Receivables Convention optional annex Article 4(1).

85 Guide, para. 13, at 151–2; for advantages, *see also* Law Commission Consultation Paper No. 176, para. 2.43 (significance of advance filing; electronic registration, simplicity and speed; simple description; unique registration number; avoiding dual registration for ships, IP and aircraft; determination of priority from the time of filing; disappearance of distinction between floating and fixed charges).

86 For a similar argument, *see* H. Beale (2008) 'The Future of Secured Credit in Europe: Concluding Remarks', in Eidenmüller and Kieninger (eds), op. cit. (f'note 7), 375, 389. For some criticism of the Law Commission's suggestions of advantages of notice filing, *see* McCormack, op. cit. (f'note 66), 292.

87 Guide, at 155–158. Cape Town Convention and Model Law support electronic based registers.

88 For example, Cape Town Convention Article 26 enables universal access to the Registry. For the operation of the International Registry system, *see* Wool, op. cit. (f'note 39), 539 *et seq.*

89 For a discussion of economic consequences of publicity and lack of publicity, *see* Fleisig, H *et al.*, (2006) *Reforming Collateral Laws to expand access to Finance.* Washington DC: The World Bank, 38 *et seq.*

registered. Specialised registries are also title registries, which function as sources of information on the current status of title to specific assets.[90] Specialised registries serve both to publicise rights and ensure third-party effectiveness. The Guide adopts the position that if States maintain a specialised registry, registration of a security right in that registry will achieve third-party effectiveness.[91] The significance of a specialised registry within the framework of the Guide is that with the exception of competing claimants who register their rights in the specialised registry and obtain third-party effectiveness, other third parties may obtain third-party effectiveness either by registering their rights in a general security rights registry or by transfer of possession.[92] The result of this is that, as there are limited types of assets that can be registered in specialised registries, essentially in a priority conflict between a security right registered in a general security rights registry and a security right registered in a specialised registry, the latter will have priority regardless of the time of registration.[93]

The publicity under the Model Law is achieved through a separate charge register.[94] This is not a general register and only registered charges envisaged under the Model Law can be registered. The Model Law reflects the fact that charges must establish public knowledge and this should be constructive knowledge. There is, however, a detail that seems to establish a difference between the Model Law and the common law systems. Under the Model Law registration is part of a procedure of creation of a registered charge.[95] Registration under the Cape Town Convention establishes the priority of an international interest against third party claims (other international interests, creditors and administrator or liquidator in the debtor's insolvency). Under the Convention, a notice registration (filing) system (Article 17(2)(i)) is adopted as it better serves the purpose, according to which a public notice is provided for the existence or the potential existence of an interest

90 For further information on the registry system and types of registries, *see e.g.* Guide, Chapter IV.

91 Recommendations 34(a)(iii) and 38(a).

92 Recommendations 32 and 34.

93 Recommendations 38, 77 and 78.

94 To assess the progress of reform in transition economies, the EBRD conducted a survey in 1999, which has been regularly updated. By 2004 all of the transition economies had undertaken reform activities, but the regional reform lacked consistency where some countries achieved publicity through registration of non-possessory charges, while others failed to achieve the same efficiency and continued to set restrictions on the use of non-possessory charges. *See* Fairgrieve, D. and Andenas, M. 'Securing Progress in Collateral Law Reform: The EBRD's Regional Survey of Secured Transactions Laws', *Law in Transition*, 28 (Autumn 2000); Dahan, F. and Simpson, J. (2004) 'Secured Transactions in Central and Eastern Europe: European Bank for Reconstruction and Development (EBRD) Assessment', 36 *U.C.C.L.J.*, 77. For some observation as to how legal efficiency can be achieved in secured transactions reform, *see* Dahan, F. and Simpson, J. (2009) 'Legal Efficiency for Secured Transactions Reform: Bridging the Gap between Economic Analysis and Legal Reasoning', 27 *Penn. St. Int'l Rev.*, 623.

95 Model Law Article 6.2 indicates that a registered charge is created by the chargor and chargeholder entering into a charging instrument and registration of the charge.

by inputting minimal data.[96] The registration in the international registry is not made against the name of the debtor but on a uniquely identifiable asset (i.e. aircraft, railway rolling stock or satellite – an asset-based system).[97] The international interest permits the secured creditor to 'preserve its priority and the effectiveness of the international interest in insolvency proceedings against the debtor'.[98] Arguably in those countries that have registration systems or registration systems for the particular equipment covered under the Cape Town Convention, it is necessary to register the international interest for third-party effectiveness rather than registering in the national/local registries. The third-party effectiveness of an international interest by registration does not denote its creation, which is done without the need for registration. Under the Cape Town Convention, registration of a validly created international interest in an international registry grants a priority status to the secured creditor against subsequent registered and unregistered interests on the same asset.[99] One of the differences between the Guide and the Cape Town registration systems is that in the former general collateral description is provided, as the Guide deals with security interests in future assets, intangibles and inventory, which cannot be described in specific detail, hence the debtor-based registration, whereas the latter requires registration of specifically identifiable assets in an asset-based registry.[100] Even though the Aircraft Protocol extends registration to outright sales, registry under the Cape Town Convention is not a title registry. The outcome is that in a conditional sale or a leasing agreement, rather than the title, the seller or the lessor will register their interests, upon which the international interest comes into existence. Registering an interest is not a presumption that the lessor, seller or buyer is the owner of the registered aircraft object and ownership is determined by the applicable law.[101] Registration of an international interest under the Cape Town Convention is 'a priority point, not merely a perfection requirement'[102] against creditors, liquidator in the event of debtor's insolvency, subsequent interest

96 For the advantages of the notice filing system, *see* Mooney, C. (1999) 'Relationship between the Prospective Unidroit International Registry, Revised Uniform Commercial Code Article 9 and national civil aviation registries', *Unif. L. Rev.*, 335, 338.

97 *See* Goode, R. (2008) *Convention on International Interests in Mobile Equipment and Protocol thereto on Matters Specific to Aircraft Equipment Official Commentary*, revised ed. Rome: UNIDROIT, at 50, paras 2.70 and 2.73. For the international registration system, *see* Stanford, M. (2002) 'From Ottawa to Cape Town: Unidroit's Role in the Modernisation of the Law Governing Leasing and the Taking of Security', in I. Davies (ed.) *Security Interests in Mobile Equipment*. Aldershot: Ashgate, 397, 439.

98 Goode, ibid., at 49, para. 2.69.

99 Goode, op. cit. (fnote 97), at 49, para. 2.69. Knowledge of an earlier unregistered interest does not affect the validity of registration. Cape Town Convention Article 29(2)(a) and (3)(b). Cape Town Convention Article 1(mm) defines unregistered interest.

100 Cape Town Convention Article 18(1).

101 Cuming, R.C. (2006) 'The International Registry for Interests in Aircraft: An Overview of its Structure' *Unif. L. Rev.*, 18, 22.

102 Ibid., at 224, para. 4.182. For the necessity of establishing clear priority status on international interest in mobile equipment, *see* UNIDROIT Study LXXII-Doc. 1, 29 *et seq.* (1989). *See also* Mooney, op. cit. (fnote 96), 336–7.

holders and buyers of the equipment. As clear and transparent priority and registration rules are key features of the Cape Town Convention, priority of claims is determined according to the date and order of registration in the International Registry. The title of the conditional seller and the lessor is limited to a security interest. The Cape Town Convention enables the registration of financial leases and retention-of-title agreements (i.e. the functional equivalents to security) and includes operating lease arrangements.[103] The extension of the registration requirement to financial leasing and title retention devices is necessary because in the absence of registration third parties cannot ascertain whether the movable tangible assets belong to a lessor or the seller. Similarly, under the Guide and the Receivables Convention the scope of the general security rights registry is extended to cover outright assignment of receivables, and assignments by way of sale and security have been combined functionally under assignment with no distinction in terms of priority and third-party effectiveness.[104] The same argument also applies to retention-of-title agreements under the Guide.[105] Another difference between the Cape Town Convention and the Guide is that in the former, retention-of-title and leasing agreements (which are not traditional security interests) are not automatically characterised as security interest (as this is left to the applicable law determined by the forum State's conflict-of-laws rules),[106] but are still required to be registered for third-party effectiveness and in the latter, depending on the choice of States as either unitary or non-unitary approach, all transactions having security functions will be treated as equally secured transactions law aspects, according to which third-party effectiveness and priority rules applicable to security rights will equally apply to acquisition and non-acquisition financing devices.[107] In some civil law jurisdictions registration is both a requirement of third-party effectiveness and effectiveness as between parties under certain transactions, typically in retention-of-title arrangements in sales contracts[108] and in title registers where aircrafts and ships are registered and all proprietary rights are publicised. Retention-of-title agreements are not registrable under English law. As the 'buyer in possession' is an

103 Guide, para. 44, at 113. Broadly, the finance lease has a security purpose, whereas the operating lease has no security function. For the difference between the financial lease and operating lease, *see* Chapter 1.

104 Recommendation 32; Receivables Convention Article 2(a) and the Optional Annex section 1 Art. 1.

105 Recommendations 2(c) and 8.

106 Cape Town Convention Articles 2(4), 5(2)(3).

107 Recommendation 178, which recommends that all acquisition financing devices be registered. Acquisition security right (both within the context of unitary and non-unitary approaches) means a security right in a tangible asset that secures the obligation to pay any unpaid portion of the purchase price of the asset, or an obligation incurred, or credit otherwise provided, to enable the grantor to acquire the asset. Thus, under the unitary approach, it encompasses rights arising out of transactions known as retention-of-title and financial leases under non-unitary approach.

108 E.g. under the Swiss Civil Code (Art. 715–716) and Turkish Civil Code (Art. 764). Compulsory registration of retention-of-title agreements also exists in Spain. *See* Kieninger, E-M. (2004) 'Evaluation: A Common Core? Convergences, Subsisting Differences and Possible Ways for Harmonisation', in E-M. Kieninger (ed.), *Security Rights in Movable Property in European Private Law*. Cambridge: Cambridge University Press, 647, 658.

exception to the *nemo dat* rule, the conditional seller may be at risk, as a consequence of which hire purchase agreements are preferred and the *nemo dat* exception does not apply to these transactions.[109] The fact that the Guide recommends creation of a general security rights registry to cover all types of assets and parties fits well with the suggestions made at European Union level.[110] Professor Kieninger makes an observation in relation to the inclusion of retention-of-title and leasing in the uniform regime, which will require general registration and the effect of this on purchase-money security interests (PMSIs).[111] PMSIs are security interests if the goods secure a purchase-money obligation, which the UCC Article 9 defines as an obligation of an obligor incurred as all or part of the price of the collateral or for value given to enable the debtor to acquire rights in or the use of the collateral if the value is in fact so used.[112] The Guide rejects the usage of the term PMSI, preferring the term 'acquisition security right'.[113] The loan under the PMSI facilitates the acquisition of new assets. The significance of the PMSIs is that when the PMSI lender extends credit, new assets purchased with this new loan are not included in the floating charge over after-acquired property. Therefore, the situational monopoly of the first creditor who previously perfected his interest on the assets already owned by the debtor will not create any risk on the potential PMSI lenders. This will prevent the potential injustice that may be caused by the secured creditor to obtain benefit to the detriment of the subsequent creditors.[114] The PMSI lender lends money to the debtor to purchase new property, thus the debtor's pool of assets is increased, whereas a general secured creditor who takes security over the already owned asset does not add new value to the debtor's assets. The former is regarded as neutral as it does not affect existing creditors whereas the latter affects existing creditors by reducing their share.[115] Thus the distinction between the two types is to grant super-priority to the PMSI lender which will have a similar position as a conditional seller.[116] PMSIs have special priority positions (UCC §9–324) and are not subject to simple first-to-file priority rule.[117] PMSIs need to be registered to have third-party effectiveness and priority towards both an unsecured and

109 On the risks involved in retention-of-title agreements for original owners and third parties, *see* Beale *et al.*, op. cit. (f'note 3), para. 7.23. Recommendations of registration were made for all-monies retention-of-title agreements as they serve for security purposes, *see* Law Commission Consultation Paper No. 164, para. 7.24. For the relationship between registration-of-title based devices and the *nemo dat* rule, *see* op. cit. (f'note 3).

110 Kieninger, in Kieninger (ed.), op. cit. (f'note 108), 670.

111 Kieninger, ibid., 672.

112 UCC§9–103(a)(1) and (2)..

113 Guide, para. 82, 29. *see* Chapter 7 for further discussion.

114 *See generally* Finch, V. (2009) *Corporate Insolvency Law: Perspectives and Principles*, 2nd edn. Cambridge: Cambridge University Press, 639.

115 *See generally* McCormack, op. cit. (f'note 66), 292 *et seq.*

116 A similar analogy can also be made to the extension of super-priority to institutional lenders: *Abbey National Building Society v Cann* [1991] 1 AC 56, [1990] 1 All ER 1085 (HL). For further discussion on this point, *see e.g.* Bridge, M. *et al.* (1999) 'Formalism, Functionalism and Understanding the Law of Secured Transactions', 44 *McGill L.J.*, 567, 593 *et seq.*

117 *See* Chapter 6 for the justification of preferential treatment to PMSIs.

secured creditor (the ones who registered their interests following the conclusion of the sales contract). Special perfection requirements also need to be fulfilled in order to obtain super-priority status and, depending on the type of goods (inventory or otherwise), either conflicting PMSI holders need to be notified, or within twenty days of acquisition of possession of collateral PMSI needs to be registered.[118] Under the Model Law (Article 9) an unpaid vendor's charge has to be registered within six months or else it needs to be transferred into a registered charge and registered after the lapse of this period. The period under the UCC Article 9 is twenty days and under the Guide that needs to be specified as a short period.[119] Thus, there seems to be a tendency to have exemption for a certain period from registration. It is believed that this is a necessary evil as a system of general security rights registry for all secured transactions will make it necessary for the reformers to have a special treatment for PMSI, and this may require a grace period (e.g. Recommendations 180 alternatives (A) and (B) and 192 alternatives (A) and (B)) for the registration of certain acquisition financing devices (PMSIs). However, in some countries retention-of-title need not be registered.[120]

In relation to aircraft,[121] in the United Kingdom mortgages should be registered against the company in the Companies House for third-party effectiveness. If the aircraft is registered in the United Kingdom, for priority purposes the mortgage will be registered with the Civil Aviation Authority.[122] The order of registration determines priority and a registered interest will have priority over the unregistered interest.[123] The usefulness of the international registry established by the Cape Town Convention can be illustrated by the fact that mortgages registered in the United Kingdom national registry may not be recognised or enforceable in countries that do not recognise aircraft mortgages or are not party to the Geneva Convention on the International Recognition of Rights in Aircraft, despite the fact that rights over aircraft are treated as rights *in rem* and governed by *lex registri*, which may not still be helpful in case of insolvency.[124]

The critical point in notice filing is the fact that it is mainly based on North American property law and presents differences to the civil law property law approach by setting distinctions between creation, attachment and perfection of

118 UCC §9–324.

119 Recommendation 180 Alternative A (a)(ii).

120 E.g. in England retention-of-title agreements need not be registered. For comparative data, *see* Kieninger, op. cit. (f'note 110), 647 *et seq.*

121 A charge over aircraft is registrable under the Companies Act 2006 s. 860(7)(h). If the charge is created by an individual, it is also registrable under the Bills of Sale Acts 1878 and 1882.

122 For more details on aircraft financing in England, *see* Edward, J. (2007) 'Aircraft', in P. Ali (ed.) *Secured Finance Transactions*. London: Globe Law and Business, 141.

123 Mortgaging of Aircraft Order 1972 (SI 1972/1268) Art. 14. The Register of Aircraft Mortgages introduced by the Order is only open to mortgages of aircraft registered on the UK nationality register. Spare parts are also registrable.

124 Edmunds, J.A. (2002) 'Mortgages of Aircraft', in I. Davies (ed.) *Security Interests in Mobile Equipment*. Aldershot: Ashgate, 145, 152–3.

security rights.[125] In English law, transaction filing, which is transaction specific, requires certain particulars of charge and the instrument to be filed with Companies House within twenty-one days as of the date of creation of charge over book debts[126] (but no registration requirement for factoring of debts where a significant difference between the Receivables Convention and the Guide's functional approach to assignment can be established), as opposed to notice filing adopted under the UCC Article 9–501 where the financing statement, which can be filed either before or at the same time as attachment, is filed to provide notice to third parties.[127] However, the perfection system under English law has been criticised for being too cumbersome and expensive, for what is registrable not being comprehensive, for there being no possibility to register charges before they are created, and for the twenty-one day requirement, during which a charge must be registered with Companies House, presenting a danger to subsequent creditors.[128]

Single filing covers multiple security transactions, having the effect of reducing the cost of credit by repeatedly preventing the requirement of individual registration of each transaction, particularly in financing the sale and supply of goods transactions.[129] The significance of single filing in the functional approach that the Guide adopts is the requirement of registration of quasi-security interests, which are not registrable in English law. The Guide, like the UCC Article 9, recharacterises certain transactions as security interests, including financial leases and retention-of-title, and registration is necessary to make them effective as against third parties.[130] Thus, there is divergence between the Guide's approach and English law. The Guide requires registration as a general requirement for quasi-security interests. Although there may be arguments to the contrary, there is wisdom in requiring quasi-security interests to be registered for third-party effectiveness. Most importantly, for predictability reasons third parties need to be informed of a prior functionally equivalent security device and, arguably, notification will have positive impact on lending decisions. As a key objective the Guide advocates that public notice be given by registration of all types of security rights in a general security rights registry, which has the general characteristics that it records notices rather than the transaction itself, that notices are made available to any interested party and except in acquisition financing transactions, where a

125 Particularly, in Scotland priority of real rights are determined in order of creation *prior tempore potior jure*. Among civil law jurisdictions, only Quebec and Louisiana introduced notice filing. For concerns of civil law and mixed legal systems on the notice filing scheme, *see e.g.* Scottish Law Commission Discussion Paper No 121 Registration of Rights in Security by Companies (Edinburgh, October 2002) paras 1.28–1.29; Final Report by the Scottish Law Commission Registration of Rights in Security by Companies (Edinburgh, September 2004), para. 1.5.

126 Companies Act 2006 Part 25.

127 UCC §9–210 also requires certain disclosure to be made by the secured creditor.

128 Law Commission Consultation Paper No. 176, para. 2.4 *et seq.*

129 *See generally* UCC §9–502 Official Comment. This is also the case under the Guide where one registration covers for multiple security rights. Recommendations 67–68.

130 Recommendation 2(d).

non-unitary approach is adopted, third party effectiveness and priority will be determined by the time of registration.[131]

The Guide envisaged a unitary or non-unitary approach in acquisition financing devices.[132] It diverges from the functional approach of UCC Article 9 in the sense that acquisition financing devices may or may not be treated substantively, in the same way as security interests. If a non-unitary approach is opted into by a State that prefers to separate security interests and quasi-security interests, the latter will be treated substantively the same way as the security interests, but the characterisation will be different.[133] The significance of this original approach to third-party effectiveness is that even though States are free to choose whether quasi-security rights may be characterised as security rights or not (States may choose to preserve retention-of-title and financial lease as independent acquisition financing transactions), they will still be under the Guide's rules and required to be registered to achieve third-party effectiveness. In that sense this aspect proves to be an exception to the first-to-file priority rule envisaged in the Guide.[134] In some jurisdictions retention-of-title and financial lease transactions do not need to be registered[135] and any additional step to make the right effective against third parties is not required. Thus, once the retention-of-title agreement is concluded the seller's ownership rights are effective as against third parties without the need for a registration. On the other hand, in jurisdictions that treat quasi-security devices as security rights,[136] thus employing the functional approach, the registration of a retention-of-title agreement for third-party effectiveness is required. Seller's ownership right in retention-of-title, or lessor's right, is transformed into an acquisition security right. The buyer may encumber the assets purchased from the seller to other creditors because seller's right on the asset is no longer an ownership right but a security right. Thus registration of notice of retention-of-title is desirable.[137] Under the Guide, there is a requirement that acquisition security rights must be registered in the general security interest registry for third-party effectiveness.[138]

The information contained in the financing statement does not provide the full details of the security agreement but it is party specific, which prompts the lender to conduct further research on the borrower by signalling the existence of a prior security interest. It has the public information function. The burden of inquiry should not be too great, as this will defeat the object of reducing the cost of credit.

131 Guide, paras 54 and 66, at 21 and 24.

132 *See below* Chapter 7. Guide Chapter IX Acquisition Financing, *see especially* paras 96–115, at 342–7.

133 For further discussion of this original aspect of the Guide, *see below* Chapter 7.

134 Recommendation 32.

135 E.g. in English law retention-of-title and financial lease transactions need not be registered.

136 E.g. UCC Article 9.

137 Guide, para. 100, 343.

138 For further details of how registration will have effect under unitary and non-unitary approaches, *see* Chapter 7.

Unlike the positions of the Receivables Convention[139] and the Guide,[140] advance registration (registration before a security right is created) has not received the support of the EBRD,[141] as rapid electronic registration possibilities diminished the significance of allowing the creditor to obtain priority during the negotiations.[142] The significance of advance registration is that potential lenders during negotiations can check the register to enquire whether the debtor has security over the assets, and register their security in order to secure their positions during the negotiation process. If advance registration is not allowed, during the negotiations the debtor may grant security to another lender, who will register and rank ahead and diminish the value of the first lender's security.[143] The Cape Town Convention also recognises the possibility to register in advance where prospective international interest[144] can be registered in advance of conclusion of the transaction that creates or provides for the interest. The significance of registering prospective international interests is that once this interest becomes an international interest no further registration is necessary.[145] From a critical point of view, advance registration particularly in notice filing systems is important in making lending decisions, as it provides an indication that a secured creditor may have a security right over the asset in question. Advance registration and reserving the rank of priority between the time of checking the registry and granting the loan may have a cost reduction function as the lender will have certainty. Furthermore, by registration and reserving the ranking, the lender prevents another secured creditor from registering during loan negotiations.[146]

Similar arguments may be made for the Receivables Convention, which treats assignment by way of sale and security on a functional basis and recommends registration of assignment of receivables. The Convention adopts the functional approach and registration of outright transfers of receivables may be contrary to both English law and some civil law jurisdictions. The Receivables Convention suggests that a registration system should be established even if States prefer to

139 Article 4(3) Optional Annex permits registration in advance of the assignment to which it relates.

140 Guide, paras 98–101, 174–5. Recommendations 67–68. Registration may be made before or after the creation of the security right or the conclusion of the security agreement.

141 Model Law Article 8(1) where commentary states that '[t]he model does not provide for advance registration'.

142 EBRD Guiding Principles, at 14.

143 Law Commission Consultation Paper No. 164, para. 3.29. Under English law advance registration is not possible, as particulars of the charge need to be registered rather than the notice of it. The Law Commission recommended the notice to be filed in advance of conclusion of the security agreement, whereby priorities set by first-to-file rule. Para. 4.110

144 Cape Town Convention Article 1(y) defines *prospective international interest* as 'an interest that is intended to be created or provided for in an object as an international interest in the future, upon the occurrence of a stated event (which may include the debtor's acquisition of an interest in the object), whether or not the occurrence of the event is certain'.

145 Cape Town Convention Articles 16, 18(3), 19(4) and 22(3).

146 For further discussion, *see* Fleisig *et al.*, op. cit. (f'note 89), at 40.

keep their priority systems.[147] This is envisaged as a notice registration.[148] It is necessary to make assignment of receivables publicly ascertainable as this will enable financiers to predict the priority status and arguably, facilitate lending decisions and receivables financing. It is clear that a perfection system based on notice registration may contradict the other two priority options envisaged in the annex (priority determined by the time of transfer and priority determined by the first notification). One of the reasons why the Receivables Convention has kept the registration system optional was the risk that some States might refuse to become signatories and the Convention might not attract sufficient interest.[149] Another reason was that there was no consensus on priority rules based on registration or on the time of filing 'due to confidentiality, data protection and competition issues'.[150] Other reasons bearing on this lack of consensus are that introducing a filing system would harm non-notification practices and would not provide sufficient assurance that a right actually existed, because this would contradict systems where issues of priority are based on the time of the assignment.[151] Arguably, the optional nature of registration is the weakest point of the Receivables Convention. Concerns in relation to registration violating privacy and confidentiality of parties' dealings and limiting competition contributed to the optional nature of registration in the Convention.[152] As prescribed under Article 42, even if States apply their domestic priority rules, the registration system can still be opted into in order to benefit from the main objectives of the Receivables Convention, and certainty in cross-border receivables financing may be created. The Receivables Convention subjects the perfection requirements to the law of the assignor's State.[153] In that sense, the law of the assignor's State governs priority of competing claimants and priority will be granted to the claimant who fulfils the perfection requirements of that State. However, if the law of the assignor's State does not contain modern perfection rules or protect the interests of assignees, the optional annex of the Receivables Convention offers the creation of a registration system. Considering complex modern financing practices, registration of assignment of receivables seems to present a predictable solution. The Receivables Convention optional annex section II Article 3 sets out the details of establishment of a registration system. This is particularly important for Contracting States that do not have a registration system. Registration is not only intended for the purposes of the Convention (i.e. assignment of international

147 Article 42(4) and optional annex Section II. Chapter V of the Guide will be useful in setting the registry system in the Contracting States.

148 Article 4(1) Optional Annex where it is stated that '. . . data registered shall be the identification of the assignor and the assignee and a brief description of the assigned receivables'.

149 Schwarcz, S.L. (1999) 'Towards a Centralized Perfection System For Cross-Border Receivables Financing', 20 *U. Pa. J. Int'l Econ., L.* 455, 462.

150 Bazinas, S. (2001) 'Lowering the Cost of Credit: the Promise in the Future UNCITRAL Convention on Assignment of Receivables in International Trade', 9 *Tul. J. Int'l & Comp. L., 259*, 285.

151 A/CN.9/434, para. 248.

152 For discussions *see* A/CN.9/445, paras 83–119.

153 Receivables Convention Article 22.

receivables or international assignment of receivables), but also for the registration of domestic assignments and receivables. Therefore, the Commission decided to prepare a registry, which is compatible even with the domestic assignments of receivables. The registry is open to any person to search its records according to identification of the assignor, and a search in writing can be obtained. The written search result issued by the registry is admissible as evidence and is proof of the registration of the data to which the search relates. The registration is proposed to be simple and inexpensive and requires a limited amount of data by virtue of Article 4, which establishes the basic characteristics for an efficient system and, therefore, an assignee and an assignor would not be required to register information that is too detailed. These basic characteristics are 'the public character of the registry, the type of data that need to be registered, the ways in which the registration-related needs of modern financing practices may be accommodated and the time of effectiveness of registration'.[154] Article 4(2) and (3) of the Optional Annex ensure the efficient operation of registration by accommodating existing or future assignments and receivables arising from one or several contracts in the registry. Thus, obstacles before registration that may render it slow, expensive and inefficient are cleared.[155] However, there seems to be still one obstacle to achieve third-party effectiveness and the ultimate goal of ascertaining priority under the Receivables Convention. If a State does not adopt the registration system under the Convention, nor enacts any other registration system, even for domestic assignments, the assignee will not be able to ascertain the priority status as expected under the Receivables Convention. Establishing a domestic registration system or a registration system purely for international assignments may not be helpful. It may be argued that the Guide will assist domestic reforms in this area and set a standard for the creation and operation of a registration system.[156]

Despite the Guide's approach to third-party effectiveness through registration, in the main civil law jurisdictions operate and achieve third-party effectiveness without a general security rights registration system. Professor Kieninger, in her report, indicates that publicity regimes in European jurisdictions are extremely divergent including denial of publicity, reliance on notification, asset-based registries, debtor-based registries or fixing the date of transaction.[157] It is clear that such divergence cannot assist the facilitation of credit regionally or globally. The fact that there is no registration or publicity system in Germany may well work in a closed market system, where flow of credit information or the standing of the debtors are communicated clearly among the creditors. However, for the success of this type of system there must be a perfect flow of information among the lenders about the creditworthiness and financial behaviour of borrowers. Previous

154 A/CN.9/489/Add. 1, para. 78.

155 Ibid., para. 79.

156 Guide, Chapter III and IV.

157 Kieninger, op. cit. (f'note 110), 670. Professor Kieninger also rightly suggests that a possible European Security Interest should be publicised in a debtor-based registry system, as asset-based registries may not be easily found by the general public to search potential security interests.

security rights are invisible due to lack of registration.[158] Here, it must be pointed out that clear flow of information depends on human and sociological factors too (i.e. both the banks and the borrowers must be open in their dealings and there must be no corruption). Arguably this system is open to abuse by misrepresentations, and there is an important element of cultural and human factor for it to operate successfully (i.e. lenders must be sure that the borrower's financial standing is what he says it is).[159] The system may have the risk of high administrative costs. Arguably registration may not be necessary when proprietary security interests are created on majority by transfer of title. Particularly among business people, the requirements for establishing good faith, which arguably has a premier status in civil law more so than it is in common law jurisdictions, could be strengthened, as businesses are supposed to know (presumption of constructive knowledge) that goods are bought on credit.[160] However, a critical review will reveal that the advantages of registration are more than its absence. The concept of good faith has different connotations in common and civil law jurisdictions and it would be unfeasible to attempt to change notions that are so deeply rooted in national legal cultures. Registration will enable creditors and investors to be certain about their priority rankings. This will in turn lower the cost of credit, as predictability, in the sense that subsequent creditors will be notified of the existence of a prior security interest over the same asset, or other assets, of the debtor, will assure secured creditors that they will be repaid. Lenders will not, under neutral conditions, include the risk premium in the interest rates. The functional approach to security and registration of all devices aiming at security will abolish the constructive knowledge requirement of prior security rights. In the absence of a registration requirement of retention-of-title clauses, unsecured creditors especially are unable to ascertain prior rights, and this increases their already risky business venture. Thus, small and unsecured creditors in particular will benefit from the functional approach and the comprehensive general security rights registration, as there will be no assumption that they have knowledge of the prior security interest.

Some civil law jurisdictions, such as Japan,[161] and transition economies, such as Poland, Slovakia, Czech Republic and Hungary,[162] adopted centralised

158 Drobnig, U. (2003) 'Present and Future of Real and Personal Security', 5 *E.R.P.L.*, 623, at 660 (stating that he '[remains] to be convinced of the true necessity of a filing system').

159 On the German position regarding registry and the system without registry, *see* Rakob, J. (2007) 'Germany', in Sigman and Kieninger (eds), op. cit. (f'note 46), 63, at 66.

160 *See generally* Drobnig, U. (2009) 'Basic Issues of European Rules on Security in Movables' in J. De Lacy (ed.) *The Reform of Personal Property Security Law Comparative Perspectives*. Abingdon: Routledge, 444, at 448.

161 The centralised registration system was established in 1998 for perfection purposes. This is a significant reform example in the sense that written notification or consent, which are obstacles before financing, are not required. *See* True, R.B. 'New Developments in Japanese Asset Securitization: Open the Floodgates', available at http://www.tuj.ac.jp/newsite/main/law/lawresources/TUJonline/Corporate/assetsecwith%20glossary.html (last accessed 10 May 2010).

162 Although a registration system is in place in Hungary, this is a paper-based document filing instead of online notice filing, and the publicity aimed at by the registration system is slow and complex. For criticism of the system and reform, *see* Csizmazia, N. (2008) 'Reform of the Hungarian Law of Security Rights in Movable Property', XIV *Juridica Internatinal*, 181, 190–1.

registration systems.[163] The aforementioned transition economies, albeit still with some shortcomings,[164] have established the centralised registration system with the assistance of the EBRD. Registration is also a feature of the Model Law.[165] The Model Law requires the registration of a registration statement (Article 8) that is not the transaction between the parties (i.e. charging instrument). The content of the registration statement is kept to a minimum. Thus, the Model Law, along with the other international instruments, provides notice registration with minimum information, where vital terms of the credit agreement are not revealed. Unlike the UCC Article 9, where perfection is a method of third-party notice of prior security interest and registration is irrelevant as to the validity of the security interest, the Model Law requires registration for the purpose of third-party notice as well as a condition of the validity of the charge. There are, however, two exceptions to registration. Possessory charges do not need to be registered. Taking possession fulfils the third-party effectiveness requirement.[166] An unpaid vendor's charge (which is a simple retention-of-title agreement) is also an exception to the registration requirement,[167] the purpose of which 'is to avoid registration for short-term credits in the context of the sales of goods'.[168] If the unpaid vendor's charge extends beyond six months, or if it is to be converted into a registered charge under the Model Law, then it needs to be registered within six months of the conclusion of the unpaid vendor's charge agreement.[169] It is arguable that the non-registration feature of the unpaid vendor's charge has a negative impact on third parties because a third party creditor may be unaware of the existence of the unpaid vendor's charge. Furthermore, the purchaser as chargor must not dispose of the property, otherwise the acquirer will have good title and in this context, registered charge offers better solutions.[170] Professor Röver submits that the rejection of registration requirement for all unpaid vendor's charges supports the idea of protection of small suppliers against the large suppliers and lenders and that no system of registration can effectively establish third-party rights over the asset that appears to be owned by the debtor and lenders can protect themselves by ensuring the seller is paid or that no title retention exists in the first place.[171] First, it is clear

163 Simpson, J. and Menze, J. (2000) 'Ten Years of Secured Transactions Reform', *Law in Transition*, (Autumn) at 20; Fairgrieve and Andenas, op. cit. (f'note 94); Dahan, F. and Simpson, J. (2005) 'Publicity of Security Rights? Setting Standards for Charge Registries', *JIBFL*, 58; Simpson, J. and Dahan, F. (2006) 'The impact of the Legal Framework on the Secured Credit Market in Poland', *JIBFL*, 174.

164 E.g. in Poland the time required for registration discourages the use of security. *See e.g.* Dahan, F. *et al.*, (2004) 'Enforcing Secured Transactions in Central and Eastern Europe: An Empirical Study', *Law in Transition*, 14.

165 Model Law Part 5 outlines the details of the registration system.

166 Model Law Articles 6.1.3, 6.4 and 10.

167 Model Law Articles 6.1.2, 6.3 and 9.

168 Röver, op. cit. (f'note 34), at 78.

169 Model Law Article 8.2 and 9.3.

170 Model Law Article 9.1.

171 Röver, op. cit. (f'note 34), at 83 paras 7.59–7.60.

that, for a small supplier, registration of rights over every supplied material may be costly and burdensome. Arguably, a critical review of this argument on registration would reveal that small suppliers might have been well protected if a registration system was required under the Model Law, or at least the length of the non-registrable period could have been shorter than six months. If the argument is protection of small suppliers, thus facilitation of credit, the lack of registration for an unpaid vendor's charge does not seem to be justifiable. Small suppliers may not have the necessary system to find out about the earlier rights on the same asset, which also applies to lenders. Second, the debtor's representations may not always be trusted. The lender is unaware of the existence of a right over the asset. The unpaid vendor obtains super-priority over other charges.[172] As the priority may be considered a balance of rights of lenders and sellers, registration is necessary for all types of transactions that serve economically similar functions for third-party effectiveness. Lenders should not be disadvantaged against the other contractual partners of debtors. Protection suggestions for lenders in the absence of a registration system can only increase the cost of credit. It is possible that the unpaid vendor's charge creates an impression of false wealth and critically has a negative impact upon the virtues of a registration system. Essentially, an unpaid vendor's charge or retention-of-title clauses should be subject to the same rule applicable for security interest for creation and third-party effectiveness.

The types of creditors against whom a security interest can be registered is also critical. On this matter, Dahan and McCormack argue that determination of the function of a register, as to whether it determines priority or provides public notice or actual knowledge, has to be addressed.[173] Under the Guide registration is necessary for third-party effectiveness and determines priority status of competing creditors. Under the Cape Town Convention, the objective of registration is to provide notice of the existence of a registered interest on a uniquely identifiable asset (registration is against the asset) and the registration takes effect against third parties for priority purposes as of 'the time [the required information entered in the International Registry data base becomes] accessible by way of search or would be accessible if the system were functioning properly'.[174] The Cape Town system, under Article 16, allows the registration of international interests (Articles 1(o) and 2(2)), assignments and subordinations of international interests and other interests.[175] The validity of registration is subject to consent in writing and the duration of registration depends on the time of discharge or the expiration period specified

172 Model Law Article 17.3. *See also* Chapter 6 for a discussion.

173 Dahan and McCormack, op. cit. (f'note 12), at 728–9. For further discussion on priority, *see* Chapter 6.

174 Goode, op. cit. (f'note 97), para 2.75, at 51–2. Cape Town Convention Article 19(2), (6). Aircraft Protocol Article XX(1). Article 26 also permits anyone interested to access the international registration facilities.

175 Prospective interests, prospective assignments of international interests (Articles 1(x) and (y)). Article III of Aircraft Protocol also prescribes the type of interests that can be registered and this includes prospective sales.

in the registration.[176] Furthermore, under Article 29(1), the creditor who registers the international interest will have priority over the subsequent registered interest as well as over the unregistered interest, whether or not registrable.[177] It is argued that this rule avoids any complexities that may arise from diverse national legal systems by giving superiority to international interests. Third parties are informed about of the existence of a prior security interest over high value mobile equipment. Registration establishes the creditor's priority and third-party effectiveness in insolvency proceedings against the debtor. Registration is not a requirement for creation or proof of existence of an international interest. Without a validly created international interest registration cannot have any effect on third parties. Following the creation of an international interest upon registration, the international interest obtains priority over subsequently registered international interests and unregistered interests.[178] However, even if an international interest is registered, it does not guarantee its existence. As retention-of-title contracts are registered under the Cape Town Convention, when the buyer pays for the asset and acquires the title, the interest is effectively discharged whether or not it is still on the registry.[179]

5.3.2 Possession

Transfer of possession of movables is a traditional method of establishing third-party effectiveness. Despite the decline of its publicity function, as it lacks practicality in modern secured transactions systems,[180] it is still necessary to achieve third-party effectiveness in certain tangibles. The actual delivery of a movable asset to the creditor, or someone designated by the creditor, serves, first, as the consent of the debtor to grant a security over the assets, and second, a third-party effectiveness according to which third parties are informed, albeit tacitly, that the debtor does not have the physical possession of the asset, and thus, in the absence of registration, cannot mislead third parties that the debtor holds unencumbered title to the assets.[181] Complementing this argument, possession also guarantees the secured creditor's priority over the pledged asset in the event of the debtor's insolvency. Transfer of possession is not suitable for intangible assets as its possessory nature makes it impossible for the intangibles to be physically transferred to the creditor. Generally speaking, as the debtor is deprived of possession the economic value of the asset cannot be utilised[182] and possession, arguably, is not essentially a useful method in the facilitation of credit. The effectiveness of possession is limited

176 Cape Town Convention Articles 19–21.
177 Goode, op. cit. (f'note 97), at 222–3.
178 Cape Town Convention Article 29(2)(a), (3)(b).
179 Goode, op. cit. (f'note 97), 49–50.
180 For a discussion on the decline of significance of possession, *see* Kieninger, op. cit. (f'note 110), at 652–3.
181 Guide, para. 47, at 114.
182 For a similar view, *see* Cuming, R. (1997) 'The Internationalisation of Secured Financing Law: The Spreading Influence of the Concepts UCC, Article 9 and its Progeny', in R. Cranston (ed.) *Making Commercial Law–Essays in Honour of Roy Goode*. Oxford: Oxford University Press, 499, 502.

vis-à-vis registration of a notice of a security right in the general security rights registry. The particular tension between possession and registration co-existing in the same legal system needs elaboration. Registration compared to possession seems to provide a better source of information as to the existence of an earlier security right over the same asset. Proof of an earlier security right is objectively established through registration. Nevertheless, as possession is necessary for certain tangible assets (e.g. negotiable instruments), it may operate in harmony with a general security rights registry.[183]

The Guide recognises the significance of possession (where the asset is capable of being transferred and when the debtor is willing to give up actual possession of the asset)[184] and recommends that for certain tangible assets (negotiable instruments), and for short-term financing business (pawnbrokers), possession may work as an alternative method to achieve third-party effectiveness.[185] For priority purposes possession will be the main method to achieve third-party effectiveness in negotiable instruments and documents.[186] Constructive possession, where actual delivery of the movable to the creditor is bypassed and the grantor or an agent of the grantor keeps possession, has been used as a substitute for non-possessory security rights in the absence of the latter.[187] However, constructive possession is not recognised under the Guide,[188] and as the establishment of a general security rights registry is recommended, there seems to be no logical reason to extend the concept of possession to cover an area that is the realm of non-possessory security rights.[189]

The Model Law recognises the significance of possession and provides a possessory charge[190] for third-party effectiveness, of which the possession of the collateral must be given and a charging instrument (a contract between the parties) must be entered into.[191] Following the introduction of the Model Law in the early 1990s, in transition economies, due to the limited number of registered financing devices, pledge has been extended to cover a non-possessory charge and developed as

183 For the rationale of establishing the general security rights registry in addition to the transfer of possession, *see* Guide, para. 49, at 115.

184 Guide, para. 50, at 115.

185 Recommendation 37.

186 For negotiable instruments and negotiable documents, possession will be the primary method of achieving third-party effectiveness and for priority purposes, whoever has the possession of these tangibles; thus, achieved third-party effectiveness will obtain priority over other creditors who have achieved third-party effectiveness through other methods. Recommendations 101 and 109.

187 Under English law constructive possession is possible, and a requirement for attachment is confined to pledges. It is possible that third parties may agree to hold physical possession for the creditor, or that the debtor in possession may create a pledge if the debtor informs the creditor that the goods are held to the creditor's order, which will be deemed to be in the possession of the creditor. For more information, *see* Gullifer, op. cit. (f'note 8), 70–1.

188 Constructive possession is not permitted under the UCC Article 9, where possession as a method of perfection must be actual.

189 Guide, para. 53, 116.

190 Model Law Articles 6.1, 6.4, 7 and 10.

191 Model Law Article 6.4.1 and 10.

constructive possession, according to which the debtor keeps possession of the asset and the creditor's right over the asset is recognised as constructive possession by the courts.[192] Professor Spanogle argued that as the Model Law did not contain clarification as to whether actual physical delivery by the debtor to the creditor was required,[193] the possessory charge was used in transition economies in a wider ambit. The main difference between the traditional pledge and possessory charge should be that in the former, which creates a right *in rem*, actual delivery of possession is needed,[194] whereas in the latter a proprietary right is established over the debtor's property to secure the obligation to a creditor and there seems to be no implication of loss of possession. The criticism was that in the absence of not requiring actual physical possession of the charged property by the creditor or creditor's agent, the constructive possession concept will provide no public notice and the utilisation of a possessory charge in this wider sense will diminish the significance of a non-possessory registered charge.[195]

Divergent approaches in the region have led the EBRD to assist transition economies to establish centralised registration systems in order to overcome the risk of secret encumbrance of property through non-possessory pledge where parties avoid registration. The EBRD Guidelines and Recommendations on Publicity of Security Rights points out that if a charges register is created, three alternative policies may be adopted in relation to possessory charges. As it is not necessary to register possessory charges they receive priority as of the time of creation. However, it is necessary to set the means of establishing the time of creation and the effect of debtor regaining possession (i.e. if the security right is created orally and possession is transferred, and subsequently the secured creditor wishes to relinquish possession, the agreement for this should be in writing).[196] When possessory and non-possessory charges work together, the possessory charge is subordinate to a subsequent registered charge, or possessory charges need to be registered, which naturally diminishes the distinction between the possessory and non-possessory charges.[197]

UCC Article 9–313 authorises perfection by possession, which fulfils enforceability[198] and perfection where the secured party perfects a security interest in negotiable documents, goods, instruments, money or tangible chattel paper by taking actual

192 Spanogle, in Norton and Andenas, op. cit. (f'note 25), 166.

193 Model Law Article 10 indicates that possession may be obtained by either the chargeholder, a person nominated by the chargeholder, or a person holding on terms agreed between the chargeholder and chargor (where parties may agree on the chargor/debtor). The Guide also confirms third party custody in place of creditor possession. Recommendations 15 and 32. UCC Article 9 also permits the possession of the third party as the secured party's agent.

194 Thus this gives a narrow ambit to pledge. *See e.g. Official Assignee of Madras v. Mercantile Bank of India Ltd.* [1935] AC 53.

195 Spanogle, in Norton and Andenas, op. cit. (f'note 25), 166. The Guide rejects the constructive possession concept, *see* above.

196 Guide, para. 33, at 72–3; Recommendation 15 and 32. This has consequences in relation to continuity and lapse of third-party effectiveness. Third-party effectiveness is continuous as long as there is no time of third-party ineffectiveness. Recommendation 46.

197 For these alternatives, *see* EBRD Guiding Principles, at 7.

198 UCC §9–203.

possession.[199] Under English law where, for instance, pledge of goods is not registered but is effective against third parties, and this is a security interest perfected by possession as it is called under North American personal property security legislations, there is no need for registration to make it effective against third parties.[200]

5.3.3 Alternative methods of achieving third-party effectiveness

Alongside a general registry for security interests there will be other methods to achieve third-party effectiveness.[201] There are various methods where, without transfer of possession, third-party effectiveness is established in response to the need for non-possessory secured financing. Although there are arguments that registration should not have too many exceptions or alternatives,[202] it is necessary to keep registration as the principal method and have alternatives to maintain an optimal third-party effectiveness regime. Sale of the movable asset to the secured creditor by the grantor, with the condition of right of redemption upon repayment of the credit equal to the sale price, may be used. This type of financing practice, where creation and third-party effectiveness are achieved through concluding a sale agreement, however, presents a risk according to which third parties have no means of verifying the existence of a prior right over the asset. Furthermore, third parties, who are unaware of prior secured creditor's rights, must be protected. Other methods include declaration of the grantor's holding the encumbered asset on behalf of the secured creditor. However, without an efficient publicity system it is clear that these various methods cannot produce workable results to facilitate credit both in domestic and international financing practices. Particularly, notwithstanding its drawbacks compared to modern financing practices,[203] traditional pledge, where the movable asset's possession is actually delivered to the creditor, is an important method of financing as far as the movable assets are concerned (Recommendation 37). The use of traditional pledge is critical in countries where receivables cannot be used due to poor enforcement prospects and banks accept only movables as collateral and so extend credit upon pledging them.[204] Alternative methods[205] include possession of a

199 For a detailed examination *see* White and Summers, op. cit. (f'note 45), at 769 *et seq.*

200 Beale *et al.*, op. cit. (f'note 3), at 328.

201 The Guide recommends alternatives and exceptions to registration for achieving third-party effectiveness. Recommendation 34.

202 Stürner, in Eidenmüller and Kieninger (eds), op. cit. (f'note 7), 169.

203 It is widely accepted that the debtor should be able to use the assets to utilise the economic value and repay the creditor.

204 For empirical figures on the use of pledge and types of acceptable collateral in unreformed economies, *see* Safavian, M. (2008) 'Firm-level Evidence on Collateral and Access to Finance', in F. Dahan and J. Simpson (eds) *Secured Transactions Reform and Access to Credit*. Cheltenham: Edward Elgar, 110, 118.

205 It can be argued that those alternative methods to registration in a general security rights registry are similar to those under UCC Article 9, where filing is not allowed for perfection of money (UCC §9–312(b)(3)), deposit accounts (UCC §9–312(b)(1)), or letter-of-credit rights (UCC §9–312(b)(2).

negotiable instrument by a secured creditor (Recommendations 51–53), registration of movables in a specialised registry or notation on the title certificate,[206] control of the bank account in the right to payment of funds credited to a bank account (Recommendation 49), in an attachment to a movable asset by registration or notation on the title certificate (Recommendation 42) or in the case of an attachment to immovable property by registration (Recommendation 43). In these alternative methods, the Guide's approach is that the agreement creates the security interest and the transfer of possession is regarded as an alternative method to registration for third-party effectiveness.

5.3.3.1 *Automatic third-party effectiveness*

Perfection of security interests upon attachment is a method of third-party effectiveness under UCC Article 9.[207] This type of third-party effectiveness is a significant method to create certainty in receivables financing where, particularly in loan participation transactions (sale of an undivided interest and security in the loan to a third party), requirement of filing may create confusion.[208] It seems that the Guide takes a similar approach and allows the automatic third-party effectiveness of a security right in proceeds and in an attachment.[209] Automatic third-party effectiveness is permissible for security rights in proceeds, in a mass or product, in an attachment to a movable asset where third-party effectiveness was achieved before the asset became an attachment. Security rights over proceeds that arise out of the encumbered asset are created as of the time these proceeds arise and as long as they remain identifiable.[210] A particular problem relates to security rights over future assets from which proceeds may arise. It is possible to register security rights in advance of the debtor acquiring rights in the assets. Once those rights are created over the assets, proceeds will automatically arise. It will not be necessary additionally to achieve third-party effectiveness because automatic third-party effectiveness will already have been achieved.[211] Thus for efficiency reasons third-party effectiveness is extended to proceeds in the form of receivables, money, negotiable instruments and rights to payment of funds credited to a bank account, provided third-party effectiveness for security rights is achieved when the proceeds arise.[212]

206 Recommendation 38. This is similar to UCC §9–311, where a secured creditor perfects its security interest by notation on the certificate in an automobile that has been issued with a certificate title.

207 UCC §9–308–310: automatic perfection is achieved when purchase-money security interest in consumer goods is perfected automatically when it attaches; UCC §9–312(e)(f)(g) and §9–315(c)(d). Automatic perfection can be for 20 days on a temporary basis UCC §9–317(e). For further information, *see e.g.* S.L. Sepinuck, *Practice under Article 9 of the Uniform Commercial Code*, American Bar Association, 2008, 95 *et seq.*; Sigman, op. cit. (f'note 46), 143, 150.

208 McCormack, op. cit. (f'note 14), 247; Bjerre, C. (1999) 'Secured Transactions Inside Out: Negative Pledge Covenant, Property and Perfection', 84 *Cornell L. Rev.*, 305, 392.

209 Recommendations 39–41, 44–45.

210 Guide, para. 87, 124. Guide recommends this approach for the creation of security rights over proceeds. Recommendation 19.

211 Recommendation 39.

212 Guide, para. 94, at 126.

Under Model Law Article 5.10 the charge holder is not granted an automatic right to have interest in the proceeds of sale in the event the charged property is sold. The proceeds of the property are not included in the charged property unless this is provided in the charge agreement prior to taking the charge. An international interest also extends to proceeds of the object under the Cape Town Convention (Article 1(w) insurance and other loss-related proceeds rather than disposition of the object) and priority also covers proceeds.[213] The Guide also adopts the approach that security follows obligation in the creation of security rights and for third-party effectiveness, in the sense that if third-party effectiveness of a security right is achieved in a receivable or negotiable instrument, this automatically extends to the accessory rights without the necessity to complete further acts.[214]

5.3.3.2 Control

Control of collateral[215] is an alternative method to registration used to achieve third-party effectiveness in funds deposited in a bank account and a right to receive the proceeds under an independent undertaking. A similar argument applies to fixed charges over financial collateral (bank accounts and shares in a company, unless the latter allow dividends, which may be considered as book debts and registrable) and floating charges over financial collateral, which are not registrable and become effective as of the time of control.[216] A charge over financial collateral need not be registered, and the Companies Act 2006 requirement of registration under s. 860 does not apply. Financial collateral is perfected through control as of the time the chargee takes control of it. A charge on a bank deposit is not treated as a book debt, thus charge-backs seem to be not registrable.[217]

The Guide permits control of the collateral (a right to payment of funds credited to a bank account) for third-party effectiveness. The deposit account is not the asset on which the security right is created. The asset on which the security right is created is 'the grantor's right to claim performance of the bank's obligation to pay the value of the funds credited to the grantor's bank account'.[218] Control can take one of the three forms. It can be automatic if the secured creditor is the

213 Articles 2(5) and 29(6).

214 Recommendation 48.

215 UCC §9–314, where security interests in investment property, deposit accounts, letter-of-credit rights or electronic chattel paper are perfected by the secured party acquiring the control of the collateral, rather than by registration.

216 This is due to Financial Collateral Arrangements (No. 2) Regulations 2003 SI 2003/3226. *See also* Beale *et al.*, op. cit. (f'note 45), at 327 and 346–7. However, had all charges been registrable, the requirement under the Financial Collateral Arrangements Regulation could have been seen as an exception (i.e. control as an exception to registration). On this matter, *see e.g.* Bridge, in Eidenmüller and Kieninger (eds), op. cit. (f'note 26), at 185–6.

217 *Re BCCI No. 8* [1998] A.C. 214, 227. For discussion on this matter, *see* McCormack, op. cit. (f'note 14), 249 *et seq.*

218 Guide, para. 138, at 137.

depository bank. This alternative has raised a debate[219] in England as to whether the depositary bank can take security over its indebtedness to the debtor. The next alternative may be called 'positive control'.[220] The grantor, the bank and the secured creditor may conclude a control agreement according to which the bank agrees to take instructions from the secured creditor to make payments from the grantor's deposit account. Alternatively, the secured creditor may replace the grantor and become the bank customer, effectively taking possession of the deposit account;[221] thus, in practice, the debtor can no longer deal with the account and this may be called 'negative control'.[222] The impracticality of this latter alternative is clear in that it does not allow the grantor to utilise its money. In order to accommodate various approaches in those countries, where general security rights registries exist, the Guide provides an option under recommendation 49, according to which third-party effectiveness through a control mechanism may be achieved either by registration or control of the funds credited to the bank account. The rationale for having alternative third-party effectiveness methods in bank accounts is that although registration provides an objective way of ensuring third-party effectiveness, until a registration system to this end is established there may be delays and banking transactions may have additional costs. The control method requires the participation of the bank as this method will operate if the bank is a secured creditor, a control agreement is concluded with the grantor and either the secured creditor or the bank establishes a new bank account in order to channel the funds from the grantor's account.[223]

On the other hand, control, under Recommendation 50, is the exclusive method of achieving third-party effectiveness of a security right to receive proceeds under an independent undertaking (such as letter-of-credit or independent guarantee) in order to protect the issuer against a secured creditor. Similarly, control or possession of the negotiable document representing a tangible asset, or registration under recommendation 32 of a security right in a negotiable document, should be sufficient to achieve third-party effectiveness.[224]

219 On one hand, arguments against pointed out that it was impossible (e.g. *Re Charge Card Services Ltd* [1987] 1 Ch. 150); on the other hand, by virtue of *Re BCCI No. 8* [1997] UKHL 44, [1998] AC 214, it was made clear that charge-backs were possible. *See e.g.* McCormack, G. (1998) 'Charge Backs and Commercial Certainty in the House of Lords', *CfiLR*, 111. The Law Commission recommended that charges over a bank account in favour of the bank itself should be possible when the bank takes control and be exempt from registration Law Commission Paper No. 164, para. 5.51.

220 For these alternatives under English law, *see* Beale, *et al.*, op. cit. (f'note 45), Chapter 10 and especially at 402–4. Under UCC §9–104 there can only be positive control, in which the bank agrees to take instructions from the secured creditor in relation to deposit accounts.

221 Guide, paras 141–6, at 138–9.

222 For further details, *see e.g.* Beale, in Eidenmüller and Kieninger (eds), op. cit. (f'note 7), 386–7.

223 Bazinas, S. (2007) 'Bank Accounts', in P. Ali (ed.) *Secured Finance Transactions Key Assets and Emerging Markets*. London: Globe Business, 101, 105.

224 Recommendations 51–53.

5.4 Conclusions

Separating the creation of security rights between parties from the third-party effectiveness is an essential element of modern secured transactions regimes. Some international instruments, prominently the Guide, contain alternative methods of achieving third-party effectiveness. These include possession, which is a traditional method of obtaining publicity; control, which is significant in UCC Article 9 type legislations and under Financial Collateral Arrangements Regulations; and automatic third-party effectiveness under certain cases. Among those, the significance of possession in modern secured transactions regimes has declined due to the increased significance of intangibles as collateral.[225] The particular problem in the third-party effectiveness of security rights is related to non-possessory security interests where intangible assets are used as collateral. It is not possible to transfer intangible assets, particularly receivables, physically. The only method to notify third parties of the existence of the security right on the asset is to register in a general security interests registry. The registry ensures practicality, predictability and transparency. The access to register and searches should be easy and inexpensive. Priority should depend on the time of registration. Registration should operate as notice filing rather than transaction filing, because the aim is to provide a notice to third parties rather than revealing all aspects of the transactions, which may not be beneficial for parties and which does not permit advance registration.[226] It should be possible to have advance registration (registration before concluding the security agreement). As Professor Goode rightly argued 'priority rules, instead of deriving from technical doctrines such as the superiority of the legal title, would be designed to produce a result that would generally be considered fair in typical situations'.[227] Generally speaking, international secured transactions instruments contain, more or less, these features. Registration is the main feature of the Guide, the Model Law and the Cape Town Convention. Although establishing registration is optional under the Receivables Convention, it is arguable that when dealing with receivables perfection, priority cannot decisively be achieved without the registration system. There are some minor variations. For instance, Model Law does not provide for an advance filing; however, the registration must be made within 30 days of the security agreement in order to avoid any secret charges. Also, even though registration is a feature of the Model Law, unlike in other instruments, it is not a separate step but is a constitutive element of creation. A legislative text on registration of security interests will be the future work of the UNCITRAL.[228] This may coincide opportunely with the possible future work and past experience of the Law Commission's work on registration of security interests.

225 Gullifer, *op cit* (f'note 8) 8, 95.

226 For example, scholars agree that a notice filing system to all assignment of receivables should apply, as this is a clear and predictable way of solving priority disputes. *See e.g.* Davies, I. (2004) 'The Reform of English Personal Property Security Law: Functionalism and Article 9 of the Uniform Commercial Code', 24 *Legal Studies*, 295, 305, fn. 61.

227 Goode, op. cit. (f'note 22), 675.

228 *See* A/CN.9/702; A/CN.9/702/Add. 1; A/CN.9/WG.VI/WP.44 and A/CN.9/WG.VI/WP.44/Add. 1 A/CN.9/WG.VI/WP.44/Add.2.

6 Priority of security interests

6.1 Introduction

A clear and predictable priority structure is said to lower the cost of credit by 'giving effect to an efficient public registration mechanism [which] can increase the accuracy of the legal risk assessment'.[1] Generally speaking, the ability to have priority distinguishes a secured lender from an unsecured lender, and grants certain rights during post-default liquidation. There has been, mostly confined to academic circles, a debate whether the secured creditor should be given full priority.[2] However, it is clear that anything less than a full priority position will clearly lead financiers to increase the cost of credit. International instruments take the view that priority should be given in full to secured creditors and no carve-out should be allowed. If a legal system offers clear and predictable priority rules facilitating low-cost credit, lenders are given the opportunity 'to assess the loan's potential risk and return based on its size, the value of collateral, and the order of priority of other creditors'.[3] Priority allows a secured creditor to assess whether recovery of the value of collateral is possible by ascertaining who has a prior right over the same asset. Further benefits of a predictable priority regime that aims to facilitate credit may be summarised as maximisation of value of the collateral and facilitation of efficient commercial practice where priority rules are ascertainable prior to entering into a commercial relationship.[4]

This chapter will discuss the approach of international instruments to the priority of security rights. The recurrent theme is that predictable rules are necessary for the facilitation of credit, and a comprehensive regime for determination of

1 Davies, I. (2002) 'Introduction' in I. Davies (ed.) *Security Interests in Mobile Equipment*. Aldershot: Ashgate, p. ix, at xii.

2 *See* Chapter 1 for the overview of the debate. For a comparison between UK and US laws, *see* e.g. McCormack, G. (2003). 'The Priority of Secured Credit: An Anglo-American Perspective', *J.B.L.*, 389.

3 Fleisig, H., Safavian, M. and De La Pena, N. (2006) *Reforming Collateral Laws to Expand Access to Finance*. Washington, DC: The World Bank, p. 30.

4 H. Sigman, 'Perfection and Priority of Security Rights' in H. Eidenmüller and E.M. Kieninger (eds) *The Future of Secured Credit in Europe*. E.C.F.L.R., Munich: De Gruyter Recht, 2008, 143, 159.

priority between claimants whose rights derive from the same grantor must be established. The Guide, as a comprehensive text, adopts the functional approach according to which, regardless of the form of the transaction or the terminology used by the parties, all rights in movable assets created by agreement and securing the payment or obligation should be implemented as security rights (recommendation 8). This denotes that the agreement will be characterised as creating a security right, and priority conflicts will be determined accordingly. However, a similar argument cannot be made to a non-unitary approach to acquisition financing (recommendation 9(b)).

6.2 Issues in priority

Often the priority dispute is not between an unsecured and a secured creditor,[5] but between a seller and a lender, where the former generally has the super-priority over the latter who registers prior to the other creditors making their claims. The dispute seems to be more critical in those jurisdictions where a formalist approach to security is applied when the asset is encumbered through different devices, such as retention-of-title and a non-possessory security interest. The question of whose priority (the lender or the seller) will prevail arises. Moreover, the multiplicity of priority rules in the same system may cause contradiction and reduce the value of collateral by diminishing the priority status.[6] Thus a comprehensive priority system regulating transactions covering all assets, obligations and parties, arguably, may achieve the desired predictability to facilitate credit. It is argued that the priorities of lenders and sellers are 'an economic question'.[7] The balance between the interests of sellers and lenders needs to be established, hence, probably the grant of super-priority for PMSI based on its economic purpose.[8] International instruments, generally, achieve predictability in priority disputes. In general, priority is determined through registration (first-in-time) and this rule has exceptions or alternatives. In certain cases, priority conflicts are directed to conflict-of-law rules backed up with optional substantive rules.

Divergent approaches and inconsistencies in priority regimes lead creditors to raise the cost of credit. These approaches include first-in-time to notify, first-in-time to register or publicise, or first-in-time to conclude the transaction giving rise to security. Achieving predictability through clear priority rules is one of the underlying principles of international instruments. International instruments, with the

5 As typically the secured creditor will obtain priority, and the unsecured creditor may have other means to protect the rights. For a number of means, *see* Guide, paras 43–44, at 195.

6 *See generally* Fleisig *et al.*, op. cit. (f'note 3), pp. 31–2.

7 Röver, J-H. (2007) *Secured Lending in Eastern Europe: Comparative Law of Secured Transactions and the EBRD Model Law*. Oxford: Oxford University Press, p. 83.

8 Veneziano, A. 'Attachment/Creation of a Security Right' in Eidenmüller and Kieninger (eds), op. cit. (f'note 4), pp. 113, 131–2 (arguing that PMSI priority is not based on the structure of the transaction but rather economic efficiency arguments).

exception of the Factoring Convention, provide detailed provisions on priorities. Priority, in those instruments, is mostly linked to registration where first-to-file is given priority.[9] For the purposes of certainty, priority should be determinable, in principle, through registration and by the order of registration. There may be exceptions to that, but these should not be too detailed. Arguably, and notwithstanding the domestic debates as to whether or not full priority is a good thing, granting full priority rights to a secured creditor is instrumental in international trade and, in law reform activities, in lowering the cost of credit. Including carve-outs does not assist debtors, rather it provokes lenders to increase their cost of credit. Further, priority is an important reflection of fair exchange and bargain for credit. Secured creditors bargained for their security and priority positions, whereas involuntary creditors and unsecured creditors have not. This issue has raised significant debate mostly confined to academic circles.[10] Full priority is important for a secured creditor who extends credit with the knowledge that, in the event of the debtor's default or insolvency, they have a priority status and will be paid. This is an illustration of the significance of determining priority for enforcement purposes. The more predictable priority rules are, the easier the enforcement. The secured creditor will be able to ascertain the amount of recovery based on his priority ranking. If the priority rules are not predictable, there may be uncertainty in the amount that may be recovered in the grantor's insolvency. This leads to the increase in the cost of credit (where a risk premium is included in the interest rate calculation) or reduction of the amount of credit available.[11] Under these circumstances priority rules generally regulate the superiority between the secured creditor and competing claimants and the insolvency administrator. Security interests provide the secured creditor with proprietary rights which, in addition to the contractual rights against the debtor, grants priority over other creditors of the debtor in the debtor's insolvency. Clear priority rules are also critical in the case of third-party claims where a non-possessory security interest is created on the asset and the grantor, notwithstanding with the charge over the asset, sells or leases the asset to a third party. The question of priority arises whether the *bona fide* purchaser/lessee or the lender has priority.[12] Priority rules are prepared on a temporal basis (i.e. ranking is made according to the date of third-party effectiveness first-in-time, first-in-right) that is combined with aspects of the claim (e.g. the method of achieving third-party effectiveness, the character of the claim and claimant, the amount of obligation due and the percentage of the outstanding obligation).[13] Arguably, and it is adopted by a majority of the international instruments, registration in a general public registry, thus achieving third-party effectiveness

9 The Receivables Convention in its optional annex provides three different substantive law options but favours the establishment of registration system even though States preserve their priority regimes.

10 *See* Chapter 1.

11 For a detailed account, *see* Guide, paras 16–19, at 189.

12 Guide, paras 12–14, at 188.

13 Guide, paras 29–32, at 192.

which will be a tool for priority, is the optimal method of achieving third-party effectiveness for the determination of priority status. However, registration cannot be used for every type of secured transaction, and naturally has exceptions and alternatives. First, possession, control and registry in a specialised registry are exceptions/alternative methods to achieve third-party effectiveness. In that context, first to obtain possession, the creditor that obtains control and registration in a specialised registry will grant priority over the registration made in a general security rights registry. Second, in relation to consumer goods, the third-party effectiveness may be automatic, which means that the time of creation of a security right will grant priority. Finally, only in limited circumstances (in acquisition financing) and in those secured transactions regimes that adopt a general security rights registry, a first-created and later-registered security right will be given priority, hence the temporal basis will be the date of creation rather than registration.[14]

Priority status among competing claimants may be obtained by achieving third-party effectiveness through registration in a general security rights registry, or through an alternative method, or a combined method. In the case of registration in a general security rights registry, essentially, the priority will be obtained as of the date when rights are acquired (i.e. a security right is created and third-party effectiveness is achieved). However, as the creation may take after third-party effectiveness, and during which the grantor may enter into loan facilities with another lender, an exception is necessary to create a balance. Accordingly, priority of security rights that are made effective against third parties through registration is given to the security right, the notice of which is registered first-in-time. So the priority is determined by the order of occurrence of registration. The rationale is to encourage advance registration so that predictability, notice and transparency are achieved. Further, in order to facilitate creation of security rights over future assets or assignment of future receivables, a single date for ascertaining priority (date of registration) is established.

The grantor may transfer, lease or license the asset that is encumbered by a secured creditor. The rights of the secured creditor and transferees, lessees and licensees must be balanced. In essence, the transferee, lessee or licensee takes the asset subject to the security right, because security follows the asset. In principle, the secured creditor's right is retained in the asset as well as the proceeds of the sale or any other transfer that may occur. However, this rule may have exceptions where the secured creditor either agrees to the transfer, or from the nature of the assets it is expected that the secured creditor authorises their sale free of encumbrance.[15] The latter exception may be illustrated in a number of avenues, among them most notably being the ordinary course of business approach.[16] The rationale of this exception is that

14 Guide, paras 35–38 and 50, at 193–4 and 197.

15 For a discussion of this rule and exceptions, *see* Guide, paras 60–89, at 200–208.

16 For the other avenues, such as the good faith approach and the time limitation approach, *see* Guide, paras 74–76, at 203–4.

> sales of encumbered assets consisting of inventory made by the grantor in the ordinary course of business will result in the automatic extinguishment of any security rights that the secured creditor has in the assets without any further action on the part of the buyer, seller or secured creditor.[17]

For the exception to be applicable the seller in his ordinary course of business must be selling the kind of assets that are sold, and the buyer must not have prior knowledge that the sale violates the secured creditor's security right over the encumbered assets. In relation to the latter point, buyer's mere knowledge of the existence of a security right on the asset is insufficient.[18] This approach is adopted by the Guide (recommendation 81(a)). Similarly, under English law, a buyer of assets subject to a floating charge will take free even if the buyer knows the floating charge.[19] However, if the buyer knows that crystallisation occurred, or disposition is not permitted under the security agreement, assets will not be taken free.[20] Conversely, under UCC Article 9–320(a), a buyer of goods takes free of a security interest created by the buyer's seller even if the security interest is perfected and the buyer knows of its existence. In relation to the rights of lessees, the main point is whether the security interest still continues over the leased asset. Similar exceptions, applicable to buyers, equally apply to the rights of lessees and either the secured creditor has to authorise the lease (recommendation 80(b) or the lessor of the tangible assets must be in the business of leasing tangibles of the kind leased (recommendation 81(b)).[21]

Recognition of full priority of secured creditors has not been recognised in all jurisdictions. Some jurisdictions require a certain percentage of the debtor's assets to be set aside for the unsecured creditors who cannot change their positions. These carve-out proposals, rightly, have not received approval in international secured transactions instruments. Particularly, the Guide does not contain any carve-out proposals, thus it seems to take a similar approach to priority of secured creditors as UCC Article 9 does. On the other hand, English law contains carve-outs under the Insolvency Act.[22] Generally speaking, under English law, priority regulation is generally fragmented and complex.[23] First-in-time to be created has priority. This is the reflection of the *nemo dat* rule (one cannot give what one has

17 Guide, para. 67, at 202.

18 Guide, para. 68, at 202.

19 *Re Castell & Brown Ltd* [1898] 1 Ch. 315.

20 Law Commission Consultation Paper No. 164, para. 2.59. It should also be mentioned that the buyer of a company's assets cannot be expected to search the register. *Asborder BV v Green Gas Power Ltd.* [2004] EWHC 1517 explains the position of a buyer or an incumbrancer in the ordinary course of business.

21 Guide, paras 77–79, at 204–5.

22 Insolvency Act 1986 s. 176A.

23 For an overview of the current state of affairs of priority under English law and criticism, *see* e.g. Gullifer, L. (ed.) (2008) *Goode on Legal Problems of Credit and Security*, 4th edn. London: Sweet & Maxwell, Chapter V; for the priority of competing interests, *see* paras 5.23–5.34.

not got). The simple idea underlying this rule is that when one gives the asset that he owns to another, he will have no rights over the asset and thus cannot give it to a third person. However, this rule has lengthy exceptions.[24] Not all security interests are registrable and among the registrable ones (enumerated under the Companies Act 2006), first-to-register will have priority.[25] There is distinction between traditional and quasi-security interests. Recent domestic reform activities recommended the introduction of a registration of security interests upon which priority will be determined, similar to UCC Article 9,[26] by the first secured party to file or perfect should have priority rule.[27] The Law Commission Consultation Paper[28] has set the weaknesses of the priority system in the absence of a comprehensive registration system that has a public function system. The weaknesses of the existing priority rules have been clearly summarised as follows:

> The rules are complex, varying from one type of asset to another and depending on a complicated interplay of factors – the date of creation, whether the competing interests were legal or equitable, whether the charge was registrable, whether it was registered within the 21 days allowed and, in some cases, whether a subsequent secured party had notice of a negative pledge clause in an earlier charge.[29]

UCC Article 9 provides a predictable priorities system, albeit extremely detailed[30] with certain exceptions (e.g. super-priority of PMSIs in consumer goods), according to which the first secured party to file the financing statement will have priority when there are competing security interests over the same collateral.[31] Registration as the centre point of obtaining priority has significance and needs to be made so

24 Purchasers of legal interests in good faith and without notice, the rule in *Dearle v Hall* where the subsequent assignee to notify the debtor without the knowledge of the first assignment will be granted priority, authority to make absolute disposition, authority to create prior ranking security interest, obtaining priority through registration under specialised legislation including Bill of Sales Act, and charges over a ship or aircraft, statutory exceptions as in Sale of Goods Act 1979 ss. 24–25, the rule against tacking and priority agreements establish exceptions to the *nemo dat* rule. For more detail, *see* Beale, H., Bridge, M., Gullifer, L. and Lomnicka, E. (2007) *The Law of Personal Property Security*. Oxford: Oxford University Press, Ch. 13; for the principle and exceptions, *see* Gullifer, ibid., 176 *et seq.*

25 However, note that the Companies Act does not regulate priority issues and this is left to the general rules of law, except for those enumerated under s. 860 where first-to-file will obtain priority. It is also important that registration establishes notice to those who could reasonably be expected to search the registry. Buyers in the ordinary course of business are excluded from this rule. For further details, *see* Beale, *et al.*, ibid., 408 *et seq.*

26 UCC §9–322 (a)(1).

27 Law Commission Consultation Paper No. 176, Part 2.

28 Law Commission Consultation Paper No. 176, para. 2.3 *et seq.*

29 Ibid., para. 2.5, at 13.

30 White, J.J. and Summers, R.S. (2000) *Uniform Commercial Code*, 5th edn. St. Paul: West, Ch. 24.

31 The rationale for specific rules was explained as minimisation for 'the need for *ex post* fact sensitive judicial determinations, [minimisation of] litigation and [providing] the greatest possible *ex ante* certainty to the actors'. *See* Sigman, in Eidenmüller and Kieninger (eds), op. cit. (f'note 4), p. 146.

that a secured creditor can obtain priority status. Apart from this main rule, a perfected security interest has priority over the unperfected security interest (UCC §9–322(a)(2)) and if the conflicting security interest is unperfected the first security interest to attach has priority (UCC §9–322(a)(3)). An unperfected security interest will be subordinate to the insolvency administrator. A buyer takes free of an unperfected security interest if value is given and without the knowledge of the security interest (UCC §9–317).

Often national laws give priority to the seller who retains title in the proceeds from the resale of goods in order to protect the seller who has the ownership rights on the goods against a good-faith buyer of the goods.[32] A particular issue in priorities is whether PMSIs should be given priority (the so called super-priority) over a previously registered security interest. The rationale for this super-priority is to enable sellers to continue to take security without their rights being affected by that earlier security right.[33] The preferential treatment in terms of granting super-priority to PMSIs is justified on the grounds that, while the general creditor who extends credit may calculate the average risk, a PMSI financier having specialist knowledge on the collateral may lend on advantageous terms.[34] Furthermore, the PMSI lender's extension of funds to the debtor increases the debtor's pool of assets and enables the debtor to be able to purchase new assets. As PMSI adds new money into the debtor's assets, the grant of super-priority decreases the risk of an earlier creditor holding after-acquired property to have situational monopoly.[35] Put another way, the super-priority will enable subsequent lenders to be able to lend, or lend at low cost, and prevent the first lender's monopoly over all of the assets of the borrower. It has, however, been argued that a rule based on time of registration determining priority will prevent the first lender from having credit monopoly.[36] PMSI lenders are granted super-priority because it is considered that the new credit extended by them is not used by the debtor to roll over old debt.[37] Finally, if super-priority exception is not permitted, the debtor will be precluded from utilising the full value of assets in obtaining further credit. Particularly, UCC Article 9 and the systems influenced by it grant super-priority to PMSI lenders.

32 A/CN.9/378/Add.3, para. 10, at 3.

33 This is the case under UCC Article 9–324. *See* Kieninger, E-M. (2004) 'Evaluation: A Common Core? Convergences, Subsisting Differences and Possible Ways for Harmonisation' in E-M. Kieninger (ed.) *Security Rights in Movable Property in European Private Law*. Cambridge: Cambridge University Press, pp. 647, 672.

34 McCormack, G. (2004) *Secured Credit under English and American Law*. Cambridge: Cambridge University Press, p. 85, fn. 66.

35 *See generally* Jackson, T. and Kronman, A. (1979) 'Secured Financing and Priorities Among Creditors', 88 *Yale L. J.*, 1143, 1171 *et seq.*

36 McCormack, G. and Dahan, F. (1999) 'The EBRD Model Law on Secured Transactions: Comparisons and Convergence', *CfiLR*, 65, 78.

37 *See* McCormack, op. cit. (f'note 34), at 86 (*citing* D.G. Baird and T. Jackson (1987) *Security Interests in Personal Property*, 2nd edn. New York: Foundation Press, at 401).

6.3 Determination of priority status under the Guide

The purpose of priority provisions under the Guide is to provide predictable rules to ascertain priority rights of competing claimants.[38] The Guide's priority rules are exceptionally detailed and aim to resolve complex priority disputes. The same rules also aim to facilitate transactions by which the grantor may grant more than one security interest over the same asset that will then permit the grantor to fully and economically utilise the value of assets.[39]

Priority under the Guide is subject to predictable and detailed rules. Priority is obtained by the time of filing or perfection. Achieving third-party effectiveness is considered as an integral element for priority. In that sense, time of creation of a security right is irrelevant for obtaining priority. The significance of this rule is that a security right over a future asset can be registered in advance of creation of a security right over the asset. This enables potential creditors to be informed of the security right over the asset. It is also an indication that advance registration is permitted under the Guide. Priority is determined by the time of registration of notice between security rights that achieved third-party effectiveness by registration.[40] If third-party effectiveness was achieved by means other than registration, priority will be determined by the order of third-party effectiveness.[41] Priority will be determined by the order of registration or time of achieving third-party effectiveness other than registration, whichever occurs first, if two competing security rights are made effective against third parties by registration and a method other than registration.[42] Knowledge of the existence of a prior security right is irrelevant in the determination of priority, as it is often impossible to establish whether the person has prior knowledge.[43] Subordination is also allowed either unilaterally or by a mutual agreement.[44]

Coordination of priority in a text where different methods of achieving third-party effectiveness exist, contributes transactional predictability. In a competition between two security rights, one registered in a general security rights registry or made effective against third parties by a method other than registration and the

38 Competing claimants under the Guide include creditors with security rights on the same encumbered asset, the seller or financial lessor who retained title in the context of a non-unitary approach to acquisition financing, another creditor of grantor with a security right on the same asset, an insolvency representative or any buyer or transferee of the encumbered asset.

39 *See* Statement of Purpose for Chapter V. Priority of a Security Right.

40 Recommendation 76(a).

41 Recommendation 76(b).

42 Recommendation 76(c).

43 Recommendation 93.

44 Recommendation 94. Subordination may have an impact during the debtor's insolvency. First, a subordination agreement on an unsecured debt may contravene the *pari passu* principle as secured creditors are not affected by this principle (as they pay for their priority positions). Second, the debtor may grant a floating and fixed charge to two different creditors over the same asset and, because of a subordination agreement floating charge, may have priority over the fixed charge creating a circularity issue. *See* Gullifer, op. cit. (f'note 23), pp. 209–213.

other registered in a specialised registry, the priority will be granted to the security right registered in the specialised registry.[45] Obtaining priority in relation to negotiable instruments and documents and money will occur by possession.[46] In the case of bank accounts, first-to-register has an exception. Under the Guide, as an alternative third-party effectiveness method, control also determines priority. A security right perfected through control will have priority over other creditors notwithstanding their method of achieving third-party effectiveness. When the bank has multiple control agreements, priority will be determined according to the order of those control agreements. If the bank has automatic control by being a secured creditor, this will grant priority over other secured creditors; however, this will not be the case if the security right of a secured creditor takes control of the deposit account, in which case that will be the account holder and he will have priority.[47] There seem to be similarities between UCC Article 9 and the Guide's approach to priority in relation to priorities over deposit accounts.[48] It has been argued that registration has advantages over control mechanisms in achieving priority.[49] These include transparency, cost and time effectiveness and simple first-to-file rule under registration that enables ascertaining priority status and relative equality offered by registration vis-à-vis control where the bank has a sort of special priority status. However, to the extent that third-party effectiveness serves as a tool for priority, control will be the premier method to achieve priority (i.e. control beats registration).[50]

Acquisition-financing security rights are exceptions to the first-to-register rule, and they are granted priority over earlier-registered, non-acquisition-financing security rights.[51] The Guide supports the position that under a unitary approach all acquisition-secured creditors (seller, lessor and lenders) are subject to the same priority regime, and in a competition between a supplier (seller or lessor) and another creditor, the former obtains priority.[52] Under the non-unitary approach, in a competition between a retention-of-title seller or a financial lessor and an acquisition-financing provider, priority is obtained by the seller or the lessor regardless of the time of registration. In the case of priority of a security right in the proceeds of a tangible asset, priority extends to the proceeds provided that third-party effectiveness is achieved.[53]

45 Recommendation 77(a). For the rationale of granting priority to registrations in specialised registries, *see* Chapter 5, fnn 81–83 and the accompanying text thereof.
46 Recommendations 101, 102, 106, 108 and 109.
47 Recommendation 103.
48 UCC §9–327.
49 Walsh, C. 'Security Interests in Receivables' in Eidenmüller and Kieninger (eds), op. cit. (f'note 4), pp. 321, 326–7.
50 Recommendations 103 and 107.
51 Recommendations 178–185 and 191–199. *See* Chapter 7.
52 Recommendation 182.
53 Recommendation 199.

6.4 Divergence in priority rules in the assignment of receivables

In the context of assignment of receivables, competing creditors' claims may arise in the assignor's insolvency, from government claims or judgment creditors, or by a prior or subsequent assignment of a receivable to an assignee, or the multiple assignments by the assignor, where the same receivable is assigned to multiple assignees.[54] A particularly troublesome successive assignment may occur where a purchaser of goods, on which the seller retains title, assigns the proceeds both to the seller retaining title and to an assignee (particularly a bank) in the form of an assignment of future receivables in order to obtain immediate cash to expand his business. Some jurisdictions grant priority to the first assignee to notify the debtor, or the first one to register, or simply to the first assignee. The Receivables Convention provides options to legal systems that wish to modernise priority rules, and attempts to regulate priority disputes through carefully designed conflict-of-laws rules and an optional annex containing substantive rules. Although the conflict-of-laws rule under the Receivables Convention has received, arguably exaggerated, criticism from both academics and non-governmental pressure groups,[55] it is a sophisticated and potentially far-reaching rule.[56]

Unlike the Receivables Convention, the Factoring Convention does not contain priority rules. This is regarded as one of the most significant drawbacks of the Factoring Convention that has prevented it being accepted widely.[57] Priority regulations in different legal systems within the context of successive assignments of the same debt, conflicts between the assignee and the assignor's creditors, the bankruptcy of the assignor and the bankruptcy of the debtor were considered during the drafting process of the Factoring Convention.[58] It was observed that,

54 UNIDROIT Study LVIII–Doc. 31, 11 *et seq.* (1987).

55 *See e.g.* Steffens, L. (2006) 'The New Rule on the Assignment of Rights in Rome I – The Solution to All our Proprietary Problems? – Determination of the Conflict-of-laws Rule in Respect of the Proprietary Aspects of Assignment', 4 *E.R.P.L.*, 543; Flessner, A. and Verhagen, H. (2006) *Assignment in European Private International Law*. Munich: Sellier; Verhagen, R. (2006) 'Assignment in the Commission's 'Rome I Proposal'', *LMCLQ*, 270; Financial Markets Law Committee, Issue 121 – European Commission Final Proposal for a Regulation on the Law Applicable to Contractual Obligations ('Rome I'), October 2006 and April 2006.

56 For further details of the application of the law of the assignor's State and Articles 22 and 30, *see* Chapter 8.

57 A conflict-of-laws rule was considered where the applicable law for priority conflicts would be the law of the supplier's principal place of business. UNIDROIT Study LVIII–Doc.10, at 4 (1982). *See also* UNIDROIT Study LVIII–Doc. 22, 2, para. 1 (1986) the Comment of Factors Chain International.

> 'To facilitate international factoring, which is . . . the aim of the Convention, it is for the factoring business of utmost importance to solve the wide discrepancy from one country to another in dealing with the question of priority of assignments. . . . [I]t would be indeed a time-consuming work to find acceptable uniform rules. . . . [M]aybe UNIDROIT can study this item at a later time and can come forward with proposals which would be highly appreciated.'

58 UNIDROIT Study LVIII–Doc. 1, 17 *et seq.* (1976).

while in international factoring transactions conflicts among the creditors were common, 'such cases would in any event be rare as most factoring contracts contain an "exclusivity" clause in favour of a factor'.[59] Following a number of proposals, mainly from jurisdictions[60] that employ a registration system in ascertaining priority status of an assignee, the Factoring Convention failed to include any provision solving the priority problem which is left to whatever may be the applicable law.[61] Failure to set a substantive, or at least a conflict-of-laws, rule only contributes to confusion and increased cost of credit in cross-border financing transactions.

In that context, the Receivables Convention seems to have more wisdom to the extent that it contains both a conflict-of-laws rule and an optional annex that serves to modernise the domestic priority rules of the Contracting State, should they opt into the Annex. While it is doubtful that a conflict-of-laws provision may lead to practical uniform results, given the fact that priorities rules are complex, it seems that there could be no possible way to regulate this matter with a substantive provision. Furthermore, the conflict-of-laws rule envisaged by the Receivables Convention and recommended by the Guide achieves transactional predictability despite the criticism it receives.[62] In this context, the Commission's decision on subjecting the law applicable to priorities to a single determinable law (i.e. the law of the assignor's State) is the right choice. This approach can receive support from another perspective. Once the conflict-of-laws rule leads the assignee and third parties to the law of the assignor's State, the substantive priority rules contained in the annex become crucial. Arguably this two-step priority solution may lead to harmonisation. This is because third parties and the assignee will have, at least, the certainty that the law of the assignor's State will apply, and this law, on the substantive basis, will be either of these substantive law priority rules in the optional annex if they opted into or another one, i.e. the substantive law of the assignor's State. In other words, from a practical point of view, lawyers acting for the assignee will have fewer problems in ascertaining the law of the assignor's State, as UNCITRAL has limited the applicable laws – which means that when a Contracting State opts into one of the options in the annex, this will be similar to one of the modern secured transactions laws on priority and not an unfamiliar one. Furthermore, generally assignors will be from developing States, who are in need of immediate liquidity, and the assignees will be from developed States that have financial power and whose legal systems are, in general terms, represented in

59 UNIDROIT Study LVIII–Doc. 32, para. 28, 10 (1987).

60 Alexander, M.R. (1989) 'Towards Unification and Predictability: The International Factoring Convention', 27 *Colum. J. Transnat'l L.*, 353, 379; Diplomatic Conference, Comments by Governments, The United States of America, UNIDROIT 1988 CONF. 7/6 Add.2, 11–12; UNIDROIT Study LVIII–Doc. 31, 11 *et seq.* (1987).

61 Committee of Governmental Experts, Commentary Prepared by the Secretariat, Study LVIII–Doc. 20, 7 (1985).

62 For discussion on the advantages and criticism against the law of the assignor's State, *see* Chapter 8.

the optional annex. Since the assignors may most likely opt into one of these priority options in the annex, assignees will have no problem in finding the applicable law, as this law will most likely be familiar to them. Therefore, it is fair to subject the applicable law on priorities to the law of the assignor's State.[63] Another argument may be that, since there may be more than one assignee, it could also be wise not to subject priorities to the law of the assignee's State. Otherwise, it would have been quite difficult to decide which law would have applied. Arguably the rationale of opting in for the law of the assignor's location as the applicable law for priority disputes is that the international secured transactions instruments generally reflect the principles more or less settled in Anglo-American jurisdictions, and assignors are generally located in those countries which are in need of credit. Thus, when the assignor's State adopts an instrument, it is basically harmonising itself with the principles of Anglo-American jurisdictions, and international lenders located in Anglo-American jurisdictions will be more certain in relation to the applicable law to their priority disputes as it will reflect the principles that they are used to.[64]

Article 22 introduces a new approach to the bulk assignments of all present and future receivables where, instead of applying different priority rules according to the value of the assigned receivable, it applies the law of the assignor's State to the priority issues. Had the Convention applied to the priority rules according to their values, especially in the bulk assignments, there would have been inadvertent results. Such a situation would have created the '[facilitation of] manipulation of the applicable priority rule by the parties'.[65] The significance of having predictable rules on priority disputes is that the cost of credit may be reduced and that assignees may advance credit without including the premium risk.

6.4.1 'Priority' and 'competing claimants'

The Convention defines *priority* under Article 5(g) and *competing claimant* under Article 5(m). The definition of *priority* seems similar to UCC Article 9's definition of 'perfection',[66] where priority means that a party may satisfy its claim in preference to other claims. In this connection, priority includes whether the claimant has a proprietary or a personal right. Hence they are not treated distinct from

63 *See also* Report of the Committee on Foreign and Comparative Law of the Association of the Bar of the City of New York (December 21, 2001), at 10 (where there is a similar approach that supports the above argument as follows: 'One of the purposes of the Annex is to provide a framework for future development of such a worldwide system, [p]erhaps if a few States create an international filing system, others will be able to observe its merits in action.')

64 E.g. the two parts of the substantive priority rules contained in the optional annex of the Receivables Convention are based on UCC Article 9 and English law.

65 A/CN.9/489/Add.1, para. 31.

66 Sigman, H. and Smith, E. (2002) 'Towards Facilitating Cross-Border Secured Financing and Securitization: An Analysis of the United Nations Convention on the Assignment of Receivables in International Trade', 57 *Bus. Law.*, 727, 747. UCC Article 9 §9–308(a).

priority, and whether an assignment is an outright assignment or an assignment by way of security, and whether the necessary requirements to render the right effective against a competing claimant have been satisfied and, by virtue of that, priority may mean validity. The definition of a *competing claimant* covers all potential priority conflicts.[67]

6.4.2 Article 22 and the conflict-of-laws rule[68]

The choice-of-laws approach for priorities in the Receivables Convention Article 22 permits the domestic law of the assignor's State to determine whether the assignee has a proprietary or contractual right, and whether the transaction is an outright assignment or an assignment by way of security.[69] Article 30, which also repeats the same conflict-of-laws rule,[70] deals with priority rules that are applicable irrespective of whether the assignor is located in a Contracting State. An assignee under the Convention's priority rule needs to comply with the priority rules of the law of the assignor's State for the purposes of perfection and priority. This causes concern in some States that require a public filing system as a condition precedent to the third-party effectiveness of an assignment.[71] The rationale is that some States where the assignor is located may not have a developed priority system or a public disclosure system. Once the conflict-of-laws rule leads the assignee and third parties to the law of the assignor's State, the substantive priority rules contained in the annex become crucial. Arguably this two-step priority solution may lead to harmonisation. This is because third parties and the assignee will have, at least, the certainty that the law of the assignor's State will apply, and this law, on the substantive basis, will be either of these substantive law priority rules in the optional annex if they opted into or another one, i.e. the substantive law of the assignor's State. The merit of the optional annex has been explained as follows:

> One of the purposes of the Annex is to provide a framework for future development of such a worldwide system, [p]erhaps if a few States create an international filing system, others will be able to observe its merits in action.[72]

The law of the assignor's State where the assignor has more than one place of business will be determined at the time of the assignment, and this is the place

67 A/CN.9/489, para. 77.

68 For more details on the conflict-of-laws rules, *see* Chapter 8.

69 Sigman and Smith, ibid., 754. Receivables Convention Article 5(i) refers to the substantive law in force in a state other than its rules of private international law.

70 Article 30(1).

71 *See* e.g. Report of the Committee on Foreign and Comparative Law of the Association of the Bar of the City of New York (December 21, 2001), at 10 (where it was stated: 'Although . . . a choice of law rule is by no means a negligible accomplishment, it is something of a disappointment for those legal practitioners and business people who operate in States which have filing systems and who were hoping to see such a system established worldwide').

72 Ibid.

where the central administration of the assignor is exercised. The location of the assignor is compatible with bulk and future assignments, because third parties do not need to search for the real place of business of the assignor. The location of the assignor 'would result in the application of the law of the jurisdiction in which any main insolvency proceeding with regard to the assignor would be most likely to commence'.[73] When an assignee has places of business in more than one State, reference will be made to the place of central administration. On the other hand, when the debtor has places of business in more than one State, then the place most closely connected to the original contract will be the place of business. The reason for this approach is to 'ensure that the debtor is not surprised by the application of legal rules to which the original contract between the debtor and the assignor has no apparent relationship'.[74] The law of the assignor's location will also resolve a priority conflict between an outright buyer of a receivable and a seller retaining title.

One of the advantages of Article 22 is that, in the event of insolvency of the assignor, the law governing the priority and the law governing the insolvency of the assignor will be the same (i.e. the law of the assignor's State). If transactions are made through branch offices, by virtue of a central administration location rule and subject to the fact that the assignor has its central administration located in a Contracting State, the Convention will apply.[75] This article is subject to Articles 23 and 24 (mandatory law and public policy exceptions and a special law on priority in proceeds). Under Article 23, mandatory rules of the forum or the applicable law cannot override the law of the location of the assignor. However, in an insolvency proceeding commenced in a State other than the assignor's State, any preferential right that arises and gives priority over the rights of the assignee in insolvency proceeding may be given priority notwithstanding the application of the law of the location of the assignor. The special proceeds priority rule, regulated under Article 24, is probably the only substantive priority rule outside the optional annex in the Convention. The Convention grants priority to an assignee over the rights of a competing claimant if the assignor receives proceeds as well as the assigned receivables, provided the assignor received the proceeds under the assignee's instructions and the proceeds are held separately, for the benefit of the assignee, by the assignor and are reasonably identifiable.

6.4.3 *Optional annex*

Third-party effectiveness of an assignment and its effects, mainly in the form of priority rankings, are also dealt with by substantive rules under the Receivables Convention contained in the optional annex. The substantive rules in the annex regulate priority disputes between competing claimants as described in the

73 A/CN.9/489/Add.1, para. 32.
74 A/CN.9/557, at 6–7, para. 19.
75 A/CN.9/557, at 7, para. 20.

Convention.[76] As the priority rule that supports the first to notify the debtor without the knowledge of an earlier assignment causes complex solutions, States have chosen to confine the notification of the debtor as a condition of effectiveness of an assignment as against the debtor. The Receivables Convention under the optional annex provides three substantive law alternatives. One alternative regulates the public registration and first-to-register, the other recommends that priority will be determined in the order of conclusion of the assignment agreement, and the final alternative supports notification of the debtor and priority is granted to the first assignee to notify the debtor.

The optional annex comprises substantive law priority rules, which the Contracting States may opt into if they 'wish to modernize or to adjust their laws to accommodate assignments under the Convention'.[77] Arguably the substantive priority rules are based on UCC Article 9 (first registration in time), English law (first to notify, *Dearle v Hall*) and the civil law system (first assignment in time). As prescribed in Article 42(4), even if a State applies its own priority rules, they can still utilise the registration system in order to benefit from the main objectives of the Convention and to create certainty in receivables financing.[78] One of the main reasons why the Commission has prepared this optional annex is that some States may have no national priority rules, or the rules that they have may be outdated or not fully adequate in addressing all relevant problems.[79]

6.4.3.1 *Priority rules based on registration*

Priority rules based on registration provide predictable and simple solutions. Sections I and II of the optional annex deal with registration, and aim to provide notice to potential financiers that certain receivables may have been assigned and establish priority. The rule on priority among several assignees, under Section I Article 1 of the optional annex, is that the assignee who registers first obtains priority. If no registration is made, priority will be determined by the order of conclusion of the respective contracts of assignment. Such registration does not intend to create or constitute evidence of property rights, but notifies third parties about assignments made, and establishes a standard for resolution of priority conflicts between competing claims.[80] Rules under this section (Article 2) regulate the priority conflict between the assignee and the insolvency administrator or

76 Competing claimant is defined in Article 5(m).

77 Bazinas, S. (2001) 'Lowering the Cost of Credit: the Promise in the Future UNCITRAL Convention on Assignment of Receivables in International Trade', 9 *Tul. J. Int'l & Comp. L.*, 259, 285; *see also* Bazinas, S. (2002) 'Multi-Jurisdictional Receivables Financing: UNCITRAL's Impact on Securitization and Cross Border Perfection', 12 *Duke J. Comp. & Int'l L.*, 365, at 380 *et seq.*

78 But for criticism of the optional nature of registration, *see* Chapter 5 and Schwarcz, S.L. (1999) 'Towards a Centralized Perfection System for Cross-Border Receivables Financing', 20 *U. Pa. J. Int'l Econ. L.*, 455, 462.

79 A/CN.9/489/Add.1, para. 72.

80 A/CN.9/489/Add.1, para. 74.

creditors of the assignor. If the receivable is assigned before the commencement of insolvency proceedings in relation to the assets and affairs of the assignor, as long as registration is made then Article 2 protects the priority status of the assignee.

The optional annex also provides the details of a registration system.[81] This is a significant guide for Contracting States that do not have a registration system. The registry is open to any person to search the records for identification of the assignor, and a search in writing can be obtained. The written search result issued by the registry is admissible as evidence and is proof of the registration of the data to which the search relates. The registration is proposed to be simple, inexpensive, and requires a limited amount of data (Article 4). These basic characteristics of a registration system are 'the public character of the registry, the type of data that need to be registered, the ways in which the registration-related needs of modern financing practices may be accommodated, and the time of effectiveness of registration'.[82]

6.4.3.2 Priority rules based on the time of the contract of assignment

The optional annex also embodies rules where priority among several assignees is determined by the order of the conclusion of the respective contracts of assignment (Article 6). Article 7 is concerned with priority between the assignee and the insolvency administrator or creditors of the assignor, where the assignee has priority over the right of an insolvency administrator and creditors. However, assignment should be made before the commencement of insolvency proceedings. Any method of proof is accepted under Article 8 for ascertaining the time of conclusion of the assignment contract.

In this option, the time of assignment determines priority, whereby after the first assignment the assignor cannot assign the same receivable to another assignee. There is no need for registration. However, the disadvantage is that third-party creditors may be unable to determine whether certain receivables have been assigned, as there is a predictable objective system to ascertain prior activity in relation to receivables. Arguably, this may increase the cost of credit. Conversely, 'in a closed market, banks can still rely on borrowers' representations and gain knowledge about their clients' financial transactions, [and] the penalty for double financing of receivables in these markets outweighs the potential benefits'.[83] This may certainly be the case in civil law jurisdictions (notably in Germany) where there is no registration system. However, in unreformed secured transactions regimes and in developing economies, it is doubtful that this system will produce results that facilitate credit. Particularly, proving the time of the contract of assignment by any means, including witnesses, may prove to be challenging.

81 Section II Article 3.

82 A/CN.9/489/Add.1, para. 78.

83 Bazinas, op. cit. (f'note 77), p. 284.

6.4.3.3 Priority rules based on the time of notification of assignment

Priority is determined by the order in which the debtor receives notifications of the respective assignments. If the subsequent assignee has knowledge of a prior assignment to the first assignee at the time of the conclusion of the contract of assignment, then the subsequent assignee cannot obtain priority on the ground that the debtor is notified.[84] In relation to priority between the assignee and the insolvency administrator or creditors of the assignor, the assignee has priority over the right of an insolvency administrator, and the creditor of the same assignor if the receivable was assigned, and notification was received by the debtor before the commencement of such insolvency proceeding or attachment by judicial act or similar act that gives rise to the right of the creditor of the assignor.[85] It is arguable that in this system potential assignees may enquire from the debtor, whose accurate and immediate response is vital, whether prior to their contract certain receivables have been assigned. Also, in the assignment of bulk and future receivables the system may not respond to the needs of potential assignees, as the identity of the debtor will be unknown or there will simply be multiple debtors. Therefore, it may not be cost effective for assignees to find out whether certain receivables have been assigned.[86]

For instance, in England an assignment made by a company will only be registrable if it is an assignment by way of security over book debts.[87] If it is an assignment by way of sale, it is not registrable. Conversely, all types of assignments (outright or for security purposes) by an individual are registrable.[88] It has been recommended that the sale of receivables by companies should be registered.[89] The significance of this fragmentation can also be acutely felt in legal and equitable security interest, a distinction that makes the priorities regime 'unnecessarily complex'.[90] The issue has wider implications. As, functionally, the sale of receivables is similar to a charge over receivables, it seems perfectly reasonable to make the sale of receivables registrable. Lack of registration causes certain problems, such as subsequent creditors or assignees having to rely on the representations of

84 Optional Annex Article 10.

85 Optional Annex Article 11.

86 For the criticism of the rule in *Dearle v Hall*, *see* e.g. de Lacy, J. (1999) 'The Priority Rule of *Dearle v Hall* Restated', 63 *Conv.*, 311.

87 CA 2006, s. 860(7)(f).

88 Insolvency Act 1986, s. 344.

89 Law Commission Report No. 296, para. 4.7 *et seq.*

90 Law Commission Report No. 296, *Company Security Interests*, para. 1.7, at 3 where it is reported that priority issues depend on

> distinguishing between legal and equitable interests and whether certain buyers should be expected to check the register. They may also take lenders by surprise, as where a charge-holder registers first finds it is subject to a charge created up to three weeks earlier that it knew nothing about. The rules for charges over receivables and sales of receivables grant priority to those who notify account debtors – a process increasingly unsuited to the needs of modern receivables financing.

the assignor and may not be informed of the existence of a functional equivalent of charge over receivables.[91] What is more striking is that the rule in *Dearle v Hall*,[92] which regulates priority over receivables, is outdated. It is not suitable for modern financing techniques. Take, as an example, assignment of bulk receivables: it seems almost impossible to notify each debtor, to fulfil the requirements of *Dearle v Hall*.[93] Failure to notify debtors will result in the loss of priority status in a subsequent assignment under *Dearle v Hall*, and in civil law jurisdictions the assignment becomes void in the insolvency of the assignor.[94] It is arguable that this is because of formal validity, and publicity requirements are considered as a condition of priority, and they have not been met. Professor Oditah succinctly explains the danger of application of this outdated rule to assignment of bulk receivables as follows:

> . . . bulk assignees of receivables, especially lenders as opposed to invoice discounters, generally do not give notice of their bulk assignments until the assignor defaults and it is necessary for the assignee to collect the assigned receivables itself.[95]

In the assignment of future receivables the rule does not produce any logical results. It is not possible to notify debtors who are unknown at the time of conclusion of the contract of assignment. However, even when the identities of future debtors are known (possibly in ongoing business relations) and notice is given prior to the coming into existence of receivables, this may not be sufficient to secure its priority, because a notice given to the debtor after the receivables have come into existence will have priority.[96]

The risk that the rule in *Dearle v Hall* offers in both assignments of bulk and future receivables is self-explanatory. The cost of credit obviously will increase, and for small businesses factoring or other types of financing will become increasingly difficult. Thus registration of the sale of receivables to give notice to other assignees, particularly in the assignment of future and bulk receivables, seems to be necessary. Registration will prevent later assignees giving notice under *Dearle v Hall*[97] and obtaining priority. This may, arguably, lift difficulties before the assignment of bulk receivables.

91 Ibid.

92 (1828) 3 Russ I.

93 Nevertheless, the rule also applies to assignment of bulk receivables, *Compaq Computer Ltd. v Abercorn Group Ltd.* [1993] BCLC 602. The rule in *Dearle v Hall* applies to both statutory and equitable assignments as explained in *Pfeiffer Weinkellerei-Weineinkauf GmbH & Co. v Arbuthnot Factors Ltd.* [1988] 1 WLR 150, 162; [1987] BCLC 522, 533.

94 For a similar assertion, *see* Oditah, F. (2009) 'Recurrent Issues in Receivables Financing' in J. Armour and J. Payne, *Rationality in Company Law Essays in Honour of DD Prentice*. Oxford: Hart, pp. 321, 351.

95 Ibid.

96 *Re Dallas* [1904] 2 Ch 385. *See also* Oditah, ibid.

97 The second limb of the rule under *Dearle v Hall* requires the subsequent assignee to have no information of the existence of an earlier assignee and to give notice.

6.4.4 Independent conflict-of-laws rules

The Convention also contains independent conflict-of-laws rules for priorities apart from the normal conflict-of-laws rules for priorities prescribed in Article 22. Article 30 prescribes the independent conflict-of-laws rules for priorities based on the law of the assignor's location, and it applies to transactions to which Article 22 does not apply due to absence of territorial connection.[98] Although the law applicable to priority is governed by the conflict-of-laws rule under Article 22, the significance of Article 30 is that it enables the application of the Convention to transactions which may not normally fall within the ambit of the Convention due to lack of territorial connection. The assignor does not have to be located in a Contracting State for the application of the Convention. This, arguably, enables assignors to enjoy the value of the Convention in those States that prefer not to adopt the Convention. The scope of application of Article 30 is reiterated in Article 1(4), according to which the provisions of Chapter V, where Article 30 is located, apply to assignments of international receivables and to international assignments of receivables independently of paragraphs 1 and 2. Article 1(1) and (2) set out the applicability of the Convention and, according to these paragraphs, the Convention applies to assignments of international receivables and to international assignments of receivables if, at the time of the conclusion of the contract of assignment, the assignor is located in a Contracting State and subsequent assignments are governed by the Convention. Since Article 30 regulates the priority issues even if the assignor's State is not a Contracting State, the applicability of the priority issues is enlarged. However, in Article 1(4) it is noted that those provisions do not apply if a State makes a declaration under Article 39. Therefore, if a State declares that it will not be bound by the provisions of Chapter V, then the law of the assignor's State shall not govern priority issues if the State of the assignor is not a Contracting State. The same goal is confirmed in Article 26(a).

6.5 Model law

Priority provisions of the Model Law seem simpler than both UCC Article 9 and, in particular, English law. The EBRD Core Principles on Secured Transactions recommends an effective system of governing competing rights, particularly in the case of persons holding security and buyers in the ordinary course of business who are not normally expected to search the register.[99]

Over the same right or thing, a chargor can grant multiple charges (Article 17). The main issue here is establishing the priority among the different types of charges (registered charge, possessory charge and unpaid vendor's charge) (Article 17.2).

98 Some writers define this type of application of priority rules contained in Article 30 as 'indirect application through the conflicts of laws provisions of the Convention'; Markell, B.A. and Broude, R.F. (2003) 'A Short Introduction to the Priority Provisions of the UNCITRAL Convention on the Assignment of Receivables in International Trade', 16 *Insolv. Int.*, 1, 2.

99 Principle 9. *See* Chapter 5, fn. 18 and the accompanying text.

Model Law, like the Cape Town Convention (which combines retention-of-title or financial lease and the security agreement under an international interest) determines the priority of a charge of different types. Thus it does not 'engage with property issues'.[100] Under the Model Law, priorities have the function of determining the order of distribution among different charge holders, as well as the right to enforcement between multiple enterprise charge holders.[101] Among different charges, as a main rule, the time of creation or deemed creation determines priority (Article 17.2). Although the Model Law does not envisage advance registration, if a State determines to establish an advance registration this will also be considered as an exception. There are, however, four significant exceptions to this general rule under Articles 17.1–17.8. If the title to charged property is acquired, that charge will have priority over any charge granted by the acquirer (Article 17.2). An unpaid vendor's charge or a possessory charge over the negotiable instruments will have priority over any prior charge (Articles 17.3 and 17.4). A security interest arising by operation of law will have priority (Article 17.6). Priority of a charge cannot be altered unless there is an agreement of charge holders (Article 17.8). Furthermore, for an enterprise charge there is a separate priority rule according to which, if additional registration is required, the charge will not have priority until this additional registration is made. However, the unpaid vendor's charge will always have priority over this type of charge.

Under the Model Law, as registration is a requirement for creation of a registered charge, and as creation is the main connection point for determining priorities, ascertaining the time of registration is critical to establish priority status (Articles 6.7, 6.8 and 17). The unpaid vendor's charge receives priority over the registered charge. As the Model Law contains several types of charges, the fact that a charge is not registered will not mean that the unregistered charge will lose priority. Indeed, the unregistered priority (i.e. the unpaid vendor's charge and the possessory charge) may have super-priority status vis-à-vis other charges including the registered charge.[102] Critiques of the unpaid vendor's charge generally argue that this type of charge diminishes the value of the registered charge as the former is not registrable and has priority over any other types of charge.[103] Particularly, the unpaid vendor's charge (which is similar to the simple retention-of-title arrangement) is not registrable and thus aims to protect the seller of goods/creditor who sells goods on credit. As the unpaid vendor's charge is unregistered, third-party creditors cannot be notified about the existence of a security right over the

100 Bridge, M. 'The Scope and Limits of Security Interests' in Eidenmüller and Kieninger (eds), op. cit. (f'note 4), pp. 180, 194.

101 Commentary to Model Law Article 17.1.

102 Model Law Article 17.3. For discussion of possessory charge and where it may undermine the significance of registered charge, *see* Chapter 5.

103 *See* Spanogle, J. (1998) 'A Functional Analysis of the EBRD Model Law on Secured Transactions' in J. Norton and M. Andenas, *Emerging Financial Markets and Secured Transactions*. The Hague: Kluwer, pp. 157, at 164 *et seq.*

asset. Thus lenders may not be protected. Arguably, in raising finance, using title for security purposes offers limited opportunities (i.e. credit is linked to the sale of the goods and offered for a short term), whereas borrowing money is critical for small businesses as this offers a long-term credit.[104] Under the Model Law, the distinctive feature of the unpaid vendor's charge is that it is limited to six months (Article 9.4.1) or until the seller is paid the full price, and it can be converted into a registered charge within the six months without affecting its priority.[105] Some commentators argue that the unpaid vendor's charge does not create a super-priority as the unpaid vendor's charge under the Model Law is only limited to unpaid vendors and treated separately.[106] A critical review of the Model Law's provisions on the unpaid vendor's charge will, however, reveal that a super-priority status is provided to the unpaid vendor as there is a secret encumbrance of rights over the asset, thus the priority of the lender is subordinate to the seller's priority.[107] However, juxtaposing a non-registered unpaid vendor's charge and a registered charge under the same framework of secured transactions regime, and thus granting super-priority to the former to the detriment of the latter, raises certain policy issues. Arguably for the Model Law, unlike the Guide, registration, as a means of obtaining priority, is not the main feature. First, a secured creditor with a registered charge will prefer to monitor the business decisions of the debtor, and an invisible encumbrance of the debtor's asset will increase the cost of this monitoring activity that will eventually increase the cost of credit. Second, when the debtor encumbers the same asset on which the unpaid vendor has rights to a lender, similar arguments may be made. Registered charge holder's (lender's) rights may be subordinated to the inventory financier's rights.[108] An unpaid vendor has the ability to ascertain whether it has priority under Article 17.3. A similar argument also applies under Article 17.2 to the registered charge holder who ascertains the priority status by searching the registry, according to which the first to file will have priority. However, as the unpaid vendor's charge is not required to be registered, there seems to be an invisible encumbrance against the lender's right. Professor Spanogle comments upon two choices which lenders (who will take security through registered charge) against credit sellers (unpaid vendors) may adopt in order to obtain priority. Under the Model Law's structure, lenders will either have to increase the cost of credit as their priority status will be subordinate to that of the unpaid vendor's, or require the debtor to make payments periodically which may be burdensome.[109]

104 For similar views, *see* Spanogle, in Norton and Andenas, op. cit. (f'note 103), at 164–5.

105 Spanogle, op. cit. (f'note 103), at 165.

106 Mistelis, L. (1998) 'The EBRD Model Law on Secured Transactions and its Impact on Collateral Law Reform in Central and Eastern Europe and the Former Soviet Union', 5 *Parker Sch. J. E. Eur. L.*, 455, 468.

107 For a similar view, *see* Spanogle, ibid., at 165.

108 Spanogle, op. cit. (f'note 103), at 165.

109 Spanogle, op. cit. (f'note 103), at 167 where these transactions are defined as 'pay-out and pay-over' transactions.

6.6 Cape Town Convention

6.6.1 Basic rule

The registration of an international interest under the Cape Town Convention is an element of priority. The simple first-to-file rule is the basic rule for priority conflicts.[110] There seems to be no distinction deriving from super-priority rules under the Convention. First, because the rationale for a super-priority is to protect from subordination of the lender with whose loan the equipment is purchased from a prior security interest over future assets. Second, because the Convention is a legal text dealing with asset-based financing rather than a general legal text, like the Guide or the Model Law which regulate general financing alongside asset-based financing, and the Convention does not cover future property not uniquely identified,[111] there seems to be no necessity to have different priority rules.[112] Thus the Convention does not make any reference to purchase-money security interests, nor does it contain any super-priority rules.

Article 29 deals with the priority of registered international interests. Priority of unregistered interests does not fall within the ambit of the Convention and is left to the applicable law. Subject to exceptions, essentially under Article 29(1), a registered interest in the international registry has priority over any other interest subsequently registered and over unregistered interests. These interests include interests arising from the Convention and from another law, consensual and non-consensual interests, subsequently registered interests and unregistered interests. The creditor who registers the international interest first will have the priority, regardless of whether it is registered with the knowledge of the existence of another interest and value given by the holder of the first interest with such knowledge.[113] The critical issue under the Convention is that registration serves as notice of the existence, or potential existence, of an international interest and is a means of obtaining priority. The third party's knowledge is irrelevant in obtaining priority of the registered interest.[114] Put

110 Cape Town Convention Article 29(1) and (2). Under English law, registered mortgages prevail over the unregistered and subsequently registered mortgages. Thus, the date of registration determines priority ranking. Registration constitutes constructive notice and fixed charges registered will have priority over the subsequently registered and earlier unregistered mortgages. Floating charges are not within the Mortgages of Aircraft Order, but they will be covered under the Companies Act s. 860. The Buyer will not be able to take free of an equitable mortgage or charge as the bona fide purchaser for value and without notice, as the registration is a constructive notice as against subsequent parties. *See* Beale, *et al.*, op. cit. (f'note 24), 471–4.

111 Note that identification of the equipment/object is necessary for it to be registered as the registration system is asset based.

112 *See also* Goode, R. (2008) *Convention on International Interests in Mobile Equipment and Protocol thereto on Matters Specific to Aircraft Equipment Official Commentary*, Revised edn. Rome: UNIDROIT, para. 2.105; for a similar argument, *see* Bridge, in Eidenmüller and Kieninger (eds), op. cit. (f'note 100), at 193.

113 Article 29(2).

114 Article 29; Cuming, R.C. (2006) 'The International Registry for Interests in Aircraft: An Overview of its Structure', *Unif. L. Rev.*, 18, 28.

another way, the international interest holder's actual knowledge of a prior interest is irrelevant and will not obstruct his obtaining priority.[115]

6.6.2 Exceptions

The Convention contains several exceptions to the first-to-file rule. An outright buyer's interest is essentially not registrable. However, the Aircraft Protocol extends the priority and registration requirements to outright sales of aircraft objects. Thus, Article 29(3) does not apply to aircraft objects. One of the exceptions to the basic rule is a rule in favour of an outright buyer, in that an outright buyer of an object acquires interest subject to an earlier registered interest. Put another way, an outright buyer takes the object free, if the international interest is not registered prior to the acquisition.[116] However, this exception also has an exception in that it does not apply to international interests in aircraft objects to the extent that the Aircraft Protocol applies. Article 41 aims to operationalise the Aircraft Protocol, which permits the outright buyer to register the interest, so that outright buyers of equipment can benefit from registration and priority linked to registration.[117] The Aircraft Protocol enables the registration of sales and prospective sales (Article III), and prospective international interests and prospective assignments of international interests are registrable (Article 16(1)). However, a prospective international interest will not have effect until it becomes an international interest, thus, its priority will be determined at the time of registration. Creditors may protect their priority by registering their prospective international interest and, when the prospective interest becomes an international interest, that international interest will be considered as registered at the time of registration of the prospective interest (Article 19(4)). The significance of registering a prospective interest is that priority is determined at the time of its registration (i.e. achieving third-party effectiveness) rather than its creation. In that context, an interest that is registered but has not been created will have priority over the prior-created but later-registered interests on the same equipment (aircraft object). This illustrates the significance of registration in achieving third-party effectiveness and priority. Unless there is a retention-of-title agreement, a prospective buyer who registers his interest, and achieves third-party effectiveness during the negotiation process of a contract of sale of an aircraft object, will have priority over a buyer who enters into a contract and registers the interest at a time between the first buyer's date of registration and the date of conclusion of the contract of sale. Thus, creation of an interest is irrelevant in obtaining priority status. Another exception deals with a problem where a conditional seller or lessor grants charge over the object, or grants a lease and after concludes a sale

115 *See also* Gopalan, S. (2003) 'Securing Mobile Assets: The Cape Town Convention and its Aircraft Protocol', 29 *N.C.J. Int'l L. & Com. Reg.*, 59, 74.

116 Article 29(3)(b).

117 Aircraft Protocol Articles III and XIV; Goode, op. cit. (f'note 112), para. 4.279.

and lease-back from the buyer.[118] Arguably, the conflict is resolved in a different way with the same outcome (first-to-register obtains priority). In order for the registration system to apply, the conditional buyer's or lessee's priority will prevail over the chargee if the seller's or the lessor's interest is registered first.[119] In sale and lease-back, the seller will in any case have the possession, and it has been argued that sale and lease-back is difficult to distinguish from a charge in English law.[120] Under the Convention, the exception in relation to sale and lease-back will lead to first-to-file as well. Another exception is the priority granted to non-consensual rights over both the registered and unregistered international interests under Article 39. These non-consensual rights or interests, under the law of that Contracting State, are those rights or interests that 'have priority over an interest equivalent to the holder of the international interest'.[121] In order for the non-consensual rights to have priority over international interests, Contracting States need to specify these rights and make a declaration. However, States may also make a declaration that specified categories of non-consensual rights or interest may be registrable (such as a judgment or orders permitting attachment of equipment covered by a relevant Protocol or State liens for taxes or unpaid charges),[122] and when they are registered they will have priority over the subsequently registered and unregistered international interest.[123]

6.6.3 Proceeds

As the international interest extends to the proceeds of the object,[124] the priority under Article 29(6) extends to proceeds only to the extent that the proceeds are those described under the Convention.[125] The Convention, in addition to priorities arising out of interests on the aircraft objects, also regulates priorities arising out of payment rights associated[126] with registered interests.[127] In those cases,

118 Article 29(4). *See also* Goode, R. (2002) 'The Cape Town Convention on International Interests in Mobile Equipment: A Driving Force for International Asset-based Financing', *Unif. L. Rev.*, 3, 9.

119 *See also* Stanford, M. (2002) 'From Ottawa to Cape Town: UNIDROIT'S Role in the Modernisation of the Law Governing Leasing and the Taking of Security' in I. Davies (ed.), *Security Interests in Mobile Equipment*. Aldershot: Ashgate, pp. 397, 442.

120 McCormack, op. cit. (f'note 34), p. 51.

121 Goode, op. cit. (f'note 117), para. 2.148.

122 Goode, op. cit. (f'note 117), para. 2.153.

123 Article 40 which states: '. . . non-consensual right or interest . . . shall be registrable . . . as if the right or interest were an international interest and shall be regulated accordingly.'

124 Article 2(5).

125 Article 1(w) defines proceeds as money or non-money proceeds of an object arising from the total or partial loss or physical destruction of the object or its total or partial confiscation, condemnation or requisition.

126 Associated rights are defined under Article 1(c) as all rights to payment or other performance by a debtor under an agreement which are secured by or associated with the object.

127 Articles 35–36.

priorities and proceeds will be determined by the Cape Town Convention if they are defined under Articles 1(w) and 36(3); otherwise, the applicable law will determine the priority. In that case the applicable law in relation to the assignment of receivables, if proceeds are receivables, may be the Receivables Convention.[128] In relation to the assignee's priority in the associated rights, if an assignment of an associated right cannot satisfy the conditions indicated under Article 36(1), thereby the Cape Town Convention does not apply, the priority of the competing assignments of associated rights will be determined by the applicable law, and this can be the Receivables Convention provided the State is its Contracting State. Thus, these provisions attempt to avoid any overlap between the applicability of the two conventions to the extent they relate to receivables arising out of aircraft objects, railway rolling stock and space assets, which are more closely connected to a specific convention, i.e. the Cape Town Convention. From another point of view, it is arguable that the same implicit reference may indicate the Guide or the Model Law, if either of these is adopted by and become substantive law of that State whose substantive law is the applicable law under Article 36(3), thus the priority provisions of these instruments may apply.

6.6.4 Priority and assignment of associated rights and international interests

Assignment of associated rights[129] is an important financing option in equipment financing transactions. However, the critical issue is whether associated rights follow international interests when assigned. Normally, security as an accessory to the obligation follows the obligation.[130] This is because security cannot exist independently from the secured debt or obligation. In the early drafts of the Cape Town Convention there was divergence in the treatment of assignment of associated rights.[131] The particular problem arises out of the security agreement, more

128 Goode, op. cit. (f'note 112), para. 4.29.

129 Associated rights (Article 1(c)) are all rights to payment or other performance by a debtor under an agreement that are secured by or associated with the object.

130 E.g. the Receivables Convention Article 10(1); UCC§9–203(g) and 9–308(e); Model Law Article 3.1 and 18.1 (if parties agree to transfer the charge, this will be understood as transfer of secured debt as well as the charge).

131 *See also* Cuming, R.C.C. (2000) '"Hot Issues" in the Development of the (Draft) Convention on International Interests in Mobile Equipment and the (Draft) Aircraft Equipment Protocol', 34 *Int'l Law*, 1093, 1102, where Professor Cuming explains the earlier position as follows:

> Conceptually this is a peculiar feature since it treats the right to the receivable arising from the financing of an object that is the subject of an international interest as accessory to the interest in the object. Under most legal systems, a security interest is accessory to the obligation. . . . Assignments of agreements providing for the lease or financing of the aircraft are very common. The commercial value of the . . . Convention would be substantially diminished if it did not extend to assignments, financing and leasing contracts and the streams of payment associated with these contracts.

so than the conditional sale or lease agreements, because the secured obligation need not have any relationship with the equipment or object used as collateral to secure it.[132] In the early drafts of the Convention, it was suggested that associated rights would follow the international interest because the main point of concern under the Convention was the assignment of international interest rather than the receivables (which in any case falls within the ambit of the Receivables Convention). However, the problem is that this approach goes against the traditional understanding that security right follows obligation (i.e. security is accessory to the main obligation). Finally, the Cape Town Convention adopted the traditional rule and provided under Article 31(1) that, unless otherwise agreed by the parties, an assignment of associated rights made in conformity with the formalities also transfers to the assignee the related international interests and all the interests and \priorities of the assignor under the Convention. Although it is possible to have an assignment of unregistered interest, assignments have to be registered in the international registry in order to obtain priority based on the first-to-file rule. In that context, when there are competing assignments of the same international interest, Article 29 (the main priority rule under the Convention) applies and priority of an assignee of associated rights prevails over the subsequent assignee.[133]

6.7 Conclusions

Predictable priority rules are at the heart of modern secured transactions regimes that aim to facilitate credit. A modern secured transactions regime must facilitate the access to low cost credit by enabling the competing creditors to be certain of their priority rankings. Grantors should be allowed to create more than one security over the same asset, and thus utilise the full economic value of their assets. Registration, being a tool of priority that derives its roots from the functionality of the security interest concept, is favoured by the international instruments for the right reasons (i.e. predictability in ascertaining priority status is said to lower the cost of credit). The Guide, the Receivables Convention and the Cape Town Convention require, in principle, priority to be determined through first-in-time registration.[134] The Model Law, conversely, adopts as a general rule of determining priority as the time of creation.[135] Particularly, the Guide has extremely detailed and carefully designed priority rules. These rules both take into account priority between competing claimants and creditors and sellers. Secured creditors

132 Mooney, C.W. (1999) 'Assignments of International Interests in Mobile Equipment and Related Receivables under the UNIDROIT Convention: When Should the Tail Wag the Dog?', 20 *U. Pa. J. Int'l. Econ. L.*, 443, 448 (discussing the earlier draft and the background problems).

133 Articles 35–36. *See also* Wool, J. (1999) 'The Next Generation of International Aviation Finance Law: An Overview of the Proposed UNIDROIT Convention on International Interests in Mobile Equipment as Applied to Aircraft Equipment', 20 *U. Pa. J. Int'l Econ. L.*, 499, 549–50; Harris, S.L. (2007) 'The International Rail Registry', *Unif. L. Rev.*, 531, 542–5.

134 There are alternatives and exceptions to registration such as possession or control. *See* Chapter 5.

135 Article 17.2.

receive full value for their priority positions. Arguably, all instruments overcome the fragmentation and complex nature of priority systems. They have a compact system to successfully achieve their purpose. They achieve risk management by enabling the competing claimants to manage their priority status, and through their registration system ensure that transparency is there for the creditors to be able to ascertain whether credit should be extended, and whether recovery is possible to the extent their ranking is concerned. The Guide, unlike the Model Law, contains exceptions for a PMSI holder's priority, thus arguably a balance is achieved between creditors and sellers.[136] Finally, the Factoring Convention does not contain any priority rules and, arguably, this is one of the main reasons why it has failed to achieve its mission.

136 For further discussion, *see* Chapter 7 below.

7 Acquisition financing devices

7.1 Introduction

Businesses often purchase assets on credit, and the rights on those purchased assets serve as security for the credit in favour of the credit provider. Under certain secured transactions systems, these are called purchase-money security interests (PMSIs). In order to establish a harmonised, secured transactions regime it is critical to ascertain whether title retention devices and PMSIs should be subject to the same rules as traditional security interests (i.e. creation, third-party effectiveness, priority). As part of the functional approach to the security element, the Guide reflects the view that retention-of-title agreements may be treated as security interests, unlike the stand taken by English law. However, States that have not adopted the UCC Article 9 type of legislation treat these transactions and other transactions based on title retention (they may also be referred to as 'quasi-security interests' in English legal terminology) distinctly, and subject them to separate rules particularly in relation to creation, third-party effectiveness, priority and remedies. International instruments have, generally, the tendency to accommodate both title devices and security agreements, and in doing that either take the functional or the formalist approach. Arguably, even if traditional security interests and quasi-security interests are combined under a single scheme (functional scheme), it is paramount to draw a distinction of how far rules applicable to traditional security interests apply to quasi-security interests.[1] International instruments reflect this tension clearly. As a fundamental policy of the Guide, balancing the interests of lenders and sellers in a comprehensive, integral and functional system is critical for the facilitation of credit; hence drafting of the unitary and non-unitary approach to acquisition financing devices. This is a unique approach to a significantly sensitive area of secured transactions law. In essence there are two methods to achieve the results desired to facilitate credit: the unitary and the non-unitary approach. This chapter will discuss the significance of acquisition financing devices and the approach of international instruments.

1 For an in-depth discussion on this matter, *see* e.g. Bridge, M. (2008) 'The Scope and Limits of Security Interests', in H. Eidenmüller and E.M. Kieninger (eds) *The Future of Secured Credit in Europe*. E.C.F.L.R., Munich: De Gruyter Recht, p. 181.

7.2 Acquisition financing devices

7.2.1 General

PMSIs are critical for enterprises and consumers as well as buyers and sellers of tangible assets. The Guide rather uses the term *acquisition financing transactions* as a generic and comprehensive concept, by being applicable to all types of transactions where the lender provides credit to the grantor to purchase tangibles while holding a security right on these assets, and the seller who retains title over the assets sold to the buyer and by being classified as a security right.[2] The rights arising out of these are referred to as *acquisition security rights*.[3] Acquisition financing transactions are economically and functionally equivalent to traditional security interests. The Guide on acquisition financing transactions states as follows:

> An acquisition financing transaction exists whenever a person (for example, a seller or lender) may claim a property right in tangible assets to secure another person's obligation to pay any unpaid portion of their purchase price . . . A transaction under which a seller retains ownership of (or title to) the assets sold for such a purpose is also an acquisition financing transaction.[4]

The key features of this transaction are that the credit obtained by the buyer or lessee is utilised specifically for the acquisition of a tangible asset; the seller or the lessor retains rights over the tangible asset that derive from the extended credit, and these rights derive from an agreement.[5] Acquisition financing devices take different forms. These transactions also include retention-of-title, financial lease, or hire-purchase agreements (lease agreements with an option to purchase).[6] The particular significance of acquisition financing devices arises out of transactions where the setting involves cash sales and sales on credit. Buyers often conclude transactions either through credit obtained from lenders (depending on the creditworthiness of the buyer as these are concluded on an unsecured basis) or by the seller retaining title on the goods sold until the full sales price is paid (retention-of-title). However, in both of these examples of financing, buyers face difficulties in accessing credit. Small businesses particularly have financing problems due to the fact that banks reject an extension of credit and the fact that separate legal identities of small businesses are blurred; thus it may not always be possible to

2 Guide, para. 57, at 332.
3 Guide, para. 82, at 29; and para. 3, at 319; 'whenever an enterprise or consumer acquires assets on credit, and rights in the acquired assets are to serve as security for credit, the transaction is a form of secured transaction . . . [called] an acquisition financing transaction.'
4 Guide, para. 7, at 320.
5 Guide, para. 7, at 320; these characteristics fall squarely within the definition of PMSI provided under UCC §9–103(a)(1) and (2). 'Purchase-money obligation' means an obligation of an obligor incurred as all or part of the price of the collateral, or for the value given to enable the debtor to acquire rights in or the use of the collateral if the value is in fact so used.'
6 For further details on the scope, *see* Guide, paras 9–12, at 320–1.

obtain credit as a corporate identity. This often requires partners or managers to apply for credit on a personal basis. In other cases, businesses grant security over the assets of the enterprise to secure the payment of credit obtained to acquire new equipment or assets.[7] However, more often, the acceptable collateral may be the asset that is being acquired[8] (in which case the lender takes security over the asset or the seller retains title). In all of these patterns, the credit derives its origins from an agreement between the buyer and the seller/lender.

7.2.2 Retention-of-title

One of the significant methods within acquisition finance is the retention-of-title where, in simple terms, the seller retains title (the seller delays the passing of title until fully paid or the title is transferred on the condition that, upon default, the seller regains title) until the buyer pays the purchase price in full.[9] Retention-of-title may also be referred to as 'conditional sales' (most prominently in common-law jurisdictions and under the Cape Town Convention).[10] Retention-of-title has different patterns, including a simple clause, a current-account clause, an extended clause, a tracing (proceeds of sale) clause, and an aggregation clause. Briefly, the *simple* retention-of-title is the most commonly used and it seems that there is strong convergence in the way they are recognised throughout the European Union member States. This is because most member States agree that the simple retention-of-title has effectiveness both among the parties and against third parties, and mostly registration is not required.[11] Complementing this finding, the Guide comments in relation to simple retention-of-title transactions that in most States the seller's retention-of-title is confined only to the tangible asset sold and not in the proceeds or products of the asset; that its original identity is retained and that it secures only the sale price rather than any other sums owed

7 The Model Law also offers an enterprise charge similar to the English floating charge concept. The enterprise granting the charge needs to be a corporate entity and the charge needs to be registered. Articles 5.6 and 6.6.

8 Guide, para. 17, at 322.

9 Guide, para. 24, at 323. For a detailed treatment of the subject, *see* e.g. McCormack, G. (1995) *Reservation of Title*, 2nd edn. London: Sweet & Maxwell; Worthington, S. (1996) *Proprietary Interests in Commercial Transactions*. Oxford: Clarendon Press.

10 In this monograph these two terms are used interchangeably. The Guide commentary, however, explains the difference as follows: *see* Guide para. 22, at 323:

> . . . the sale itself is not conditional (that is, the actual sale agreement is not dependent on the occurrence of some future and uncertain event not related to the sale itself). Rather, . . . it is only the transfer of ownership to the buyer that is conditional. The seller reserves ownership of the asset sold until the purchase price has been paid in full or the buyer has complied with any other conditions prescribed in the sale agreement.

11 Kieninger, E-M. (2004) 'Evaluation: A Common Core? Convergences, Subsisting Differences and Possible Ways for Harmonisation', in E-M. Kieninger (ed.), *Security Rights in Movable Property in European Private Law*. Cambridge: Cambridge University Press, pp. 647, 658–9.

between the seller and buyer.[12] A *current account* (all-monies) clause is a variation according to which until all outstanding monies owed by the buyer to the seller (in addition to the price arising out of the contract of sale giving rise to the clause) are paid, the seller retains title. This type may often occur in contracts of supply. It has been commented that the practical significance of this type is that it allows 'the repeat seller to assert title to fungible goods supplied without having to trace these goods back to a particular contractual consignment'.[13] The effectiveness of this type of retention-of-title clause was recognised in *Armour v Thyssen Edelstahlwerke AG*[14] where reference was made to the Sale of Goods Act 1979, setting out the incidents where the parties to a sales contract have the autonomy to decide when the title passes to the buyer and the title may be transferred until certain conditions in the contract are fulfilled.[15] In *products* clauses, the seller's rights extend to the products of the asset manufactured out of the asset on which title is originally retained. A *proceeds* clause is also a significant one, in that the seller's rights extend to the proceeds of the asset (such as receivables) on which the title is retained by the seller. It has been argued that the existence of the retention-of-title clause does not automatically give rise to the extension of the seller's rights to the proceeds.[16] Particularly, the proceeds clause, where the seller retains title even in the resale of the goods, has been a point of debate by virtue of the *Romalpa*[17] decision. The proceeds clause has been considered as a charge, and required registration.[18] If in the proceeds of a sale an interest is created that may also create a charge and thus will be registrable.[19]

12 Guide, para. 28, at 324.

13 Bridge, M. (2002) 'The English law of Real Security', 4 *E.R.P.L.*, 483, 489.

14 [1991] 2 AC 339. *See also* Law Commission Consultation Paper No. 164, para. 6.18, '. . . an all monies clause does not convert the transaction into a charge and thus the clause need not be registered in order to be valid'.

15 Sale of Goods Act 1979 ss. 17 and 19. For further details, *see* Bridge, ibid., at 489; McCormack, G. (2004) *Secured Credit under English and American Law*. Cambridge: Cambridge University Press, p. 177.

16 McCormack, op. cit. (f'note 15), 181. All sums clauses, or proceeds and products clauses, are treated as true security devices. Guide, para. 20, 69.

17 *Aluminium Industrie Vaassen BV v Romalpa Aluminium Ltd* [1976] 1 WLR 676; for further discussion on this matter, *see* e.g. Bradgate, R. (2002) 'Twenty-Five Years of Romalpa' in I. Davies (ed.) *Security Interests in Mobile Equipment*. Aldershot: Ashgate, p. 29; De Lacy, J. (1995) 'Romalpa Theory and Practice under Retention of Title in the Sale of Goods', 24 *Anglo-American L. Rev.*, 327.

18 The Guide comments that in States 'that permit "proceeds" clauses, . . ., the seller's right in the proceeds is not ownership, but is an ordinary security right that does not benefit from any special priority'. Para. 27, at 324. *See also* Worthington, op. cit. (f'note 9), 8–9, arguing that proceeds or products clauses are 'construed as registrable, but unregistered, charges created by the buyer'; Law Commission Consultation Paper No 164, para. 6.20, under the proceeds clause '. . . the assumed intention is that the seller will receive or retain only such part of the proceeds as equals what is due to it'. *E. Pfeiffer Weinkellerei-Weineinkauf GmbH & Co v Arbuthnot Factors Ltd* [1988] 1 WLR 150 (where the Court of Appeal held that the retention-of-title clause in a sales contract created charge over book debts and required registration and was void for failure of registration).

19 *Compaq Computer v Albercorn Group Ltd.* [1991] BCC 484.

In England, a retention-of-title agreement is not subject to the same rules applicable to security interests (such as creation, third-party effectiveness, priority and enforcement). There are certain reasons for the use of retention-of-title clauses in commercial relations. Retention-of-title clauses ensure that the purchase price is paid. The clause protects the seller from the buyer who may become insolvent before paying the full price.[20] In the event that the purchase price is unpaid, the seller has the right to repossess the asset. In comparison to charges that are registrable, retention-of-title clauses are not generally registrable.[21] The ownership right granted through retention-of-title confers more superior rights than the limited rights granted by a security interest (charge). An all-monies retention-of-title clause does not convert the clause into a charge, thus under English law it is not registrable. Under English law, retention-of-title is not treated as a security interest, thus the functional approach to security is, at least at the present time, rejected.[22] Moreover, extended retention-of-title clauses will be considered as a charge. If the asset is converted or manufactured into a new material, the seller may have the right on the finished product.[23] Further, a floating charge holder will have priority in competition with subsequent creditors, and the floating charge holder will be accountable for the surplus (only entitled to the loan amount plus interest) after the realisation of assets.[24] However, a seller retaining title will have prevailing priority over the prior chargee, and will be entitled to retain[25] the surplus as a result of the sale of assets. The simple reason of super-priority may be explained as follows:

> the unpaid seller never becomes involved in a priority battle with a lender who has taken an earlier security over the buyer's assets . . . [as this] security attaches only to the buyer's assets, which by definition never include the goods until the property in them is transferred to the buyer when payment is made.[26]

The Law Commission, in line with the previous studies,[27] had agreed that retention-of-title clauses serve for security purposes (particularly in the all monies retention-of-title pattern where security is created over the goods delivered and paid for) and should be registrable.[28]

20 *Clough Mill Ltd v Martin* [1985] 1 WLR 111, 122.

21 For a criticism of this, *see* Law Commission Consultation Paper No. 164, paras 7.24–7.26.

22 Law Commission Consultation Paper No. 164 recommended that retention-of-title agreements should be registrable. Paras 7.24–7.26.

23 McCormack, op. cit. (f'note 15), 166.

24 Beale, H., Bridge, M., Gullifer, L. and Lomnicka, E. (2007) *The Law of Personal Property Security*. Oxford: Oxford University Press, p. 180.

25 This is so, unless one of the exceptions to *nemo dat quod non habet* apply. *See* ibid., at 180.

26 Bridge, op. cit. (f'note 13), 488.

27 E.g. Diamond, A.L. (1989) *A Review of Security Interests in Property*. London: HMSO, paras. 17.1–17.4.

28 Law Commission Consultation Paper No. 164, para. 7.24. One of the reasons why retention-of-title agreements are not registrable is the avoidance of 'administrative burdens and unwelcome publicity'. *See* Beale *et al.*, op. cit. (f'note 24), at 180.

Retention-of-title agreements may pose disadvantages. Third parties, particularly lenders, in the absence of publicity (registration) may not obtain reliable information on the creditworthiness of the buyer and have to rely on buyer's representation.[29] This has a negative impact on the cost of credit. The buyer may not always be able to grant the assets as collateral to obtain second-ranking security interest. Furthermore, a buyer's unsecured creditors may have the risk of not being able to enforce their rights without the seller's consent.[30]

7.2.3 Leases[31]

A lease is also a critical transaction that enables the use of the asset without paying the full purchase price. The lessor retains the ownership of the equipment and receives payments from the lessee during the course of the lease agreement. The distinction between an operational and a financial lease can mostly be felt in their function, length and registrability. However, for a lease to be categorised as an acquisition financing transaction, it is necessary to ascertain whether 'the lessee [acquires] the use of the asset for at least most of its useful life, in exchange for notional rental payments that represent the economic equivalent of its price if it had been sold in an instalment sale'.[32] This is an indication that a finance lease, as opposed to an operating lease, qualifies as an acquisition-financing transaction.

7.3 The new frontier: unitary and non-unitary approaches to acquisition financing

The Guide adopts a flexible approach in allowing States to choose between a unitary and a non-unitary approach to acquisition financing devices. However, conversely, recommendations made by the Guide state that States should adopt a unitary, functionally integrated approach to non-acquisition secured transactions (i.e. all transactions that create a right in any type of asset, meant to secure the performance of an obligation, should be considered to be secured transactions and regulated by the same rules).[33] The perception of Recommendation 9, which deals with the unitary and non-unitary approach, is that all financiers (sellers that retain title or lenders using security) should be treated equally (a functionally integrated approach to all acquisition financing transactions). The application of a secured transactions regime equally to all financiers, so that businesses are provided with low-cost credit, is a key objective and a fundamental policy of the Guide.[34] The rights of sellers and lenders are distinguished in many jurisdictions

29 Guide, para. 99, at 54.
30 Ibid.
31 For a further discussion, *see* Chapter 1 (f'notes 76–79) and the accompanying text thereof.
32 Guide, para. 31, 325.
33 Guide, para. 62, at 23; paras 64–65, at 334.
34 Guide, para. 52, at 20 and para. 72, at 26.

where sellers have the right to retain title until the buyer pays in full, and lenders have the right to take security over assets which are purchased with the credit provided by lenders. These are treated distinctly in creation, third-party effectiveness and priority.

The purpose of the Guide in adopting a unitary and non-unitary approach to acquisition financing is to recognise the importance and facilitation of acquisition financing as a source of access to low-cost credit for small businesses, while treating all providers of acquisition financing equally, and the creation of a transparent system for acquisition financing (i.e. registration in a general security rights register).[35] The purpose clarifies that an acquisition security right, whether or not it is under the unitary or non-unitary approach, should be subject to the same rules as general security rights, including the application of the general security rights' rules on creation, third-party effectiveness and priority.[36] The same argument applies equally to the non-unitary approach because, under Recommendation 188, it is necessary that the rules governing acquisition financing produce functionally equivalent economic results, regardless of whether the creditor's right is a retention-of-title or financial lease right, or an acquisition security right.

Differences of approach to non-possessory security rights over tangible assets led legal systems to develop certain approaches to acquisition of tangible assets. On the one hand, States preferred the protection of sellers by permitting the use of retention-of-title and other title-based devices exclusively to sellers in the hope that small businesses were protected, and would not be vulnerable against large financial institutions which had a stronger bargaining position.[37] On the other hand, in those systems that had a tendency to promote seller- and lender-based acquisition financing, they permitted sellers to contractually extend their rights deriving from the retention-of-title agreements to the proceeds and the products, thereby subjecting the seller equally to the regime applicable to security interests, and the regime applicable to retention-of-title.[38] Finally, and arguably, the optimal approach that promotes seller and lender acquisition financing is a fully integrated approach that works in tandem with the single functional security right. The aim is to integrate various acquisition financing rights, including retention-of-title and financial lease, into one functional and single security right while treating these rights equally for sellers and lenders. This is also the fundamental policy of the Guide in achieving equality of lenders and the rights of sellers in an extension of credit to the grantor by enhancing competition between the sellers and lenders which will eventually reduce the cost of credit.[39] The fact that an acquisition

35 Statements of Purpose for Options A and B under Chapter IX, Acquisition Financing.

36 Recommendation 178.

37 *See generally* Guide, paras 46–51, at 329–30; for a similar line of argument, *see also* Davies, I. (2002) 'Retention-of-title Clauses and Non-Possessory Security Interests: A Secured Credit Regime within the European Union?' in I. Davies (ed.) *Security Interests in Mobile Equipment*. Aldershot: Ashgate, pp. 335, 337–8.

38 *See generally* Guide, paras 52–55, at 330–1. *See also* op. cit. (f'note 16).

39 Guide, para. 72, at 26 and para. 57, at 332.

security right is a security has an exception 'where the particular circumstances of acquisition financing require a special rule applicable only to such rights, all the rules applicable to security rights generally also apply to acquisition security rights'.[40] In order to frame acquisition security rights within the fully integrated comprehensive PMSI approach, the Guide discusses the key features. These include, first and foremost, the equality of sellers (the suppliers of tangible assets) and lenders or lessors; preference to a security right given to a secured creditor, regardless of whether a secured creditor retains title or lends; the ability of a buyer to utilise the full value of assets by offering the same assets to multiple creditors and offering lower-ranking priority; the ability to register in the general security rights register the security right regardless of its denomination (retention-of-title, financial lease or security agreement) and achieving third-party effectiveness through registration in the general security rights register; the ability to have super-priority provided registry is made within a short period of time after delivery of the assets or prior to delivery in the case of inventory;[41] and finally, the ability to enforce rights outside insolvency.[42]

It is often the case that PMSI is an exception to the first-to-file registration that leads to priority status. The characteristic of the PMSI is that the seller's non-possessory security interest is similar to the lender's security interest, and that it has a preferential priority position compared to general secured creditors.[43] It gives super-priority status to the PMSI lender over the earlier registered security interest holder, and a PMSI is perfected upon attachment.[44] Otherwise the interest of the purchase-money lender will always be automatically subordinate to an earlier security right which is registered and has achieved third-party effectiveness securing present and future rights. The super-priority status is automatically given to retention-of-title transactions. The simple rationale is that, as the debtor has never obtained the ownership rights over the assets on which a charge is established, a seller retaining title will have priority over the chargee. Professor Bridge, in line with the Guide's perspective on a functionally integrated approach to acquisition financing,[45] commented that separating PMSI from retention-of-title

40 Ibid.

41 The significance of registration in order to make the PMSI enforceable with priority towards unsecured and subsequently registered secured creditors, EBRD Model Law Article 9 suggests a six months period after the conclusion of the sales contract. Under UCC Article 9–324 this period is 20 days, and under the Guide this period is envisaged as, depending on the choice of the legislator, either 20 or 30 days (Recommendation 180 A and B). For a suggestion of a short period for EU Member States, *see* Kieninger, op. cit. (f'note 11), 671–2. For a European concept of retention-of-title, see e.g. Milo, J.M. (2003) 'Retention of Title in European Business Transactions', 43 *Washburn L. J.*, 121, 134.

42 Guide, para. 58, at 332.

43 For more discussion, *see* Guide, paras 37–39, at 327.

44 UCC §9–309.

45 Guide, para. 68, at 335, '. . . buyers should be permitted to seek the best deal possible to satisfy their acquisition financing needs'.

gives the buyer a broader spectrum by introducing this credit to other creditors.[46] It has been argued that this traditional super-priority position enjoyed by the seller retaining title may also be extended to purchase-money lenders.[47]

The Guide, as a key policy choice, opts for the functionally integrated and unitary approach in relation to non-acquisition secured transactions.[48] Recommendation 8 also confirms this, according to which all types of rights serving for security purposes will be abolished and the transactions and financing practices they aim at will be incorporated under a single security right (a functionally integrated approach to non-acquisition secured transactions). In the implementation of a functional approach, however, acquisition financing presents an exception to the general rule adopted under the Guide (Recommendation 8, second sentence). Under this approach, the system recharacterises all types of transactions fulfilling the economic function of a security device as security rights. The characterised transactions are not, strictly speaking, a security agreement but rather transactions where ownership is held with the seller or lessor.[49] This is the integrated and functional approach combining a number of advantages for all parties, including facilitation of credit by having competition among credit providers and a simpler legislation cleared of fragmentation.[50] Under both the unitary and non-unitary approaches, all types of financiers (sellers or creditors) must be treated equally. The Guide, while justifying the application of a functional approach to finance leases and other title-based devices as to the ownership concept that underlies them, is reduced to only a security interest, and recognises the complexity of including lenders and sellers in the same scheme. The Guide pointed out as follows: '[w]hen the obligation being secured is the payment of the purchase price of a tangible asset, [. . .] a conceptually more complex issue is presented, since the parties involved are not all lenders. They are also sellers.'[51] The disadvantage of re-characterisation of transactions that are not traditional security interests, but have the same economic function as security interests, is that certain States that treat quasi and traditional security interests distinctly will be compelled to adjust their secured transactions laws. In those States, security rights are an exception to the equality of creditors (i.e. on the one hand, secured creditors with security interests who paid for their bargains and priority positions and, on the other, unsecured creditors who cannot adjust their positions and have

46 Bridge, in Eidenmüller and Kieninger (eds), op. cit. (f'note 1), at 197.

47 Kieninger, E-M. 'The Scope and Limits of Security Interests' in Eidenmüller and Kieninger (eds), op. cit. (f'note 1), 215, 219.

48 Functional approach is a fundamental policy under the Guide. Guide, para. 62, at 23.

49 Guide, para. 65, at 334,

> [a]ll transactions where rights in the grantor's assets, including ownership, are used to secure an ordinary repayment obligation by a borrower to a provider of credit should be treated as security devices, and identified as such, in contexts of both inside and outside the insolvency.

50 Ibid.

51 Guide, para. 66, at 334.

no priority) and with the introduction of the functional and integrated approach to security, secured credit must be spread.[52]

The term 'acquisition financing devices' under a unitary approach includes financing patterns such as retention-of-title and financial lease, whereas under the non-unitary approach retention-of-title and financial lease are not included within the term and can be used separately. In relation to acquisition financing devices, Recommendation 9 provides two options to States that aim to modernise their secured transactions regimes. States may either adopt the unitary or non-unitary approach to secured transactions where acquisition security rights are involved. Under unitary approach (Recommendation 9(a)) all acquisition financing transactions will be subject to one single security right and are classified as rights that secure payment or performance of an obligation. In this context, retention-of-title and financial leases are included in the term acquisition security right, and they have no distinction from security interests. This approach treats an acquisition financing device as a security right. Put simply, the unitary approach eliminates all distinctions between title devices and security interests. While the unitary approach denotes abolishing the distinctions between forms of acquisition financing transactions and characterising them as a security right, the non-unitary approach prefers to retain the distinct acquisition financing transactions. The unitary approach allows all acquisition financing devices to be classified as a security right and that title-based devices will be regulated in the same way as an acquisition security right taken by a lender and, in a sense, a seller's ownership rights are reduced to a limited security right by considering the buyer to have acquired ownership of the asset.[53]

On the other hand, the Guide recommends that, under the non-unitary approach, the functional equivalence between the rights of sellers and lenders can be achieved either through treating all acquisition financiers the same, but with an exception provided to financiers who retain title or, again, treating all acquisition financiers the same but the secured creditors and non-acquisition secured creditors are subject to different rules.[54] The non-unitary approach reflects the distinction between retention-of-title, a financial lease, and other acquisition financing devices. Even though transactions are not viewed functionally as a security interest, results as to priority and third-party effectiveness will lead to the same point. Put another way, under the non-unitary approach even though retention-of-title will be retained, the seller, as in the unitary approach, will be required to register (unlike many legal systems including English law) to achieve third-party effectiveness and for priority purposes. Failure of registration will convert the seller into an unperfected security right holder, and retention of ownership will not be effective. The non-unitary approach to acquisition financing also produces a result where the acquisition security financier will have the same priority status as a

52 Guide, para. 108, at 57.

53 Guide, para. 78, at 337.

54 Guide, paras 80–81, at 338.

competing claimant, such as financial lessor or the seller retaining title.[55] Under Recommendation 9(b)(i), with the exception of retention-of-title and financial leases, which will be treated distinctly for third-party effectiveness and priority purposes, all other security rights will be categorised as acquisition security rights, and thus governed by the rules that govern acquisition financing transactions. Moreover, although the ownership rights of the seller and lessor will continue (rather than these rights being treated as security interests, i.e. lower status than ownership rights), in order to achieve functionally equivalent outcomes similar to an acquisition security right, rules governing them will be modified (Recommendation 9(b)(ii)) so that all acquisition financing providers are treated equally.[56]

In this sense, the Cape Town Convention provides valuable wisdom. Retention-of-title, financial lease and security interests can be registered in the international registry, but this does not make them altogether a security interest. Characterisation is left to contracting States. The significant feature of the Cape Town Convention is that even though three distinct transactions are combined under the Convention, and they are registered in an international registry, there is no requirement of super-priority for title-based devices and PMSI holders are not granted super-priority. This means that a first-filed interest will have priority over the subsequently registered interests (which may be a retention-of-title or financial lease).[57] The first-to-file rule under the Cape Town Convention provides clear and predictable priority, without the need to resort to a functional approach to security and to re-characterise title-based devices as security interest, or to distinguish three distinct transactions for the purposes of establishing priority. Arguably, it is this aspect that makes the Cape Town Convention unique and acceptable to most jurisdictions, hence the high number of ratifications. The simple first-to-file rule for obtaining priority, registration for third-party effectiveness and rejection of re-characterisation, makes this conceptually complex area of secured transactions law easily understandable and practical. Many States that prefer to preserve their title-based devices may do so without the need to re-educate the legal and financial community with the concepts underlying the functional approach to security. Arguably, the non-unitary approach is similar to the status of chargee, the conditional seller and the financial lessor under the Cape Town Convention. The Cape Town Convention that regulates security rights over a specific category of mobile equipment, on the other hand, clearly opts for the non-unitary approach in leaving

55 For a discussion of unitary and non-unitary approach, *see below*; Sigman, H. 'Perfection and Priority of Security Rights' in Eidenmüller and Kieninger (eds), op. cit. (f'note 1), at 164–5, stating that 'successful implementation of the non-unitary approach, which requires modifying the existing rules (not only those governing priority) to achieve functional equivalence of outcomes under the unitary approach, would not be easy to accomplish'.

56 Guide, para. 111, at 58. For discussion, *see* Guide, paras 101–12, at 55–8.

57 This is not possible, for instance, under English law as a seller will have priority over the charge even though the charge is made effective against third parties earlier.

the characterisation of the security device to contracting States. It combines security interests, retention-of-title and financial lease agreements under one uniform concept of international interest[58] without converting them into one uniform concept of security interest in the sense that it is understood under a UCC Article 9 type of functional approach to security.[59] Thus all of these devices are treated distinctly, yet are subject to the same third-party effectiveness (registration) and priority rules. On the other hand, basic default remedies under security interests (Articles 8–9) and retention-of-title and financial lease (Article 10) are distinguished.

A similar argument can be made for the Model Law which, arguably, opts in for the non-unitary approach where the concept of charge combines different types of security devices (possessory charge, registered charge, unpaid vendor's charge and enterprise charge) while their distinctive legal nature is recognised,[60] and Articles 17 to 21 regulating third-party effectiveness and priority conflicts (involvement of third parties) apply to all charges. The clear distinction under the Model Law between the unpaid vendor's charge (retention-of-title) and the registered charge, although both are addressed as charge, is that the former is not required to be registered for six months[61] and can be converted into a registered charge.[62] Under Article 9.1, the Model Law clearly suggests that a seller by delivering goods under the unpaid vendor's charge takes charge (security interest) over the goods. The operation of the unpaid vendor's charge is not exactly as retention-of-title, 'but rather as a transfer of title to the purchaser and the simultaneous grant back of a security interest to the seller'.[63] The unpaid vendor's charge seems to be a simple retention-of-title as it allows for securing the unpaid price, interest and realisation expenses.[64] This, in comparison to English law,[65] grants limited protection to the seller,[66] because the seller cannot extend the retention-of-title until all debts and obligations are paid so that there is no indebtedness between the seller and the buyer (the current account method). The same inability to extend the contract under the Model Law equally applies to extended, proceeds, or aggregation clause retention-of-title types.[67] Under the Model Law, retention of title arrangements are replaced by the unpaid vendor's charge according to which 'ownership passes to

58 *See generally* Cuming, R. (2002) 'The Characterisation of Interests and Transactions under the Convention of International Interests in Mobile Equipment, 2001' in I. Davies (ed.) *Security Interests in Mobile Equipment*. Aldershot: Ashgate, p. 377.

59 UCC Article 9 has the unitary approach, where all secured transactions having the same economic functions are treated as security interests.

60 Röver, J-H. (2007) *Secured Lending in Eastern Europe: Comparative Law of Secured Transactions and the EBRD Model Law*. Oxford: Oxford University Press, p. 75–6.

61 Model Law Article 9.4.1.

62 Model Law Article 8.2.

63 McCormack, G. and Dahan, F. (1999) 'The EBRD Model Law on Secured Transactions: Comparisons and Convergence', *CfiLR*, 65, 74.

64 Ibid. 74.

65 In English law retention-of-title is quite extensively developed. There are at least five types of retention-of-title agreements; *see* below.

66 Ibid. 75.

67 *See* op. cit. (f'note 16) and accompanying text thereof.

the purchaser and simultaneously a charge is given in favour of the vendor'.[68] The unpaid vendor's charge is exempt from registration. Article 17.3 sets aside what is similarly and generally found in registration-based priority systems, the first-to-file rule, and grants priority to the unpaid vendor's charge. Although this is similar to the super-priority of PMSIs, the Model Law does not contain a provision on PMSIs. The unpaid vendor's charge has a six months' lifetime (Article 9.4.1). However, if the goods subject to the unpaid vendor's charge are disposed of within this period, and as this type of charge is not required to be registered, the third party purchasing these goods from the chargor cannot make an enquiry and, in any case, the quest for enquiry is impracticable.[69] The third party purchaser will take these goods free of the charge and obtain good title.[70]

The critical issue under the functional approach to security is that normally, under national secured transactions regimes, traditional and quasi-security interests are treated distinctly. This is so in most jurisdictions except those that reflect the UCC Article 9 structure and philosophy. There are certain concerns in those jurisdictions that have not adopted the functional approach to security. The particular concern is related to remedies. If the functional approach to security is accepted, retention-of-title devices will be re-characterised as security interests. However, title finance devices generally grant better rights than security interests (super-priority and remedial superiority). The rationale is that the title financier holds ownership rights over the assets, often until the buyer pays for the assets in full. Arguably it is this full ownership right that gives an advantageous position to the seller. An automatic right to proceeds for secured party was not kept under the scheme recommended by the Law Commission Report and the automatic right to proceeds for secured party 'was an advantage that held out to [retention-of-title] suppliers (who currently are not entitled to the proceeds of sale unless they make special provision and, even if they do so, normally do not register a floating charge).'[71] Professor Beale succinctly argued that it should be optional whether the surplus should be paid to the debtor. Normally, the title retainer can retain any surplus from the sale of the asset upon default of the debtor whereas the security interest creditor must return any surplus to the debtor.[72] This is because the creditor has limited property rights over the asset and not the owner, unlike the lessor and the seller. Security rights do

68 Röver, op. cit. (f'note 60), 78.

69 Commentary to Article 9.1.

70 Article 21.2.7, *cf.* Sale of Goods Act 1979 s. 25(1), similarly good faith and no previous notice of any encumbrance of the original seller in respect of the goods are required. This is also an exception to the *nemo dat* rule. For an examination of exceptions to the *nemo dat* rule, *see also* Merrett, L. (2008) 'The importance of delivery and possession in the passing of title', *C.L.J.*, 376.

71 Law Commission Report 296, para. 3.56 and fn. 86.

72 Beale, H. 'The Future of Secured Credit in Europe: Concluding Remarks' in Eidenmüller and Kieninger (eds) op. cit. (f'note 1), 375, 393. UCC §9–601(g) regulates that in an outright sale of receivables the buyer collects the receivables in full and no surplus is left to the debtor. *See also* Law Commission Consultation Paper No. 164, para. 6.4. For some arguments on the surplus issue, *see* e.g. Gullifer, L. (2007) 'Retention of Title Clauses: A Question of Balance' in A. Burrows and E. Peel (eds) *Contract Terms*. Oxford: Oxford University Press, pp. 285, 291.

not permit deprivation of surplus value from the debtor.[73] Under UCC Article 9, the surplus is limited to the amount of debt secured. Under the Cape Town Convention, the surplus goes to a subsequent chargee and other registered interest holders, and after satisfaction of registered interest holders, unregistered chargees will be satisfied, and if any surplus is left that will be paid to the debtor.[74] On the other hand, a conditional seller or lessor upon termination of the contract either takes possession or control of the equipment.[75] The significance of this provision is that jurisdiction that treats retention-of-title and financial lease as security interests will not apply this article, but rather will apply Cape Town Convention Articles 8 and 9.[76] The Guide suggests that the grantor should receive any remaining surplus after all claims have been satisfied (Recommendation 152).

The other critical concern is for third-party effectiveness, and to obtain priority whether it is necessary to subject a retention-of-title agreement to a registration requirement. The concern must be separated into two parts. First, whether it should be necessary to register retention-of-title agreements for third-party effectiveness and secondly, whether registration should be a priority point. For traditional security interests it is necessary to have the interest registered for third-party effectiveness in order for subsequent secured creditors to be informed of any prior rights on the asset. However, when a debtor has a security interest over his assets, and a seller retains title over these, it will be necessary for secured creditors (lenders) to be able to ascertain whether the debtor owns these assets. For a debtor to be able to give his assets as collateral, he needs to have full ownership rights over the asset. In the case of retention-of-title or financial lease, as the seller or the lessor has superior rights the debtor will not be in a position to claim against their property rights. For example, the seller retaining title will have super-priority over any registered charge (earlier or later). Even though the buyer grants a charge to a third-party creditor on future assets and the third party registers the floating charge on the future assets, as the buyer has no ownership rights over the assets and the seller has, the seller retaining title will beat the earlier charge. Thus the seller with title retention will have super-priority as it will not be bound by first-to-file. However, without a registration requirement for retention-of-title, lenders will be misled that the debtor owns the assets. Thus, a full general security rights registry is necessary so that both retention-of-title and traditional security interests are registered for third-party effectiveness. However, this could mean that retention-of-title arrangements are re-characterised as security interests.[77]

In England the list of registrable charges is short and outdated. The Law Commission's recommendations indicated that registration should be required

73 Guide, para. 35, at 245.

74 Cape Town Convention Article 8.6.

75 Cape Town Convention Article 10.

76 Goode, R. (2008) *Convention on International Interests in Mobile Equipment and Protocol thereto on Matters Specific to Aircraft Equipment Official Commentary*, revised edn. Rome: UNIDROIT, p. 187.

77 *See generally* Beale, op. cit. (f'note 72), at 393.

for all types of security devices, including the title-retention arrangements.[78] Registration is overwhelmingly an important method for achieving third-party effectiveness for security over intangible property, without which subsequent secured creditors cannot be able to ascertain earlier security rights. The information obtained from the debtor may not be trusted. Registration also serves as an element of priority in those jurisdictions where the general security right registry is established, because registration serves as an information conduit and establishes a comprehensive priority regime. If retention-of-title agreements are registrable under a notice-filing system, retention-of-title agreements will have third-party effectiveness and obtain priority. This is because under notice filing, priority will be established at the time of registration, which may be in advance of creation, rather than time of creation of security interest, or conclusion of the retention-of-title agreement. Among European Union member states, third-party effectiveness (publicity) differs particularly in the context of different types of title-based devices.[79] In some countries, extension of retention-of-title to the products may amount to a hidden charge and cannot be enforceable against third parties.[80] Under the UCC Article 9 scheme, in addition to registration, the supplier of goods is protected through special priority rules and granted a super-priority status. These are called the PMSI holders, and the PMSI ranks ahead of earlier security interests. However, this is an exception to the main priority rules.[81] There is no need to register PMSI in consumer goods in order to avoid registration of too many small-scale interests filling up the register.[82] The perfection occurs in the case of goods at the time the grantor receives possession, or within 20 days of receiving possession (UCC §9–324(a)). In the case of inventory other than goods, perfection occurs at time of possession and, additionally, a PMSI secured creditor must send a notification to the earlier security interest holder (UCC §9–324(b) and (c)). The rationale was explained as follows:

> in the case of inventory financing, the lender will typically make ongoing advances against receipt of invoices reflecting newly-acquired inventory and does so without conducting a new search of the filing system before making each advance, in reliance on its priority based on its first filed position. . . . notification is the source of warning that the first-filer cannot so rely with respect to the new inventory described in the notification.[83]

78 Law Commission Consultation Paper No. 164.

79 These extend from retention-of-title in raw material with a products clause to retention-of-title with an all-monies clause. *See* Kieninger, in Kieninger (ed.), op. cit. (f'note 11), 656.

80 Kieninger, in Kieninger (ed.), op. cit. (f'note 11), 657.

81 Law Commission Consultation Paper No. 176, para. 3.209.

82 For a similar view, *see* Bridge, M. (1992) 'Form, Substance and Innovation in Personal Property Security Law', *J.B.L.*, 1, 13. Under the Guide, third-party effectiveness for consumer goods does not require registration (Recommendation 191).

83 Sigman, op. cit. (f'note 55), 163.

The super-priority also extends to proceeds in the case of goods but not in inventory.[84] Arguably, this rule where super-priority does not extend to PMSI in inventory, protects the receivables financier who is already subordinated in relation to PMSI in inventory, from being subordinated for the second time (i.e. the second time in relation to receivables).[85] English law gives effectiveness to PMSIs, and under it the PMSI of a seller who financed the acquisition of assets is limited to only the original goods supplied.[86] It has also been suggested, in the Law Commission's Consultation Paper,[87] that PMSIs would be the exception to the notice filing and would be given super-priority status over previously registered security interests on the same asset.[88] However, PMSIs had not been included in the Law Commission's Report, as retention-of-title agreements were excluded from the current scope of the Report due to opposition from the legal and finance sector. However, it could have been acceptable had retention-of-title agreements been included and made registrable. This development could have still made them work in tandem with PMSIs just like under UCC Article 9.[89]

The registration requirement of acquisition security rights is important, as registration provides transparency and notice of the possible existence of a security right. If title-based devices and security agreements are all included in one scheme, it is necessary to grant super-priority to PMSIs (acquisition financing rights) over the non-acquisition security rights. Thus, registration in that sense for acquisition financing rights does not become a priority point as first-to-file does not work for acquisition financing rights. The Guide recommends registration to achieve third-party effectiveness for title retention devices both under the unitary and the non-unitary approach to security.[90] Under the non-unitary approach, the registration in the general security rights registry needs to be done within 20 to 30 days after the possession of the asset. Acquisition financing transactions present exceptions to the first-to-register priority rules, and an acquisition financing right will have priority over an earlier registered non-acquisition security right (that is general security right). As to the creation of an acquisition security rights under the unitary approach, there seems to be no difference between acquisition security rights and non-acquisition security rights (Recommendation 178). In relation to

84 UCC§9–324(a) and 327(1).

85 Sigman, op. cit. (f'note 16) 55, 163 points out the rationale as follows:

> '. . . the advance rate . . . for receivables is usually higher than that for inventory, the amount of the receivables will be higher than the cost to the grantor of the inventory and, . . . it will usually be the advance by the receivables financier that enables the grantor to pay its inventory supplier.'

86 Bridge, M., MacDonald, R., Simmonds, R. and Walsh, C. (1999) 'Formalism, Functionalism and Understanding the Law of Secured Transactions', 44 *McGill L.J.*, 567, 647.

87 Law Commission Consultation Paper No. 176, para. 2.43.

88 Ibid. para. 3.208.

89 For a similar line of arguments, *see* Bridge, M. (2006) 'The Law Commission's Proposals for the Reform of Corporate Security Interests' in J. Getzler and J. Payne, *Company Charges Spectrum and Beyond*. Oxford: Oxford University Press, pp. 267, 279–280.

90 Recommendations 178 and 192, Alternatives A and B.

non-acquisition security rights, in order to achieve the functionally equivalent results, formalities are reduced to writing or evidence by writing where the seller's or lessor's intent to retain ownership is clear, and the writing must take place before the buyer or lessee obtains possession of the asset (Recommendation 189).

7.4 Conclusions

An innovative feature of the Guide is its efforts of combining traditional security interests and quasi-security interests under a single scheme. This requires harmony in the creation, third-party effectiveness, priority and remedies. However, differences of national legal systems' approaches to title retention devices make this argument more significant. The Guide, in order to facilitate credit and establish a balance between sellers and lenders, created an alternative where, depending on their policy choices, States can either choose a unitary or non-unitary approach to acquisition financing rights. However, whatever the States choose, the rules are carefully designed to produce the functionally equivalent results. The Guide's apparent tendency to a unitary approach is in line with its mission: in order to facilitate credit lenders, the sellers must be treated equally so that there is competition and this can be achieved by transparent rules in third-party effectiveness and priority. However, this approach may bring along the problem of resembling retention-of-title to security interests by reducing the value of full ownership rights to a limited right.

The unitary approach resembles the UCC Article 9 functionality. The functionality concept is important by being efficient and creating predictable results and reducing the cost of credit, albeit one has to go through a myriad of complex rules. However, UCC Article 9 is a *sui generis* legislation taking its genesis from the domestic American business traditions. Its relation to other articles of the UCC should also be considered and debated before transplanting it. It is arguable that recommending registration for title retention devices may be controversial for those jurisdictions that do not adopt UCC Article 9 type legislation, and these jurisdictions may be compelled to change their judicial attitudes on this matter. Nevertheless, registration will provide transparency and any concerns that these jurisdictions may have can be overcome by the introduction of a acquisition financing right into their legislations, which will then grant the holder a super-priority right.

8 Choice-of-law issues

8.1 Introduction

Choice-of-laws rules have a significant role in the facilitation of credit. In the international context, choice-of-laws serve as a means to determine the applicable substantive law on creation, third-party effectiveness and priority of a security interest. In cross-border secured transactions, international financiers are often concerned about the recognition of creation, third-party effectiveness and priority of security interests, hence efforts to create a comprehensive international secured transactions regime to overcome complexities. In this context, achieving predictability and certainty through choice-of-laws may reduce the cost of credit.

It seems a remarkably feasible approach to combine substantive and choice-of-laws rules within the framework of a single international instrument. Simply harmonising choice-of-laws rules cannot provide a satisfactory approach. Equally, since substantive secured transactions laws vary among States, creating a purely substantive law instrument may not always be possible.[1] Even though there may be similarities in the way jurisdictions regulate creation and perfection, this is not sufficient to establish certainty in international secured transactions because a harmonised application is necessary. This may be achieved through international instruments that address these problems and offer solutions through either substantive or choice-of-laws rules. Some instruments address these issues through a mixture of rules.[2]

This chapter aims to illustrate the significance of choice-of-law provisions of international secured transactions instruments. The chapter suggests that

1 For a similar view with reservations, *see* Kreuzer, K. (2008) 'Conflict-of-Laws Rules for Security Rights in Tangible Assets in the European Union', in H. Eidenmüller and E-M. Kieninger (eds) *The Future of Secured Credit in Europe*. E.C.F.L.R, Munich: De Gruyter Recht, 297, at 314.

2 E.g. The Receivables Convention addresses the issue of priorities through substantive (optional annex) and conflict-of-laws rules (Article 22). For a similar view, *see* Beale, H., Bridge, M., Gullifer L. and Lomnicka, E. (2007) *The Law of Personal Property Security*. Oxford: Oxford University Press, 741.

choice-of-laws rules are essential features of international secured transactions instruments. For the purposes of certainty and predictability in the applicable law, the chapter argues that *lex situs* should only be applicable to tangible assets to the extent that they are not border crossing[3] and the law of the grantor's (assignor) location for intangibles (particularly, for receivables) is the only feasible connecting factor in international secured transactions. Furthermore, it is argued that party autonomy should not be allowed for the proprietary aspects of secured transactions, since party autonomy adversely affects third party rights. Part two examines choice-of-laws rules and international instruments. Part three explores the Guide and the Receivables Convention's approach to choice-of-laws. In that context, particular attention will be on the significance of an innovative but unfairly criticised feature of the Guide and the Receivables Convention – the law of the grantor's (assignor) location as a general connecting factor in receivables. It is argued that problems are most likely to present themselves under this connecting factor. The applicability of this to creation, third-party effectiveness and priority problems, particularly in receivables, is appropriate because it has a positive impact on the facilitation of credit by establishing certainty and predictability through the application of single law. Part four examines the Cape Town Convention's relationship with choice-of-laws rules and argues that the traditional *lex situs* rule is not appropriate for mobile assets that cross borders. Conclusions will be in part five. The chapter will not be discussing the Model Law and the Factoring Convention, as they do not contain choice-of-laws rules.

8.2 Choice-of-laws and the international instruments

Globalisation of commerce means that commercial activities occur more often at cross-border level, which raises the critical question of what should be the style of rules in international instruments. The nature of the law of secured transactions requires a substantive and choice-of-law rules structure in international instruments. International instruments tend to harmonise certain areas (e.g. priorities, third-party effectiveness or form) of secured transactions law through choice-of-laws rules in order to achieve comprehensiveness[4] and to supplement substantive rules (choice-of-laws rules may act in filling gaps in the instruments) where there is already consensus, in order to achieve certainty and predictability (the two critical objectives central to international instruments). From another angle, choice-of-laws rules are considered to have a positive impact on international instruments in achieving wider acceptance on areas in which there is almost no possibility to

3 If tangibles cross borders, the feasible approach will be the Cape Town Convention's approach. *See below*.

4 E.g. Receivables Convention Article 22 and Chapter V; A/CN.9/397, paras 40 *et seq*.

establish substantive rules that may be acceptable to every State.[5] Parties in their transactions often select an applicable law, but this may not always be possible or the selected law may be set aside by the mandatory rules of the forum. In any case, party autonomy cannot be used to override the rights of third parties[6] and is inappropriate in transactions concerning proprietary matters. Choice-of-laws must be mandatory for the proprietary aspects of a secured transaction[7] (in any case, party autonomy is permitted for the contractual aspects of a secured transaction) and the law should not permit party autonomy to be used so to avoid application of referred substantive law rules. Otherwise, the aim of predictability, for example, in priority disputes may be defeated. In other words, choice-of-laws rules in secured transactions should be responsive to parties' commercial expectations. The grantor should not be allowed to choose different laws to priority disputes in two different contracts concluded with two competing creditors, as each creditor has a property right on the grantor's collateral and this will cause uncertainty. Any agreement between the grantor and each creditor should not have adverse affects on the other competing creditor or on third parties.[8] This risk increases the cost of credit as secured lenders wish to be certain in relation to their priority positions.

The question of whether a single choice-of-laws rule should govern the creation, perfection and priority of security interests has been a tension point in choice-of-laws. This may seem to be a feasible approach to the extent that certainty and simplicity govern the philosophy underlying secured transactions law. However, third parties' interests may be protected better if there are different rules applicable to priorities. Complementing this matter is the issue of whether choice-of-laws rules for creation, third party effectiveness and priority should be the same for intangible and tangible assets.[9] However, this has the risk of straight-jacketing particularly receivables to the rule of *lex situs*, which will not provide feasible solutions. *Lex situs* is mainly suitable for tangible and immovable assets. Intangibles, especially receivables, do not have a physical location. The Receivables Convention and the Guide have adopted the approach that receivables should be

5 Some commentators in the early 1990s argued that choice-of-laws problems in receivables financing would be reduced by the Factoring Convention because it was an instrument that harmonised substantive laws rather than introducing new choice-of-laws rules. E.g. Moshinsky M. (1992) 'The Assignment of Debts in the Conflict of Laws', *L.Q.R.*, 591, 612. However, the Factoring Convention is in force in only seven countries. It is arguable that one of the main reasons why it has received little acceptance, even from the factoring industry, is the fact that it does not contain a choice-of-laws rule governing the formal validity of assignment or priority of competing claims. On the other hand, the Receivables Convention contains a choice-of-laws rule (the law of the assignor's State), applicable to formal validity and priority matters, as well as an autonomous chapter. A similar approach is also adopted by the Guide. *See below.*

6 *See e.g.* Receivables Convention Article 6.

7 Deschamps, M. (2008) 'Conflict-of-Laws Rules for Security Rights: What Should be the Best Rules?', in Eidenmüller and Kieninger (eds), op. cit. (f'note 1), 284, at 285.

8 Deschamps, ibid., at 285 *et seq.*

9 Guide, paras 18–9, at 390.

governed by the law of grantor's (assignor) location,[10] as opposed to the law of the location of the debt or the encumbered asset. The law of the location of debt[11] is artificial because book debts as intangibles cannot have a location.[12] The rationale of applying *lex situs* to intangibles is that the debt is considered to be located in the place where it can be recovered (enforced), thus the forum is deemed to have control over the debtor and the asset.[13] However, controlling the intangible asset and attributing a physical location is not easy. A debt may have multiple *situs* and thus be enforceable in multiple jurisdictions,[14] so that a debtor, which may be a company operating its business in more than one jurisdiction, may be sued in any of the jurisdictions where it operates.[15] The application of the law of the grantor's (assignor) location has the benefit of bypassing fictional attribution of locations, such as the law of place payment, the law governing the receivable, location of the debtor of the receivable, law of location of enforcement, or the law governing the relationship between the grantor and creditor. The law of the grantor's location, however, does not apply to negotiable instruments, intellectual property rights and investment securities, hence the application of *lex situs* to these assets.[16]

The general principle for tangible assets that do not move across borders is that the law of the location of the tangible governs the validity and priority of the security interest (*lex situs or lex rei sitae*). If the encumbered asset moves to a new location, the law of the new location determines 'the impact of subsequent events (such as a sale or pledge by the debtor or the secured party's failure to observe a (re)perfection requirement)'[17] over the validly created security interest in the first location.

The Guide and the Receivables and Cape Town Conventions have rules that regulate creation, third-party effectiveness, priority and enforcement of security rights. These instruments provide a comprehensive, predictable and innovative regime for the type of assets and transactions that they govern. Their treatment is

10 Receivables Convention Article 22 and Guide, recommendation 208. It should be noted that under the Guide different rules apply to intangibles other than receivables.

11 The law of the debtor's place of residence has practical disadvantages, such as multiple debtors, and in the case of bulk assignment of receivables, may cause unpredictability as to which law applies. For cases that apply the law of the debtor's place of residence, *see e.g. Wight v Eckhardt Marine GmbH* [2003] UKPC 37, [2004] 1 AC 147; *Deutsche Schachtbau-und TiefbohrgesellschaftmbH v Shell International Petroleum Co Ltd* [1990] 1 AC 295.

12 For a criticism of attributing a *situs* to book debts, *see* Rogerson, P. (1990) 'The *Situs* of Debts in the Conflict of Laws–Illogical, Unnecessary and Misleading', 49 *C.L.J.*, 441, 453 *et seq.* A/CN.9/489/Add.1, para. 30: 'there is no universal agreement on where a receivable is located'.

13 *See* Moshinsky, op. cit. (f'note 5), at 607 (citing cases that reflect otherwise *Cammell v Sewell* (1860) 5 H.& N. 728 and *Winkworth v Christie Manson & Woods Ltd.* [1980] Ch. 496); Rogerson, ibid., at 453.

14 Rogerson, op. cit. (f'note 12), at 450.

15 Brussels I Regulation on Jurisdiction and the Recognition and Enforcement of Judgments in Civil and Commercial Matters, Articles 2 and 5(1); Moshinsky, op. cit. (f'note 5), at 607.

16 The Guide has different rules for these. *Lex situs* applies to these but the law of the location of the grantor applies to receivables as pure intangibles. However, there has been criticism, which suggests that the law of the grantor's location should apply to these altogether. *See* Deschamps, in Eidenmüller and Kieninger (eds), op. cit. (f'note 8), at 294 *et seq.*

17 World Bank Report of Working Group on Debtor Creditor Rights, para. 20, 1999.

innovative because their choice-of-laws rules aim to create predictability and, in that sense, some of the rules (e.g. the law of the assignor's State) depart from the anticipated current approach. First, the Guide and the Receivables Convention's connecting factor for intangible assets is the law of the grantor's (assignor) location. However, this has attracted unfair criticism.[18] Second, as part of functionalism, the Guide's choice-of-laws rules apply to both security interests and title-based devices even though they are not governed substantively by the same rules.[19] This is a critical matter because if choice-of-laws rules are broad enough to include both security interests and title-based devices, it will not be necessary to have multiple rules for priority of competing claimants where one is a secured creditor and the other retains title.[20] A functional approach also avoids the risk that the forum has to apply different priority rules and allows predictable results by preventing burdensome enquiries. Thirdly, the Receivables Convention (Article 2(a)) applies to both assignments by way of sale and security. This positively triggers the possibility of the application of Articles 22 and 30[21] that apply to priority disputes where the law of the assignor's location is the connecting factor. Thus, the Convention does not distinguish priority rules between assignment by way of sale and security. Moreover, the formal validity of the assignment under the Receivables Convention is governed by the law of the assignor's location as a condition of priority.[22] This is also reflected under the autonomous choice-of-laws chapter's formal validity of the contract of assignment as between the parties.[23] The Guide adopts a similar rule (Recommendation 208), in which the law of the grantor's location applies to creation, third-party effectiveness and priority issues. Finally, as the Cape Town Convention's subject matter involves mobile assets that move across borders, *lex situs* is not suitable, hence the rejection of the traditional rule and introduction of an international registry and interest.

The particular problem common to most of the above illustrations is the inadequacy of *lex situs* in cross-border transactions. The rule is not useful in the case of intangible property and is problematic in the case of border-crossing mobile

18 This is discussed in more detail below. *See e.g.* Steffens, L. 'The New Rule on the Assignment of rights in Rome I – The Solution to All our Proprietary Problems? – Determination of the Conflict of Laws rule in Respect of the Proprietary Aspects of Assignment', 4 *E.R.P.L.*, 543 (2006); Flessner A. and Verhagen, H. (2006) *Assignment in European Private International Law*. Munich: Sellier; Verhagen, R. (2006) 'Assignment in the Commission's "Rome I Proposal"', *L.M.C.L.Q.*, 270; Financial Markets Law Committee, Issue 121 – European Commission Final Proposal for a Regulation on the Law Applicable to Contractual Obligations ("Rome I") October 2006 and April 2006.

19 Guide, Recommendation 202 and para. 10, at 385. For the Guide's approach to unitary and non-unitary security interests, *see* Chapter 3 and Chapter 7.

20 *See* Deschamps, in Eidenmüller and Kieninger (eds), op. cit. (f'note 8), at 287–8.

21 Article 30 is under Chapter V, the application of which does not depend on the assignor or debtor being located in Contracting States (Articles 26 and 1(4)).

22 Receivables Convention Articles 5(g) and 22.

23 Receivables Convention, Article 27.

property or space objects, particularly in relation to validity of security interests, third-party effectiveness and priority issues.[24]

8.3 The Guide and the Receivables Convention

The Guide's choice-of-laws rules apply to creation, third-party effectiveness, priority and enforcement of security interests and supplement its substantive law rules while determining the territorial scope of application of the Guide's substantive rules.[25] There are several rules for the assets covered under the Guide.[26] The applicability of choice-of-laws recommendations under the Guide is subject to enactment by the Forum State.[27] The Guide's choice-of-laws rules simplify instances of creation and registration of security interests and obtaining priority. Similarly, the Receivables Convention has individual choice-of-laws rules in addition to an autonomous choice-of-laws chapter.

8.3.1 Connecting factors

There are two main connecting factors under the Guide.[28] For tangible assets, the law of the location of the encumbered asset (*lex situs*) and for intangible assets (mostly for receivables), the law of the location of the grantor[29] operate as connecting factors. The rule for tangible assets demonstrates a 'factual relation to the situation to be governed by that law'.[30] The rule for intangibles illustrates the reality that intangibles, particularly receivables, should be governed by the law of the assignor's location to achieve predictability. Two key policy objectives, 'certainty' and 'predictability', are critical in rationalising choice-of-laws rules envisaged under the Guide. The particular concern of an international lender is to make sure that the security interest is validly created, has third-party effectiveness and grants priority rights. As secured transactions laws are deeply rooted in domestic laws, which impede the creation of substantive rules that are generally acceptable by all legal systems, it is necessary to regulate certain aspects through choice-of-laws rules.

24 In relation to the Cape Town Convention, *see e.g.* Gopalan S. (2003) 'Harmonization of Commercial Law: Lessons from the Cape Town Convention on International Interests in Mobile Equipment', 9 *L. & Bus. Rev. Am.*, 255, 257.

25 Guide, para. 2, at 386. Bazinas, S. (2006) 'Modernising and Harmonising Secured Credit Law: the Example of the UNCITRAL Draft Legislative Guide on Secured Transactions, Part 2', *BJIBFL*, 58, at 61.

26 For a general overview, *see e.g.* Machoka, P.M. (2006) 'Towards Financial Sector Development – The Role of the UNCITRAL Guide on Secured Transactions', *JIBLR*, 529, at 534.

27 Guide, para. 3, at 383.

28 There are several exceptions, e.g. Recommendations 204–207, 209, 210–211 and 212–214.

29 This is also adopted as the law of the assignor's State under the Receivables Convention (Article 22 as the law applicable to competing rights).

30 Deschamps, in Eidenmüller and Kieninger (eds), op. cit. (fnote 8), at 287; Beale, Bridge et al., op. cit. (fnote 2), at 686.

8.3.2 The scope of the Guide's choice-of-law rules

The scope of the Guide's choice-of-laws rules on creation, third-party effectiveness and priority is limited to the proprietary aspects of the transaction and does not apply to the mutual rights and obligations of parties to a security agreement.[31] On the other hand, parties' (grantor and secured creditor) mutual rights and obligations in relation to the security interest are governed either by the law chosen by them or, in absence of choice, by the law governing the security agreement.[32] These rights and obligations are governed through party autonomy,[33] as these are contractual in character. This rule is in line with the Rome I Regulation on the Law Applicable to Contractual Obligations.[34]

8.3.3 The Receivables Convention: individual rules and Chapter V

The Receivables Convention contains several choice-of-laws provisions that regulate the rights of the assignee and competing creditors[35] and an autonomous choice-of-laws chapter. Due to great divergences among legal systems on priorities, there was no consensus on a substantive priority rule, which is why the Convention has no substantive rules for the formal validity of the assignment and priority rights.[36] Nevertheless, it is submitted that the Receivables Convention's approach to priorities is commendable as it, at least, achieves a degree of predictability in ascertaining the applicable law to priority among competing creditors by restricting potential jurisdictions, the laws of which might apply to priority disputes and assist the reduction of cost of credit.[37] Similar arguments are equally applicable to the formal validity of assignments. Formal validity of the

31 Guide, para. 12, at 386.

32 Recommendation 216; Guide, para. 61, at 397.

33 On party autonomy and choice-of-laws, *see e.g.* Zhang, M. (2006) 'Party Autonomy and Beyond: An International Perspective of Contractual Choice of Law', 20 *Emory Int'l L. Rev.*, 511, 511; Heiss, H. (2009) 'Party Autonomy', in F. Ferrari and S. Lieble (eds) *Rome I Regulation: The Law Applicable to Contractual Obligations in Europe*. Munich: Sellier, 1.

34 Guide, paras 12 and 61, at 386 and 397. Rome I Regulation Articles 3 (freedom of choice) and 4 (applicable law in the absence of choice). *See e.g.* Tang, Z. 'Law Applicable in the Absence of Choice – The New Article 4 of the Rome I Regulation', 71 *M.L.R.*, 785 (2008); Briggs, A. (2009) 'When in Rome, Choose as the Romans Choose', 125 *L.Q.R.*, 191; Bridge, M. (2009) 'The Proprietary Aspects of Assignment and Choice of Law', *L.Q.R.*, 671.

35 Article 22. This article is subject to Articles 23 and 24 (mandatory law and public policy exceptions and special law on priority in proceeds).

36 United Nations (2004) *The Explanatory Note by the UNCITRAL Secretariat on the United Nations Convention on the Assignment of Receivables in International Trade*, New York: United Nations, at 40 ('Explanatory Note'). It should be noted that the optional annex contains substantive rules, which may be opted in or out.

37 For a similar view, *see* Sigman, H. and Smith, E. (2002) 'Toward Facilitating Cross-Border Secured Financing and Securitization: An Analysis of the United Nations Convention on the Assignment of Receivables in International Trade', 57 *Int'l Law.*, 727, 754. The Factoring Convention has not achieved this predictability, as it has no priority provisions.

assignment is a condition of priority,[38] thus it will also be governed by the law of the assignor's State.

In addition to individual rules, the Receivables Convention contains a comprehensive autonomous choice-of-laws chapter (Chapter V). This chapter was addressed as a 'mini convention'.[39] Chapter V provisions apply to transactions to which the Convention's provisions would not apply due to lack of connection, such as where the assignor or the debtor is located in a non-contracting State or the law governing the receivable is the law of a non-contracting State.[40] Chapter V, in general, governs the form of the contract of assignment (formal requirements for contract will be satisfied by adhering to either the law of the assignor or assignee's location or, if they are located in different States, to the law of either State),[41] the rights and obligations of the assignor and assignee,[42] the assignee and debtor,[43] law applicable to priority[44] and mandatory rules and public policy.[45] Chapter V has been designed to have a gap-filling character and comprehensively deals with two main issues; first, matters within the scope of the Convention where territorial scope is not an issue, in the sense that for the application of this Chapter there is no need for an assignment to be connected to the assignor or the debtor's State and, second, matters within the scope of the Convention but not settled elsewhere in it.[46] Unless the Receivables Convention's general principles resolve a dispute, when the

38 Article 5(g).

39 Walsh, C. (2001) 'Receivables Financing and the Conflict of Laws: The UNCITRAL Draft Convention on the Assignment of Receivables in International Trade', 106 *Dick. L. Rev.*, 159, 164; A/CN.9/466, para. 146: 'from a legislative point . . . it would not be appropriate to attempt, in essence, to prepare a mini private international law convention within a substantive law convention'.

40 Explanatory Note, op. cit. (f'note 36), at 43; Article 1(4). E.g. if the assignor is located in a non-contracting State and the debtor in a contracting State, the rules of Chapter V shall apply.

41 Article 27.

42 Article 28 regulates contractual aspects between the assignor and assignee (mutual rights and obligations of assignor and assignee will be governed by their chosen law and in the absence of choice it will be the law most closely connected to the assignment contract), and is similar to Articles 3(1) and 4(4) of Rome I Regulation. The Receivables Convention includes a separate chapter (Chapter IV) containing default rules (Article 11–14) on mutual rights and obligations of assignor and assignee where party autonomy is allowed by virtue of Article 6 subject to Article 19. UCC §1–301(c) has a liberal approach that the parties to a transaction can choose any law applicable to their transaction, whether or not this law bears any relation to the State designated.

43 Article 29 regulates the relationship between the assignee and debtor (the law applicable to the underlying contract shall determine the assignability of the receivable and the debtor's defences and rights of set-off). The time when the right of set-off is available to the debtor under Article 18 is not covered by the substantive rules and thus Article 29 will be helpful in the determination of the time.

44 Article 30.

45 The applicability of Article 27–29 is subject to mandatory rules and public policy exceptions envisaged under Articles 31–32. The Forum may refuse to apply the law specified under Chapter V if that law is *manifestly contrary* to the public policy of the forum State. The rationale is that the forum must act cautiously before refusing to apply the chosen law.

46 Article 26. For the scope of application, *see* Chapter 3.

assignor or the debtor is located in a contracting State or the law governing the receivable (original contract) is the law of a contracting State, the autonomous choice-of-laws rules will have a gap-filling role.[47] During the preparation phase of the Receivables Convention, Chapter V was rightly criticised, as it was unnecessarily extending and complicating the broad applicability of the Convention.[48] Chapter V is optional and contracting States may opt out of its application under Article 39, which enables States to adopt the Convention without being hindered by the autonomous choice-of-laws rules, as they may be inconsistent with their choice-of-laws rules.[49] Arguably, this certainly will have a positive impact on the future applicability of the Convention.

8.3.4 **Lex situs** ***for tangible assets***

8.3.4.1 General rule

The general rule of *lex situs*[50] (the law of the State in which the encumbered asset is located) is envisaged for tangible assets under recommendation 203 with exceptions.[51] The rule, however, does not distinguish between possessory and non-possessory security interests. This is reflected when an intangible asset is assimilated to a tangible one (e.g. a negotiable instrument) and treated as a tangible asset. In this case, the law of the location of the instrument will govern creation, third-party effectiveness and priority matters.[52] The Guide draws a distinction between pure intangibles and documentary intangible assets (such as bill of lading) that can be subject to possessory security interests, where the latter is treated in the same way as tangibles[53] and *lex situs* (the law of the location of the negotiable instrument) applies.[54]

47 Article 7(2) is the provision in relation to interpretation.

48 Ferrari, F. (2000) 'The UNCITRAL Draft Convention on Assignment in Receivables Financing: Critical Remarks on Some Specific Issues', in J. Basedow, I. Meier, A.K. Schnyder, T. Einhorn and D. Girsberger (eds) *Private Law in the International Arena – Liber Amicorum Kurt Siehr*. The Hague: T.M.C. Asser Press, 181 *et seq.* (criticising Article 1(4)); Bazinas, S. (2002) 'Multi-Jurisdictional Receivables Financing: UNCITRAL's Impact on Securitization and Cross-Border Perfection', 12 *Duke J. Comp. & Int'l L.*, 365, 370 (discussing concerns about the extension of applicability by reference to choice-of-laws rules that are not harmonised.)

49 *See also* Bazinas, S. (2003) 'Key Policy Issues of the United Nations Convention on the Assignment of Receivables in International Trade', 11 *Tul. J. Int'l & Comp. L.*, 275, 298.

50 For the unsuitability of this rule for mobile goods, *see* section 8.4 below, International Interests in Mobile Equipment and Choice-of-Laws.

51 These exceptions are envisaged where the *lex situs* rule would not be sufficient to establish the applicable law. Exceptions include mobile assets and tangible assets subject to specialised registration or notation on a title certificate.

52 Guide, paras 26 and 30, at 388–90.

53 For some supporting English case law, *see e.g. Embiricos v Anglo-Austrian Bank* [1905] 1 KB 677, 683; *Alcock v Smith* [1892] 1 Ch 238.

54 Guide, para 27, at 389. Priority issues between the security interest over the document and the holder of a non-possessory security right over the tangible assets will be governed by the law of the State in which the document is located (Recommendation 206).

Under the Guide, in relation to the law applicable to tangibles, there have been arguments that the application of traditional rule of *lex situs* is not justified as to whether the rights have been validly created, and the 'great advantage of permitting the creation of rights to other rights is that it allows commercial parties freedom of choice'.[55] However, this approach modifies proprietary and contractual rights. Changing the traditional rule of *lex situs* for tangible assets in favour of the law governing the contract, thereby allowing party autonomy to the proprietary aspects of a secured transaction, cannot create correct results. It is unnecessary in cross-border secured transactions to have multiple applicable laws for creation and third-party effectiveness of security interests.[56] Distinct treatment of security interests involving outright transfer of ownership where *lex situs* is the governing law and transfer for security purposes where it is not, involves the risk of contradiction with the international instruments that treat outright and security transfers the same for the purposes of perfection and priorities but differently for enforcement purposes.[57] Moreover, choosing the law applicable to priority through party autonomy has the risk of creating unfairness against third parties who are not in privy,[58] as well as being incompatible with the key objectives of certainty and predictability enshrined in international instruments. This argument equally applies to intangibles (particularly receivables).

For tangible assets in transit and export goods, the Guide contains additional rules for creation and third-party effectiveness of security interests.[59] The Guide supports the approach that creation and third-party effectiveness of goods in transit and export goods will either take place at the original location (location of the asset at the time of creation of security interest – recommendation 203) or provided that the asset reaches within a prescribed period to the ultimate location (destination) under the law of the ultimate location.[60] Recommendation 207 seems to present a part autonomy option in the determination of the applicable law to the proprietary aspects. The particular issue in relation to these assets is that the priority of competing claimants will be subject to the law of the location of the goods at the time priority disputes arise, hence there is no need for an additional rule.[61]

The Guide contains special rules for creation, third-party effectiveness and priority of a security interest in a negotiable instrument. The law of the location of the negotiable instrument governs creation, third-party effectiveness and the priority of a security interest (Recommendation 203). However, for the purposes

55 R. Stevens, (2008) 'Choosing the Right Approach for European Law Making', in Eidenmüller and Kieninger (eds) op. cit. (f'note 1), 83, at 96 (citing *Re Harvard Securities Ltd* [1997] 2 BCLC 369 (Neuberger J)).

56 Beale, H. (2008) 'The Future of Secured Credit in Europe: Concluding Remarks', in Eidenmüller and Kieninger (eds) op. cit. (f'note 1), 375, at 378–9.

57 E.g. the Guide and the Receivables Convention treat outright and security assignments alike.

58 Deschamps, in Eidenmüller and Kieninger (eds), op. cit. (f'note 8), 285 *et seq.*

59 Guide, paras 31–33, at 390.

60 Guide, Recommendation 207; Bazinas, op. cit. (f'note 25), at 61. Kreuzer indicates that a number of conditions need to be met for the proper applicability of the law of the destination to export goods rule. *See* Kreuzer, in Eidenmüller and Kieninger op. cit. (f'note 1), at 313–14.

61 Guide, para. 33, at 390.

of achieving third-party effectiveness only, if registration is a requirement to achieve third-party effectiveness in the grantor's State, the law of the grantor's location will govern third-party effectiveness so as to determine this is achieved through registration (Recommendation 211). Notwithstanding with this rule, *lex situs* will continue to be applicable law for creation and obtaining priority.

It seems that English secured credit law takes a similar approach in tangible assets. For tangible movables, the *lex situs* is the connecting factor[62] for the proprietary validity, though there are exceptions.[63] The creation of a security interest on tangible property (the distinction, here, is made between possessory and non-possessory security interests – on intangible property – where the latter is mainly governed by the Rome I Regulation) is governed by the *lex situs* of the movable.[64] Third-party effectiveness (perfection) of security interests, depending on the perfection method (possession or registration), is governed either by *lex situs* (in the case of perfection by possession whether possession has been transferred or retained) or in the case of perfection by registration, the law of the location of tangible property[65] or, for intangibles, the law governing the proprietary right for intangible property.[66] The Companies Act 2006 s. 860 requires that certain charges have to be registered[67] (in the chargor's location) in order to have third-party effectiveness, including towards liquidators, insolvency administrators and company creditors.[68] The rule supersedes *lex situs* for tangible movables as the

62 *See e.g. Cammell v Sewell* (1858) 3 H & N 617, *affd* (1860) 5 H & N 728 (Exch Ch); *Winkworth v Christie Manson & Woods Ltd.* [1980] Ch 496; *Glencore International AG v Metro Trading Inc. (No. 2)* [2001] 1 Lloyd's Rep. 284; *Air Foyle Ltd v Center Capital Ltd* [2002] EWHC 2535 at [42]; *Kuwait Airways Corpn v Iraqi Airways Co (Nos 4 and 5)* [2003] 2 Lloyd's Rep 753, [2002] 2 AC 883, [2002] UKHL 19 at [13] and [161]. For an overview of conflict-of-laws rules on secured transactions in England, and particularly for tangible movable property, *see e.g.* Stevens, R. (2001) 'The English Conflict of Laws Rules', in M. Bridge and R. Stevens (eds) *Cross Border Security and Insolvency*. Oxford: Oxford University Press, 205, at 210 *et seq.*; *see also* Beale, Bridge *et al.*, op. cit. (f'note 2), 683 *et seq.*

63 The rule in *Winkworth* has exceptions. Generally, exceptions to the *lex situs* rule are movables in transit (the law of the transfer may be the appropriate applicable law), acquirer not in good faith, public policy (in the last two exceptions either the law of the transfer or the law of the forum applies), statutory provisions of the forum State cannot be overridden and general assignment of movables arising on bankruptcy or succession. *See* Beale, Bridge *et al.*, op cit (f'note 2), at 687 *et seq.*

64 Beale, Bridge *et al.*, op. cit. (f'note 2), 707 *et seq.*

65 Professor Bridge makes a suggestion, similar to Recommendation 45 of the Guide, that when the tangible property moves to another jurisdiction, after a grace period from the arrival of the tangible property to the new jurisdiction, English courts should recognise the invalidity of the security for failure to comply with the registration requirements of the new jurisdiction. *See* Beale, Bridge *et al.*, op. cit. (f'note 2), 711.

66 Beale, Bridge *et al.*, op. cit. (f'note 2), 709–10, para. 20.62; but *cf.* Moshinsky, op. cit. (f'note 5), at 617, where he suggests that in the case of receivables the law of the assignor's place of business should govern.

67 Section 860(7) CA 2006. Section 860 has extraterritoriality as demonstrated by s. 866 CA 2006.

68 The charge may be retrospectively registrable if an overseas company has no assets in England at the time of granting charge and subsequently obtains assets beyond the 21-day period. *NV Slavenburg's Bank v Intercontinental Natural Resources Ltd* [1980] 1 All E.R. 955. However, the outcome of this decision has been abolished by the Overseas Companies Regulations 2009, which came into force on 1 October.

charge over the movable needs to be registered regardless of the location of the movable (i.e. even if the movable is not located in England). In relation to receivables, s. 860 seems to be consistent with the Rome I Regulation Article 14. The latter, like Rome Convention Article 12, does not address third-party effectiveness in the assignment of receivables by way of security; thus, the application of the law of the assignor's location seems appropriate.[69] A similar argument applies equally in relation to the Receivables Convention, which suggests the approach of the law of assignor's location, that is, the assignor's place of business (the central administration in the case of multiple places of business). The priority of tangible movables is determined by the *lex fori*; however, in accordance with *Macmillan Inc v Bishopsgate Investment Trust plc (No 3)*,[70] the applicable law may be *lex situs*.[71] Professor Bridge rightly suggests that the application of *lex situs* in a successive assignment of tangible movables enables the first transferee to avoid the risk of the transferor in possession to move the assets to another country and, in the case of a priority conflict involving a transferee and owner who has acquired movables bona fide, the *lex situs* provides a fair solution.[72] If there is a priority agreement between secured creditors, the priority will be governed by the law chosen in the contract and, in the absence of choice, the characteristic performance (in this case it is the place of business of the creditor that gave up priority status) of the contract will govern.[73]

On the other hand, the UCC Article 9 departs from the *lex situs* rule in favour of the application of the law of the location of debtor (grantor/assignor) in the determination of the law governing perfection[74] and priority of security

69 For a similar view, *see generally* Beale, Bridge *et al.*, op. cit. (f'note 2), at 711–2; Bridge, op. cit. (f'note 34), 696; Struycken, T.H.D. (1998) 'The Proprietary Aspects of International Assignment of Debts and the Rome Convention, Article 12', *L.M.C.L.Q.*, 345, 359; *Re Oriel Ltd.* [1986] 1 W.L.R. 180 (C.A.). However, it should be noted that under the Rome I Regulation Article 19(1) the habitual residence of a company is the place of central administration.

70 [1996] 1 WLR 387.

71 Stevens, in Bridge and Stevens (eds), op. cit. (f'note 62), at 211–3 arguing that there may be difficulties with the *lex situs* in mobile equipment and ascertaining the scope of foreign law. Stevens also correctly argues that the *lex fori* leads to forum shopping issues in order to obtain advantageous priority rules. It can be argued that forum shopping in priority rules may be detrimental to third party rights, thus *lex fori* does not represent a correct approach.

72 Beale, Bridge *et al.*, op. cit. (f'note 2), at 729.

73 Beale, Bridge *et al.*, op. cit. (f'note 2), at 729.

74 For an in-depth analysis, *see e.g.* McCormack, G. (2004) *Secured Credit Law under English and American Law*. Cambridge: Cambridge University Press, 76 *et seq.* Some security interests under the UCC are perfected upon attachment (UCC §9–308(a) and 309), by filing (registration) (UCC §9–310), by delivery of possession (UCC §9–313) and by control (UCC §9–314). The registration feature of UCC Article 9 for perfection of security interests may have a negative impact on certain parties that do not have the sophistication to check the registry to ascertain whether there is any previous security interest over the same asset. However, this may not be a valid argument for parties that deal with high value mobile equipment, as these parties have the necessary legal knowledge of the sector and rules. UNIDROIT Study LXXII-Doc. 1, at 27 (1989) and *see also* below, the discussion on the Cape Town Convention, under which an international registry is a key feature. For more discussion on perfection, *see* Chapter 5.

interests.[75] However, to the extent that the collateral is tangible (e.g. negotiable document or chattel paper), the law of the location of the collateral (*lex situs*) applies.[76] This leads to two different laws being applicable to perfection (law of the debtor's location)[77] and to priority (*lex situs*) for certain types of collateral.[78]

It is arguable that the rules in international instruments demonstrate similarity to modern secured transactions regimes. The connecting factor for intangibles is similar to the rule under UCC Article 9. The rule departs from the traditional *lex situs* approach and the law of the location of the debtor governs perfection by registration, its effects and priority matters (UCC §9–301(1)), as opposed to the law of the location of the asset at the date the security interest is created (i.e. *lex situs*).[79] Professor Beale argues that the rule '. . . avoids many of the problems of re-registration within "grace periods" when goods are moved from one jurisdiction to another'.[80]

8.3.4.2 Exceptions

There are two exceptions to *lex situs* under the Guide. In the following two exceptions the law of the origin applies in order to avoid applying multiple laws to assets that move across borders to re-establish third-party effectiveness and priority status. Commentators have correctly argued that these exceptions aim to establish automatic recognition of a security interest's priority and third-party effectiveness in a foreign country by presupposing both the uniformity of choice-of-law rules under the Guide's recommendations and of substantive rules applicable to security interests.[81] The application of the law of origin can only be feasible, first, when

75 UCC §9–301(1); UNIDROIT Study LXXII-Doc. 1, at 27 (1989).

76 UCC §9–301(3).

77 Under UCC Article 9 there is a unified single filing rule, according to which the secured creditor files only one financing statement, which combines local and state filings. The same rules determine the filing jurisdiction and perfection requirements. *See* Cohen N.B. and Smith, E.E. (1999) 'International Secured Transactions and Revised UCC Article 9', 74 *Chi-Kent L. Rev.*, 1191, 1200 *et seq.* Professor Mooney argues that the application of the location of debtor (assignor/grantor) rule reduces the burden of filing statements in multiple states. In particular, the significance of the rule may be felt if the debtor's assets are abroad, in which case it is sensible to look at one certain, single location (i.e. the location of the debtor). *See* Mooney, C. (2001) 'Extraterritorial Impact of Choice of Law Rules for Non-United States Debtors under Revised Uniform Commercial Code Article 9 and a New Proposal for International Harmonisation', in M. Bridge and R. Stevens (eds) *Cross Border Security and Insolvency*. Oxford: Oxford University Press, 187, at 198.

78 For further information, *see also* Sepinuck, S.L. (2008) *Practice under Article 9 of the Uniform Commercial Code*. American Bar Association, 95 *et seq.*

79 But *cf.* UCC §9–301(3).

80 *See* Beale, op. cit. (f'note 56), at 395. Creation of a security interest (attachment under the UCC Article 9) is not addressed under Part 3 of the UCC; as all states adopted Article 9, there is no need to have a particular choice-of-laws rule for the *inter partes* effectiveness. This is left to UCC Article 1–105(1), where this section determines the applicable law governing a UCC transaction. *See* Cohen and Smith, ibid., 1221 *et seq.*

81 *See e.g.* Kreuzer, in Eidenmüller and Kieninger, op. cit. (f'note 1), at 313.

the forum or the *situs* of the asset applies the law of the origin and, second, the forum or the *situs* of the asset recognises the security interest created under the law of the origin as it is.[82]

First, mobile assets by their nature cannot be subject to *lex situs*.[83] If *lex situs* applies, the secured creditor will be forced to complete relevant requirements for third-party effectiveness of each country to which the goods move. Furthermore, as there is the risk of movement of goods, the secured creditor may not be certain in advance on the law applicable to priority of claims.[84] In that context, the application of the location of the grantor's law to creation, third-party effectiveness and priority of security interests serves for certainty and predictability.

Second, if ownership of mobile assets is registered to a specialised registry (such as aircraft or motor vehicles), and to the extent that this registry permits the registration of security interests, the law of the State that maintains the specialised registry shall govern creation, third-party effectiveness and priority of a security interest.[85] Although the 'rule takes precedence over the mobile goods rule and is aimed at ensuring that the same law [governs] an absolute transfer of ownership of and a security right in the asset',[86] there are some concerns with regard to its clarity, namely, that the Guide only deals with security interests as opposed to ownership issues. It may rarely be the case that the choice-of-law rules of third States point to the State where the registry is located for ownership and, as this exception applies to mobile goods to which the location of the grantor applies, the location of the grantor must be different from the location of the registry, since third parties first search the location of the grantor.[87]

8.3.5 Law of the grantor's (assignor's) location and other alternatives

8.3.5.1 The law of the grantor's (assignor's) location

The law of the grantor's (assignor's) State is the second main connecting factor under the Guide. This rule is particularly applicable to receivables as opposed to other intangibles (such as bank deposits and proceeds from letters of credit) as the Guide contains different rules for the latter. The Receivables Convention, too,

82 Ibid., at 313.
83 For more information on the unsuitability of *lex situs*, *see* the discussion on the Cape Town Convention below.
84 *See also* Deschamps, in Eidenmüller and Kieninger (eds), op. cit. (f'note 7), at 292.
85 Recommendations 204 and 205.
86 Deschamps, in Eidenmüller and Kieninger (eds), op. cit. (f'note 7), at 292.
87 Deschamps, in Eidenmüller and Kieninger (eds), op. cit. (f'note 7), at 292, where it is also argued that the adoption of the Cape Town Convention may enable the disclosure of ownership and security interests over mobile assets by introducing the international registry.

adopts this rule according to which formal validity of assignments and priority disputes[88] are subject to the law of the assignor's State (location).[89]

The law of the assignor's State provides an efficient and predictable connecting factor for assignment of future and bulk receivables. It has undisputable significance in the context of proprietary aspects of assignment of receivables. It is a pragmatic property-based approach in cross-border assignment of receivables transactions.[90] The connecting factor provides more predictable results than the application of *lex situs,* the place of payment of receivables or the law of the location of the debtor of the receivable by providing a single point of reference. The Receivables Convention's approach in that sense aims to establish a transparent system through publicity (registration) that enables access to low-cost credit and protects all participants to a financial transaction.[91] The effect of assignment on third parties is measured through priority and the law of the assignor's location (the actual centre of administration) provides a suitable method to achieve certainty.[92] The law of the assignor's location is ascertainable at the time of the contract of assignment, even when the debt has not yet come into existence (future receivables). In the case of bulk receivables the assignee will not be required to do extensive due diligence to ascertain what the applicable law is in relation to priorities. If there is a requirement for registration of the assignment, the connecting factor provides a single and determinable location for assignees to search at the assignor's place of business to determine whether there is a prior assignment of the same receivables.[93] Particularly at the time of the assignment of future receivables, the debtor is unknown but the assignor's location is ascertainable. In securitisation, where a pool of future receivables is assigned to a special purpose vehicle,

88 Receivables Convention Articles 22 and 29 governing priority. Priority is defined under Receivables Convention Article 5(g) and includes third-party effectiveness, publicity and the formal validity (effectiveness as between parties) of assignment. It is important to note that if the assignor's law has modern rules, there will be certainty. A/CN.9/489/Add.1, para. 34. Arguably, the optional substantive priority rules of the Receivables Convention guarantee modernisation of domestic substantive priority rules. For a detailed discussion, with comparisons to a number of instruments and jurisdictions, *see* Sigman, H. and Kieninger, E-M. (2009) *Cross-Border Security Over Receivables*. Munich: Sellier, 60 *et seq.*

89 For the discussion of the meaning of location, *see below*. It is sufficient here to indicate that location is understood as the assignor's place of business.

90 The Guide (recommendation 2) and the Receivables Convention (Article 4(2)) mainly apply to trade receivables; under the Guide there are exceptions for security interests in bank deposits and proceeds from letters of credit and they do not apply to intellectual property rights and securities.

91 *See generally* the Preamble of the Receivables Convention.

92 Walsh, op. cit. (f'note 39), 176.

93 A/CN.9/397, para.41; for a similar view in relation to the applicability of the law of assignor's location, *see* Moshinsky, op. cit. (f'note 5), at 611. For example, under UCC §9–301(1), for perfection the security interests must be registered at the location of the debtor (assignor). *See also* Professor Mooney's arguments, op. cit. (f'note 77). Registration is not the pre-condition of the law of the assignor's location. For example, under the Receivables Convention, registration is not a requirement but is only suggested under Article 42(4). Furthermore, traditional civil law jurisdictions such as Belgium and Luxembourg have adopted the law of the assignor's location approach for securitisation transactions. The Law Commission for England and Wales also recommended establishing a priority scheme inspired by UCC Article 9. *See* Law Commission Report No. 296, at 30 (2005).

the application of *lex situs* as the governing law for priority disputes[94] cannot provide efficient results.[95] First, there may be different priority rules applicable to numerous future receivables, which may be impossible for the assignee to ascertain the applicable law to priorities. The choice-of-laws approach for priorities in the Receivables Convention Article 22 permits the domestic law of the assignor's State to determine whether the assignee has a proprietary or contractual right and whether the transaction is an outright assignment or assignment by way of security.[96] The Receivables Convention under Article 2(a) covers the assignment both by way of sale and security.[97] Third parties can identify the applicable law efficiently. The rationale is the expectation that competing claimants,[98] subsequent assignees, assignor's creditors and the insolvency administrator (the group of people who are concerned with the assignment and proprietary aspects) can make enquiries at the location of the assignor's wealth as to whether the assignor is solvent and could be sued. This is a favourable approach as it leaves characterisation to states and achieves results that could not have been achieved through a substantive rule as it might have imposed a stricter rule. Second, as the debtor is unknown at the time of assignment, subjecting the assignee to an unknown law would go against the fundamental principle of certainty and may increase the cost of credit. Third, when multiple debts are owed by debtors located in various jurisdictions, *lex situs* (payment place of the receivable or the location of the debtor) will suggest that the assignee has to meet the requirements of all of these jurisdictions, hence the significance of the law of the assignor's location.[99] Deschamps correctly argues that a single law such as *lex situs* cannot apply to bulk assignment of present and future receivables unless they have the same location.[100] As future receivables come into existence

94 Priority disputes are normally governed by *lex situs*. A/CN.9/489/Add.1, para. 30.

95 But *cf*, Bridge, M. (2001) 'English Conflicts Rules for Transfers of Movables: A Contract-based Approach?', in M. Bridge and R. Stevens (eds) *Cross Border Security and Insolvency*. Oxford: Oxford University Press, 123, at 126, where he argues that the place where the debtor resides is considered to be the place where the debt exists, the law of which may be beneficial for asset financiers when they establish an SPV in securitisation transactions by providing consistency.

96 Sigman and Smith, op. cit. (f'note 37), 754. Receivables Convention Article 5(i) refers to the substantive law in force in a state other than its rules of private international law.

97 For a suggestion on the same direction, *see also* Struycken, op. cit. (f'note 69), at 357. The concept of assignment under the Rome I Regulation covers both the outright and security assignments (Article 14(3)).

98 For a definition of 'competing claimant', *see* Receivables Convention Article 5(m).

99 For a similar view, *see* Moshinsky, op. cit. (f'note 5), at 611.

100 Deschamps, in Eidenmüller and Kieninger (eds), op. cit. (f'note 7), at 293. But *cf.* Verhagen, op. cit. (f'note 18), 274, arguing that at the time of assignment of bulk and future receivables, the law of the assigned receivables will be clear and, thus, should be applicable as opposed to the law of the assignor's location. However, the law of the assigned receivables may not have the necessary rules that protect the priority position of the assignee, which increases the cost of credit. Professor Verhagen's arguments are supported by Professor Flessner, who suggests that priority should be determined by the *situs* of the receivable at the '*time of the transaction*'. *See* Flessner, A. (2008) 'Security Interests in Receivables – A European Perspective', in Eidenmüller and Kieninger (eds), op. cit. (f'note 1), 336, at 345. Receivables cannot have a natural *situs* and this suggestion arguably only serves to further complicate the determination of priority.

after the time of the conclusion of the assignment contract, in the above example, the assignee has to meet the requirements of different laws, which contains the risk of increasing the cost of credit. In the case of assignment of bulk receivables, the assignee is not in a position to check each assignment to see which law applies, thus the law of the assignor's State facilitates access to credit by reducing burdensome administrative matters. Finally, the application of the law of the grantor's State (assignor's central administration) has the advantage of being the law of the State where the insolvency proceedings against the grantor are to be administered.[101] The significance of this approach is that when the assignor and assignee choose the law applicable to assignment[102] that law applies to the insolvency. This law may not be recognised by the insolvency forum on the basis of public policy. Thus, the application of the law of the assignor's state provides predictability and avoids non-recognition of the applicable law.

The location of intangibles, particularly the receivables, is extremely difficult to ascertain and any fictitious attribution of location is not significantly helpful in cross-border credit transactions.[103] The law of the grantor's State provides a single and predictable rule. Even if an assignment transaction involves multiple debtors and receivables, there will be only one assignor and thus, predictability will be achieved by subjecting creation, third-party effectiveness and priority rules to one law. There are various approaches, such as the law of the place where payment is to be made, the domicile of the creditor (owner of the debt),[104] the business place of the debtor of the receivable,[105] or the place referred to by the law governing the debt.[106] The place of the business of the debtor and the place of payment may not be clear and definition of location needs to be established precisely. Both

101 Guide, para. 41, at 393; *see below* (f'note 139 and accompanying text). For some interesting discussion on the possibility of manipulability of the 'centre of main interest (COMI)' under the European Insolvency Regulation, *see* McCormack, G. (2009) 'Jurisdictional Competition and Forum Shopping in Insolvency Proceedings', 68 *CLJ* 169, 185 *et seq*. For suggestions to make the habitual residence definitive so that it coincides with the COMI, *see* Alferez, F.J.G. (2009) 'Assignment of Claims in the Rome I Regulation: Article 14', in F. Ferrari and S. Lieble (eds) *Rome I Regulation The Law Applicable to Contractual Obligations in Europe*. Munich: Sellier, 217, 248.

102 They may choose a law that is favourable to the assignee upon subjecting credit to the choice of favourable law.

103 For criticism of attribution of location to intangibles, *see* Rogerson, op. cit. (f'note 12), 442, 453 *et seq*.

104 *Lex domicilii*. This is an unsatisfactory connecting factor for commercial and international transactions and its use is limited to bulk assignments of 'assets on death, marriage and bankruptcy'. *See* Moshinsky, op. cit. (f'note 5), at 591.

105 Guide, para. 42, at 393. *See also* Rogerson, op. cit. (f'note 12), at 442–3; *see e.g. New York Life Insurance Co v Public Trustee* [1924] 2 Ch 101; companies with multiple locations, *F. & K. Jabbour v Custodian of Israeli Absentee Property* [1954] 1 WLR 139; 1 All E.R. 145. This may also be called the law of the place where the debtor resides. *Commissioner of Stamps v Hope* [1891] A.C. 476, 481, where the rationale of choosing the law of the location of the debtor as the *situs* is that recovery of monies from the debtor can take place at the personal residence of the debtor, where his assets are located.

106 *Joachimson v Swiss Bank Corporation* [1921] 3 KB 110.

approaches have the risk of increasing the cost of credit by imposing upon the assignee the unnecessary burden of investigation, the cost of which may be reflected in the interest rate applied on the credit. Thus, application of *lex situs* for intangibles may be unfeasible; hence the necessary promotion of the law of the assignor's State in the assignment of receivables.

Some commentators argue that the Receivables Convention's connecting factor for priority disputes (the law of the assignor's location) mainly suits jurisdictions with registration requirements[107] and 'prioritises the interests of assignees at the expense of debtors'.[108] The argument is that the Principles of European Contract Law (PECL) serves better for European systems as, unlike the Receivables Convention, the PECL has rules for third-party effectiveness that do not require registration of assignment for third-party effectiveness, and for priority disputes the PECL relies on notification of debtor.[109] This argument sets forth that if parties are free to choose the applicable law under which the security interest is granted, the priority rule can be determined by the law under which the second interest is granted.[110] A critical review of this argument may establish the unfeasibility and the high cost of notification of debtors in the assignment of future and bulk receivables. What is more important is that the proprietary aspect of assignments is irrelevant to debtors. For instance, under English law proprietary aspects of assignments can be seen in the effectiveness of an assignment between the assignor and assignee, third-party effectiveness of assignees' rights against assignor's creditors, liquidator or insolvency representative and priority between competing assignees.[111] The debtor is, in any case, protected by the law governing the assigned receivables. Professor Beale correctly argues that the critiques' solution does not seem to be workable, as

> it might cause considerable anxiety to first secured parties who, although they had done all they could to secure priority under the law under which they had taken their interests, would be at risk of being displaced by a provision of some other, as yet unknown, law.[112]

107 *See generally e.g.* Flessner, in Eidenmüller and Kieninger (eds), op. cit. (f'note 100), 336 *et seq.*; Steffens, L. (2006) 'The New Rule on the Assignment of Rights in Rome I – The Solution to All our Proprietary Problems? – Determination of the Conflict of Laws Rule in Respect of the Proprietary Aspects of Assignment', 4 *E.R.P.L.*, 543; Perkins, J. (2008) 'A Question of Priorities: Choice of Law and Proprietary Aspects of the Assignment of Debts', 2 *L. & F.M.R.*, 238, 240.

108 Perkins, ibid., at 240.

109 E.g. Flessner, in Eidenmüller and Kieninger (eds), op. cit. (f'note 100), 339. PECL is only a general set of contractual principles. Lando, O. (1998) 'Principles of European Contract Law in the Third Millennium', in Centre for Transnational Law (ed.), *Transnational Law in Commercial Legal Practice*. Centre for Transnational Law, at 76. However, the PECL does not have a universal significance and as it is a first draft there will be further changes. *See* Bergsten, E. (2006) 'Foreword', in J. Felemegas (ed.) *An International Approach to the Interpretation of the United Nations Convention on Contract for the International Sale of Goods (1980) as Uniform Sales Law*. Cambridge: Cambridge University Press, at xi.

110 Beale (summarising Flessner's argument) op. cit. (f'note 56), at 378–9 and fn. 19. *See* ibid., at 344–5. *See also* Flessner and Verhagen, op. cit. (f'note 18), 32–6.

111 *See* Bridge, op. cit. (f'note 34), at 687–8.

112 Beale, op. cit. (f'note 56), in Eidenmüller and Kieninger (eds), at 378–9 and fn. 19.

Complementing Professor Beale's argument, it is submitted that the suggested approach by commentators is too complicated to create predictability and presumes that all states have a similar approach to priority disputes. The primary reason for taking security is to ensure that the secured creditor has a priority right and will be recouped. Why would a financier risk extending credit if the law applicable to priority would be unknown in advance and *forum shopping* was allowed, granting better priority rights and adversely affecting the third parties?

The concern with respect to the insolvency of an assignor whose inefficient law applies to the secured transaction and insolvency process seems to be unnecessary. The concern is understandable where the assignee wishes to apply its law and may suggest that the assignor set a company in the assignee's country so that domestic insolvency law of the assignee's state applies. However, this is unnecessary. Arguably, the implementation of international instruments, which are mostly based on similar rules to modern secured transactions regimes, is expected to modernise developing economies' secured transactions laws. Since assignors are often from emerging economies that are in need of low-cost credit, the application of the law of the assignor (assuming the assignor's country adopts international instruments) seems to correspond with the expectations of assignees and other financiers. It is argued that the Legislative Guide in particular will have the necessary merits to achieve overall modernisation and to meet expectations.

8.3.5.2 The law of the assigned receivable

As an alternative, the law governing the assigned receivables (the law governing the original contract from which the receivable arises) may be used as a connecting factor.[113] In *Raffeisen Zentralbank Österreich AG v Five Star General Trading LLC*[114] it was held that contractual and proprietary aspects of the assignment could not be distinguished and the assignment was within the scope of Article 12(2), according to which the law of the receivables governed the proprietary aspects of assignment (in this case, to whom the debtor must pay). The advantage of this approach is, first, that creation, third-party effectiveness and priority of a security interest will be governed by the same applicable law that applies to effects of the security interest against the debtor. Second, in terms of validity of an assignment made notwithstanding anti-assignment, application of the law of receivables prevents a situation where a different law enables the creation of a security right over the receivables or permits the assignability of the receivable. Third, the risk that the

113 *See e.g.* Moshinsky, op. cit. (f'note 5), at 610 discussing the unsuitability of the law governing the receivables. Rome I Regulation Article 14(2) deals with the law governing the assigned receivables, according to which assignability, the relationship between the assignee and debtor, conditions to invoke an assignment against the debtor and the discharge of debtor's obligations. For a discussion of Rome Convention, *see* Bridge, op. cit. (f'note 95), 140–2.

114 [2001] 3 All ER 257. The decision is the central authority on the choice-of-law rules for assignment of receivables in England by interpreting Rome Convention Article 12.

grantor may be relocated and make subsequent assignments is prevented by this approach.[115]

However, the law governing the receivables has several serious drawbacks. First, although the law governing receivables may be perfectly acceptable for the assignment of a single receivable or financial contracts, receivables arising from securities, swap agreements, claims arising from bank accounts and foreign exchange transactions,[116] in the assignment of bulk receivables it proves to be burdensome for the assignee to check each document to ascertain whether the receivable is assignable. Furthermore, as all receivables of the assignor cannot have the same *situs* (e.g. the assignor's receivables originate from different countries with varying laws), the assignee will be forced to conduct due diligence, upon which the cost of credit will increase.[117] Second, it can be submitted that application of different laws to the validity and priority of an assignment causes inconvenience for the assignee. The assignee may be required to fulfil formal requirements for multiple legal systems.[118] Third, it is arguable that allowing party autonomy (the possibility that the debtor and assignor choose a law that may be disadvantageous for the assignee) for property aspects of an assignment,[119] and to govern priority of competing assignees, cannot provide correct results. This has the risk of increasing the cost of credit for assignors, despite the possibility that assignees may subject credit

115 Guide, para. 44, at 393–4.

116 The Receivables Convention Article 4(2) and the Guide recommendation 4(c)–(e) exclude these transactions and receivables from their scope. The rationale of the Rome I Regulation excluding the law of the assignor's location was the concern that it was unsuitable in the context of high value single receivables transactions. However, it should be noted that by 17 June 2010, according to Rome I Regulation Article 27, the Commission will submit a review of the provision on assignment and subrogation, and it is hoped that the law of the assignor location may be included in Article 14 so that this provision becomes more compatible with the Receivables Convention and the Guide. The Guide applies the law governing receivables to the right to payment of funds credited to a bank account (recommendation 210B). For some suggestions and brief overview, *see* Walsh, C. 'Security Interests in Receivables', in Eidenmüller and Kieninger (eds) op. cit. (f'note 1), 321, 333–4.

117 This is particularly the case in jurisdictions where assignment by way of security is not required to be registered, but when the law of the assigned receivable, which requires registration, governs this assignment, the assignee will not be able to verify whether the assignor is the owner of the receivable. This is an example of the significance of the registration and publicity requirements in lowering the cost. For more discussion, *see* Krupski, J. (2007) 'Cross-Border Receivables Financing at the Crossroads of Legal Traditions, Capital Markets, Uniform Law and Modernity', *Unif. L. Rev.*, 57, at 83–4.

118 For a similar argument, *see* Struycken, T.H.D. and Stevens, R. (2002) 'Assignment and the Rome Convention', *L.Q.R.*, 15, 19; for similar arguments pointing out the disadvantages of the law governing the receivable, *see* Deschamps, in Eidenmüller and Kieninger (eds), op. cit. (f'note 7), at 293.

119 It is established that the proprietary aspects of assignment are outside the scope of Rome I Regulation. This includes priority involving third parties. For the Rome Convention (which is almost identical to the Rome I Regulation), *see e.g.* Goode, R. (2004) *Commercial Law*, 3rd edn., London: Butterworths, 1111; but *cf.* Stevens, in M. Bridge and R. Stevens (eds), op. cit. (f'note 62), 214.

to the selection of favourable law.[120] Under Receivables Convention Article 6, party autonomy is subject to two strict conditions. The chosen law by the assignor and assignee by derogating from or varying by agreement the provisions of the Convention cannot adversely affect the rights of third parties and force the debtor to waive certain defences. Pure party autonomy cannot allow third parties or the debtor to be informed about their rights. Furthermore, unlike the law of the assignor's location, which is a neutral location, the assignee's imposition of a favourable law may have adverse effects on the assignor's other creditors and subsequent assignees. Fourthly, the law of the receivable 'exposes retrospective assignees to the burden of having to determine the notional *situs* of each receivable separately'.[121] In bulk assignments the assignee will not be able to ascertain the governing law of receivable to decide the law governing priorities, as this will take considerable time, and be impractical. Finally, in the assignment of future receivables the assignment transaction is concluded before the original contract from which the receivables arise. Therefore, it is not possible for the assignee to ascertain which law shall apply, because the *situs* of receivables is unidentifiable[122] and the assignee may often have no means to identify the applicable law in advance. The cost of credit may increase for the assignee who wishes to ascertain in advance the applicable law or the requirements to be met.[123] Some commentators argue that the law governing the assigned receivable (the law chosen between the assignor and debtor) is more suitable as a choice-of-law rule and that the law of the assignor's location ignores the debtor protection rule and, therefore, is inconsistent with party autonomy.[124] Debtor protection is, naturally, critical in assignment transactions and the Receivables Convention adopts debtor protection as a principle. However, the debtor has no interest in third-party effectiveness, priority of an assignee against competing creditors or the creation of a security interest.[125] Rules governing debtor protection and third-party effectiveness are separate. Thus, subjecting third-party effectiveness matters to the law of the assignor's location and the debtor protection issues to the law of the assigned receivable will only lead to the increased cost of credit and due diligence.[126] It is arguable that party autonomy is inconsistent with

120 The inequality of bargaining position in this example is evident.

121 A/CN.9/489/Add.1, para. 30.

122 For arguments against attributing a *situs* to receivables and in favour of the law of the assignor's location, *see* Deschamps, M. (2002) 'The Priority Rules of the United Nations Receivables Convention', 12 *Duke J. Comp. & Int'l L.*, 389, 393–394.

123 A/CN.9/489/Add.1, para. 30.

124 Financial Markets Law Committee, Issue 121 – European Commission Final Proposal for a Regulation on the Law Applicable to Contractual Obligations ('Rome I'), at 5 (October 2006); Financial Markets Law Committee, Issue 121 – European Commission Final Proposal for a Regulation on the Law Applicable to Contractual Obligations ('Rome I'), at 21 (April 2006); Perkins, op. cit. (f'note 107), 241 *et seq*; Flessner and Verhagen, op. cit. (f'note 18), 21 *et seq.*, (arguing that party autonomy provides certainty for the parties as to the applicable law).

125 For similar views, *see* Walsh, in Eidenmüller and Kieninger (eds), op. cit. (f'note 116), at 334; Bridge, op. cit. (f'note 34), at 696–7; Krupski, op. cit. (f'note 117), at 77.

126 For a similar argument, *see* Sigman and Kieninger, op. cit. (f'note 88), 61, fn. 187.

proprietary aspects of the assignment of receivables.[127] Proprietary aspects of assignment affect third party rights. Therefore, party autonomy and the application of the law governing the receivable should not be allowed. Professor Walsh argues that the rationale for incorporating the law of the assigned receivable is to allow the assignee to subject the extension of credit to the assignor by forcing the assignor to choose a law in the agreement with the debtor that is more favourable to the assignee.[128] This argument illustrates that the law of the assigned receivable may well be against the interests of the debtor. This approach pressurises the assignor to accept, possibly in return for much-needed credit, a law that may be detrimental. It is also argued that the law of the assigned receivable does not protect the debtor and that it only contributes to complexity and unfairness in the assignment of receivables and in securitisation transactions.

8.3.5.3 The law of the assignment

The law of the assignment may be considered as a possible connecting factor, but it does not provide appropriate results. This is the law that governs the relationship between the grantor (assignor) and secured creditor (assignee). In *Brandsma q.q. v Hansa Chemie AG*,[129] the Dutch Hoge Raad has applied the law of the assignment to both the contractual and proprietary aspects of the assignment.[130] The law of the assignment avoids problems presented by the law of the assigned receivables and allows the application of a single law chosen by the grantor and secured creditor to govern creation and third-party effectiveness of a security interest. However, it does not consider third party rights, particularly, in determining priority between competing assignments and cannot protect debtor's rights.[131] It is also unfair to permit the grantor and secured creditor to choose a law that applies to proprietary aspects (e.g. priority of competing claims) and is unknown by third parties at the time of choice. This may have negative impacts on third parties who are not privy to this relationship and increase the costs of credit.[132] If the law chosen by the assignor and the assignee governs priorities, the assignor will be allowed to have a special benefit to determine the priority among several

127 A/CN.9/489/Add.1, para. 30 (it was noted that 'such a result would run counter to the principle of party autonomy as limited in Article 6'); for the applicability of Article 6 of the Receivables Convention, *see* A/CN.9/489, para. 78; but *cf.* Flessner, in Eidenmüller and Kieninger (eds), op. cit. (f'note 100), at 344 arguing that a transfer may have third-party effects without the consent of the creditor in property law.

128 Walsh, in Eidenmüller and Kieninger (eds), op. cit. (f'note 116), 334.

129 Hoge Raad, 16 May 1997, Rechtspraak van de Week 126.

130 The Dutch court applied Rome Convention Article 12(1) for a dispute between the assignee and the assignor's liquidator. This is now Article 14(1) of the Rome I Regulation. For a criticism of the decision, *see e.g.* Struycken, op. cit. (f'note 69), 355.

131 Debtor protection is a principle under the Receivables Convention.

132 For a similar view, *see* Rühl, G. 'Party Autonomy in the Private International Law of Contracts: Transatlantic Convergence and Economic Efficiency', *CLPE Research Paper 4/2007*, 3(1) (2007), at 34–5

claimants.[133] Under Receivables Convention Article 6, the debtor and the assignee may derogate or vary by agreement from their respective rights in the Convention; however, this derogation cannot affect the rights of any person who is not a party to the agreement.[134] Thus, there is limitation to avoid any negative effects on third parties. The law of the assignment may lead to divergent laws applicable to two competing security interests.[135] The appropriate method of determining the applicable law for the proprietary aspects is to direct parties to a single neutral, in the sense that it is known by all parties and is an easily determinable connecting factor (i.e. the law of the grantor's location). There are views that the grantor and secured creditor should be allowed to choose the law applicable to their contract despite the fact that the assignor's creditors may be affected by an assignment that takes place without their consent and this is the very essence of property law.[136] However, the grantor's other creditors may not allow the grantor to choose a law that will place them behind other creditors or assignees. What is important is not the consent of third parties but the proprietary aspects of a transaction on which party autonomy may have effects. Party autonomy, in this context, poses the risk of increasing the cost of credit. Parties with stronger bargaining powers will always attempt to impose favourable laws applicable to the assignment contract irrespective of whether party autonomy is allowed or not.[137] Thus, the law of the assignor's location, once again, provides a predictable and neutral port of call.

From the cost effectiveness perspective, if third parties (such as assignor's creditors or the insolvency administrator) need to ascertain the applicable law to the security interest, they should not be subject to either the grantor or secured creditor who may not be cooperative in assisting third parties. When the same receivable is assigned to multiple assignees under different applicable laws, it may not be possible to ascertain which law grants the priority position.[138] On the other hand, if the connecting factor is the law of the grantor's location, there will be single

133 A/CN.9/489/Add.1, para. 30.

134 'The party autonomy provision applies to agreements between the assignor and the assignee, between the assignor and the debtor or between the assignee and the debtor as long as they vary or derogate from provisions of the Convention'. A/CN.9/489, para. 78.

135 Guide, para. 13, at 386.

136 *See e.g.* Flessner, in Eidenmüller and Kieninger (eds), op. cit. (f'note 100), 344 *et seq.*

137 Henry Gabriel correctly argues that

> . . . uniform laws favor the parties with the strongest bargaining positions as it is the representatives of these parties who have been most active in the processes of formulating uniform law. It is these parties who have the most to gain by uniform laws and tend to have the bargaining position to insure that these laws will be the chosen sources of laws in their respective transactions. . . . [T]hose parties . . . are often sophisticated enough to provide specific terms that contract around many of the default provisions otherwise provided by the uniform law instrument . . . [and] the rules will be replaced with specific terms that reflect party choice.

Gabriel, H. (2010) 'Choice of Law, Contract Terms and Uniform Law in Practice', *Congress to Celebrate the fortieth annual session of the UNCITRAL*, 4, online available at <http://www.uncitral.org/pdf/english/congress/Gabriel-rev.pdf> (last accessed 30 January 2010).

138 *See generally* Deschamps, in Eidenmüller and Kieninger (eds), op. cit. (f'note 7), at 293.

and easily determinable law applicable to creation, third-party effectiveness and priority rules for the assignment of receivables.

8.3.5.4 Location

Defining 'location' for determining the law applicable to intangible assets is critical. Unlike the location of tangibles, which is not problematic since tangibles are physically located, location of intangibles is not ascertainable, hence the synchronised definition under the Guide and the Receivables Convention. 'Location' under the Convention, as well as the Guide, 'was considered as being the real location of the [assignor] and . . . it leads to the law of the State in which the main insolvency proceedings [against the assignor] would most likely be opened'.[139] Professor Walsh focuses on two possible methods to define location. These are the assignor's actual centre of administration or the legal centre of the assignor's business, which may be either the place under whose laws it is constituted or where it is registered.[140]

Under the Guide and the Receivables Convention, the location of grantor[141] refers to the grantor's place of business.[142] Thus, these two instruments' location is defined by the *de facto* centre of the assignor's business (centre of administration). If the grantor has multiple places of business, the location will be deemed to be the place where the central administration of the grantor is exercised.[143] If the grantor has no place of business then the location is to be understood as the grantor's habitual residence. The Guide and the Receivables Convention depart from the law of the place with the closest relationship to the relevant transaction in favour of application of the law of the central administration.[144] This rule provides for a

139 Guide, para. 21, at 388.

140 Walsh, op. cit. (f'note 39), at 175.

141 Recommendation 219; Receivables Convention Article 5(h). On location and priority relationship, *see* Chapter 6.

142 The Guide and the Receivables Convention illustrate similarity to the UCC §9–307(b), according to which the location is based on the individual's residence or the individual's primary residence, and if the assignor is a company, it is the company's place of business or chief executive office. For a comparative chart, *see also* Sigman and Smith, op. cit. (f'note 37), at 764–6. If the individual's residence does not have a public filing system, the individual will be deemed to be located, for the purposes of UCC Article 9, in the District of Columbia. For further discussion on the location of the debtor, *see* Cohen and Smith, op. cit. (f'note 77), 1201 *et seq*. Possessory security interests on collateral point to the law of the location of the collateral that governs perfection, the effects of perfection and priority. UCC §9–301(2). Goods covered by a certificate of title, such as motor vehicles, the law of the location under whose certificate of title the goods are covered governs perfection, the effects of perfection and priority matters. UCC §9–303(c).

143 Under the Receivables Convention Article 36, if the assignor is located in a federal state and if it has multiple places of business in multiple states, then it will be deemed to be located in the state in which it has its central administration.

144 A/CN.9/557, para. 19; Explanatory note, op. cit. (f'note 36), para. 19. For the definition under the Guide, *see above*. *See also* Bazinas, op. cit. (f'note 49), 295 (arguing that the choice-of-laws rule in relation to priority of competing rights 'centralize[s] all priority conflicts to the law of the assignor's location').

clear determination of the law applicable to the priority issues as a connecting factor.[145] On the other hand, if the debtor has multiple places of business, reference is made to the place most closely connected to the original contract (i.e. the contract between the assignor and the debtor). Thus, debtor protection is maintained by preventing the debtor from being adversely affected by the application of rules that may arise from a contract to which the debtor is not party.[146] If the transactions are made through branch offices, then by virtue of the central administration location rule, and subject to the fact that the assignor has its central administration located in a State party to the Convention, the Convention will apply.[147]

The time for the determination of location under Article 22, for predictability purposes, is the time of conclusion of the contract of assignment.[148] The test of determination of the assignor's location has raised concerns to the extent that the assignor's change of location may adversely affect the debtor since the assignor's action may result in a change of priority rules.[149] It has been put forward that in securitisation transactions, the risk of change of the central administration of the special purpose vehicle (SPV) may have adverse effects on assignees and the investors of receivables.[150] Indeed, in securitisation transactions where there is a chain of assignments, there may be multiple assignors and the determination of the exact time of the contract of assignment is critical. However, possible changes in priority rules and the resulting uncertainty as to who the debtor should pay to get a good discharge seems to be irrelevant in the context of the applicability of the law of the assignor's State to priority disputes. The argument that 'the debtor cannot always know who to pay',[151] arguably, does not concern priority (i.e.

145 Professor Flessner argues that the law of the assignor's location is unconstitutional under EU law. *See* Beale, op. cit. (f'note 56), in Eidenmüller and Kieninger (eds), at 396 and fn. 116; Professor Beale correctly points out that Flessner's argument of unconstitutionality of the law of the assignor's location will depend on 'whether . . . priority disputes can be solved effectively and efficiently under a scheme under which the parties may choose which system of law is to govern the priority of the assignment'.

146 A/CN.9/557, para. 19.

147 A/CN.9/557, para. 20.

148 Receivables Convention Article 1(1)(a): '. . . if, at the time of conclusion of the contract of assignment, the assignor is located in a Contracting State . . .'. One particular point of concern relates to assignor's change of location, particularly after establishing third-party effectiveness. A grace period provided for compliance with the new location's rules was not accepted in order not to complicate the provision under the Receivables Convention. Since the location is fixed to the place of central administration, change of location need not be separately regulated. *See* A/CN.9/455, paras 19 and 21. On the other hand, under the Guide, recommendation 220(b) if the dispute is between competing claimants whose rights became effective as against third parties before the change of location of the asset or the grantor, the initial location will govern priority and third-party effectiveness. For a similar determination of time formula, *see* Rome I Regulation Article 19(3).

149 Perkins, op. cit. (f'note 107), 240.

150 Alferez, op. cit. (f'note 101), 242.

151 Perkins, op. cit. (f'note 107), 240.

proprietary aspects that are irrelevant vis-à-vis the debtor), but rather concerns discharge of debt that is protected under the law of receivables (e.g. Rome I Regulation Article 14(2)). Under the Guide,[152] for creation of a security right, the time for determining the location of the assignor is the time of the purported creation of a security right, and for priority and third-party effectiveness is the location at the time the issue arises. In that context, if the assignor becomes insolvent and changes the central administration location, it is appropriate that the insolvency proceedings commence in the new location.[153]

The location of the assignor is compatible with bulk and future assignments because third parties do not need to search for the real place of business of the assignor. The location of the assignor 'would result in the application of the law of the jurisdiction in which any main insolvency proceeding with regard to the assignor would be most likely to commence'.[154] Moreover, the law of assignor's location closely corresponds to 'the basis for jurisdiction of the main proceeding in the event of the insolvency of the assignor'.[155] In this context, one of the advantages of Article 22 is that in the event of insolvency of the assignor, the law governing the priority and the law governing the insolvency of the assignor will be the same (i.e. the law of the assignor's state). If transactions are made through branch offices, by virtue of the central administration location rule and subject to the fact that the assignor has its central administration located in a contracting State, the Convention will apply.[156] However, if insolvency proceedings are commenced in a State other than the State of the assignor, Article 23, which addresses public policy and mandatory rules, applies. It stipulates that the application of the law of the location of the assignor may be refused if it is manifestly contrary to the public policy of the forum. The critical point under Article 23 is that mandatory rules of the forum or the applicable law cannot override the law of the location of the assignor. However, in an insolvency proceeding commenced in a State other than the assignor's State, any preferential right that arises and is given priority over the rights of the assignee in an insolvency proceeding may be given priority notwithstanding the application of the law of the location of the assignor. This limitation over the application of the law of the assignor's location facilitates certainty and, thus, appears sensible, as it 'does not empower the forum court to disregard the applicable rule; it . . . preserves whatever power to disregard that rule may exist under the law of the Forum State'.[157] Article 23(2) ensures that the application of

152 Recommendation 220(a).

153 *See* Kieninger, E-M. and Sigman, H. (2006) 'The Rome-I Proposed Regulation and the Assignment of Receivables', *The European Legal Forum* 1, 6.

154 A/CN.9/489/Add.1, para. 32.

155 Kieninger and Sigman, op. cit. (f'note 153), at 2. Under the EU Insolvency Regulation (Council Regulation No. 1346/2000) insolvent's 'centre of main interests' corresponds to the place of central administration.

156 A/CN.9/557, at 7, para. 20.

157 Sigman and Smith, op. cit. (f'note 37), at 758. Sigman and Smith argue that the manifest violation requirement indicates that the law of the assignor's location may be used in case of doubt.

the law of the assignor's State may not be prevented on the grounds that a mandatory rule of the Forum State or another State exists.[158] The application of the law of the assignor's State (which manifestly contradicts the public policy of the forum state) may only be refused on grounds of public policy.[159] This approach is justified in achieving third-party effectiveness and priority. Article 23(3) addresses the issue that preferential claims that arise by operation of law (such as tax or wage claims)[160] under the law of the Forum over the interest of the assignee in the assigned receivables are given priority (if the Forum State gives priority to them over the interest of the assignee), notwithstanding a contrary rule under the law of the assignor's location.

8.3.5.5 Exceptions to the law of the grantor's location

The Guide diverts from the law of the grantor's location in a number of categories of intangible assets. These include rights to payment of funds credited to a bank account, rights to receive the proceeds under an independent undertaking and receivables related to immovable property. The Receivables Convention Article 4(2)(f) excludes bank deposits and, thus, does not contain any special rule to refer priority rules to the law of the state where the branch is located.[161] Professor Walsh analyses the complexity of creating rules for banks separate from the law of the location where the central administration of the bank is exercised. The analysis focuses on four significant points. There is a challenge in defining concepts such as 'bank' and 'branch'. The legal personality argument affecting local branches of foreign banks is significant in banking regulation and supervision but not as much so in the private law field. There is further public policy challenge related to subjecting banks to separate rules not applicable to other businesses. The structure of banks, in this context, should be considered, as they operate through their branches rather than subsidiaries. In the assignor's insolvency a branch office exception would cause unpredictability. As noted earlier, the law of the assignor's location is normally the law applicable to insolvency; therefore, any exception will increase multiplicity of applicable laws in the case of insolvency. Assignees in a branch exception may also have to conduct further due diligence in order to conform to the requirements of priority and third-party effectiveness, which may lead to the risk of increasing the cost of credit. Finally, a separate rule may confuse

158 A/CN.9/557, at 14, para. 50.

159 This is also followed by the Guide recommendation 222. Receivables Convention Article 30(2) stipulates that to achieve certainty correctly, the application of the law of the assignor's State to third-party effectiveness and priority matters.

160 Ibid.

161 One of the particular concerns in relation to the application of the law of the assignor's location is that banks will not be able to apply the law of the bank's location when foreign bank account holders assign their claims. This would have left banks with less protection and probably with less modern law applicable to the contract. For a similar view, *see e.g.* Flessner and Verhagen, op. cit. (f'note 18), at 66–7, who suggest, in those cases, a solution based on party autonomy.

the assignor's other creditors, in the sense that there may be confusion as to whether the law of the assignor's place of business or the law of the location of the branch applies.[162] With these points in mind, it can be argued that excluding bank deposits and relevant legal matters from the scope of the Receivables Convention seems to be the correct approach because a separate rule might have complicated the determination of location and weakened the significance of the law of assignor's location.

The Guide considered three approaches and introduced two alternatives in relation to rights to payment of funds credited to a bank account.[163] Firstly, as bank deposits are receivables, the law of the assignor's location (as applied to receivables) may apply in order to maintain simplicity.[164] Secondly, the law of the branch's location that maintains the account is a transparent approach that establishes certainty (Recommendation 210 A).[165] The law of the branch's location is easily determinable. Furthermore, 'the location of the branch is often viewed as the *situs* of a bank account for regulatory or other matters in respect of which the *situs* of the account must be ascertained'.[166] This approach is similar to UCC §9–304, according to which the law governing perfection and priority of security interests in a deposit account will be governed by the local law of the bank's jurisdiction. A third approach refers to the law specified in the account agreement as governing the agreement (Recommendation 210 B). In the absence of choice of law, the Guide follows Article 5 of the Hague Convention on the Law Applicable in Respect of Securities Held with an Intermediary, according to which the applicable law will be the law of the intermediary's office location through which the intermediary concluded the account agreement; alternatively, the applicable law will be the law of the place where the intermediary is located or failing this the applicable law will be the law of the place of business of the intermediary.[167] This approach provides certainty for third parties, as well as reflecting the expectations of parties to the account agreement,[168] and the law specified in the account agreement (provided the depositary bank has a branch in the State whose law is specified) will govern creation, effectiveness against third parties and priority of a security interest in a bank deposit.[169] If third party effectiveness in security

162 For these issues, *see* Walsh, op. cit. (f'note 39), at 179–180.

163 Recommendations 210 alternative A or B.

164 Guide, para. 49, at 395; but *cf.* Flessner and Verhagen, op. cit. (f'note 18), at 66–7.

165 This is also the approach under English law. *R. v Lovitt* [1912] A.C. 212; *Re Russian Bank for Foreign Trade* [1933] 1 Ch. 745.

166 Guide, para. 49, at 395; *see also* Deschamps, in Eidenmüller and Kieninger (eds), op. cit. (f'note 7), at 294, arguing that this approach is similar to the determination of the *situs* of the receivable (the payment place of the receivable or the location of the receivable's debtor) and that the law applicable to a security interest in bank accounts will be the same as the law that applies to attachment or seizure of a credit balance in the account.

167 Guide, Recommendation 210 B. The Hague Convention Article 5 (1), (2) and (3).

168 Guide, para. 50, at 395.

169 Deschamps, in Eidenmüller and Kieninger (eds), op. cit. (f'note 7), at 294, arguing that this approach is similar to the law governing the receivable, according to which the law governing the security interest and the contractual obligations of parties will be the same.

interests on funds credited to a bank account is achieved through registration, the law of the grantor's location shall apply.[170] Deschamps rightly argues that the alternatives in the Guide generally have the same outcome (i.e. the account agreement will be governed by the law of the State where the branch is located), thus for the predictability and simplicity the law of the grantor's location should be applicable to bank deposits, as they are a form of receivable.[171]

In relation to rights to receive the proceeds under an independent undertaking, the creation of a security interest will be governed by the law of the grantor's location. Third-party effectiveness and priority of a security interest are governed by the law specified in the independent undertaking (Recommendation 212) and, in the absence of specification of applicable law, the law of the location of the relevant office of the person that has provided the undertaking will govern (Recommendation 213). If the undertaking guarantees the performance of an obligation under a receivable or negotiable instrument, the law governing the creation and third-party effectiveness in the receivable or the negotiable instrument may be extended, for the purposes of certainty, to the independent undertaking (Recommendation 214).

Finally, although the Guide does not directly apply to immovable property, it applies to receivables arising from the sale or lease of immovable property. The Guide also applies when a receivable is secured by an immovable property. Priority of competing interests will be governed by the law of the State where registry is maintained (Recommendation 209). This also provides clarity and predictability so that competing parties can rely on the registry.

8.3.6 Choice-of-law rules on security interest in proceeds

Both the Receivables Convention and the Guide contain rules on the law applicable to the proceeds of an assigned receivable or a security right. The Receivables Convention contains a substantive law rule (Article 14) applicable as between the assignor and the assignee. Article 14 enshrines the principle that the assignee has a legal right on the assigned receivable, as well as the proceeds of its collection. The legal right is applicable between the assignor and the assignee notwithstanding the fact that proceeds are paid directly to the assignee, or assignor or a third party over whom the assignee has priority.[172] This substantive law rule is complemented by a choice-of-law rule (Article 24). Article 24 is a limitation on Article 22, which regulates priority of competing rights. Special rule on proceeds is a significant provision that aims to overcome the differences among different legal

170 Guide, para. 51, at 395 and Recommendation 211.

171 Deschamps, in Eidenmüller and Kieninger (eds), op. cit. (f'note 7), at 295–6.

172 The assignee cannot retain more than the value of his right in the receivable, indicating the fact that this is only possible when there is an assignment by way of security (Article 14(2)).

traditions in this field.[173] The law of the assignor's location determines priority of the assignee's right in the proceeds, first, when the assignee receives and retains the proceeds, provided the assignee has priority over the right of a competing claimant in the same assigned receivable and, second, when proceeds are held by the assignor separately from its assets, where the proceeds are reasonably identifiable from the other assets, for the benefit and under the instructions of the assignee.[174] The latter situation is limited by Article 24(3), according to which the law of the assignor's location does not apply to priority disputes where one party has a right of set-off against the proceeds or where the right is created by an agreement and not derived from a right in the receivables. This possibility has a significant applicability in a priority dispute of a receivables assignee and a claimant who is a party to a contract that covers the proceeds of inventory as receivables (typically the inventory financier who lends to a manufacturer using the raw material or other inventory as collateral), in which case the law of the assignor's location seems to be unsuitable for priority disputes.[175]

Under the Guide, the creation of security rights in proceeds and third-party effectiveness and priority of security rights in proceeds are governed by separate rules. The aim is to encompass the interests of all parties related to the same proceeds. The main concern is between where the security interest is in receivables as proceeds of inventory and receivables as original encumbered assets. Although a solution in terms of subjecting creation, third-party effectiveness and priority to the law of the location of the inventory may be favourable to the inventory financier, the same argument may not be applicable to the receivables assignee. One of the significant concerns for the receivables assignee is the unpredictability of the applicable law, particularly whether a priority dispute will be with an inventory financier or another receivables assignee.[176] The application of the law of the inventory financier will not provide appropriate results and will increase the cost of credit for assignors who conduct business with receivable assignees. The Guide balances the interests of the inventory financier and receivables assignee

173 For further discussion, *see* Bazinas, op. cit. (f'note 49), at 297; A/CN.9/466, paras 45–6. Different opinions on this matter are based on priorities over proceeds that are receivables and goods. If priority over proceeds is governed by the law of the assignor's location, the expectations of third parties in the location of the goods may be frustrated and, in any case, a distinction between goods received in total or partial satisfaction of the receivable and goods returned must be drawn. With regard to the latter, goods received in total or partial satisfaction of the receivable are another form of the same receivable and should be subject to the same priority rules as the receivables; the goods returned have no relation to the receivable and, therefore, should be subject to the law of their location.

174 Article 24(1) and (2)(a), (b). Particularly Article 24(2) is designed to facilitate securitisation and undisclosed invoice discounting, where the assignor in agreement with the assignee collects and holds payments in a special client account. *See* Bazinas, S. (2004) 'The United Nations Convention on the Assignment of Receivables in International Trade: Insolvency Aspects', 13 *Int'l Insol. Rev.*, 155, 164.

175 *See generally* Walsh, op. cit. (f'note 39), at 185–6.

176 Guide, para. 57, at 397.

by subjecting the creation of a security interest in proceeds to the same law that applies to the creation of a security interest on the assets from which the proceeds arise, and third-party effectiveness and priority of a security interest in proceeds to the same law that applies to the same kind as the proceeds (if proceeds are tangible, the law of the location of inventory, and if intangible, the law of the grantor's location).[177] The significance of this separate treatment is that it provides predictability to all parties (especially the receivables assignee and inventory financier) on the law applicable to their transactions, whether the security interest extends to proceeds and whether formalities to obtain priority against competing claimants are fulfilled.

8.4 International interests in mobile equipment and choice-of-laws

The Cape Town Convention, as an influential instrument, governs agreements that create or provide for an international interest. It aims to establish certainty and predictability in the validity, enforceability and priority rules in high value mobile equipment. The Convention is the product of inadequacy of *lex situs* or *lex rei sitae* (the law of the location of the encumbered asset that governs the proprietary rights).[178] The application of the law of the physical location of movables may seem to be simple, easily ascertainable by the parties and commercially certain to protect the commercial interests of parties.[179] Furthermore, there are some perspectives that suggest that the rule allows parties to restrict their search to the country of the *situs*.[180] The rule, in reality, does not seem to assist the facilitation of credit in cross-border acquisition of mobile equipment.

The *lex situs* rule presents serious disadvantages for international lenders as far as it is applicable to cross-border mobile equipment (such as aircraft that can move across multiple borders within a short period of time) and space object transactions (since the space object has no fixed location, the *situs* rule is illogical). For example, under English law, there is no predictable authority that distinguishes aircraft from tangibles. Application of cases such as *Cammell v Sewell*[181] to aircraft

177 For further information, *see* Guide, paras. 59–60, at 397; Bazinas, op. cit. (f'note 25), at 61; Recommendation 215.

178 *See e.g.* Stanford, M. (1999) 'A Broader or a Narrower Band of Beneficiaries for the Proposed New International Regimen?: Some Reflections on the Merits of the Convention/Protocol Structure in Facilitating the Former', *Unif. L. Rev.*, 242, 242; Goode, R. (2008) *Convention on International Interests in Mobile Equipment and Protocol thereto on Matters Specific to Aircraft Equipment Official Commentary*. Rome: UNIDROIT, revised edn. para. 2.5; Wool, J. 'The Next Generation of International Aviation Finance Law: An Overview of the Proposed Unidroit Convention on International Interests in Mobile Equipment as Applied to Aircraft Equipment', 20 *U. Pa. J. Int'l Econ. L.*, 499, 501 *et seq.* (1999).

179 Lalive, P.A. (1955) *The Transfer of Chattels in the Conflict of Laws*, Oxford: Clarendon Press, 114–15.

180 *See e.g. Winkworth v Christie Manson & Woods Ltd.* [1980] Ch 496.

181 (1860) 5 H.& N. 728 holds that proprietary interest on a tangible asset will be decided by *lex situs*.

aligns them with tangibles.[182] However, it is argued that general tangibles and aircraft are not alike, particularly when it is considered that *lex situs* is unsuitable for border-crossing tangible assets. In that sense, the Cape Town Convention will make a positive impact in the change of application of *lex situs* to mobile equipment. From another angle, a uniform choice-of-laws rule, which is impossible to achieve, cannot provide results as this rule may depend on national laws whose secured transactions regimes differ on their regulation of interests or rights arising from security agreement or title-based devices. It is argued in this context that a particular difficulty is experienced between the systems that have a functional approach to secured transactions and the others that are not so favourable to the functional approach or to non-possessory security interests. The *lex situs* rule does not serve for the facilitation of credit in the realm of border-crossing mobile equipment, as it does not assist certainty in creation, third-party effectiveness, priority and enforcement of interests securing the claim of the creditor. This may deter financiers from extending credit and, thus, work against the basic philosophy of facilitation of credit.[183] The uncertainty particularly stems from questions of whether a validly created security right in one State may be recognised in the new location and if it is recognised whether its value is diminished by *in rem* rights on the same asset in the new location.[184] In other words, is there a need to create a new security interest and, if there is no need, does the originally created security interest grant priority rights in the new location of the asset? International financiers need predictability in order to facilitate the financing of acquisition of mobile equipment other than that offered by traditional choice-of-laws rules, which are mainly based on the *lex situs* rule. When the mobile equipment changes *situs*, the security interest created over the mobile equipment in the original *situs* may not always be recognised in the next *situs*. The civil law notion of *numerus clausus* may restrict the recognition of certain types of security interests as the foreign security interest may not be accommodated under the domestic security interests, due to not having a corresponding counterpart.[185] The same argument does not seem to be equally applicable in some common law jurisdictions, where there is flexibility of equity enabled through equitable mortgage and charge and where the original location's categorisation and

182 For a similar assertion, *see* Osborne, D. (2004) '*Lex Situs* and Aircraft', *L.M.C.L.Q.*, 303, 312. Osborne wrote that '[a]ircraft were treated by English domestic law no differently from general chattels in relation to their mortgaging until the Mortgaging of Aircraft Order 1972 [which is an operator's register rather than a register of title]' at 303. Although the Order determines priority of mortgages over aircraft in the UK through registration, Article 13 of the Order states that 'registration of a mortgage shall not be evidence of its validity'.

183 UNIDROIT Study LXXII-Doc. 3, at 6–7 (1991); lack of an international system is a negative factor on the recognition of security interests and secured creditor rights by the law of other states which affects lenders' decisions.

184 UNIDROIT Study LXXII-Doc. 1, at 7 (1989); *see also* Kreuzer, in Eidenmüller and Kieninger, op. cit. (f'note 1), at 299 arguing that public notice requirements create impediment to recognition of foreign non-possessory security interests.

185 *See* T. Schilling, 'Some European Decisions on Non-Possessory Security Rights in Private International Law', 34 *I.C.L.Q.*, 87, 97–8 (1985).

characterisation of security interest is looked to, rather than attempting to fit the interest to the second location's categorisation or simply refusing it.[186] In jurisdictions that adopted functionalism in their approach to secured transactions where substance over form takes precedence and a security interest is a proprietary interest that is created or provided for by agreement,[187] a foreign security interest must meet the requirement to be recognised as a validly created security interest. Common law treats foreign security interests 'as valid in the new *situs* unless and until it is displaced by a new security interest acquired in accordance with the law of the new *situs*'.[188] A list that provides similarities between different security interests may prove to be impractical; as new financing techniques arise, this list will require updating.[189]

The inadequacy of the *lex situs* rule is further coupled with the question of recognition of the priority status of the security interest in the second location. It is generally recognised and shaped by public policy considerations that a security interest's priority status in the original location may be transposed to the second location by granting it a status of similar security interests, as opposed to recognising its effectiveness between parties and priority status attributed under the original location.[190] However, the danger with this approach is that often a creditor having a security interest in the original location may end up in the second location with either a better priority right or, more often, with less favourable priority status. This is particularly the case if the original location attributes greater significance to non-possessory security interests.[191] Transposition of foreign security interests should provide connectedness between the foreign and the domestic security interest.[192] This will preserve the interests of the creditor both in the original and subsequent location. This approach has some impact on public notification. However, the difficulty for the foreign security interest is that the secured creditor may not be able to know the requirements and time limits of public notification of the second location, which may eventually reduce the original status of the foreign security interest. Thus, even though the foreign security interest is

186 UNIDROIT Study LXXII-Doc. 1, at 7 (1989).

187 *See e.g.* the definition of security interest under UCC§1–201(37).

188 Gopalan, S. (2003) 'Harmonization of Commercial Law: Lessons from the Cape Town Convention on International Interests in Mobile Equipment', 9 *Law & Bus. Rev. Am.* 255, 257; *see also* Cuming, R.C.C. (1990) 'International Regulation Aspects of Security Interests in Mobile Equipment', *Unif. L. Rev.*, 62, 83.

189 UNIDROIT Study LXXII-Doc. 1, at 26–7 (1989).

190 *See generally* op. cit. (f'note 184), at 8–9.

191 Ibid., at 8. This is particularly a critical matter between common law and civil law systems, where the latter generally frowns upon non-possessory security interests where the debtor holds the collateral and which prefers generally possessory security interests. Although recently, most notably in France, reform on recognition of non-possessory security interests has been undertaken in civil law jurisdictions. *See e.g.* Ancel, M.E. (2008) 'Recent Reform in France: The Renaissance of a Civilian Collateral Regime?', in F. Dahan and J. Simpson (eds) *Secured Transactions Reform and Access to Credit*. London: Edward Elgar, 259.

192 Gopalan, op. cit. (f'note 188), at 258.

recognised the practical utility of it may be diminished by the different priority regimes. In sum, the *lex situs* rule does not seem to be appropriate for cross-border transactions involving mobile equipment.

In view of these arguments, it was necessary to establish an international registry and a concept of international interest through the Cape Town Convention. The Convention's approach to security interests in mobile equipment is a rejection of the traditional *lex situs* rule.[193] The Convention harmonises interests over mobile equipment, which has been attempted in a fragmented style in the past.[194] The Convention establishes an innovative international interest concept, which is created under the rules set out in the Convention and perfected globally by registration in an international registry. The idea is that international interest is recognised by all contracting states and the register in which it is registered, for the effectiveness against third parties can provide an international public disclosure system to all parties. International interest does not take the characteristics of civil law systems, where security interests are enumerated through the *numerus clausus* concept, but takes the common law systems' functional approach to security, where there is a generic description of transactions that fall within their scope.[195] According to Article 2(4), which is a uniform choice-of-laws rule, the Convention does not determine whether an international interest in mobile equipment falls within the category granted by the chargor under a security agreement or vested in the conditional seller under a retention-of-title agreement or lessor under the leasing agreement; rather, this is determined by the applicable law. In other words, characterisation of an international interest, mainly for the purposes of determination of applicability of default remedies, is made by the 'domestic rules of the law applicable by virtue of the rules of private international law of the Forum State (Article 5(3))'.[196] If the applicable law is *lex fori*, that law determines the characterisation issue. Apart from the rule under Article 2(4), the Convention '[dispenses] with the need to resort to [choice-of-laws] rules as regards [the mobile

193 Op. cit. (f'note 184), at iii (Appendix A): 'The effect of the proposed Convention would be to displace the *lex situs* as the law applicable to validity of a security interest'.

194 E.g. UNIDROIT Convention on International Financial Leasing 1980 (which deals with security interest over movable goods but is not a comprehensive text on international financial leases); Geneva Convention on the International Recognition of Rights in Aircraft 1948 (the choice-of-laws rule of which determines the validity and the place of registration of security interest in aircraft, and provides for the recognition of contractually created mortgages, hypothèques and other similar rights in aircraft, and that these rights are created in accordance with the law of the Contracting State in which the aircraft is registered as to nationality [Article 1(1)(d)(i)–(ii)]. However, a contracting state has the right to refuse recognition of foreign security rights that do not fit into domestic types of security rights, provided that national law does not prohibit registration of a foreign right that can be validly created in accordance with the national law [Article 2(3)]. This requirement constitutes a disadvantage for aircrafts that are transferred from one country to another one.)

195 For an early view, *see* op. cit. (f'note 184), at 28.

196 Goode, op. cit. (f'note 178), at 169.

equipment]'.[197] The significance is that in all cases *renvoi* is excluded,[198] as it may provide solutions contrary to the expectations of parties. The importance of leaving characterisation to the applicable law is that it is easier to meet the requirements of the security interest in that domestic applicable law. Thus, in one sense, certainty is established and the international interest becomes widely acceptable. Finally, under Aircraft Protocol Article VIII, parties are allowed to choose the applicable law to their contract and this law may be the law to which parties have no connection.

The main connecting factor for the applicability of the Convention, which must be satisfied at the time of the conclusion of the agreement creating or providing for the international interest, is that the debtor[199] must be located in a contracting State (Article 3(1)). It is not necessary for the creditor to be located in a contracting State (Article 3(2)). Similarly, the mobile equipment does not have to be a type that can or does cross borders. Thus, there are no specific requirements of internationality, meaning that, subject to Article 50, the Cape Town Convention may even apply to internal transactions.[200] There are a number of alternatives to test the location of the debtor. The debtor is considered to be situated in a contracting State if it is incorporated or formed under the law of that Contracting State, if it has a registered office, a statutory seat or its centre of administration there, or if it has its place of business, principal place of business or its habitual residence there (Article 4(1)). Thus, the Convention seems to present a wider array of locators for the debtor to fulfil the connecting factor for the wider applicability and acceptance of the Convention by contracting states. The Convention applies to helicopters or airframes (i.e. the body of the aircraft without its engines)[201] if the helicopters or airframes are registered in the registry of a contracting State.[202]

8.5 Conclusion

It is critical and necessary to have choice-of-laws rules in international secured transactions instruments supplementing substantive rules. Divergent approaches to creation, third-party effectiveness and priority of security interests can best be solved through a mixture of substantive law and choice-of-law rules. However, extending the scope of application of international instruments through choice-of-law rules may have a negative impact, as choice-of-law rules are not harmonised[203] and may contradict national laws.

197 Goode, op. cit. (f'note 119), at 1107.

198 For a similar regulation, *see* Guide, recommendation 221, where *renvoi* is excluded and any reference to the law applicable is to the substantive law in force in that State.

199 The term 'debtor' under Cape Town Convention Article 1(j) means a chargor under a security agreement, a conditional buyer under a retention-of-title and a lessee under a leasing agreement.

200 'Internal transaction' is defined under Cape Town Convention Article 1(n).

201 Aircraft Protocol Article I(e).

202 Aircraft Protocol, Article IV(1).

203 Walsh, op. cit. (f'note 39).

The *lex situs* is adopted generally as the main connecting factor for tangible assets. However, its unsuitability in the context of border-crossing, high value mobile equipment and international assignment of receivables is evident. In the former type of assets, the *lex situs* cannot achieve efficient third-party effectiveness and priority. The Cape Town system enables third-party effectiveness and priority through registration of a unique international security interest in an international registry. This presents a reliable, predictable and more efficient reference point and certainly facilitates credit. In the latter, as receivables do not have any location and may move across borders, the *lex situs* is unsuitable. The connecting factor, '*the law of the assignor's location*' in the assignment of receivables, is a feasible method in an uncertain area to establish third-party effectiveness and priority. Both the Receivables Convention and the Guide adopt the law of the assignor's (grantor) location for receivables. This approach departs from traditional methods of the law of the assigned receivables or the law of the assignment. Although counter arguments have been forwarded,[204] suggesting that it may not be the best solution for certain types of transaction,[205] it provides, most importantly, predictability and among all options it provides the best solution.[206] This is so, provided that the location of the assignor and the time of establishing this location are clear. For intangibles other than receivables, separate rules seem to be more appropriate. Finally, party autonomy should not be considered as part of the proprietary aspects of a transaction. Proprietary aspects of a security transaction affect third parties' rights, hence the unsuitability of party autonomy.

204 *See e.g. generally* Flessner, A. and Verhagen, H. (2006) *Assignment in European Private International Law*. Munich: Sellier.

205 Op. cit. (f'note 116). In any case, the Receivables Convention and the Guide have exceptions.

206 Sigman and Kieninger, op. cit. (f'note 88), 60 *et seq*.

Conclusion

This monograph has focused on international secured transactions instruments. The arguments made during the distillation of the underlying principles intensified around the idea that harmonised modernisation of the law of credit and security was important and it would assist the facilitation of credit. The following conclusions can be drawn from the analysis of the topic.

Security is important. It lowers the cost of credit, enables investment and expansion of business for SMEs, allows self-help and affords, more importantly, priority status. Full priority is necessary for creditors. The reality in international commercial dealings is that no lender will lend without security and a bargained priority status. All international instruments discussed in this monograph confirm this and do not permit carve-outs. The ability to grant security affects lending decisions. Lenders prefer immovable or movable assets. Ninety-seven per cent of businesses globally are SMEs, which provide 50 per cent of employment worldwide.[1] The negative impact of restrictions has been proved by the empirical data provided by the World Bank.[2] Inability to use receivables as collateral, which is normally acceptable in modern legal and financial systems, and the restrictions that give rise to assignment of receivables, adversely affect SMEs' access to credit. Arguably, it is this aspect that led the UNCITRAL to remove obstacles before receivables financing and modernise domestic systems[3] to 'unlock the dead capital'.[4]

Harmonisation can only be achieved if the international instrument considers different legal cultures rather than imposing rules from above. The support and input from the private sector in the drafting process always helps the acceptability of an international instrument. The clear example of this is the recent success of

1 http://www.ifc.org/ifcext/media.nsf/AttachmentsByTitle/AM09_SME/$FILE/AM09_SME.pdf (last accessed 10 June 2010).

2 For some empirical data, *see* Safavian, M. (2008) 'Firm level evidence on collateral and access to finance', in F. Dahan and J. Simpson (eds) *Secured Transactions Reform and Access to Credit*. Cheltenham: Edward Elgar.

3 *See e.g.* A/CN.9/378/Add.3; A/48/17, paras 297–301.

4 Safavian, M., Fleisig, H. and Steinbuks, J. (2006) 'Unlocking the Dead Capital', *View Point*. Note Number 307 (March).

the Cape Town Convention. It was argued that even if the working methods of international organisations were not legitimate, the identification of this claim was fortuitous, as those claims of certain States lacked clear theoretical and most importantly practical support. These claims seem to be somewhat political. The more transparent the working methods of an organisation, the harder for certain States to influence other members and the agenda of the organisation.[5] It is clear that States attempt to achieve in one organisation what they cannot achieve in another.[6] What seems extraordinary is that it is those States' laws that need modernisation, break the chains of nineteenth-century rules and accept with open arms those instruments that aim to modernise secured transactions law as well as facilitate access for small businesses to low-cost credit. Party autonomy should not be allowed to the extent this affects third party rights.

Facilitation of credit can only be achieved if there are clear and predictable rules in relation to creation, third-party effectiveness and priority of security interests. There should not be fragmentation in the way obligations and assets can be used to create security interests. A comprehensive security interest concept should be established. Registration should be used for all types of security interests. All assets and obligations should be available to be used as collateral. All persons (legal and natural) should be able to grant security. Grantors should be able to utilise the full economic value of their assets by granting multiple security rights with varying priority rankings. This will enable the availability of more credit as well as creating competition among financiers, who will, arguably, provide security with low cost in return for higher ranking priority status. Creation of security should be possible with minimum formalities. For the creation of a security there should not be any requirement for registration. Registration, rather, should be expected for third-party effectiveness with some alternatives/exceptions (possession or control). Third-party effectiveness and creation of security interest should be separate procedures. Third-party effectiveness should normally be a point of priority. In order to achieve these general security rights registry should be operational, which will provide transparency and predictability for potential creditors of the debtor. This registry should provide notice to potential creditors. It should be electronic and only include minimum information with the possibility of advance filing.[7] Priority, in line with the Guide, Cape Town Convention and optional annex Section I of the Receivables Convention, should be determined according to first-in-time registration. This provides clear and simple determinability, because it is transparent and includes all types of transactions that are

5 *See* Introduction and Chapter 1 above.

6 For an in-depth explanation of the input of countries and its criticism, *see* Farnsworth, E.A. (1996) 'Unification and Harmonization of Private Law', 27 *Canadian Bus. L. J.*, 48, at 56–60. A/RES/57/20 Enlargement of the Membership of the United Nations Commission on International Trade Law.

7 Both the Guide and the Receivables Convention require that registration should permit notice filing as well as advance filing.

functionally equivalent to security rights. General security rights registry should be debtor-based.[8] There have, understandably, been certain doubts about the inclusion of retention-of-title transactions in the registration scheme; however, this may be bypassed by providing acquisition security rights.[9] Otherwise, it may be necessary to fine-tune separate types of title-based devices, such as retention-of-title and financial lease, and subject them to separate rules.

The Guide has a wide scope with unique features. The rules envisaged under the Guide are very detailed, resembling the UCC Article 9 type legislation, though substantively they differ in many instances. One of the unique features of the Guide is the acquisition financing devices and functional approach to security, where a unitary and non-unitary approach has been introduced. These devices are in essence transactions where the seller retains title, the lessor leases tangible assets or lenders lend by taking security. The Guide refrains from using the North American legal jargon that refers to purchase-money security interests. It has a very detailed set of rules on acquisition financing devices. As part of the fundamental policies of the Guide the aim is to establish equality between lenders and sellers in financing the buyer. This fundamental policy, where all devices serving for the acquisition of tangible assets (seller with title retention, lessor under financial lease and lender with a security interests) combined under PMSI with the same third-party effectiveness and priority rules, is based on economic ideas and efficiency in secured transactions rather than formalism. In both the unitary and non-unitary approach to acquisition financing it seems that jurisdictions will be compelled to make adjustments to their domestic laws and will need to re-educate lawyers. In that context, even if States choose the non-unitary approach to acquisition financing, as the Guide has a clear tendency to the unitary approach and the expectation is to have functional equivalence, legal traditions and knowledge will need to be adjusted. However, this is a positive development, as an integrated approach to acquisition financing promotes competition between sellers and lenders based on price, which may increase the availability of credit and, arguably, simplifies a complex area by combining all transactions that fulfil the same economic function of security and referring them as security rights.[10] Other instruments also adopt this approach. The Cape Town Convention, while respecting the distinct nature of retention-of-title, financial lease and security interests, combines them under the concept of international interest. Third-party effectiveness by registration is necessary to obtain priority, and registration requirement also applies to retention-of-title and financial lease agreements. The Receivables Convention similarly abolishes the distinction between assignments by way of sale and security, and correctly avoids a distinction between title devices and security rights. This certainly has effects in the

8 It should be noted that the Cape Town Convention has an asset-based registry as the Convention only deals with equipment financing rather than general financing.

9 Beale, H. (2008) 'The Future of Secured Credit in Europe: Concluding Remarks', in H. Eidenmüller and E.M. Kieninger (eds) *The Future of Secured Credit in Europe* E.C.F.L.R, Munich: De Gruyter Recht, 375, 398.

10 Guide, paras 64–65, at 334.

reduction of cost of credit. In any case, it is often difficult to ascertain the difference between outright and security transfers. Thus, the Receivables Convention illustrates preference to functionality rather than formalism. More importantly, Receivables Convention Article 22 deals with priority conflicts between competing claimants (Article 5(m)). Article 5(m) clearly makes a reference to the fact that priority conflict may be between the assignee of receivables (Article 5(m)(i)) and creditor of the assignor, who may be a seller retaining title (Article 5(m)(ii)). Similarly the Model Law also contains an unpaid vendor's charge (Article 9) and is similar to the Guide in acquisition financing aspects.[11]

Conflict-of-laws solutions in international instruments to complex areas where divergence can be felt acutely, provide valuable wisdom. The law of the assignor's location under the Receivables Convention and the Guide has received an antagonistic reception on the basis that it did not reflect the interests of parties but rather protected assignees, that it was best suited to those jurisdictions with a general security interests registry system, that it did not protect the debtor, as the debtor was not in a position to know who to pay, and that it only applied to competing claimants and thus had very limited third-party effectiveness scope, ignoring party autonomy. Debtor protection has no link with establishing priority of assignees. Priority deals, whether with the secured creditor or assignee, could be recouped in the insolvency of the debtor. Party autonomy should have no place in proprietary aspects of a transaction. Registration, in any case, is foreseen and recommended by the international instruments, which means that the law of the assignor's State may well be suitable once these instruments are implemented. Protection of assignees is important, as it is their protection that facilitates credit by having predictable rules in the instruments. Finally, the law of the assignor's location points parties to a single and determinable law for priorities, which will also be the applicable law in the insolvency of the debtor. The definition of competing claimants is quite broad both under the Receivables Convention and the Guide and includes both the insolvency administrators, competing assignees of the same receivable and creditor of the assignor.[12] The conflict-of-laws rules of the Guide and the Receivables Convention should be utilised, as they have the necessary wisdom to facilitate credit.

Enforcement is critical, but this is mostly in national prerogatives. In the international context, it is not possible to establish enforcement mechanisms. Thus, rules on enforcement in international instruments (Model Law and the Guide) are mostly suggestions to nations on how to reform their rules so that credit can be facilitated. One of the most pressing matters for small businesses is that receivables are not accepted as collateral and only immovables or movable assets are. The main reasons for this are that secured credit laws in those countries are not efficiently endorsing security or the enforcement mechanisms are not efficient. Thus, lenders or creditors prefer to have tangible collateral.

11 *See* Chapter 7.

12 Receivables Convention, Article 5(m).

Clearly, some instruments, arguably the UNIDROIT Convention on International Factoring with its limited scope of applicability and lack of critical features necessary to facilitate credit (priority provisions and formal validity rules), will have limited contribution to the facilitation of credit. Finally, international modernisation and harmonisation efforts of, particularly, the UNCITRAL, UNIDROIT, the EBRD, the World Bank and other international organisations should be supported and States, as well as regional organisations, should make every effort to contribute to the international harmonisation efforts. Regionalism and regional harmonisation solutions can only produce further divergence, which will work against facilitation of credit internationally.

Bibliography

Selected Travaux Préparatoires

When references are made in the footnotes to the Guide, the following document or website is used: UNCITRAL Legislative Guide on Secured Transactions, New York: United Nations Publications, 2010; also available at http://www.uncitral.org/pdf/english/texts/security-lg/e/09-82670_Ebook-Guide_09-04-19English.pdf.

A/32/17
A/35/17
A/56/17
A/61/17
A/CN.9/WG.VI/WP.21/Add. 3
A/CN.9/130
A/CN.9/131 and Annex
A/CN.9/132
A/CN.9/378/Add.3
A/CN.9/412
A/CN.9/397
A/CN.9/432
A/CN.9/434
A/CN.9/445
A/CN.9/455
A/CN.9/456
A/CN.9/466
A/CN.9/470
A/CN.9/472/Add.2
A/CN.9/472/Add.3
A/CN.9/475
A/CN.9/486
A/CN.9/489
A/CN.9/489/Add.1
A/CN.9/496
A/CN.9/512
A/CN.9/557
A/CN.9/631
A/CN.9/631, Add. 1–11 (A/62/17, Part I)

A/CN.9/635
A/CN.9/637, Add. 1–8 (A/62/17, Part II)
A/CN.9/639
A/CN.9/660
A/CN.9/670
A/CN.9/689
A/CN.9/702
A/CN.9/702/Add. 1
A/CN.9/WG.6/WP.2
A/CN.9/WG.II/WP.105
A/CN.9/WG.VI/WP. 42
A/CN.9/WG.VI/WP.27/Add. 1
A/CN.9/WG.VI/WP.3
A/CN.9/WG.VI/WP.44
A/CN.9/WG.VI/WP.44/Add. 1
A/CN.9/WG.VI/WP.44/Add. 2
http://siteresources.worldbank.org/DATASTATISTICS/Resources/GDP.pdf
http://www.fsb.org.uk/
http://www.ifc.org/ifcext/media.nsf/AttachmentsByTitle/AM09_SME/$FILE/AM09_SME.pdf
http://www.uncitral.org/uncitral/en/about/methods.html
http://www.unidroit.org/english/implement/i-2001-convention.pdf

Unidroit 1988 CONF. 7/6 Add.2
Unidroit DC9/DEP-Doc. 8
Unidroit Study LVIII-Doc. 1
Unidroit Study LVIII-Doc. 10
Unidroit Study LVIII-Doc. 14
Unidroit Study LVIII-Doc. 20
Unidroit Study LVIII-Doc. 22
Unidroit Study LVIII-Doc. 25
Unidroit Study LVIII-Doc. 31
Unidroit Study LVIII-Doc. 32
Unidroit Study LVIII-Doc. 33
Unidroit Study LXXII-Doc. 1
Unidroit Study LXXII-Doc. 2
Unidroit Study LXXII-Doc. 3
Unidroit Study LXXII-Doc. 5
Unidroit Study LXXII-Doc. 6 Add. 2
Unidroit Study LXXII-Doc. 7
Unidroit Study LXXII-Doc. 8
Unidroit Study LXXII-Doc. 10
Unidroit Study LXXII-Doc. 35
Unidroit Study LXXIIJ-Doc. 13
Unidroit Study LXXIIJ-Doc. 14

Cited works

Ajani, C. (1995) 'By Chance and Prestige: Legal Transplants in Russia and Eastern Europe', 43 *Am. J. Comp. L.*, 93.

Akseli, O. (2008) 'On the Methods of International Harmonisation of Secured Transactions Law' in C.B. Andersen and U.G. Schroeter (eds) *Sharing International Commercial Law across National Boundaries: Festschrift for Albert H. Kritzer on the Occasion of his Eightieth Birthday.* London: Wildy, Simmonds & Hill.

Akseli, O. (2009) 'Contractual Prohibitions on Assignment of Receivables: An English and UN Perspective', *J.B.L.*, 650.

Alexander, K. (2009) 'Global Financial Standards Setting, the G10 Committees and International Economic Law', 34 *Brook. J. Int'l L.*, 861.

Alexander, M.R. (1989) 'Towards Unification and Predictability: The International Factoring Convention', 27 *Colum. J. Transnat'l L.*, 353.

Alferez, F.J.G. (2009) 'Assignment of Claims in the Rome I Regulation: Article 14' in F. Ferrari and S. Lieble (eds) *Rome I Regulation: The Law Applicable to Contractual Obligations in Europe.* Munich: Sellier.

Allcock, B. (1983) 'Restrictions on the Assignment of Contractual Rights', 42 *C.L.J.*, 328.

Ancel, M. (1976) 'From the Unification of Law to its Harmonisation', 51 *Tul. L. Rev.*, 108, 114–17.

Ancel, M.E. (2008) 'Recent Reform in France: The Renaissance of a Civilian Collateral Regime?' in F. Dahan and J. Simpson (eds) *Secured Transactions Reform and Access to Credit.* London: Edward Elgar.

Annex I-Cape Town Papers Series vol. 1, *Contract Practices under the Cape Town Convention* http://www.awg.aero/pdf/Annex5.pdf.

Ansaloni, G. (2009) 'Reflection on the Implementation of a Floating Security Interest over Tangible Property in French Law (Study of the New Non-Possessory Pledge)', *IBLJ*, 35.

Armour, J. (2008) 'The Law and Economics Debate About Secured Lending: Lessons For European Lawmaking?' in H. Eidenmüller and E.M. Kieninger (eds) *The Future of Secured Credit in Europe.* E.C.F.L.R., Munich: De Gruyter Recht.

Bailey, S.J. (1932) 'Assignment of Debts in England from the Twelfth to the Twentieth Century', 48 *L.Q.R.*, 248, 249.

Baird, D. (1983) 'Notice Filing and the Problem of Ostensible Ownership'. 12 *J. Legal Studies*, 53.

Baird, D. and Jackson, T. (1984) 'Corporate Reorganisations and the Treatment of Diverse Ownership Interests: A Comment on Adequate Protection of Secured Creditors in Bankruptcy', 51 *U. Ch. L.Rev.*, 97, 112–14.

Baird, D. (1994) 'Security Interests Reconsidered', 80 *Va. L. Rev.*, 2249.

Baird, D. (1997) 'The Importance of Priority', 82 *Cornell L. Rev.*, 1420, 1422.

Bazinas, S. (1998) 'An International Regime for Receivables Financing: UNCITRAL's Contribution', 8 *Duke J. Comp. & Int'l L.*, 315.

Bazinas, S. (1998) 'UNCITRAL's work in the field of secured transactions' in J.J. Norton and M. Andenas (eds) *Emerging Financial Markets and Secured Transactions.* The Hague: Kluwer.

Bazinas, S. (2001) 'Lowering the Cost of Credit: the Promise in the Future. UNCITRAL Convention on Assignment of Receivables in International Trade', 9 *Tul. J. Int'l & Comp. L.*, 259.

Bazinas, S. (2002) 'Multi-Jurisdictional Receivables Financing: UNCITRAL's Impact on Securitization and Cross-Border Perfection', 12 *Duke J. Comp. & Int'l L.*, 365.

Bazinas, S. (2002) 'UNCITRAL's Contribution to the Unification of Receivables Financing Law: The United Nations Convention on the Assignment of Receivables in International Trade', *Unif. L. Rev.*, 49.

Bazinas, S. (2003) 'Key Policy Issues of the United Nations Convention on the Assignment of Receivables in International Trade', 11 *Tul. J. Int'l & Comp. L.*, 275.

Bazinas, S. (2004) 'The United Nations Convention on the Assignment of Receivables in International Trade: Insolvency Aspects', 13 *Int'l Insol. Rev.*, 155.

Bazinas, S. (2004) 'UNCITRAL's Work in the Field of Secured Transactions', 36 *UCC.L.J.*, 67.

Bazinas, S. (2006) 'Modernising and Harmonising Secured Credit Law: The Example of the UNCITRAL Draft Legislative Guide on Secured Transactions, Part 1', *BJIBFL*, 20.

Bazinas, S. (2006) 'Modernising and Harmonising Secured Credit Law: The Example of the UNCITRAL Draft Legislative Guide on Secured Transactions, Part 2', *BJIBFL*, 58.

Bazinas, S. (2007) 'Bank Accounts' in P. Ali (ed.) *Secured Finance Transactions Key Assets and Emerging Markets*, London: Globe Business.

Bazinas, S. (2008) 'UNCITRAL' in W. Johnston (ed.) *Security over Receivables: An International Handbook*. Oxford: Oxford University Press.

Beale, H. (2002) 'Finding the Remaining Traps' in S. Grundman and J. Stuyck (eds) *An Academic Green Paper on European Contract Law*. The Hague: Kluwer.

Beale, H. (2008) 'The Future of Secured Credit in Europe: Concluding Remarks' in H. Eidenmüller and E.M. Kieninger (eds) *The Future of Secured Credit in Europe*. E.C.F.L.R., Munich: De Gruyter Recht.

Beale, H., Bridge, M., Gullifer, L. and Lomnicka, E. (2007) *The Law of Personal Property Security*. Oxford: Oxford University Press.

Bebchuk, L.A. and Fried, J.M. (1996) 'The Uneasy Case for the Priority of Secured Claims in Bankruptcy', 105 *Yale L. J.*, 857.

Bebchuk, L.A. and Fried, J.M. (1997) 'The Uneasy Case for the Priority of Secured Claims in Bankruptcy: Further Thoughts and a Reply to Critics', 82 *Cornell L. Rev.*, 1279.

Beck, T., Demirguc-Kunt, R. and Levine, R. (2002) 'Law and Finance: Why Does Legal Origin Matter?', *Policy Research Working Paper No 2904*. Washington, DC: World Bank.

Beck, T., Demirguc-Kunt, A., Laeven, L. and Levine, R. (2004) 'Finance, Firm Size and Growth', *NBER Working Paper No. 10983*. Cambridge, MA: NBER.

Beck, T., Demirguc-Kunt, A. and Levine, R. (2004) 'Law and Firms' Access to Finance' *Policy Research Working Paper No 3194*. Washington, DC: World Bank.

Beck, T. Demirguc-Kunt, A. and Maksimovic, V. (2005) 'Financial and Legal Constraints to Firm Growth: Does Size Matter?', 60 *Journal of Finance*, 137.

Bell, A.P. (1989) *Modern Law or Personal Property in England and Ireland*. London: Butterworths.

Berg, A. (2004) 'Charges over Book Debts: Spectrum case in the Court of Appeal', *J.B.L.*, 581.

Berg, A. (2006) 'The cuckoo in the nest of corporate insolvency: Some aspects of the Spectrum case', *J.B.L.*, 22.

Bergsten, E. (2006) 'Foreword' in J. Felemegas (ed.) *An International Approach to the Interpretation of the United Nations Convention on Contract for the International Sale of Goods (1980) as Uniform Sales Law*. Cambridge: Cambridge University Press.

Berkowitz, D., Pistor, K. and Richard, J.-F. (2003) 'The Transplant Effect', 51 *Am. J. Comp. L.*, 163.

Bjerre, C. (1999) 'Secured Transactions Inside Out: Negative Pledge Covenant, Property and Perfection', 84 *Cornell L. Rev.*, 305.

Black, J. and Rouch, D. (2008) 'The Development of the Global Markets as Rule-makers: Engagement and Legitimacy', 2 *Law and Financial Markets Rev.*, 218.

Block-Lieb, S. and Halliday, T. (2006) 'Legitimation and Global Lawmaking', *Fordham Law Legal Studies Research Paper No. 952492* (December).

Block-Lieb, S. and Halliday, T.C. (2007) 'Incrementalisms in Global Lawmaking', 32 *Brook. J. Int'l L.*, 851.

Bonell, M.J. (2005) 'Soft Law and Party Autonomy: The case of the UNIDROIT Principles', 51 *Loy. L. Rev.*, 229.

Boodman, M. (1991) 'The Myth of Harmonization of Laws', 39 *Am. J. Comp. L.*, 699, 707.

Bradgate, R. (2002) 'Twenty-Five Years of Romalpa' in I. Davies (ed.) *Security Interests in Mobile Equipment*. Aldershot: Ashgate.

Bridge, M. (1992) 'Form, Substance and Innovation in Personal Property Security Law', *J.B.L.*, 1.

Bridge, M. (1992) 'The Quistclose Trust in a World of Secured Transactions', 12 *O.J.L.S.*, 333.

Bridge, M. (1996) 'How Far is Article 9 Exportable? The English Experience', 27 *Canadian Bus. L.J.*, 196.

Bridge, M. (2001) 'English Conflict Rules for transfers of Movables: A Contract-Based Approach?' in M. Bridge and R. Stevens (eds) *Cross-Border Security and Insolvency*. Oxford: Oxford University Press.

Bridge, M. (2002) *Personal Property Law*, 3rd edn. Oxford: Oxford University Press.

Bridge, M. (2002) 'The English Law of Real Security', 4 *E.R.P.L.*, 483.

Bridge, M. (2006) 'The Law Commission's Proposals for the Reform of Corporate Security Interests' in J. Getzler and J. Payne *Company Charges Spectrum and Beyond*. Oxford: Oxford University Press.

Bridge, M. (2008) 'The Scope and Limits of Security Interests', in H. Eidenmüller and E.M. Kieninger (eds) *The Future of Secured Credit in Europe*. E.C.F.L.R., Munich: De Gruyter Recht.

Bridge, M. (2009) 'The Proprietary Aspects of Assignment and Choice of Law', *L.Q.R.*, 671.

Bridge, M., MacDonald, R., Simmonds, R. and Walsh, C. (1999) 'Formalism, Functionalism and Understanding the Law of Secured Transactions', 44 *McGill L.J.*, 567.

Briggs, A. (2009) 'When in Rome, Choose as the Romans Choose', 125 *L.Q.R.*, 191.

Buckley, F.H. (1986) 'The Bankruptcy Priority Puzzle', 72 *Va. L. Rev.*, 1393, 1444.

Burman, H.S. (2003) 'The Commercial Challenge in Modernizing Secured Transactions Law', *Unif. L. Rev.*, 347.

Buxbaum, H.L. (2003–1/2) 'Unification of the Law Governing Secured Transactions: Progress and Prospects for Reform', *Unif. L. Rev.*, 322.

Calnan, R. (2006) *Taking Security Law and Practice*, Bristol: Jordans.

Carlson, D.G. (1994) 'On the Efficiency of Secured Lending', 80 *Va. L. Rev.*, 2179.

Carsella, M.B. (1998) 'UNCITRAL: First Step in the Globalization of Asset-based Lending', 54 *The Secured Lender*, 108.

Chaves, R., Fleisig, H. and de la Pena, N. (2004) 'Secured Transactions Reform: Early Results from Romania', *CEAL Issue Brief* (September).

Chinkin, C. and Kessedjian, C. (1999) 'The Legal Relationship between the Proposed Unidroit Convention and its Equipment-Specific Protocols', *Unif. L. Rev.*, 323.

Chiu, I.H-Y. (2006) 'The Legal Fabrication of Security Interests in the United Kingdom', 31 *N.C. Int'l L. & Com. Reg.*, 703.

Claps, G.A.M. and McDonnell, J.B. (2002) 'Secured Credit and Insolvency Law in Argentina and the US: Gaining Insight from a Comparative Perspective', 30 *Ga. J. Int'l & Comp. L.*, 393.

Clark, L. and Wool, J. (1999) 'A Report on the Development of the Proposed Unidroit Convention on International Interests in Mobile Equipment as Applied to Aircraft Equipment', 31 *UCC L.J.*, 389.

Cohen, N.B. (1998) 'Harmonizing the Law Governing Secured Credit: The Next Frontier', 33 *Tex. Int'l L. J.*, 173, 184.

Cohen, N.B. (1999) 'Internationalizing the Law of Secured Credit: Perspectives from the U.S. Experience', 20 *U. Pa. J. Int'l Econ. L.*, 423.

Cohen, N.B. and Smith, E.E. (1999) 'International Secured Transactions and Revised UCC Article 9', 74 *Chi-Kent L. Rev.* 1191.

Collins, H. (1995) 'European Private Law and Cultural Identity of States', *E.R.P.L.*, 353.

Cook, C.M. (1981) *The American Codification Movement: A Study of Antebellum Legal Reform*, Westport: Greenwood.

Cooter, R. (1997) 'Normative Failure Theory of Law', 82 *Cornell L. Rev.*, 947.

Cooter, R. and Ulen, T. (2004) *Law and Economics*, International edition: 4th edn. Harlow: Pearson.

Cork Committee (Insolvency Law and Practice (1982)) Cmnd 6556.

Cranston, R. (1995) 'Credit, Security and Debt Recovery: Law's Role in Reform in Asia and the Pacific', 39 *St. Louis Univ. L. J.*, 759.

Crowther Committee Report on Consumer Credit (Cmnd 4596, 1971).

Csizmazia, N. (2008) 'Reform of the Hungarian Law of Security Rights in Movable Property', XIV *Juridica International*, 181.

Cuming, R.C.C. (1990) 'International Regulation Aspects of Security Interests in Mobile Equipment', *Unif. L. Rev.*, 62.

Cuming, R.C.C. (1997) 'The Internationalization of Secured Financing Law: The Spreading Influence of the Concepts UCC, Article 9 and its Progeny' in R. Cranston (ed.) *Making Commercial Law Essays in Honour of Roy Goode*. Oxford: Clarendon.

Cuming, R.C.C. (1998) 'Modernizing the Secured Financing and Lease Financing Laws of Developing Nations, with Particular Focus on the West Bank and Gaza' in J.S. Ziegel and S. Lerner (eds) *New Developments in International Commercial and Consumer Law: Proceedings of the 8th Biennial Conference of the International Academy of Commercial and Consumer Law*. Oxford: Hart.

Cuming, R.C.C. (2000) ' "Hot Issues" in the Development of the (Draft) Convention on International Interests in Mobile Equipment and the (Draft) Aircraft Equipment Protocol', 34 *Int'l Law.*, 1093.

Cuming, R.C.C. (2002) 'The Characterisation of Interests and Transactions under the Convention of International Interests in Mobile Equipment, 2001' in I. Davies (ed.) *Security Interests in Mobile Equipment*. Aldershot: Ashgate.

Cuming, R.C.C. (2006) 'The International Registry for Interests in Aircraft: An Overview of its Structure', *Unif. L. Rev.*, 18.

Dahan, F. (2000) 'Secured Transactions Law in Western Advanced Economies: Exposing Myths', *Law in Transition*, 37 (Autumn).

Dahan, F., Kutenicova, E. and Simpson, J. (2004) 'Enforcing Secured Transactions in Central and Eastern Europe: An Empirical Study', *Law in Transition*, 14.

Dahan, F. and McCormack, G. (2002) 'International Influences and the Polish Law on Secured Transactions: Harmonisation, Unification or What?', *Unif. L. Rev.*, 713.

Dahan, F. and Simpson, J. (2004) 'Secured Transactions in Central and Eastern Europe: European Bank for Reconstruction and Development (EBRD) Assessment', 36 *UCC L.J.*, 77, 101.

Dahan, F. and Simpson, J. (2004) 'The European Bank for Reconstruction and Development's Secured Transactions Project: a model law and ten core principles for a modern secured transactions law in countries of Central and Eastern Europe (and elsewhere!)' in E.M. Kieninger (ed.) *Security Rights in Movable Property in European Private Law*. Cambridge: Cambridge University Press.

Dahan, F. and Simpson, J. (2005) 'Publicity of Security Rights-Setting Standards for Charge Registries', *JIBFL*, 58.

Dahan, F. and Simpson, J. (2008) 'Legal Efficiency of secured transactions reform: Bridging the Gap between economic analysis and legal reasoning' in F. Dahan and J. Simpson (eds) *Secured Transactions Reform and Access to Credit,* London: Edward Elgar.

Dahan, F. and Simpson, J. V. (2009) 'Legal Efficiency for Secured Transactions Reform: Bridging the Gap between Economic Analysis and Legal Reasoning', 27 *Penn St. Int'l L. Rev.*, 623.

Davies, I. (1988) 'The Reform of Personal Property Security Law: Can Article 9 of the US UCC be a Precedent? 37 *I.C.L.Q.*, 465.

Davies, I. (2002) 'Introduction' in I. Davies (ed.) *Security Interests in Mobile Equipment.* Aldershot: Ashgate.

Davies, I. (2002) 'Retention-of-title Clauses and Non-Possessory Security Interests: A Secured Credit Regime within the European Union?' in I. Davies (ed.) *Security Interests in Mobile Equipment.* Aldershot: Ashgate.

Davies, I. (2003) 'The New Lex Mercatoria: International Interests in Mobile Equipment', 52 *I.C.L.Q.*, 151.

Davies, I. (2004) 'The Reform of English Personal Property security law: functionalism and Article 9 of the Uniform Commercial Code', 24 *Legal Studies*, 295.

de Lacy, J. (1995) 'Romalpa Theory and Practice under Retention of Title in the Sale of Goods', 24 *Anglo-American L. Rev.*, 327.

de Lacy, J. (1999) 'The Priority Rule of *Dearle v Hall* Restated'. 63 *Conv.*, 311.

de Lacy, J. (2001) 'Constructive Notice and Company Charge Registration', *Conv.*, 122.

de la Pena, N. (1999) 'Reforming the Legal Framework for Security Interests in Mobile Equipment', *Unif. L. Rev.*, 347.

de la Pena, N. (2008) 'Challenges in Implementing Secured Transactions Reform in Latin America' in F. Dahan and J. Simpson (eds) *Secured Transactions Reform and Access to Credit.* Cheltenham: Edward Elgar.

de la Pena, N. and Fleisig, H. (2002) 'SMEs and Collateral', *CEAL Issues Brief No. 3* (October).

Demirguc-Kunt, A. and Maksimovic, V. (1998) 'Law, Finance and Firm Growth', 53 *J. Finance*, 2107.

Derham, R. (2003) *The Law of Set-Off*, 3rd edn. Oxford: Oxford University Press.

Deschamps, M. 'United Nations Convention on the Assignment of Receivables in International Trade Implementation in Canada' http://www.uncitral.org/pdf/english/colloquia/3rdSecTrans/Deschamps_Implementation_Edited.pdf.

Deschamps, M. (2002) 'The Priority Rules of the United Nations Receivables Convention', 12 *Duke J. Comp. & Int'l L.*, 389.

Deschamps, M. (2008) 'Conflict-of-Laws Rules for Security Rights: What should be the Best Rules?' in H. Eidenmüller and E-M. Kieninger (eds) *The Future of Secured Credit in Europe*, E.C.F.L.R, Munich: De Gruyter Recht.

de Vries Robbé, J.J. (2008) *Securitization Law and Practice in the Face of the Credit Crunch.* Alphen aan den Rijn: Kluwer.

Diamond, A. (1989) A Review of Security Interests in Property. DTI, London: HMSO.

DiLuigi, M.C. (2008) 'Divergence of Security and Property Law in the European Union: The Need for Action', *J.B.L.*, 526.

DiMaggio, P.J. and Powell, W.W. (1983) 'The Iron Cage Revisited: Institutional Isomorphism and Collective Rationality in Organizational Fields', 48 *American Sociological Review*, 147.

Dolan, J.F. and Vegter, J.B. (1996) 'A Voluntary Filing System for Secured Financing Transactions in the European Union', 6 *E.R.P.L.*, 195.

Drobnig, U. (1998) 'Secured Credit in International Insolvency Proceedings', 33 *Tex. Int'l L. J.*, 53.

Drobnig, U. (2003). 'Present and Future of Real and Personal Security', 5 *E.R.P.L.*, 623.

Drobnig, U. (2009) 'Basic Issues of European Rules on Security in Movables' in J. De Lacy (ed.) *The Reform of Personal Property Security Law: Comparative Perspectives,* Abingdon: Routledge.

EBRD (2004) Publicity of Security Rights Guiding Principles for the Development of a Charges Registry.

Edmunds, J.A. (2002) 'Mortgages of Aircraft' in I. Davies (ed.) *Security Interests in Mobile Equipment.* Aldershot: Ashgate.

Edward, J. (2007) 'Aircraft' in P. Ali (ed.) *Secured Finance Transactions.* London: Globe Law and Business.

Eidenmüller, H. and Kieninger, E.M. (eds) (2008) *The Future of Secured Credit in Europe.* E.C.F.L.R, Munich: De Gruyter Recht.

Engelhardt, T. and Regitz, B. (2008) 'The state of nature and lending in an unreformed environment: experience from early transition countries' in F. Dahan and J. Simpson (eds) *Secured Transactions Reform and Access to Credit.* London: Edward Elgar.

Explanatory Note of the UNCITRAL Secretariat on the United Nations Convention on the Assignment of Receivables in International Trade. New York: United Nations Publication (2004).

Fairgrieve, D. and Andenas, M. (2000) 'Securing progress in collateral law reform: The EBRD's Regional Survey of Secured Transactions Laws', *Law in Transition,* 28 (Autumn).

Faria, J.A.E. (2009) 'Future Directions of Legal Harmonisation and Law Reform: Stormy Seas or Prosperous Voyage?' *Unif. L. Rev.*, 5.

Farnsworth, E.A. (1990) *Farnsworth on Contracts,* 2nd edn. New York: Aspen.

Ferran, E.V. (1988) 'Floating Charges–the Nature of the Security', *C.L.J.*, 213.

Ferrari, F. (1997) 'The International Sphere of Application of the 1988 Ottawa Convention on International Factoring', 31 *Int'l Law.*, 41.

Ferrari, F. (1999) 'General Principles and International Uniform Commercial Law Conventions: A Study of the 1980 Vienna Sales Convention and the 1988 Unidroit Conventions on International Factoring and Leasing', 10 *Pace Int'l L. Rev.*, 157.

Ferrari, F. (1999) 'The International Sphere of Application of the 1988 Ottawa Convention on International Factoring', *IBLJ*, 895.

Ferrari, F. (2000) 'The UNCITRAL Draft Convention on Assignment of Receivables Financing: Applicability, General Provisions and the Conflict of Conventions', 1 *Melbourne J. Int'l L.*, 1.

Ferrari, F. (2000) 'The UNCITRAL Draft Convention on Assignment in Receivables Financing: Critical Remarks on Some Specific Issues', in J. Basedow, I. Meier, A.K. Schnyder, T. Einhorn and D. Girsberger (eds) *Private Law in the International Arena–Liber Amicorum Kurt Siehr.* The Hague: T.M.C. Asser Press.

Ferrari, F. (2001) 'Applying the CISG in a truly uniform manner: Tribunale di Vigevano (Italy), 12 July 2000', *Unif. L. Rev.*, 203.

Ferrari, F. (2001) 'How to Create One Uniform Contract Law', 5 *VJ*, 3.

Ferrari, F. (2003) 'The Relationship between International Uniform Contract Law Conventions', 22 *J.L. & Com.*, 57.

FIAS/IFC PEP China (2007) Reforming Collateral Laws and Registries: International Best Practices and the Case of China (March).

Financial Markets Law Committee (2006) Issue 121 – European Commission Final Proposal for a Regulation on the Law Applicable to Contractual Obligations ("Rome I") (October and April).

Finch, V. (1999) 'Security Insolvency and Risk', 62 *M.L.R.*, 633.

Finch, V. (2008) 'Corporate Rescue in a World of Debt', *J.B.L.*, 756.

Finch, V. (2009) *Corporate Insolvency Law: Perspectives and Principles*, 2nd edn. Cambridge: Cambridge University Press.

Fleisig, H. (1998) 'Economic Functions of Security in a Market Economy' in J.J. Norton and M. Andenas (eds) *Emerging Financial Markets and Secured Transactions*. The Hague: Kluwer.

Fleisig, H. (1999) 'The Proposed Unidroit Convention on Mobile Equipment: Economic Consequences and Issues', *Unif. L. Rev.*, 253.

Fleisig, H. (2008) 'The economics of collateral and of collateral reform' in F. Dahan and J. Simpson (eds) *Secured Transactions Reform and Access to Credit*. Cheltenham: Edward Elgar.

Fleisig, H. and de la Pena, N. (1997) 'Peru: How Problems in the Framework for Secured Transactions Limit Access to Credit', 3 *NAFTA: L. & Bus. Rev. Am.*, 33.

Fleisig, H. and de la Pena, N. (2002) 'Microenterprises and Collateral', *CEAL Issue Brief No. 2*.

Fleisig, H. and de la Pena, N. (2002) 'SMEs and Collateral', *CEAL Issues Brief No 3*.

Fleisig, H., Safavian, M. and de la Pena, N. (2006) *Reforming Collateral Laws to Expand Access to Finance*, Washington, DC: The World Bank.

Flessner, A. (2008) 'Security Interests in Receivables–A European Perspective' in H. Eidenmüller and E.M. Kieninger (eds) *The Future of Secured Credit in Europe*. E.C.F.L.R., Munich: De Gruyter Recht.

Flessner, A. and Verhagen, H. (2006) *Assignment in European Private International Law*. Munich: Sellier.

Frankel, T. (2002) 'The Law of Cross-Border Securitization: Lex Juris', 12 *Duke J. Comp. & Int'l L.*, 475.

Gabriel, H. 'Choice of Law, Contract Terms and Uniform Law in Practice' *Congress to Celebrate the Fortieth Annual Session of the UNCITRAL*, 4, online available at <http://www.uncitral.org/pdf/english/congress/Gabriel-rev.pdf> (last accessed 30 January 2010).

Gabriel, H. (2009) 'The Advantages of Soft Law in International Commercial Law: The Role of Unidroit, UNCITRAL and the Hague Conference', 34 *Brook. J. Int'l L.*, 655.

Garro, A. (1990) 'The Reform and Harmonization of Personal Property Security Law in Latin America', 59 *Revista Juridica Universidad de Puerto Rico*, 1.

Garro, A. (1998) 'Difficulties in Obtaining Secured Lending in Latin America: Why Law Reform Really Matters?' in J.J. Norton and M. Andenas (eds) *Emerging Financial Markets and Secured Transactions*. The Hague: Kluwer.

Gennaioli, N. and Perotti, E. (2007) 'Codification, Access to Justice and Contractual Innovation'. Oxford: Oxford Financial Research Centre Law and Finance Seminars.

Gilmore, G. (1954) 'The Commercial Doctrine of Good Faith Purchase', 63 *Yale L.J.*, 1057.

Gilmore, G. (1964) 'The Assignee of Contract Rights and His Precarious Security', 74 *Yale L.J.*, 217.

Gilmore, G. (1965) *Security Interests in Personal Property*, Vol. 1. Boston: Little, Brown & Co.

Gilmore, G. (1968) 'Security Law, formalism and Article 9', 47 *Nebraska L. Rev.*, 659.

Gilmore, G. (1981) 'The Good Faith Purchase Idea and the UCC: Confessions of a Repentant Draftsman', 15 *Ga. L. Rev.*, 605.

Glenn, P. (2003) 'Harmony of Laws in the Americas', 34 *U. Miami Inter-Am. L. Rev.*, 223.

Goode, R. (1979) 'Inalienable Rights', 42 *M.L.R.*, 553.

Goode, R. (1982) 'Some Aspects of Factoring Law: I. The Acquisition of Rights in the Receivables', *J.B.L.*, 240.

Goode, R. (1983) 'Is the Law too Favourable to Secured Creditors?', 8 *Canadian Bus. L.J.*, 53.

Goode, R. (1984) 'The Modernisation of Personal Property Security Law', 100 *M.L.R.*, 234.

Goode, R. (1984) 'Uniform Law on International Factoring' in *Unification and Comparative Law in Theory and Practice Contributions in Honour of Jean Georges Sauveplanne, Deventer*. The Hague: Kluwer.

Goode, R. (1987) 'The Legal Aspects of International Factoring' in K.F. Hagenmüller and H.J. Sommer (eds) *Factoring Handbuch National–International*. Frankfurt: Fritz Knapp Verlag.

Goode, R. (1988) 'Conclusions of the Leasing and Factoring Conventions–II', *J.B.L.*, 510.

Goode, R. (1988) 'The Codification of Commercial Law', 14 *Mon. L.R.*, 135.

Goode, R. (1990) 'Why Compromise Makes Sense', *The Times*, 22 May.

Goode, R. (1993) 'Reflections of the Harmonization of Commercial Law' in R. Cranston and R. Goode (eds) *Commercial and Consumer Law National and International Dimensions*, Oxford: Clarendon.

Goode, R. (1996) '*The Exodus of the Floating Charge*' in D. Feldman and F. Meisel (eds) *Corporate and Commercial Law: Modern Developments*. London: Lloyds of London Press.

Goode, R. (1997) 'International Restatements of Contract and English Contract Law', *Unif. L. Rev.*, 231.

Goode, R. (1998) *Commercial Law in the Next Millennium: The Hamlyn Lectures Forty-Ninth Series*. London: Sweet & Maxwell.

Goode, R. (1998) 'Security in Cross Border Transactions', 33 *Tex. Int'l L. J.*, 47.

Goode, R. (1998) 'The Preliminary Draft Unidroit Convention on International Interests in Mobile Equipment', *Unif. L. Rev.*, 265.

Goode, R. (1998) 'Transcending the Boundaries of Earth and Space: The Preliminary Draft Unidroit Convention on International Interests in Mobile Equipment', *Unif. L. Rev.*, 52.

Goode, R. (2001) 'Insularity or Leadership? The Role of the United Kingdom in the Harmonization of Commercial Law', 50 *I.C.L.Q.*, 751.

Goode, R. (2001) 'The Unidroit Mobile Equipment Convention' in M. Bridge and R. Stevens *Cross Border Security and Insolvency*. Oxford: Oxford University Press.

Goode, R. (2002) 'Assignment Clauses in International Contracts', 3–4 *I.B.L.J.*, 389.

Goode, R. (2002) 'Harmonised Modernisation of the Law Governing Secured Transactions, Outline' in Worldwide Harmonisation of Private Law and Regional Economic Integration, Congress for the Celebration of 75th Anniversary of Unidroit, Rome.

Goode, R. (2002). 'The Cape Town Convention on International Interests in Mobile equipment: A Driving Force for International Asset-Based Financing', *Unif. L. Rev.*, 3.

Goode, R. (2003) 'Harmonised Modernisation of the Law Governing Secured Transactions: General–Sectorial, Global–Regional', *Unif. L. Rev.*, 341.

Goode, R. (2004) *Commercial Law*, 3rd edn. London: Butterworths.

Goode, R. (2005) *Principles of Corporate Insolvency Law*, 3rd edn. London: Sweet & Maxwell.

Goode, R. (2008) *Convention on International Interests in Mobile Equipment and Protocol Thereto on Matters Specific to Aircraft Equipment Official Commentary*. Rome: Unidroit.

Goode, R. (2009) 'Contractual prohibitions against assignment', *L.M.C.L.Q.*, 300.

Gopalan, S. (2003) 'Harmonization of Commercial Law: Lessons from the Cape Town Convention on International Interests in Mobile Equipment', 9 *L. & Bus. Rev. Am.*, 255.

Gopalan, S. (2003) 'Securing Mobile Assets: The Cape Town Convention and Its Aircraft Protocol', 29 *N.C.J. Int'l L. & Com. Reg.*, 59.

Gopalan, S. (2003) 'Transnational Commercial Law: The Way Forward', 18 *Am. U. Int'l L. Rev.*, 803.

Gopalan, S. (2004) 'New Trends in the Making of International Commercial Law', 23 *J. L. & Com.*, 117.

Gopalan, S. (2004) 'The Creation of International Commercial Law: Sovereignty Felled?', 5 *San Diego Int'l L.J.*, 267.

Gopalan, S. (2008) 'A Demandeur-Centric Approach to Regime Design in Transnational Commercial Law', 39 *Georgetown J. Int'l L.*, 327.

Gordley, J. (2000) 'The Common Law in the Twentieth Century: Some Unfinished Business', 88 *Cal. L. Rev.*, 1817.

Gray, C.W. and Jarosz, W.W. (1995) 'Law and the Regulation of Foreign Direct Investment: The Experience from Central and Eastern Europe', 33 *Colum. J. Transnat'l L.*, 1.

Gretton, G. (1998) 'Mixed Systems: Scotland' in J. Norton and M. Andenas (eds) *Emerging Financial Markets and Secured Transactions*. The Hague: Kluwer.

Gullifer, L. (2003) 'Will the Law Commission sink the floating charge?', *L.M.C.L.Q.*, 125.

Gullifer, L. (2005) 'Quasi-Security Interests: Functionalism and the Incidents of Security' in I. Davies (ed.) *Issues in International Commercial Law*. Aldershot: Ashgate.

Gullifer, L. (2007) 'Retention of Title Clauses: A Question of Balance' in A. Burrows and E. Peel (eds) *Contract Terms*, Oxford: Oxford University Press.

Gullifer, L. (2008) 'The reforms of the Enterprise Act 2002 and the Floating Charge as a security device', 46 *Canadian Bus. L. J.*, 399.

Gullifer, L. (ed.) (2009) *Goode on Legal Problems of Credit and* Security, 4th edn. London: Sweet & Maxwell.

Haag, H. and Peglow, O. (2008) 'Germany' in W. Johnston (ed.) *Security over Receivables: An International Handbook*. Oxford: Oxford University Press.

Halliday, T. and Carruthers, B. (2009) *Bankrupt: Global Lawmaking and Systematic Financial Crisis*. Stanford: Stanford University Press.

Hansmann, H. and Kraakman, R. (2002) 'Property, Contract and Verification: The *Numerus Clausus* Problem and the Divisibility of Rights', 31 *J. Legal Studies*, 373.

Hansmann, H. and Kraakman, R. (2002) 'Property, Contract and verification: The Numerus Clausus Problem and the Divisibility of Rights', *John M. Olin Centre for Law, Economics and Business Discussion Paper No. 388*. Cambridge, MA: Harvard Law School.

Harris, S.L. and Mooney Jr., C.W. (1994) 'A Property Based Theory of Security Interests: Taking Debtors' Choices Seriously', 80 *Va. L. Rev.*, 2021.

Harris, S.L. and Mooney, C.W. (1997) 'Measuring the Social Costs and Benefits and Identifying the Victims of Subordinating Security Interests in Bankruptcy', 82 *Cornell L. Rev.*, 1349.

Haselmann, R., Pistor, K. and Vig, V. (2006) 'How Law Affects Lending' *Columbia Law and Economics Working Paper No. 285*.

Hausmann, J. (1996) 'The Value of Public-Notice Filing Under Uniform Commercial Code Article 9: A Comparison with the German Legal System of Securities in Personal Property', 25 *Ga. J. Int'l & Comp. L.*, 427.

Head, J.W. (1996) 'Evolution of the Governing Law for Loan Agreements of the World Bank and Other Multilateral Development Banks', 90 *Am. J. Int'l L.*, 214, 217.

Heiss, H. (2009) 'Party Autonomy' in F. Ferrari and S. Lieble (eds) *Rome I Regulation: The Law Applicable to Contractual Obligations in Europe*. Munich: Sellier.

Hermann, G. (2001) 'The Role of UNCITRAL' in I. Fletcher, M. Cremona and L. Mistelis (eds) *Foundations and Perspectives of International Trade Law*. London: Sweet & Maxwell.

Hill, C.A. (1996) 'Securitization: A Low Cost Sweetener For Lemons', 74 *Wash. U. L. Q.*, 1061.

Hobhouse, J.S. (1990) *International Conventions and Commercial Law: The Pursuit of Uniformity*, 106 *L.Q.R.*, 531.

Honnebier, B.P. and Milo, J.M. (2004) 'The Convention of Cape Town: The Creation of International Interests in Mobile Equipment', 12 *E.R.P.L.*, 3.

Hurst, T. (2009) 'The Role of Credit Rating Agencies in the Current Worldwide Financial Crisis', *Comp. Law.*, 61.

Hyland, R. (2004) 'The American Experience: Restatements, the UCC, Uniform Laws and Transnational Coordination' in A. Hartkamp and E. Hondius (eds) *Towards a European Civil Code*, 3rd edn. The Hague: Kluwer.

IFC/MPDF (2007) 'Vietnam Increasing Access to Credit through Collateral (Secured Transactions) Reform'. Brighton: Eldis.

Jackson, T. and Kronman, A. (1979) 'Secured Financing and Priorities Among Creditors', 88 *Yale L. J.*, 1143.

Jackson, T. and Scott, R. (1989) 'On the Nature of Bankruptcy: an Essay on Bankruptcy Sharing and the Creditors' Bargain', 75 *Va. L. Rev.*, 155.

John, M. (1989) *Politics and the Law in Late Nineteenth-Century Germany: The origins of the Civil Code.* Oxford: Clarendon Press.

Johnson, G. (2000) 'Towards International Standards on Insolvency: The catalytic role of the World Bank', *Law in Transition*, 69 (Spring).

Kanning, A.J. (2007) 'The Emergence of a European Private Law: Lessons from 19th Century Germany', 27 *O.J.L.S.*, 193.

Kelly, C.R. (2009) 'The Politics of International Economic Law: Legitimacy and the UNCITRAL Working Methods', *Brooklyn Law School Legal Studies Research Papers Working Paper Series No. 140.*

Kieninger, E-M. (2004) 'Evaluation: A Common Core? Convergences, subsisting differences and possible ways for harmonisation' in E-M. Kieninger (ed.) *Security Rights in Movable Property in European Private Law.* Cambridge: Cambridge University Press.

Kieninger, E-M. (2008) 'The Scope and Limits of Security Interests–Commentary' in H. Eidenmüller and E.M. Kieninger (eds) *The Future of Secured Credit in Europe.* E.C.F.L.R., Munich: De Gruyter Recht.

Kieninger, E-M. and Sigman, H.C. (2006) 'The Rome-I Proposed Regulation and the Assignment of Receivables', *The European Legal Forum*, 1.

Kilborn, J. (1996) 'Securing Russia's Future: A Plea for Reform in Russian Secured Transactions Law', 95 *Mich. L. Rev.*, 255.

Klee, K.N. (1997) 'Barbarians at the Trough: Riposte in Defense of the Warren Carve-out Proposal', 82 *Cornell L. Rev.*, 1467.

Kohn, R. 'Possible Future Work on Security Rights in Directly Held Securities' http://www.uncitral.org/pdf/english/colloquia/3rdSecTrans/Richard_Kohn_Edited.pdf.

Kohn, R.M. (2007) 'Promoting the Implementation of the United Nations Convention on the Assignment of Receivables in International Trade and the UNCITRAL Legislative Guide on Secured Transactions', *Comments at the Congress to Celebrate the 40th Annual Session of UNCITRAL*, Vienna 9–12 July 2007.

Kötz, H. (1991) *International Encyclopaedia of Comparative Law – Rights of Third Parties, Third Party Beneficiaries and Assignment.* Boston, MA: Brill.

Kötz, H. (1997) *European Contract Law – Volume 1: Formation, Validity, and Content of Contracts, Contract and Third Parties.* Oxford: Clarendon Press.

Kozolchyk, B. (2007) 'Secured Lending and Its Poverty Reduction Effect', 42 *Texas Int'l L. J.* 727.

Kozolchyk, B. and Wilson, J. (2002) 'The Organization of American States: The New Model Inter-American Law on Secured Transactions', *Unif. L. Rev.*, 69.

Kozolchyk, B. (2009) 'Modernization of Commercial Law: International Uniformity and Economic Development', 34 *Brook. J. Int'l L.*, 709.

Kozuka, S. (2007) 'The Economic Implications of Uniformity in Law', *Unif. L. Rev.*, 683.

Kreuzer, K. (2008) 'Conflict-of-Laws Rules for Security Rights in Tangible Assets in the European Union' in H. Eidenmüller and E-M. Kieninger (eds) *The Future of Secured Credit in Europe*, E.C.F.L.R, Munich: De Gruyter Recht.

Kripke, H. (1985) 'Law and Economics: Measuring the Economic Efficiency of Commercial Law in a Vacuum of Fact', 133 *U. Pa. L. Rev.*, 929.

Kronke, H. 'Why Transplants Rarely Work – Why Convergence is Insufficient in Commercial Law – Methodical Changes in Paradigm in the Harmonisation of Commercial Law' http://www.law.qmul.ac.uk/events/docs/London_February_2008_Kronke.ppt#1.

Kronke, H. (2005) 'Methodical Freedom and Organizational Constraints in the Development of Transnational Commercial Law', 51 *Loy. L. Rev.*, 287.

Krupski, J. (2007) 'Cross-Border Receivables Financing at the Crossroads of Legal traditions, Capital Markets, Uniform Law and Modernity', *Unif. L. Rev.*, 57.

Lalive, P.A. (1955) *The Transfer of Chattels in the Conflict of Laws*. Oxford: Clarendon Press.

Lando, O. (1998) 'Principles of European Contract Law in the Third Millennium' in Centre for Transnational Law (ed.), *Transnational Law in Commercial Legal Practice*. Köln.

Lasfer, M.A. (2000) 'Debt Structure, Agency Costs and Firm's Size: An Empirical Investigation', *Working Paper*. London: Cass Business School.

Law Commission Consultation Paper on Company Security Interests No. 164 (2002).

Law Commission Consultation Paper on Company Security Interests No. 176 (2004).

Law Commission Report on Company Security Interests No. 296 (2005).

Lawrence, W., Henning, W. and Freyermuth, W. (2004) *Understanding Secured Transactions*, 3rd edn. Newark, NJ: Lexis Nexis.

Leavy, J. (2007) 'France' in H.C. Sigman and E.M. Kieninger *Cross Border Security over Tangibles*. Munich: Sellier.

Leebron, D.W. (1996) *Claims for Harmonization: A Theoretical Framework*, 27 *Canadian Bus. L.J.*, 63.

Legrand, P. (1997) 'Against a European Civil Code', 60 *M.L.R.*, 44.

Legrand, P. (2002) 'On the Unbearable Localness of the Law: Academic Fallacies and Unseasonable Observations', *E.R.P.L.*, 61.

Legrand, P. (2006) 'Antivonbar', 1 *J.C.L.*, 1.

Levine, R. (2004). 'Finance and Growth: Theory and Evidence', *National Bureau of Economic Research, Working Paper 10766*. Cambridge, MA: N.B.E.R.

Levmore, S. (1994) 'Explaining Creditor Priorities', 80 *Va. L. Rev.*, 2103.

Llewellyn, K. (1957) 'Why We Need the Uniform Commercial Code', 10 *U. Fla. L. Rev.*, 367.

Lopez-De-Silanes, F. (2008) 'Turning the Key to Credit: Credit Access and Credit Institutions' in F. Dahan and J. Simpson (eds) *Secured Transactions Reform and Access to Credit*. Cheltenham: Edward Elgar.

LoPucki, L.M. (1994) 'The Unsecured Creditor's Bargain', 80 *Va. L. Rev.*, 1887.

LoPucki, L.M. (1997) 'Should the Secured Credit Carve-Out Apply Only in Bankruptcy? A Systems/Strategic Analysis', 82 *Cornell L. Rev.*, 1483.

Lukas, M. (2008) 'Attachment/Creation of a Security Interest' in H. Eidenmüller and E.M. Kieninger (eds) *The Future of Secured Credit in Europe*. E.C.F.L.R., Munich: De Gruyter Recht.

Macdonald, R. 'A Model Law on Secured Transactions: A Representation of Structure? An Object of Imitation? A Type or Design?' available at http://www.uncitral.org/pdf/english/colloquia/3rdSecTrans/Roderick_Macdonald_Edited-ML.pdf.

Macdonald, R. (2007) 'Unitary Law Reform, Pluralistic Law Resubstance: Illuminating Legal Change', 67 *La. L. Rev.*, 1114.

Macdonald, R. (2009) 'Three Metaphors of Norm Migration in International Context', 34 *Brook. J. Int'l L.*, 603.

Mann, R.J. (1997) 'Explaining the Pattern of Secured Credit', 110 *Harvard L. Rev.*, 625.

Markell, B. (2002) 'UNCITRAL's Receivables Convention: The First Step, But Not the Last', 12 *Duke J. Comp. & Int'l L.*, 401.

Markell, B.A. and Broude, R.F. (2003) 'A Short Introduction to the Priority Provisions of the UNCITRAL Convention on the Assignment of Receivables in International Trade', 16 *Insolv. Int.*, 1.

Marshall, O.R. (1950) *The Assignment of Choses in Action*. London: Pitman's Equity Series.

Mattei, U. (2000) *Basic Principles of Property Law: A Comparative Legal and Economic Introduction*. Westport: Greenwood.

McCormack, G. (1994) *Registration of Company Charges*. London: Sweet & Maxwell.

McCormack, G. (1995) *Reservation of Title*, 2nd edn. London: Sweet & Maxwell.

McCormack, G. (1987) 'Fixed Charges on Future Book Debts', *Co. Law.*, 3.

McCormack, G. (1998) 'Charge Backs and Commercial Certainty in the House of Lords', *CfiLR*, 111.

McCormack, G. and Dahan, F. (1999) 'The EBRD Model Law on Secured Transactions: Comparisons and Convergence', *CfiLR*, 65.

McCormack, G. (2000) 'Debts and Non-assignment Clauses', *J.B.L.*, 422.

McCormack, G. (2002) 'Notice filing versus Transactions Filing–A Comparison of the English and US Law of Security Interests', *Insolvency Lawyer*, 166.

McCormack, G. (2002) 'Personal Property Security Law Reform in England and Canada', *J.B.L.*, 113.

McCormack, G. (2002) 'Security Interests in Deposit Accounts: An Anglo-American Perspective', *Insolvency Lawyer*, 7.

McCormack, G. (2002) 'The Nature of Security over Receivables', 23 *Co. Law.*, 84.

McCormack, G. (2003) '"Quasi-securities" and the Law Commission Consultation paper on security interests–a brave new world', *L.M.C.L.Q.*, 80.

McCormack, G. (2003) 'Rewriting the English Law of Personal Property Securities and Article 9 of the US Uniform Commercial Code', 24 *Co. Law.*, 68.

McCormack, G. (2003) 'The Priority of Secured Credit: An Anglo-American Perspective', *J.B.L.*, 389.

McCormack, G. (2004) *Secured Credit under English and American Law*. Cambridge: Cambridge University Press.

McCormack, G. (2005) 'The Law Commission Consultative Report on Company Security Interests: An Irreverent Riposte', 68 *M.L.R.*, 286.

McCormack, G. (2005) *Registration of Company Charges*, 2nd edn. Bristol: Jordans.

McCormack, G. (2007) 'The UNCITRAL Legislative Guide on Secured Transactions Functionalism and Form' in B. Foëx, L. Thévenoz, and S.V. Bazinas (eds) *Réforme des sûretés mobilières. Les enseignements du Guide législatif de la CNUDCI/Reforming secured transactions, The UNCITRAL legislative guide as an inspiration*. Genève-Zurich-Bâle: Schulthess.

McCormack, G. (2008) *Corporate Rescue Law–An Anglo-American Perspective*. Cheltenham: Edward Elgar.

McCormack, G. (2008) 'The CFR and Credit Securities: A Suitable Case for Treatment?', *WG Hart Legal Workshop Paper*. London: The Institute of Advanced Legal Studies (24 June).

McCormack, G. (2008) 'The CFR and Credit Securities: A Suitable Case for Treatment?' in A. Vaquer (ed.) *European Private Law beyond the Common Frame of Reference: Essays in Honour of Reinhard Zimmermann*. Groningen: Europa Law Publishers.

McCormack, G. (2009) 'Jurisdictional Competition and Forum Shopping in Insolvency Proceedings', 68 *C.L.J.*, 169.

McDonnell, J. (1999) 'Is Revised Article 9 a Little Greedy?', 104 *Com. L. J.*, 241.
McKnight, A. (2002) 'Restrictions on Dealing with Assets in Financing Documents: Their Role, Meaning and Effect', 17 *J.I.B.L.*, 193.
McKnight, A. (2003) 'Contractual Prohibitions on a Creditor's Right to Alienate Debts', 18 *J.I.B.L.I.*, 1.
McKnight, A. (2003) 'Contractual Restrictions on a Creditor's Right to Alienate Debts: Part 2, 18 *J.I.B.L.*, 43.
McMeel, G. (2004) 'The Modern Law of Assignment: public policy and contractual restrictions on transferability', *L.M.C.L.Q.*, 483.
Merrett, L. (2008) 'The importance of delivery and possession in the passing of title', *C.L.J.*, 376.
Merrill, T. and Smith, H. (2000) 'Optimal Standardization in the Law of Property: The Numerus Clausus Principle', 110 *Yale L. J.*, 1.
Mestre, F. (1987) 'Explanatory Report on the draft Convention on International Factoring', *Unif. L. Rev.*, 85.
Miller, G.P. (1997) 'The Legal-Economic Analysis of Comparative Civil Procedure', 45 *Am. J. Comp. L.*, 905.
Milo, J.M. (2003) 'Retention of Title in European Business Transactions', 43 *Washburn L. J.*, 121.
Mistelis, L. (1998) 'The EBRD Model Law on Secured Transactions and Its Impact on Collateral Law Reform in Central and Eastern Europe and the former Soviet Union', 5 *Parker Sch. J.E.Eur.L.*, 455.
Mistelis, L. (2000) 'Regulatory Aspects: Globalization, Harmonization, Legal Transplants and Law Reform–Some Fundamental Observations', 34 *Int'l Law.*, 1055.
Mistelis, L. (2001) 'Is Harmonisation a Necessary Evil? The Future of Harmonisation and New Sources of International Trade Law' in I. Fletcher, M. Cremona and L. Mistelis (eds) *Foundations And Perspectives of International Trade Law*. London: Sweet & Maxwell.
Mitchell, C. (2007) *Subrogation: Law and Practice*. Oxford: Oxford University Press.
Modigliani, F. and Miller, M. (1958) 'The Cost of Capital, Corporation Finance and the Theory of Investment', 48 *Am. Econ. Rev.*, 433.
Mokal, R. (2001) 'Priority as Pathology: The *Pari Passu* Myth', 69 *C.L.J.*, 581.
Mooney, C. (1999) 'Assignments of International Interests in Mobile Equipment and Related Receivables under the Unidroit Convention: When Should the Tail Wag the Dog?', 20 *U. Pa. J. Int'l. Econ. L.*, 443.
Mooney, C. (1999) 'Relationship between the Prospective Unidroit International Registry, Revised Uniform Commercial Code Article 9 and National Civil Aviation Registries', *Unif. L. Rev.*, 335.
Mooney, C. (2001) 'Extraterritorial Impact of Choice of Law Rules for Non-United States Debtors under Revised Uniform Commercial Code Article 9 and a New Proposal for International Harmonisation' in M. Bridge and R. Stevens (eds) *Cross Border Security and Insolvency*. Oxford: Oxford University Press.
Moshinsky, M. (1992) 'The Assignment of Debts in the Conflict of Laws', *L.Q.R.*, 591, 612.
Moyle, J.B. (trans.) (1913) *The Institutes of Justinian* 3.14.4, 5th edn. Oxford: Clarendon Press.
Nussbaumer, M. and Barut, Ö. (2009) 'Assessing Turkey's Commercial Laws: An EBRD Perspective', *Law in Transition*, 60 (Spring).
Oditah, F. (1991) '*Legal Aspects of Receivables Financing*', London: Sweet & Maxwell.
Oditah, F. (2009) 'Recurrent Issues in Receivables Financing' in J. Armour and J. Payne *Rationality in Company Law Essays in Honour of DD Prentice*. Oxford: Hart.

Ogus, A. (1999) 'Competition Between National Legal Systems: A Contribution of Economic Analysis to Comparative Law', 48 *I.C.L.Q.*, 405.

Örücü, E. (2000) 'Critical Comparative Law: Considering Paradoxes for Legal Systems in Transition', 4.1 *Electronic Journal of Comparative Law* http://www.ejcl.org/41/art41-1.html.

Osborne, D. (2004) 'Lex Situs and Aircraft', *L.M.C.L.Q.*, 303, 312.

Perkins, J. (2008) 'A Question of Priorities: Choice of Law and Proprietary Aspects of the Assignment of Debts', 2 *L. & F.M.R.*, 238.

Philbrick, W.C. (1994) 'The Use of Factoring in International Commercial Transactions and the Need for the Legal Uniformity as Applied to Factoring Transactions between the United States and Japan', 99 *Com. L.J.*, 141.

Prentice, D. (2004) 'Bargaining in the Shadow of the Enterprise Act 2002', 5 *E.B.O.R.*, 153.

Rajski, J. (1998) 'The Challenge of Adapting Law to Market Economies in Post Communist Central European Countries' in S. Ziegel and S. Lerner (eds) *New Developments in International Commercial and Consumer Law Proceedings of the 8th Biennial Conference of the International Academy of Commercial and Consumer Law*. Oxford: Hart.

Rakob, J. (2007) 'Germany' in H.C. Sigman and E.M. Kieninger *Cross Border Security over Tangibles*. Munich: Sellier.

Reisman, A. (1988) 'The International Factoring Convention', 44 *The Secured Lender*, 26.

Reisman, A. (1990) 'The Uniform Commercial Code and the Convention on International Factoring', 22 *UCC.L.J.*, 320.

Report of the Committee on Foreign and Comparative Law of the Association of the Bar of the City of New York (21 December 2001).

Ribstein, L.E. and Kobayashi, B.H. (1996) 'An Economic Analysis of Uniform States Laws', 25 *J. Legal Studies*, 131.

Rogerson, P. (1990) 'The Situs of Debts in the Conflict of Laws–Illogical, Unnecessary and Misleading', 49 *C.L.J.*, 441.

Röver, J-H.M. (2007) *Secured Lending in Eastern Europe: Comparative Law of Secured Transactions and the EBRD Model Law*. Oxford: Oxford University Press.

Rühl, G. (2007) 'Party Autonomy in the Private International Law of Contracts: Transatlantic Convergence and Economic Efficiency', *CLPE Research Paper 4/2007*, Vol. 03, No. 1.

Rutgers, J.W. 'Secured Credit and the Internal Market: The Fundamental Freedoms and the EU's Mandate for Legislation' available at SSRN: http://ssrn.com/abstract=1099893.

Ryan Jr., R.H. (1999) 'Trade Receivables Purchases', *SD71 ALI-ABA*, 305.

Safavian, M. (2008) 'Firm level evidence on collateral and access to finance' in F. Dahan and J. Simpson (eds) *Secured Transactions Reform and Access to Credit*. Cheltenham: Edward Elgar.

Safavian, M. Fleisig, H. and Steinbuks, J. (2006) 'Unlocking Dead Capital', *Viewpoint*, Note Number 307 (March).

Safavian, M. and Sharma, S. (2007) 'When do Creditor Rights Work?', *Policy Research Working Paper No 4296*. Washington, DC: World Bank.

Salinger, F. (2006) *Factoring: The Law and Practice of Invoice Finance*, 4th edn. Sweet & Maxwell: London.

Saunders, A., Srinivasan, A. and Walter, I. (2006) 'Innovation in International Law and Global Finance: Estimating the Financial Impact of the Cape Town Convention', *NYU Working Paper No. FIN-06-037*. New York: New York University.

Saunders, A., Srinivasan, A., Walter, I. and Wool, J. (1999) 'The Economic Implications of International Secured Transactions Law Reform: A Case Study', 20 *U. Pa. J. Int'l Econ. L.*, 309.

Saunders, A. and Walter, I. (1998) 'Proposed Unidroit Convention on International Interests in Mobile Equipment as Applicable to Aircraft Equipment through the Aircraft Equipment Protocol: Economic Impact Assessment'. New York: INSEAD and New York University.

Schäfer, H-B. (2008) 'The Law and Economics Debate About Secured Lending: Lessons for European Lawmaking?' in H. Eidenmüller and E.M. Kieninger (eds) *The Future of Secured Credit in Europe*. E.C.F.L.R., Munich: De Gruyter Recht.

Schilling, T. (1985) 'Some European Decisions on Non-Possessory Security Rights in Private International Law', 34 *I.C.L.Q.*, 87.

Schnader, W.A. (1967) 'A Short History of the Preparation and Enactment of the Uniform Commercial Code'. 22 *U. Miami L. Rev.* 1.

Schwartz, A. (1981) 'Security Interests and Bankruptcy Priorities: A Review of Current Theories', 10 *J. Legal Studies*, 1.

Schwartz, A. (1989) 'A Theory of Loan Priorities', *J. Legal* Studies, 209.

Schwartz, A. (1994) 'Taking the Analysis of Security Seriously', 80 *Va. L. Rev.*, 2073.

Schwartz, A. (1997) 'Priority Contracts and Priority in Bankruptcy'. 82 *Cornell L. Rev.* 1396.

Schwartz, A. and Scott, R. (1995) 'The Political Economy of Private Legislatures', 143 *U. Pa. L. Rev.*, 9.

Schwarcz, S.L. (1994) 'The Alchemy of Asset Securitization', 1 *Stan. J. L. Bus. & Fin.*, 133.

Schwarcz, S.L. (1998) 'The Universal Language of Cross Border Finance', 8 *Duke J. Comp. & Int'l L.*, 235.

Schwarcz, S.L. (1999) 'Towards a Centralized Perfection System For Cross-Border Receivables Financing', 20 *U. Pa. J. Int'l Econ. L.*, 455.

Schwarcz, S.L. (2004) 'Securitization Post-Enron', 25 *Cardozo L. Rev.*, 1539, 1540.

Scott, R. (1986) 'A Relational Theory of Secured Financing', 86 *Columbia L. Rev.*, 901.

Scott, R. (1994) 'The Politics of Article 9', 80 *Va. L. Rev.*, 1783.

Scott, R. (1997) 'The Truth about Secured Financing', 82 *Cornell L. Rev.*, 1436, 1437–8.

Scottish Law Commission Discussion Paper No 121, Registration of Rights in Security by Companies. Edinburgh, October 2002.

Sealy, L.S. and Hooley, R.J.A. (2003) *Commercial Law Text, Cases and Materials*, 3rd edn. London: Butterworths.

Sepinuck, S.L. (2008) *Practice under Article 9 of the Uniform Commercial Code.* Saratoga, NY: American Bar Association.

Serick, R. (1990) *Securities in Movables in German Law: An Outline.* London: Kluwer.

Sheppard, H.E. (2001) 'Overcoming Apathetic Internationalism to Generate Hemispheric Benefits: An Analysis of and Arguments for Recent Secured Transactions Law in Mexico', 10 *Fla. St. U. J. Transnat'l L. & Pol.*, 133.

Sigman, H.C. (1998) 'The case for Worldwide Reform of the Law Governing Secured Transactions in Movable Property' in J. Ziegel (ed.) *New Developments in International Commercial and Consumer Law.* Oxford: Hart.

Sigman, H.C. (2004) 'Security in Movables in the United States–Uniform Commercial Code Article 9: A Basis for Comparison' in E-M. Kieninger (ed.) *Security Rights in Movable Property in European Private Law.* Cambridge: Cambridge.

Sigman, H.C. (2008) 'Perfection and Priority of Security Rights' in H. Eidenmüller and E.M. Kieninger (eds) *The Future of Secured Credit in Europe.* E.C.F.L.R., Munich: De Gruyter Recht.

Sigman, H.C. and Kieninger, E-M. (eds) (2007) *Cross-Border Security over Tangibles.* Munich: Sellier.

Sigman, H.C. and Kieninger, E-M. (eds) (2009) *Cross-Border Security over Receivables.* Munich: Sellier.

Sigman, H.C. and Smith, E. (2001) 'The Draft UNCITRAL Convention on Assignment of Receivables in International Trade: A Summary of the Key Provisions as Completion draws near', 33 *UCC L. J.*, 344.

Sigman, H.C. and Smith, E. (2002) 'Toward Facilitating Cross Border Secured Financing and Securitization: An Analysis of the United Nations Convention on the Assignment of Receivables in International Trade', 57 *Bus. Law.*, 727.

Simpson, J. and Dahan, F. (2006) 'The Impact of the Legal Framework on the Secured Credit Market in Poland', *JIBFL*, 174.

Simpson, J. and Menze, J. (2000) 'Ten Years of Secured Transactions Reform', *Law in Transition* (Autumn).

Simpson, J. and Menze, J. (2000) 'Ten Years of Secured Transactions Reform', *Law in Transition*, Part 2 (Autumn).

Simpson, J.L. and Röver, J-H.M. (1994) 'Model Law on Secured Transactions completed', *Law in Transition*, 1 (Spring).

Simpson, J.L. and Röver, J-H.M. (1997) 'General Principles of a Modern Secured Transactions Law', *NAFTA: L. & Bus. Rev. Am.*, 73.

Simpson, J.L. and Röver, J-H.M. (1998) 'General Principles of a Modern Secured Transactions Law' in J. Norton and M. Andenas (eds) *Emerging Financial Markets and Secured Transactions*. The Hague: Kluwer.

Spanogle, J.A. (1998) 'A Functional Analysis of the EBRD Model Law on Secured Transactions', in J.J. Norton and M. Andenas (eds) *Emerging Financial Markets and Secured Transactions*. The Hague: Kluwer.

Stanford, M. (1999) 'A Broader or a Narrower Band of Beneficiaries for the Proposed New International Regimen? Some Reflections on the Merits of the Convention/Protocol Structure in Facilitating the Former', *Unif. L. Rev.*, 242.

Stanford, M. (2002) 'From Ottawa to Cape Town: Unidroit's Role in the Modernisation of the Law governing Leasing and the Taking of Security' in I. Davies (ed.) *Security Interests in Mobile Equipment*. Aldershot: Ashgate.

Steffens, L. (2006) 'The New Rule on the Assignment of Rights in Rome: I – The Solution to All our Proprietary Problems? – Determination of the Conflict of Laws rule in respect of the Proprietary Aspects of Assignment', 4 *E.R.P.L.*, 543.

Stephan, P.B. (1999) 'The Futility of Unification and Harmonization in International Commercial Law', 39 *Va. J. Int'l L.*, 743.

Stephen, F.H. (1988) *The Economics of the Law*. Hertfordshire: Harvester Wheatsheaf.

Stevens, R. (2001) 'The English Conflict of Laws Rules' in M. Bridge and R. Stevens (eds) *Cross Border Security and Insolvency*. Oxford: Oxford University Press.

Stevens, R. (2008) 'Choosing the Right Approach for European Law Making' in H. Eidenmüller and E-M. Kieninger (eds) *The Future of Secured Credit in Europe* E.C.F.L.R., Munich: De Gruyter Recht.

Steyn, J. (1994) 'A Kind of Esperanto' in P. Birks (ed.) *The Frontiers of Liability*, Vol. 2. Oxford: Oxford University Press.

Struycken, T.H.D. (1998) 'The Proprietary Aspects of International Assignment of Debts and the Rome Convention, Article 12', *L.M.C.L.Q.*, 345.

Struycken, T.H.D. and Stevens, R. (2002) 'Assignment and the Rome Convention', *L.Q.R.*, 15, 19.

Stürner, R. (2008) 'Perfection and Priority of Security Rights Commentary' in H. Eidenmüller and E.M. Kieninger (eds) *The Future of Secured Credit in Europe*. E.C.F.L.R., Munich: De Gruyter Recht.

Sundahl, M.J. 'The "Cape Town Approach": A New Method of Making International Law' 44 *Colum. J. Transnat'l L.* 339 (2006).

Tang, Z. (2008) 'Law Applicable in the Absence of Choice–The New Article 4 of the Rome I Regulation', 71 *M.L.R.*, 785.

Tata, V. (2007) 'The Role of Multilaterals in the Promotion of Modern Securities Law', *Comments at the Congress to Celebrate the 40th Annual Session of UNCITRAL*. Vienna 9–12 July.

Tettenborn, A. (1998) 'Trust of Unassignable Agreements', *L.M.C.L.Q.*, 498.

Tettenborn, A. (1999) 'Trusts and Unassignable Agreements – Again', *L.M.C.L.Q.*, 353.

Thorne, P. (2006) 'Goodbye Geneva, Hello Cape Town', *BJIBFL* 439.

Tomasic, R. (2008) 'Corporate Rescue, Governance and Risk-Taking in Northern Rock' (Part 1) and (Part 2), *Company Lawyer*, 29(10): 297–303 and 29(11): 330–337.

Treitel, G. (2003) *The Law of Contract*, 11th edn. London: Sweet & Maxwell.

Triantis, G. (1992) 'Secured Debt Under Conditions of Imperfect Information', 21 *J. Legal Studies*, 225.

True, R.B. 'New Developments in Japanese Asset Securitization: Open the Floodgates', available at http://www.tuj.ac.jp/newsite/main/law/lawresources/TUJonline/Corporate/assetsecwith%20glossary.html.

van Erp, S. (2003) 'A Numerus Quasi-Clausus of Property Rights as a Constitutive Element of a Future European Property Law?', 7 *E.J.C.L.*, www.ejcl.org/72/art72-2.html.

van Erp, S. (2003) 'Civil and Common Property law: Caveat Comparator–The Value of Legal Historical-Comparative Analysis', *E.R.P.L.*, 394.

Veneziano, A. (2008) 'Attachment/Creation of a Security Right' in H. Eidenmüller and E.M. Kieninger (eds) *The Future of Secured Credit in Europe*. E.C.F.L.R., Munich: De Gruyter Recht.

Verhagen, R. (2006) 'Assignment in Commission's Rome I Proposal', *L.M.C.L.Q.*, 270.

von Ziegler, A. (2000) 'Particularities of the Harmonisation and Unification of International Law of Trade and Commerce' in J. Basedow (ed.) *Private Law in the International Arena–Liber Amicorum Kurt Siehr*. The Hague: T.M.C. Asser Press, p. 875.

Wälde, T. and Gunderson, J. (1994) 'Legislative Reforms in Transition Economies: Western Transplants – A Shortcut to Social Economy Status', 43 *I.C.L.Q.*, 345.

Walsh, C. (1997) 'Registration, Constructive Notice and the Rule in Dearle v Hall', 12 *Banking & Finance L.R.*, 129.

Walsh, C. (2001) 'Receivables Financing and the Conflict of Laws: The UNCITRAL Draft Convention on the Assignment of Receivables in International Trade', 106 *Dick. L. Rev.*, 159.

Walsh, C. (2003) 'Super-Priority for Asset Acquisition Financing in Secured Transactions Law: Formalism or Functionalism?' in S. Worthington (ed.) *Commercial Law and Commercial Practice*. Oxford: Hart.

Walsh, C. (2008) 'Security Interests in Receivables' in H. Eidenmüller and E.M. Kieninger (eds) *The Future of Secured Credit in Europe*. E.C.F.L.R., Munich: De Gruyter Recht.

Walt, S. (1999) 'Novelty and the Risks of Uniform Sales Law', 39 *Va. J. Int'l L.*, 671.

Warren, E. (1997) 'Making Policy with Imperfect Information: The Article 9 Full Priority Debates', 82 *Cornell L. Rev.*, 1373.

Watson, A. (1976) 'Legal Transplants and Law Reform', 92 *L.Q.R.*, 79.

Watson, A. (1974) *Legal Transplants An Approach to Comparative Law*. Edinburgh: Scottish Academic Press.

Watson, A. (1981) *The Making of the Civil Law*. Cambridge, MA: Harvard University Press.

Weatherill, S. (2004) 'Why object to Harmonization of Private Law by the EC?', *E.R.P.L.*, 633.

Weber, L. and Espinola, S. (1999) 'The development of a new Convention relating to international interests in mobile equipment, in particular aircraft equipment: a joint ICAO-UNIDROIT project', *Unif. L. Rev.*, 463.

Wheatley, D. (1990) 'Why I oppose the Wind of Change?', *The Times,* 27 March.

White, J.J. and Summers, R.S. (2000) *Uniform Commercial Code*, 5th edn. Eagan, MN: West.

Wilson, J.M. (2007). 'Movable Equipment Financing in Latin America: Application of the OAS Model Law, the Cape Town Convention and the Luxembourg Rail Protocol', *Unif. L. Rev.*, 473.

Winship, P. (1998) 'Selected Security Interests in the United States' in J.J. Norton and M. Andenas (eds) *Emerging Financial Markets and Secured Transactions.* The Hague: Kluwer.

Winship, P. (2001) 'The Legal Framework to Secure Loans in the United States: A Comprehensive System for Creating Security Interests', *CEAL Issues Brief No. 2* (April).

Wood, P. (2005) *Maps of World Financial Law*, 5th edn. London: Allen & Overy LLP.

Wood, P. (1997) 'Comparative Financial Law: A Classification of the World's Jurisdictions' in R. Cranston (ed.) *Making Commercial Law Essays in Honour of Roy Goode.* Oxford: Clarendon.

Wood, P. (2002) 'Fixed and Floating Charges', *C.L.J.*, 472.

Wood, P. (1998) 'World-Wide Security-Classification of Legal Jurisdictions' in J.J. Norton and M. Andenas (eds) *Emerging Financial Markets and Secured Transactions.* The Hague: Kluwer.

Wood, P. (1989) *English and International Set-off.* London: Sweet & Maxwell.

Wood, P. (2008) *Law and Practice of International Finance.* London: Sweet & Maxwell.

Woodward, W. (1997) 'The Realist and Secured Credit: Grant Gilmore, Common Law Courts and the Article 9 Reform Process', 82 *Cornell L Rev.*, 1511.

Wool, J. (1999) 'The Next Generation of International Aviation Finance Law: An overview of the Proposed Unidroit Convention on International Interests in Mobile Equipment as applied to Aircraft Equipment', 20 *U. Pa. J. Int'l Econ. L.*, 499.

Wool, J. (1997) 'Rethinking the Notion of Uniformity in the Drafting of International Commercial Law: A Preliminary Proposal for the Development of a Policy Based Unification Model', *Unif. L. Rev.*, 46.

Wool, J. (1999) 'The Case for a Commercial Orientation to the Proposed Unidroit Convention as applied to aircraft equipment', *Unif. L. Rev.*, 289.

World Bank FDP Forum (2007) 'Making Finance Work for Africa: What Role for Collateral Reform'. Washington, DC: World Bank.

Worthington, S. (2007) 'The Disappearing Divide between Property and Obligation: The Impact of Aligning Legal Analysis and Commercial Expectation', 42 *Tex. Int'l L. J.*, 17.

Worthington, S. (1996) *Proprietary Interests in Commercial Transactions.* Oxford: Clarendon Press.

WTO News (2008) 'Lamy warns trade finance situation "deteriorating"', 12 November. Geneva: WTO.

Zamora, S. (1995) 'NAFTA and the Harmonization of Domestic Legal Systems: The Side effects of Free Trade', 12 *Ariz. J. Int'l & Comp. L.*, 401.

Zhang, M. (2006) 'Party Autonomy and Beyond: An International Perspective of Contractual Choice of Law', 20 *Emory Int'l L. Rev.*, 511.

Ziegel, J. (1997) 'Harmonization of Private Laws in Federal Systems of Government: Canada, the USA and Australia' in R. Cranston (ed.) *Making Commercial Law Essays in Honour of Roy Goode.* Oxford: Clarendon.

Zimmerman, R. (2004) 'Roman Law and the Harmonisation of Private Law in Europe' *in* A. Hartkamp and E. Hondius (eds) *Towards a European Civil Code*, 3rd edn. The Hague: Kluwer.

Zimmermann, R. (2004) *Roman Law, Contemporary Law, European Law The Civilian Tradition Today*. Oxford: Oxford University Press.

Zwalve, W. (2004) 'A Labyrinth of Creditors: A Short Introduction to the History of Security Interests in Goods' in E-M. Kieninger (ed.) *Security Rights in Movable Property in European Private Law*. Cambridge: Cambridge University Press.

Zweigert, K. and Kötz, H. (1998) *An Introduction to Comparative Law*, 3rd edn. Oxford: Oxford University Press.

Index